METROPOLIS

—— METROPOLIS ——

The American City in Popular Culture

Robert Zecker

Westport, Connecticut
London

Library of Congress Cataloging-in-Publication Data

Zecker, Robert, 1962–
    Metropolis : the American city in popular culture / Robert Zecker.
        p.   cm.
    Includes bibliographical references and index.
    ISBN: 978-0-275-99712-0 (alk. paper)
        1. Cities and towns—United States—History.   2. Urbanization—United States—History.
    3. Human geography—United States—History.   4. City and town life—United States—
    History.   I. Title.
        HT123.Z423   2008
        307.760973—dc22   2007036455

British Library Cataloguing in Publication Data is available.

Library of Congress Catalog Card Number: 2007036455
ISBN: 978-0-275-99712-0

First published in 2008

Praeger Publishers, 88 Post Road West, Westport, CT 06881
An imprint of Greenwood Publishing Group, Inc.
www.praeger.com

Printed in the United States of America

The paper used in this book complies with the
Permanent Paper Standard issued by the National
Information Standards Organization (Z39.48-1984).

10 9 8 7 6 5 4 3 2 1

Contents

1. Introduction   1

2. Next Stop, the Ghetto: Tours of Ethnic Exotica in the Popular Press   15

3. "A Problem That We, the Public, Must Solve": The Gangster Film   71

4. "Certain Sociological Realities There": A City for the
    1960s and Beyond   117

5. "All of Life Was There Before": The Urban Nostalgic Memoir   165

6. "We Never Locked Our Doors at Night": Newark on the Net,
    minus the Mob   201

Conclusion   221

Notes   225

Index   267

—— 1 ——

Introduction

When a man is tired of London he is tired of life.

Samuel Johnson

This city here is like an open sewer, you know, it's full of filth and scum.
'Cause sometimes I can hardly take it. . . . Sometimes I go out and I smell it,
I get headaches it's so bad, you know? Sometimes they just, they never go
away, you know? I think the president should just clean up this whole mess
here, he should just flush it right down the f'ing toilet.

Travis Bickle in *Taxi Driver*, on Times Square, circa 1976[1]

Ever since the rise of mass culture, the idea of The City has played a central role
in the imagined landscape of many Americans. Whether in print, film, or television, the sidewalks of New York (and often Philadelphia, Detroit, Los Angeles,
San Francisco, and even Newark) have thrilled and repulsed consumers in just
about equal measure, maybe attracting readers and viewers precisely because
the city streets and the disreputable types who skulked in their shadows were so
repulsive.

Certainly some writers and filmmakers have depicted the city as a site of fun,
with Woody Allen, for example, presenting a love letter to photogenic parts of his
city like the Upper West Side, home to affluent, well-read (albeit neurotic) intellectuals with a ready blend of witty patter equal parts Noel Coward and Borscht
Belt. In the early twentieth century, too, Tin Pan Alley in particular reassured
mainstream America that "the city's a wondrous toy, just made for a girl and
boy." "East Side, West Side, all around the town," colorful New Yorkers were
offered as amusing, even if a little exotic, objects of spectacle. When city dwellers
were presented as colorful Rosie O'Grady, it was easy for listeners to convince
themselves that it was still possible to "turn Manhattan into an island of joy."[2]

Still, after non–New Yorkers finished whistling about Mott Street's gently glid-
ing pushcarts, they often turned to fictional portrayals of the city that were a little
more somber or enjoyed a fictional city in which the thrills were often illicit.
Popular song versions of Manhattan had to vie with more threatening portrayals
of immigrant thugs or lawless gangsters. And from the 1970s to the present, for
every lovable, neurotic New Yorker Woody Allen offers up, there's one of Scorsese's Brooklyn *Goodfellas* or, more ominously to middle-class white viewers,
some *Boyz 'n the Hood*. Indeed, by and large, in whatever era one chooses, the
view from the city street has been more Bickle and less Johnson.

Even as early as the mid-nineteenth century, dime novels and journalistic accounts viewed the city and its denizens as a threat to the republic, with the voices
of alarm crying fortissimo once mass immigration turned cities decidedly non-
Nordic. What devotee of *The Wire* wouldn't nod his head in recognition, if not
outright agreement, at this nightmarish account of dystopic future Philadelphia as
a city ready to implode from a surfeit of greed, vice, hedonism, poverty, and ethnic and racial tension:

'The lordlings of the Quaker City have sold their father's bones for gold, they have robbed
the widow and plundered the orphan, blasphemed the name of God by their pollution of his
faith and church, they have turned the sweat and blood of the poor into bricks and mortar,
and now as the last act of their crime, they tear down Independence Hall and raise a royal
palace on its ruins!' . . . He passed along among the crowd of gay wayfarers, he passed
many a gay equipage, many a gorgeous chariot, and here and there at the corners of the
streets or among the gayest of the laughing throng, he beheld a squalid beggar crouching to
the earth as he asked for bread, or a pale-faced mechanic in worn and tattered clothes, who
shook his hands in impotent rage as he beheld the stares of wealth which flashed from the
lofty windows as if to tantalize him with their splendor. . . . 'Cursed be the city,' cried that
solitary voice, leading the supernatural choir. 'Its foundations are dyed in blood. The curse
of the poor man is upon it, and the curse of the orphan. The widow, with her babes starving
at her breast, raises her hands and curses it in the sight of God. Wo unto Sodom!'[3]

Yet this depiction of a city decidedly short of brotherly love did not spill from
the laptop of a screenwriter pitching a new series for Fox or HBO. Rather, George
Lippard caused a sensation in 1844 with his novel *Quaker City, or The Monks of
Monk Hall*. Lippard's work spawned an entire genre, the "city mystery," with a
slew of authors exposing the "darkness and daylight" of New York, Philadelphia,
and other cities in novels disguised as moral tract or guidebook to urban vice
districts (it was often hard to tell the difference between condemners and the
promoters of the nineteenth-century sin cities). After the Civil War, publishing
houses such as Beadle made their fortune churning out dime novels that were
snapped up by readers eager to be titillated with the sins of the cities. Lippard and
his imitators often condemned the poor and the decadent upper-class urbanites
alike, for foppish plutocrats' effete love of luxury and sins of the flesh were also
seen as endangering the egalitarian republic of producers.[4]

Whether the United States, even in its first decades, ever truly was a nation of rough economic equality—even for native-born white Protestant males—is beside the point. This belief in what Glenn Altschuler calls the "rude republic" prevailed as a powerful myth, and if we discount the archaic language and lack of urban realism in the absence of "street cred" profanity, nineteenth-century fictional city hoods conveyed the same message as our contemporary television and film narratives of urban pathology: The city is corrupting the nation. Rich city leeches bleed the body politic from the top, while desperate, alien vultures prey from below.[5]

From the nation's beginning the deck was stacked against urban America. Political leaders of the early republic such as Thomas Jefferson regarded cities as the seats of chimerical mobs of landless laborers beholden to the nearest demagogue promising them a job in return for their vote. And just like Lippard, Jefferson worried about would-be aristocrats in big, bad New York and Philadelphia. It was only in the countryside, among a self-sufficient yeomanry, that political virtue could triumph. To the degree that America urbanized, Jefferson and his many protégés such as James Madison believed, the nation would descend down a rocky path to European-style corruption, in which men of means eyed the penniless rabble warily and relied on hireling armies to keep restless city folk at bay. Southern agrarians saw to it the new nation's capital was moved to a planned, semirural town to avoid the evils of cities and their sullen rabble and would-be aristocrats.[6]

Whether Jefferson's self-conception of the white rural yeoman as completely virtuous and self-reliant was accurate (for one thing, it leaves aside any consideration of the degree to which Jefferson and his peers were indebted to hundreds of slave "servants"), it became an enduring antiurban foundational myth. Only by developing western farm lands, what Jefferson called "an empire for liberty," could America counter the corrupting effects of large, vice-ridden cities. In subsequent decades this Jeffersonian ideal remained powerful in shaping many Americans' conceptions of cities, even as western metropolises such as Detroit, Chicago, and San Francisco were added to the roster of decadent, suspect, un-American places. And when such places became less Protestant and western European in composition, the alarms over the dangers of the city took on a strident tone. Historian Frederick Jackson Turner in 1893 warned that the closing of the frontier might spell the end of rugged individualism and democracy as previous generations of Americans had known it. But his jeremiad also suggested it was the sort of person streaming into the cities by 1890, not just mere numbers and urban congestion, that was alarming many middle-class academics. New York or Chicago, each with close to half its residents foreign-born and many of these from eastern and southern Europe to boot, couldn't be trusted to carry the sacred lamps of the republic's institutions with the skill of a previous generation.[7]

Turner was not alone in worrying about cities that seemed increasingly alien to Protestant, middle-class American values. Even though he went on to lose three presidential elections, William Jennings Bryan was preaching to an antiurban choir when he compared places such as Chicago and New York to farmlands and found them wanting. "Burn down your cities and leave our farms, and your cities will spring up again as if by magic," Bryan thundered in his 1896 "Cross of Gold" speech. "But destroy our farms and the grass will grow in the streets of every city in the country."[8] While this was no way to win votes in the immigrant wards of Philadelphia or Manhattan, even many middle-class, WASP urbanites alarmed at the state of "their" cities likely secretly agreed with Bryan. The nation's virtues were embodied in the rural heartland, reformers such as Charles Loring Brace had long argued in advocating the removal of city orphans to foster care on midwestern farms, a tonic to cure the sickness of city living. When Manhattan, Newark, Philadelphia, and other cities were constantly highlighted by journalists, academics, and settlement house workers as hopelessly in need of a slew of repairs, no wonder the city was, almost as a matter of course, regarded as a threat to national purity. These fears of the urban mob were raised to a full-bore, Code Red panic attack when native-born agrarians beheld their cities in the grip of Irish Catholic political machines like Boston's Fitzgerald and Curley clubs or New York's Tammany Hall. Jefferson's agrarian ethos and its suspicion of cities continued to resonate at the turn of the nineteenth century.[8]

Still, with all due respect to Jefferson, Brace, and other political leaders, most Americans received their information on the city poor from popular culture, not congressional speeches or sociological exposés. Americans, even affluent urbanites, developed a conception of the city and its immigrant millions after reading novels, plays, fictionalized magazine tours of the city's ethnic exotica, cartoons, and comic strips. In subsequent decades film and television dramas enhanced this process, and fictionalized cityscapes took on a life of their own that affected the political climate in which harsh policies were demanded to contain the country's chaotic urban hordes. These imagined urban others have changed over time, as the descendants of late-nineteenth- and early-twentieth-century immigrants regarded as "not quite white" have been rendered acceptable ("white") citizens of the republic.[9] But the fictional productions of a threatening city and its alien residents have remained remarkably constant.

Around 1900, when the mass-circulation newspaper and magazine were relatively new inventions, middle-class readers often formed their opinion on "the truth" of the city after reading a magazine exposé, with the "city mysteries" or dime novels—and more genteelly, a fictional work like Stephen Crane's *Maggie: A Girl of the Streets,* or the work of Frank Norris or Theodore Dreiser offering corroborating evidence for those who sought to rein in city vices. Across the gamut of "high" and "low" culture the city reared its threatening, phrenologically challenged head. Issue after issue of magazines such as *Century* or *McClure's* offered short fictional pieces that allowed readers voyeuristically to visit slums, in which magazine writers warned readers to beware of stiletto-wielding Italians, unscrupulous "Asiatic" Jews, and thoroughly corrupt, chiefly Irish big-city political machines. Sometimes the cast of characters was augmented by the bomb-wielding German anarchist.[10] Magazine writers often expanded their exposés into muckraking books, where they assured readers their purposes were to inform, not titillate. Still, even ostensibly earnest efforts to reform cities were crammed full of lurid accounts of the hordes of homeless "street arabs," Irish ladies of the evening, and waterfront toughs, who all waylaid the careless traveler who strayed even a few blocks off his usual respectable path into the "shadows of New York life."[11]

Whether high or low, popular-culture depicters of the city mixed amusement with dire warnings of the chaotic city and the threat it posed if left unchecked. In the 1890s and 1900s, the nation laughed at the antics of barroom philosopher Mr. Dooley, but his neighborhood of "Archie Road," in Chicago's Bridgeport area, was a violent and seedy place in which many newspaper readers only vicariously trod.[12] Even drawers of comic strips or cartoons of the turn of the century that savagely mocked the supposedly unassimilable Jewish, Irish, Italian, German, and Slavic urban hordes had a pedantic purpose. In one *Puck* cartoon a bewildered Uncle Sam found himself surrounded by a mob of street urchins from an array of stereotypically "foreign" ethnicities, who set about picking Sam's pockets (surely a metaphor that wasn't lost on native-born middle-class American readers alarmed at the Slavic-Jewish-Celtic invasion of their America).

Fictional portrayals of the Progressive Era reinforced an antiurbanist or anti-immigrant bias among many U.S. citizens, and even those sympathetic to reform causes, such as housing reform, often concluded that city dwellers were helpless in the face of the daunting ecological problems the metropolis offered. In popular culture the penniless, foreign city dweller almost always became an object of pity or scorn—take your pick—but very rarely someone capable of working out his own destiny.

Indeed, the city and its not-so-delightful residents often seemed to be dragging the entire nation, even its wholesomely WASP and rural components, down to ruin. Popular novelists of a futuristic bent ominously warned of a not-so-distant day when *The Last American* would live as a Cro-Magnon hermit in the ruins of the Capitol, the sole survivor after the "Mur-fee Dynasty" seized power in the United States around 1920 and slaughtered all the Protestants.[13] Less fancifully, naturalist writers such as Theodore Dreiser, Frank Norris, and Upton Sinclair cautioned readers that in urban America violence, seduction, and a pauper's death were never far away the moment one strayed too far down a dank alley or trusted a smooth-talking city stranger. Certainly many Progressive Era writers, journalists as well as fiction writers (and the line between the two categories was quite fluid), wrote with a great deal of empathy for the urban ghetto dwellers caught between a slumlord and a sweatshop. Yet the sympathy writers expressed with one paragraph they often took away with belittling portrayals of the hopelessly improvident, violent, or criminal residents of Hester Street or Mulberry Bend.[14]

Whatever sympathetic or noble intentions some writers and illustrators had in exposing unhealthy conditions in the Progressive Era slums, the overall impression many readers drew was that cities were beyond redemption, and many "Goo Goos" (Teddy Roosevelt's term for good government types) acted accordingly. Middle-class decision makers who read magazine, novel, or "city mystery" accounts of the dangerous, foreign, unhealthy cities were the same people, after all, who passed legislation severely limiting city dwellers' self-government. Regional commissions were imposed on cities as diverse as Newark, Jersey City, Boston, and New York by state legislatures overrepresenting rural districts. Progressive reformers championed the city manager form of government, substituting university-trained "expertise" for the whims and vices of urban immigrant voters.[15] The antiurban biases that led to such attempts to impose reform on a recalcitrant and foreign city population had to have come from somewhere, and I shall argue that middle-class reformers' conception of the city and unruly urbanites stemmed in large measure from the way popular culture characterized the city.

A few decades after the Progressive era, even as cheerful Broadway tunes remained the sound track to everyday life, gangsters in films such as *The Public Enemy*, *Dead End*, *Angels with Dirty Faces*, *Scarface*, *The Roaring Twenties,* and *Little Caesar*, to name only a few, were a franker admonition of the city's lawlessness, even if the ethnic danger to wholesome American virtues from such Irish, Italian, and Jewish mobsters was merely hinted at. Still, the gangster's very foreignness to all that was wholesome and American was a marker of the depths of despair into which Prohibition- and Depression-era Chicago and New York had plunged. Film noir, too, presented urban jungles as "tangles of urban pathology" that were every bit as dense as those that Daniel Patrick Moynihan twenty years later argued lay behind much of black Americans' woes.

Just as turn-of-the-century fictions often influenced reformers determined to clean up the Lower East Side, gangster films dovetailed with the political and journalistic world's coverage of and crusades against organized crime. In the very years Humphrey Bogart and James Cagney rose to prominence as fictional tough guys, Thomas Dewey, William O'Dwyer, and other crime fighters made their careers on the prosecution of Meyer Lansky, "Gurrah" Shapiro, and Louis "Lepke" Buchalter. And while not quite a fiction writer, the adeptly self-promoting columnist Walter Winchell helped sell quite a few copies of *The New York Daily Mirror* when he scooped the rest of the New York press and persuaded Buchalter to turn himself in. Life and the movies imitated each other in portraying Irish, Italian, and Jewish criminality in the 1930s and 1940s big, bad city.[16]

Post–World War II, and into the 1970s, cities left behind by federally financed suburbanization and redlining of the poor and minorities appeared on movie and television screens alike as almost beyond redemption, and fictional police and detectives who bent the rules to the point of breaking were excused as the only hope for an urban society teetering on the brink of the abyss. Problem films as well as the film noir genre worried that slums were still a black mark on an otherwise prosperous postwar America, and just as Michael Harrington was soon to alert his complacent countrymen to the existence of "the other America," gritty urban films like *The Blackboard Jungle* questioned the Eisenhower-era consensus.[17]

In the aftermath of the 1964–1968 urban disturbances, or riots (as those who conveniently forgot the anti-integrationist riots that greeted blacks trying to buy homes in many white enclaves in 1940s and 1950s Chicago, Detroit, and Philadelphia labeled them), popular filmmakers and television producers raised ever shriller alarms on the state of inner-city decay. Urban cowboys like *Mannix* and, a little later, *Dirty Harry,* were not above breaking a few rules or heads to uphold law and order, and many viewers from the 1960s to the present likely thought it was a small price to pay as they watched the evening news tell of the problems of the real-life streets of San Francisco (Detroit, Harlem, Newark, or Watts). Police officers were posted to *Fort Apache The Bronx,* keeping a lid on a simmering caldron. Other films similarly wrote miles of cities off.[18]

Successors to television and film portrayals of 1970s cities still do quite well in the ratings by documenting urban crime and perceived collapse. These shows and films play a powerful role in shaping the ongoing conception of cities as beyond repair, a self-fulfilling prophecy considering the disinvestment in social spending from schools to mass transit to recreational and health care facilities voted in by some of the very viewers who wouldn't miss an episode of *Cops.* In these shows it is the straightlaced forces of law and order that battle against the remnants and legacies of the permissive society. Just as in 1900 WASP magazine readers never had to venture to the Lower East Side to know all they needed to know about immigrant New York, today such TV viewings often suffice.

There have been occasional answers to this unending story of Manhattan misery or South Chicago sorrow. If we take a brief detour from this urban safari and let the subaltern speak, or at least sing, it is important to note that there have been many moments and media in which demonized city residents have talked back to the fictional representations of them and their cities as agents of decline. As early as the 1950s, Chicago and Detroit blues artists gave voice to protests against redlining, police brutality, and indifference to their problems by many whites fleeing to the suburbs. With the 1967 urban disturbances/riots in Detroit, Newark, and other cities, a series of songs such as John Lee Hooker's "Motor City's Burning" and Juke Boy Bonner's "Goin' Back to the Country" desperately tried to give context to the despair of urban black America. A short while later George Clinton's "Chocolate City" offered hope of a different kind of urban renaissance, even as the "vanilla suburbs" continued to view cities such as Detroit warily.

Hip-hop continues this culture of resistance, while visual artists have often sardonically commented on the poverty existing in the parts of postindustrial cities that have all but been abandoned by cash-starved city governments. The artists involved in Detroit's Heidelberg Project literally turned uncollected garbage into art with their evocative architectural collages on the Motor City's grim East Side. These creations out of trash were often harsh critiques of the abandonment many Detroiters felt, facing vacant houses; weedy fields overgrown with discarded refrigerators and baby buggies; and a city administration incapable of offering city services taken for granted a few miles away in Grosse Pointe.[19] Indicative of the scramble of many deindustrialized cities, desperate to replace vanished manufacturing with tourism and culture cottage industries, Detroit gave up on its original goal of bulldozing the Heidelberg Project houses and finally started marketing these artistic creations as tourist destinations.[20] Still, when some artistic creations were accepted as installations at the elite Detroit Institute of the Arts, city fathers made sure to fumigate this people's art before it entered the museum. Such artistic projects offer a way for city residents to talk back, albeit in an unequal "speech act" to those who imagine Detroit through a different lens.

As cities rebounded from the precipice of financial collapse over which municipal and national leaders once seemed determined to shove them, urban filmmakers have also capitalized on the images of Manhattan and other cities as sites of fun and desire. Filmmakers such as Woody Allen and Martin Scorsese, in very different ways, capitalized on images of a desirable city current in the gentrifying late 1970s and 1980s. Allen's city was the wonderland of jazz at Elaine's and struggling, neurotic writers and intellectuals somehow living in fabulous prewar Riverside Drive apartments in which one could land a small plane.

Scorsese and his emulators, on the other hand, presented conflicted looks at urban neighborhoods of yesteryear. Certainly these places are often as psychotically violent as any 1900 magazine slumologist's account of the Mulberry Bend's Black Hand. However, the Bronx or Brooklyn Little Italys, or even Murder Inc.'s stomping ground in *Once upon a Time in America,* also convey a longing for a time and place of roots and belonging, where moral verities were enforced one way or the other, and the code of honor was respected by everyone on the block. In *A Bronx Tale,* the recollections of the narrator present the Italian Fordham section of the Bronx as preferable to the chaos on the other, "black" side of the tracks (literally) that, by the 1960s' end, is encroaching ever closer on the clubhouse of the mob. This is a complex movie, in which the narrator expresses ambivalence about both his father and the gangster who takes him under his wing, but at least part of the message is that this neighborhood remained stable and safe as all else crumbled around hardworking white ethnics. In 1968 Fordham remained safe—if not for "outsiders" who trespassed on Belmont Avenue, at least for Italian grandparents and children—paradoxically because of "our" hoodlums holding court on the block. Such messages abound in gangster films.[21]

Novelists, too, have become adept in the last twenty or so years at fashioning urban memoirs in which older residents think back across the decades and recall pre-white-flight cities as functioning and nurturing places. In postindustrial America, the process of distinguishing between us and them begun in the Progressive Era continues. But now, ironically, it is that earlier Irish, Italian, Jewish, or other white ethnic neighborhood, once a menace to society, that is regarded as a bygone Utopia of morality and hard work, valorized compared to present-day, majority black and Hispanic cities. Film, television, and print memoirs often contain recognitions that criminality, whether bootlegging or numbers running, permeated the immigrant city, but these sins (if sins they be) are shrugged off or winked at as great viewing or reading fun. In Philip Roth's Newark there are tough guys and poverty in Jewish Weequahic (even real-life mobster "Longy" Zwillman finally makes an appearance in Roth's Weequahic, in his recent *The Plot Against America).*[22] Still, many other characters pine for the white Newark of the past, a functioning, thriving place, and agonize in primal rage at the chaos, danger, and despair of a city now 70 percent nonwhite. Jeffrey Eugenides, in his award-winning *Middlesex,* more explicitly spells out in one-sided rage the anger whites (even immigrant whites) feel, convinced they were somehow forced out of Detroit following 1967. In these works, as on Web sites of virtual cities, a fiction of white victimhood has developed. The city has once again done us in, but the miscreants of the immigrant city of 1900 identified by Progressive Era reformers are now recast in these "urban memoirs" as the good guys.[23]

This process has continued on HBO's popular urban series. In Tony Soprano's recollections, bygone Newark, when "all Italian," was a thing of beauty, hard work, and respect. That these recollections come from a man who makes his living in "waste management" lends irony to this nostalgia, but the white memories of the way Newark was, and is, are nevertheless privileged in the series. In one episode, Tony laments the filth and decay he sees all around him as he visits the old neighborhood with his son. These are pointedly a result, Tony stresses, of the fact that the neighborhood is no longer Italian, for his people "built something here." The comparison between builders (even shady builders) and present-day welfare recipients and the like is periodically stressed, even if the viewer gets violence-tinged flashbacks to how Tony's uncle and father went about their business back in the day.[24]

Likewise, the white ethnic characters of *The Wire* are often depicted robbing the port facilities and city treasury of Baltimore, and yet it is the black drug gangs that preoccupy the police force, whose upper-level officers frequent the same taverns and parishes as the thieving dockworkers. Nostalgia infuses *The Wire*, too, with a recent "white hope" mayoral candidate getting advice from Tony Junior, an ex-mayor whose career was ruined by "the riots" of 1968. HBO's particular brand of urban commentary continues the trend of selectively rendering the city exotic.[25]

And just as for readers of dime novels or "city mysteries" at the turn of the nineteenth century, part of the attraction of these tales of urban deviance is being a fly on the clubhouse wall, voyeuristically enjoying the violence of Baltimore or Newark while knowing that one can walk out of Satriale's Pork Store alive.

Both shows, too, consider another threat to the old neighborhood, gentrification, which is beginning to rear its upscale head even in Tony Soprano's formerly comfortably dowdy ethnic North Ward Newark. When a live poultry store loses its lease to upscale Jamba Juice, the gangster Patsy Parisi not only loses one of his sources of money in the protection rackets but also glumly wonders, "What the f** is happening to this city?!"[26]

Finally, a recent innovation in urban fictions might give Patsy and the other urban exiles heart. Internet posters have recently developed a string of virtual cities, which have enabled those who left "the old neighborhood" to share memories and re-create the kind of city they imagine 1930s–1960s to have been. On Internet sites, suburban exiles can return, virtually, to a time and place of their imagining, "visiting" Newark, Cleveland, or Jersey City (there are dozens of such virtual cities) in voyeuristic safety without fear of conflict or contradiction. In this respect, visitors and contributors to Web virtual cities are no less secure than a 1930s viewer of gangster films or a reader of earlier ghetto exposés.

Indeed, one of the most elaborate such sites is www.virtualnewarknj.com, and such cyber cities have enabled chiefly white ex-urbanites to imagine the places of their youth as primarily conflict-free, functioning, and harmonious, unlike the cities of the early twenty-first century, minority-majority places that posters rarely, if ever, visit. And now it is cultural consumers themselves who can readily create the kind of fictive cities that they like, by posting to these sites, a process of cyber urbanism that Alison Adam and Eileen Green aptly characterize as an "escape from a world gone wrong."[27]

For at least the last hundred years, then, the partial view of the city presented in many fictionalizations has been a grim one, and it is these darker cityscapes that this book will chiefly address. Certainly some popular culture cityscapes were joyous, as when three sailors on leave *On the Town* in 1949 manage to find true love—for example, on the subway with Miss Turnstiles—before their one-day pass expires. Nevertheless, it is my contention that such wonderland depictions of Manhattan (and far less frequently other cities—Vincente Minnelli's *Meet Me in Saint Louis* comes to mind) have been less prominent in fixing an image of the city in the public's minds than the darker scenarios of life in the concrete jungle. Musical comedies of city life have certainly been enjoyed, just as many who visit Manhattan's Upper West Side secretly hope to run into Woody Allen, or at least Annie Hall, at some little jazz club. But such urban fantasies, although enjoyed by millions, have not provided the political will for fully funded urban schools or other necessities.[28]

Certainly, the kinds of city dystopias I've been describing did not, all by themselves, create white flight or disinvestment in the metropolis, or lead to any of the very real problems that some city dwellers may have brought on themselves. But the ghetto exposé, gangster film, urban cop drama, or latest episode of *The Wire* certainly didn't make it easy for a big-city mayor to defend his community, not in 1900, 1940, 1970, or even our time. After all, as even Alvy Singer in *Annie Hall* complained to his best friend, "The rest of the country looks upon New York like we're left-wing communist Jewish homosexual pornographers. I think of us that way sometimes, and I live here."[29]

And so the American middle-class reading public, theatergoer, or comic strip reader preferred his cities dark. So what? If dreadful tales of city corruption and squalor, or the thieving propensities of Italian criminals, Irish ward heelers, and then black drug gangs, had only served as entertainment, such fiction could be dismissed as merely a distraction, even if one filled with offensive stereotypes. But readers rarely compartmentalize the information they receive from popular culture into "just fiction" and facts suitable as a basis for developing one's political beliefs. Film, novels, cartoons, and other popular cultural productions work in tandem with journalism, history, and other supposedly serious genres to construct a worldview that is unitary, even if conflicted and contradictory. Thus the city can be a site of fun, even dangerous and thrilling in illicit ways, but sinful and corrupt, hopeless in terms of any commitment of tax dollars to governmental programs. The city is a site of consumption and a throwaway all at once, a conclusion viewers/voters seem to draw at least partially based on the images they consume in popular-culture dramatizations.

Depictions of urban America in popular culture reinforced the messages "serious" opinion molders held about the New Yorks and Chicagos of America, but this process was a mutually reinforcing one. Political actors are often informed, even if subconsciously, by the preconceptions they have learned through popular culture. A schema is developed that makes political, maybe even moral, sense of the world through the reading of novels, the viewing of films and television programs, and now the downloading of Internet content. This process is a two-way data stream, though, for cultural producers often receive their ideas on the state of urban America—or any topic, for that matter—through the "serious," supposedly factual reports that come their way in the daily newspaper, nightly newscast, or university curriculum.

Thus, for at least a hundred years, members of Congress, journalists, academics, and voters have formed their views of the city at least in part, too, from what they have learned from writers, illustrators, filmmakers, and TV producers. Order is imposed on a seemingly chaotic (urban) world through our choices of fiction. The consumers of "city mysteries" or alarmist fiction warning of "an Asiatic Jewish invasion" of New York were also citizens and voters, taking their antiurbanist biases and determination to impose order on the unruly street and its urchins into the voting booths, universities, and urban reform leagues in which Progressive Era public policies were shaped. Likewise, their peers screening gangster films or urban dramas of the 1930s, and nightmare dramas of the black and supposedly dysfunctional city of the 1960s and 1970s, developed their political visions of what could or could not be accomplished for the city in some measure through the fictions they enjoyed. Those fleeing the cities emblematized by burning Newark and Detroit, 1967, and then hesitantly, voyeuristically returning as gentrifiers and tourists, to say nothing of quite a few "tough-on-crime" politicians, from Philadelphia mayor Frank Rizzo to Vice President Spiro Agnew—all of these and other political phenomena have operated in milieus in which fictional New York, Chicago, Detroit, and Newark are the places Americans have often learned to love to hate.

While the objects of scorn have changed, the city and its residents remain problematic for a new crop of cultural trend setters. Innately violent Italian gangsters of the Black Hand, or "Asiatic" Jews invading New York, have been supplanted by the African-American "underclass" and new "illegal aliens" who cause almost as much consternation as "the Slav," who sociologist Edward Alsworth Ross in 1914 was certain "could live in dirt that would kill a white man."[30] For new reasons and with a new round of usual suspects, cities such as New York and Chicago have remained a problem for most consumers of popular culture, and ironically today it is often the grandchildren or great-grandchildren of an earlier era's demonized urban ethnic other who now learn all they feel they need or care to know about the city via fictionalized mean streets. Those who view the city through the lens of *Cops, The Wire, The Sopranos,* or *CSI,* this book will argue, do not necessarily file the depictions of the city that these shows offer under "fiction" or "entertainment," nor do they delete these shows' images of Los Angeles, New York, or Baltimore (all stand-ins for urban America at large) when they enter the voting booth or consider the nightly news and its supposedly more factually based presentation of postindustrial America. Just as in 1900 or 1940, this book will argue, the fictional presentations of urban America that consumers enjoy have very real political effects and at least partially begin to explain the antiurban bias in the policymaking by America's elected and appointed officeholders in the eras under consideration.

The city was regarded as a violence-soaked threat to the nation a hundred years before the dawn of gangsta rap. One reason this is not more widely acknowledged is that journalistic, and then movie conventions, made the overt depictions of graphic violence or realistic profanity taboo. Certainly violence has become more permissible in the genres that we'll be studying in the later era. Nevertheless, within the Victorian conventions of the day, newspaper and magazine writers of around 1900, and then Hollywood moguls beholden to the Hays Code, often portrayed urban America as just as chaotic, violent, and amoral as any twenty-first-century screenwriter. Correcting for an earlier era's more genteel conventions, popular-culture purveyors offered consumers a city in 1844, 1900, and the 1930s that was often just as blood-soaked as on the screens—large, small, and laptop—of our own day.

Lippard's spirit shrieking "Cursed be the city, wo unto Sodom!" might have a few more choice Anglo-Saxon epithets if he were today railing against Baltimore or post-1967 Newark on *The Wire* or *The Sopranos,* but the spirit of condemnation is the same. And even when correcting for production codes, public sensibilities, and rudimentary technology in the novels and films of an earlier era, the streetscape presented is often quite blood-soaked and immoral. When rival gangsters truss up the corpse of Tom Powers and leave his body teetering on his mother's doorstep as she's preparing dinner for her boy, 1931's *The Public Enemy* gives any gangsta rapper a run for his money in gritty urban pathologies.[31]

So how do we know the effect that these popular-culture depictions of the city had on middle-class consumers? Simply put, we don't, at least with any mathematical degree of certainty. As a matter of full disclosure, I am a big fan of gangster films and Tony Soprano (and not just because at least once an episode I recognize some candy store, diner, or Newark street corner from my New Jersey youth). Certainly my devotion to this genre hasn't hardened me to the plight of city dwellers, and there is no reason to suppose that all of the millions of popular cultural consumers draw the same antiurban message embedded in many fictions.

However, reading these novels and films in tandem with what "serious" opinion molders were saying about urban America and city residents in the various eras in question suggests that there was a dialogue between the fictional city and those seeking to contain its supposed excesses and vices in the public policy realm. Works of art have often been cited as evidence when an official sought to make hay out of an era's urban underclass. Vice President Dan Quayle and the *Murphy Brown* televised single-parent debate was not an isolated incident, and the condemners of rap music for supposedly mirroring, and glorifying, city violence are the cultural descendants of earlier cultural critics who warned that the gangsters played by Cagney, George Raft, Edward G. Robinson, and Bogart might be making crime look too much like fun. The 1950s anti-comic-book crusaders, too, denounced the graphic depiction of blood and gore. When novels, magazine tales of the ghetto, and crime dramas are used by policymakers to justify their antiurbanist agendas, such works of popular culture become more than "just stories."[32]

This book, then, will look at a selection of popular-culture depictions of the city at discrete times. New York, Chicago, and other cities have been in the foreground of many popular-culture treatments of urban America, and it would be foolhardy to pretend to be exhaustive of every type of urban appearance in American fiction. Rather, I propose to present a select group of fictionalizations of the city that have endeavored to address the urban crisis as it was perceived at a few key moments, moments when many in America were willing to be tutored by writers, filmmakers, television producers, and others on the dark side of the city.

Chapter 2 will look at the magazine and "city mystery" tours of ethnically exotic city slums around the turn of the century. These and the more high-brow, naturalist novels set in San Francisco, Chicago, or New York, together with the urban safaris of Progressive Era journalists, established immigrant districts as, in the public's eye, sites of amusement, exotica, danger, and, never too far below the surface, a threat to the Protestant white republic.

Chapter 3 focuses on the gangster films of the 1930s and 1940s that explored the criminal element lurking within the slum. The original "G," Edward G. Robinson, made his mark as the quintessential urban hood, Little Caesar. This Jewish actor with leftist leanings often played an Italian gangster, while another star of early crime films, George Raft, was a boyhood Brooklyn pal of the real "Bugsy" Siegel. Other problem films of this era and the immediate aftermath of World War II questioned the place of the city as a stubborn problem in a suburbanizing, seemingly uniformly affluent society.

Chapter 4 will look at cultural productions in another moment of urban crisis, the 1960s and early 1970s. Here, urban-based films and television shows presented the city as in need of vigilante justice, and the crime and social decay of cities that were by now majority nonwhite were often implicitly regarded as of an order of magnitude far greater than any lawbreaking that had occurred back in "the good old days" of Jewish, Irish, or Italian neighborhoods. Here, too, the "mean streets" of Scorsese, Coppola, and other practitioners of gangster cinema set up a distinction between function in urban then and alarming now. For all their faults, unlike ghetto "rioters," Henry Hill, Don Corleone, and the like were fun to watch and easily cheered on as urban (anti)heroes.

In Chapter 5 a brief detour will be made to consider a few of the counterhegemonic messages that minority artists have employed to defend their beleaguered cities. After that, the relatively new genre, the urban memoir novel, will be explored. Here, the past of cities such as Jeffrey Eugenides's Detroit or Philip Roth's Newark are collectively presented approvingly, as model civic citizens look back to a time when white ethnics were poor but honest, or at least entertainingly shady in ways that novels such as *Middlesex, The Plot against America,* and *The Human Stain* have invariably seemed to condone. These novels, and the cinematic memoirs of vanished places that have begun to accompany them, offer a primal scream or lament for the changed demographics of inner cities. Even when sympathetic and nuanced, the best of these novels and films, I will argue, offer a sepia-toned portrait of the past that sets up invidious comparisons in the viewer or reader to the urban here and now. The political purposes of nostalgia will be interrogated in this and the subsequent chapter, too.

HBO's urban series, also under examination in Chapter 5, arguably offer a blend of sly nostalgia and selective memory for a better, white ethnic city, as well as a gritty depiction of the challenges postindustrial Baltimore and northern New Jersey face. In many ways *The Wire* and other pseudodocumentaries offer an unflinching look at the problems that cities such as Baltimore face. However, it is the white middle-class gaze that is privileged and pronounces judgment on the real threat that America faces down in the ghetto. Finally, Chapter 6 examines the selective version of urban nostalgia and history on display in the virtual cities online. Courtesy of the newest fictionalizing technology, a selective portrait is once again drawn, dividing imagined Newarks between good times and places and threatening ones.

The city, exciting, thrilling, dirty, dangerous and not quite like respectable, suburban, hardworking white "us"—the city, God love it, continues to be the star of Americans' imaginings and longings, the lead character in the longest ongoing morality play. This book intends to examine a few of the genres and roles in which New York and its costars have enthralled and appalled "normal people," and to suggest some of the political and social implications such popular fictions have had.

——— 2 ———

Next Stop, the Ghetto: Tours of Ethnic Exotica in the Popular Press

As early as 1844, fiction writers regarded the American city as an open sewer, a blind pig, a train wreck. One of the first novelistic attempts to exploit and further inflame the nation's suspicion of all things urban was George Lippard's *Quaker City,* which endeavored to expose the urban cesspool of Philadelphia to America's book-reading public. The novel's plot is as labyrinthine as the dank multilevel dungeons that meander for miles under the city's whorehouses. In brief, two dissolute young dandies plot the seduction of a young girl they have just met. Lorrimer promises to introduce his friend to the city's secret cabal of hedonists, who meet in déclassé Southwark in the "rookery, the den, the pest-house"—Monk Hall![1] Here he promises to deliver the young girl, daughter of a destitute artisan, so that his friend can plot her debauch. Monk Hall, it turns out, is where the city's elite go when they wish to indulge their corrupt tastes for sins of the flesh. There the young hedonists hobnob with licentious judges, lawyers, editors, and various other city elite, and the delighted-repulsed reader learns that for all the surface show of prosperity and respectability, Philadelphia is one big pit of shame. The army of libertines who pass in and out of Monk Hall is enough to fill a police lineup a mile long.

The real master of Monk Hall, though, is the malevolent hunchbacked mulatto Devil Bug, who with his army of black henchmen arranges the seductions, murders, and saturnalias of his aristocratic employers. He keeps a full house of fallen women, those who have become "a common creature of the town," to satisfy his wealthy clientele.[2] Devil Bug is aided, too, by other women who he has formerly lured into Monk Hall. One of them, Bess, plots the abduction of yet another innocent Philadelphia girl, asking, "Why should I regret? Have I not as good a right to the comforts of a home, to the smile of a father, the love of a mother, as she? Have I not been robbed of all these? Of all that is most sacred to woman? . . . I feel happy—aye, happy—when I can drag another woman into the same foul pit, where I am doomed to lie and rot."[3]

Lippard seems to have been particularly appalled by the white slavery in his midst, and he had good reason to be so alarmed. A few decades later, in the midst of the Civil War, the city's prostitution problem got so out of hand that the city published an official prostitutes' register to learn a bit more about who these women were and what had caused so many of them to fall into sin.[4] In Lippard's novelistic city, though, it seems that the race mixing of a mulatto procurer serving wealthy white clients was an especially sinful blot on the city. For all the faults of the white aristocrats of the Quaker City, no character is as grotesquely portrayed as Devil Bug, and his physical deformities are a fitting wrapper for a soul of utter depravity. In decades to come, the dive that he runs would have been called a black and tan, a saloon and whorehouse where blacks and whites fraternized freely. In the 1890s and later, black and tans were condemned repeatedly in New York's Progressive Era press, a tradition that was begun in Gothic prose in Lippard's exposé.[5] To be sure, Lippard despised slavery, and during Devil Bug's reverie in which he witnesses the future destruction of the American republic, an antiquarian who sells him a forbidden relic of the distant "past" (the American flag) tells him who killed the republic: "She was massacred by her pretended friends. Priest-craft, and Slave-craft, and Traitor-craft were her pretended friends."[6]

Nevertheless, like many opponents of the "peculiar institution," Lippard detested slavery as an emblem of the brakes that were beginning to be applied to poor whites' socioeconomic advancement in America. How was a yeoman farmer to compete against a southern aristocrat like Colonel Fitz-Cowles, with a hireling army of hundreds of black "servants" ready to do his bidding. Slavery had to be removed so that all whites in America could, supposedly, once again be equal. The slaves themselves, like Devil Bug, were often an object of utter derision and detestation.

As America's economy seemed to force more and more men and women of the 1840s into lives of sometimes not-so-quiet desperation, Lippard imagined the city's army of the poor as a potential army doing the bidding of the mulatto Devil Bug:

These were the Outcasts of Quaker City! In the daytime, vagabond man and woman and child lay quiet and snug, in the underground recesses of Monk Hall; in the night, they stole forth from the secret passage thro' the pawnbroker's shop in the adjoining street, and prowled over the city, to beg, to rob, or perchance to murder.

. . . On every side was filth and rags. The rags, indeed, were a wonder. Had the heavens on some stormy day, rained rags, and our friends, the vagabonds been caught in the shower, they could not have been better furnished with tatters than they were now. . . . And among this haggard crowd were women, who twenty years ago had been belles, in the saloons of fashion; men who had been educated by rich and aristocratic fathers . . . But the mass had been born in misery, Baptized by Starvation, and Confirmed at the altar of Poverty, by the good old Bishop Crime . . . Here they stood the Heathens and Outcasts of the Christian Quaker City, rotting in misery and sin, while Bibles . . . were on their way to degraded Hindoostan . . .

It is apparent that, for Lippard, savages were taking over America's cities. Such a fear would be reiterated more than forty years later, when the cartoonist for the humor magazine *Puck* suggested that New York's immigrant ghettos, already teeming with Irish dynamiters, German anarchists, and just generally disreputable southern and eastern Europeans, were a better target for missionaries than Africa or Asia. "Why send our missionaries to Africa's sunny fountains?" the cartoonist asked. "Let them stay here and labor among the barbarous tribes of the metropolis."[7]

Yet the army of the rag-clad vagabonds hadn't yet committed its greatest atrocity. To conclude the Monk Hall meeting Devil Bug asks the throng, "Wot I wants to know is this: Have I been a father to ye, ye ugly devils?" at which "the Thieves, Cut-throats and Vagabonds" exclaim as one, "Hurray for old Devil-Bug!"[8] A threat of a biracial army of the poor in 1840s America—and even, as we'll see, a hundred years later—was not something many readers were prepared to accept. No doubt vagabonds hailing a mulatto pimp alarmed 1840s Americans almost as much as if Lippard had set his words to a gangsta rap beat. Indeed, if Lippard denounced the nation's aristocrats and idle rich for allowing the growth of an army of the rag-clad, the novel's most nightmarish scenes are reserved for depictions of the poor, black and white alike, making war on their betters, and taking their grievances into their own hands.

Of course, in the real America of the 1840s and later, race more frequently divided, than united the dispossessed. The real Philadelphia saw a series of brutal antiblack riots when white workingmen grew enraged at the city's small free black population using recreational facilities in the city. An especial target for the white rioters were the marriages in the city between free blacks and poor white women. These were the transgressions that really enraged the mob. Already Americans were learning to draw the color line that sadly still spells the borderline for urban fictional and real-life crime fantasies. So, too, did popular culture teach urban newcomers, who ironically themselves were often stigmatized as undesirable, just whom to hate and how to fit in. The minstrel show was perhaps America's fist mass popular entertainment, and Irishmen such as Dan Emmett made their fortunes imitating the supposedly comical ways of plantation blacks and urban dandies among the northern freemen. As Eric Lott has documented, a macabre form of "love and theft" occurred, in which urban immigrant northerners consumed racialized tales of black comic exploits but also blacked up to fit into the white republic.

Far more frequently, white crowds, vagabond or not, mocked Devil Bug in "Jim Crow" entertainments, rather than hailing him as their savior.[9] Indeed, elsewhere in *Quaker City*, Pump Handle, another down-and-out character, boasts that the city knows how to deal with its black populace. "Why, you see," he tells another resident of Monk Hall, "a party of us one Sunday afternoon had nothing to do, so we got up a nigger riot. We have them things in Phil'delphy, once or twice a year, you know? I helped to burn a nigger church, two orphans' asylums and a school-house. And happenin' to have a pump handle in my hand, I aksedentally hit an old nigger on the head. Konsekance wos he died. That's why they call me Pump Handle."[10]

Pump Handle's blasé assertion that the riot started because he and his cronies had nothing better to do one day, and that the riots are a regular occurrence, indicates that these ritualized occasions to assert their primacy allowed unemployed white workers, displaced by the country's emerging speculator class of idle rich and emerging industrialists' discarding of skilled craftsmen, to take out their fury on an even more helpless cast of characters rather than assault the rich speculators and bankers who had caused their plight to begin with. Here was Thomas Jefferson's fear of the city writ large: An army of dispossessed, landless paupers fighting over crumbs to the amusement of the idle rich. Throw in the specter of race wars, which Philadelphia and other antebellum cities knew all too well, as when enraged Philadelphians in 1834 ransacked black taverns and residences after some blacks dared patronize a carousel amusement in Moyamensing, and urban America was already on the way to becoming a nightmare terrain.[11]

The long list of characters and sins of Monk Hall includes, too, an avaricious Jewish pawnbroker, "Von Gelt"; a penniless con man masquerading as a southern aristocrat; stock swindlers passing through the city on their way back to New York, another legendary sin city; robbers; bigoted anti-Catholic preachers; and scandal-sheet newspaper editors who lament when "there hasn't been a suicide for a week, not even a downtown murder, nor a nigger baby killed" to put on page one. One can't help feeling that what really alarmed Lippard was this amorphous mass of racial, ethnic, and class types mixing so freely and cynically on the republic's streets.

For Lippard, the city, with all its anonymous crowds of nobodies masquerading as somebodies, embodied the destabilizing and threatening uncertainties of America's early industrial revolution that caused a great deal of consternation in the 1840s. By then, teenaged immigrant girl textile operatives had replaced skilled weavers at places such as Lawrence and Lowell, Massachusetts, and then in Philadelphia's own mill districts, such as Kensington and Manayunk. The factory mode of production destroyed the old promise of a "producer's republic," and even if industrialization was imperfectly realized before the Civil War compared to what would come later, artisans had no crystal ball to see that deskilling might make their lives even harder in twenty or thirty years. By the 1830s the first strikes of threatened craftsmen shoemakers and tailors occurred in Lippard's own city, and the cry to preserve the Jeffersonian egalitarianism of society (again, at least for white Protestant males) spread to dozens of workingmen's movements in urban America before the Panic of 1837 wiped away the seemingly growing strength of "the Workies." Lippard's fictionalized impoverished mechanics cowering before a secret cabal of the city's licentious rich would have resonated with his readers, worried as they were by the vanishing dream of a city of self-sufficient artisans earning a competence.

The mushrooming growth of cities alarmed Americans in the decades leading up to the Civil War, too. Upper-class diarists Philip Hone and, a little later, George Templeton Strong bemoaned the loss of their comfortable, knowable Manhattan, where everyone, or at least anyone who mattered, was a familiar face one could place at a glance.[12] The ballooning population of New York, and to a lesser extent Philadelphia, Baltimore, and Boston, brought in its wake by the 1840s hordes of strangers, an unsettling phenomenon reflected in *Quaker City,* too. The southern gentleman who greeted one on the streets of Lippard's Philadelphia within sight of the venerable Independence Hall turned out to be a con artist; a prominent Protestant revivalist was more interested in picking one's pocket than in saving souls. Just as in Herman Melville's *Confidence-Man,* with its riverboat full of shape shifters, in Lippard's Philadelphia, no one was what he seemed, and every city dweller incapable of trusting a single soul was despairing of the future of the republican community.[13] Ironically, a mirror image of the republican ideal—in which all are equal and anyone of lowly origin could through hard work come to be his own master—was thrown in the American reader's face, and it proved to be a nightmare, a nation of plotters and schemers and frauds who employed shady black and immigrant underlings to complete the subjugation of the virtuous.

That there was a lot to clean up in Philadelphia was beyond dispute. Further anti-Irish and antiblack rioting to the southwest of the old colonial city flared up throughout the next decade, and ad hoc attempts by neighborhood notables to provide the various squabbling districts and ethnic groups with some order may have only inflamed the situation. Voluntary fire companies and militia societies often proved to be little more than ethnic gangs in polyglot places such as Kensington and Southwark (home to the fictional Monk Hall). Indeed, in many antebellum cities workingpeople used their volunteer fire and militia companies to mark their turf and battle their enemies, and raucous squabbles between Irish and nativist companies punctuated life in the cities of what Glenn Altschuler has called "the rude republic." And come election time, such fire companies were often employed to stuff the battle box, rough up adherents of the other party, and protect ballots in reliable wards. Already by the 1840s, then, cities were coming to be seen as dens of political corruption and ethnic brawling.[14]

Other features of Philadelphia were equally alarming. Sam Alewitz notes that into the twentieth century, the city's rivers and streams were used as convenient dumping grounds for all manner of human and animal waste. Night carts took away the offal from the lucky, but in working-class districts outdoor privies sometimes were emptied once every decade, whether they needed it or not. Heavily urbanized parts of Philadelphia, such as the old colonial city, and the mill districts, such as Kensington and Northern Liberties, were denounced by reforming doctors for the "pestilential effluvia" that littered the back alleys and gutters of the "trinity house" districts. Indeed, when ten such "trinities" (narrow colonial row houses of three stories) might share one alley outhouse, it's hard to downplay the degree to which effluvia littered the Quaker City.[15]

The problem was an enduring one. In 1894, Carroll Wright of the U.S. Census Bureau noted the deplorable lack of indoor plumbing in immigrant neighborhoods such as Northern Liberties, and a 1946 Settlement House survey of these blocks north of the old city indicates the problem had still not been entirely corrected by that late date.[16] When surveying the situation in the Liberties for the Works

Progress Administration's Ethnic Group Survey, a writer noted that the district contained "housing conditions almost as bad as in the worst parts of South Philadelphia." In the 1860s, owners built the trinities in backyards, without taking care to ensure that enough air or light or amenities reached the back houses. "If the street had been filled above its former level, the lower room was often partially underground. . . . One unsewered out-house and one hydrant for six or eight families living around the courtyard were the only attempt at modern convenience . . . , and if there was a stable on the block the manure might be piled high against the wall of the bandbox row."[17] For all that a writer for *The Century* in 1882 attempted to divert his readers with "A Ramble in Old Philadelphia," the illustrations accompanying the article make clear that such housing stock, colonial as well as recent, was already quite dilapidated, not quaint.[18]

Beyond the city center, industrial districts were separated by unimproved marshes, fields, and meandering creeks, with paved streets not coming to such areas as Point Breeze and its noxious gasworks until the 1940s. The "swamps of Point Breeze" and the squalid rural shanties of South Philly's "Neck" were repeatedly singled out by doctors and sanitary reformers as particularly unhealthy places. To the north, the Manayunk mill district as late as 1898 was reported to be spewing raw sewage and industrial waste into the Schuylkill River, as a jerry-rigged 1880 sewer line was already obsolete. Elsewhere in the city, Frankford's creeks were similarly used as do-it-yourself sewers, and the result was a typhoid epidemic in both districts, the sort of early-nineteenth-century semiannual occurrence that the city's neoclassical waterworks of 1828 (situated on the beautiful, blue Schuylkill) was supposed to have solved. As in Detroit and Pittsburgh, in Philadelphia's working-class districts, pipes and sewers were often of an inferior quality, and frequently even those with indoor plumbing found they had minimal water pressure or effective sanitary facilities. In Philadelphia, the Delaware River into the twentieth century frequently overflooded the narrow alley streets of Northern Liberties and Southwark, bringing garbage, excrement, and dead animals in its wake.[19] Even this cursory stroll through Philadelphia might be enough to illuminate how the place earned its nineteenth-century nickname, "Filthy-Dirty."

Physical filth had its moral equivalent, too. The streets just to the west and south of the old colonial city in the traditional Black Belt between South and Spruce Streets remained a notorious vice district of blind pigs (illegal saloons), whorehouses, and gambling dens throughout the nineteenth century.[20] While Monk Hall is an exaggeration, Lippard located his den in this Southwark vice zone, which was indeed where the city's grand dissolute sons would have gone if they needed the services of a black pimp like Devil Bug. And during the Civil War, the city fathers were so alarmed at the proliferation of Philadelphia's ladies of the evening seeking out soldiers in transit to Virginia that they established a municipal Prostitutes' Register, which provided detailed information on the birthplace, age, residence, employment history, and reason for entering the "trade" of the city's prostitutes.[21]

Not surprisingly, then, Lippard urged his Philadelphians to heal their own wounds before reforming others. While a high-society Protestant minister denounces the sins of "Pagan Rome," an elderly "American citizen" whose father had fought with Washington at Monmouth, Trenton, Germantown, and Brandywine quietly asks the revival meeting, "Do we not want Missionaries in this our good city? Are there no holes of vice, to be illuminated by the light of God's own Gospel? . . . Are there no hideous moral sores to be examined and healed by the Missionary of Jesus in this our moral heart of Philadelphia, ere we cut off the limb of Pagan Rome, or bind up the wounds of idolatrous Hindoostan?" The pious crowd hoots the old son of a veteran out of the meeting hall, but we have already been taken by the author on a shameless tour of Philadelphia's red-light district, and we know the answer to the citizen's heretical rhetorical question.[22]

If Lippard was overdramatizing the sins of the Quaker City, he couldn't have picked a more opportune year in which to do it. Philadelphia witnessed in May 1844 the first large-scale rioting against Irish Catholic newcomers, riots that "arose out of the hostility of the Native Americans, probably aided by Orangemen, against the Catholics." A public meeting of nativist mechanics and weavers was held in Nannygoat Square in Kensington, which already had an appreciable Irish Catholic population. The crowd was worked into a frenzy by speakers denouncing the slavish nature of papists who were stealing the jobs of "real Americans" (some things never change) at the district's textile mills. Nativists marched for the districts' Catholic churches but were at first repulsed by Irish residents bombarding them with bricks and curses. True Americanism's defenders regrouped, however, and after a rally at Independence Square burned down two Catholic churches, a rectory, and a Catholic orphanage. As Philadelphia's volunteer town watch looked on helplessly, or maybe indifferently, at the burning spires of St. Augustine's and St. Michael's, the patriotic arsonists made their escape by walking a mere two blocks out of the old colonial city and into the safety of Northern Liberties.[23]

Surely this cataclysm's similarity to the fiery destruction of Philadelphia in Devil Bug's dream was mere coincidence: Not even the most calculating press agent or author could have arranged this kind of media tie-in. Indeed, Lippard presented a "fictional" Philadelphia in which "Justice" turns her back and allows churches to be burned down, and in which "a licentious mob administers justice with the Knife and the Torch."[24] Lippard also included a mocking send-up of hypocritical Protestant revivalists, whose Universal Patent Gospel Missionary Society promised their followers, "We hold it to be a comfortable doctrine, to abuse the Pope o' Rome afore breakfast, and after breakfast, and all day long! . . . Our Gospel is a gospel of fire and brimstone and abuse o' the Pope o' Rome, mingled in equal quantities . . . that's what our Gospel is!"[25]

To be sure, in the book Lippard seems to have been mocking the sham revivalists, who make a very nice living by bilking their credulous sheep, as much as the followers of "the old Pagan in the Vatican." He has his fake evangelist, The Rev. F.A.T. Pyne, conclude his sermon with an odd mixture of sentiments: "Down with

the Pope—up with fire and brimstone; up with toleration; up with the Bible!"
Nevertheless, Pyne's warning of the pope's "grand plan of buying up the state of
Missouri" and moving the College of Cardinals to Faneuil Hall resonated with
many real Philadelphians. Not for the last time, as we'll see, enraged Americans
regarded Catholic newcomers as a threat to the virtue of the American republic.[26]
And when Lippard ended his novel with a vision of an entire city burning to the
ground as a just climax to the accumulated weight of municipal sins, he was
feeding on respectable society's fears of just such outcomes in the real antebellum
city. Rioting nativists battling an Irish and black "underclass" may have inspired
no less horror than the later 1960s urban disturbances in Detroit and Newark. At
least, judging from the secret fears of upper-class diarists such as Philip Hone and
George Templeton Strong, Lippard wasn't overstating the case; in their eyes,
Philadelphia, New York, and other cities were in danger of burning.

Whether because he had proved such an accurate prophet of Philadelphia's sin,
or because he told a city-phobic public what it wanted to hear, Lippard remained
a popular and prolific chronicler of the urban cesspool until his untimely death in
1854 at age thirty-two. And he was not alone. Dozens of similar fictional guides
to the urban warrens of vice were rushed into print in the next several decades.
Accounts warned out-of-towners that New York, Chicago, Philadelphia, and other
cities were hotbeds of vice, violence, pitiless conmen, and toughs. George Foster's
1850 *Celio, or New York Above Ground and Under Ground,* unmasked in fiction
the vices that supposedly infested Manhattan, and this fifty years before the
subway whisked the great unwashed so rapidly around the anonymous city. Indeed, it was the anonymity of the urban crowd and the promiscuous mixing of
classes that caused great alarm in these novels. Foster's *New York by Gas-Light*
presented a city of decadent, effete aristocrats seeking their thrills among the
lower depths, and both the fabulously wealthy and the utterly destitute were
depicted as a threat to the virtuous republic of rough egalitarianism. "What a task
we have undertaken!" Foster gushed in 1850, "to penetrate beneath the thick veil
of night and lay bare the fearful mysteries of darkness in the metropolis." The
mysteries Foster and others lay bare invariably involved the dissipations of the
decadent rich and the depravities of the desperate poor, so that, as Stuart Blumin
rightly notes, the vast majority of the middle sort with their predictable but unin-
candescent round of work and occasional play were largely missing from the work
of "Gaslight" Foster and other novelists of New York, Philadelphia, and other
lurid cities.[27]

Lippard repeated this scenario in his own New York novels, *The Empire City*
and *New York: Its Upper Ten and Lower Million,* in which the entire city has been
undermined by a honeycomb of vice and cabal, tying the wealthy and penniless
together in a plot on the virtuous middle. In Lippard's New York it was the Jesuits
who were plotting to subvert the republic. Other popular authors got in on the act,
with Ned Buntline publishing *The Mysteries and Miseries of New York* in 1848.
Many imitators followed, for city dreadfuls far outpaced pastoral novels in the
mid nineteenth century; it seems Americans wanted to be appalled by their own

dens of vice. As Paul Erickson notes, these novels of urban mysteries tied together the twin perils of "rum and starvation wages to the urban poor alongside
the perils of the combination of excessive wealth and weak moral fiber to the
urban elite." Whether on Fifth Avenue or in Five Points, New York was a threat to
the republic of virtue.[28]

Erickson argues that some books, such as *New York by Gas-Light,* that offered
"urban sketches" were a distinct genre from city mystery novels, since they presented several discrete slices of urban life rather than one grand baroque plot of
interlocking cabals of the high and mighty and the wretched urban cutpurse.[29]
While not full-scale novels, these urban sketches nevertheless seemed fully capable of producing the same city-phobia in middle-class American readers. Both
created a sense in the reading public of cities as chaotic and dangerous places,
even if they might be entertaining so long as one only read of Five Points or South
Philadelphia's warrens, from the safety of one's library. Moreover, both genres
were practiced by the very same authors, such as Foster, and even in urban sketches
great liberties were taken with the facts in pursuit of a good story or portrait of an
urban jungle. Whether in novels or slice-of-life sketchbooks, the city suffered.

Even smaller cities—such as Pittsfield, Massachusetts; Rochester, New York;
and Lowell, and Fitchburg, Massachusetts—were said to contain their own urban
"mysteries" of vice in need of exposure! An 1848 exposé of *Life in Rochester* was
subtitled *Scenes of Misery, Vice, Shame, and Oppression in the City of the Genesee.*
The blind pigs, whorehouses, and palaces of the shamelessly wealthy were just as
shockingly good copy in a city of fifty thousand as a city of five hundred thousand.
At mid century most Americans preferred to look back to their agrarian roots;
even as recently as 1800 only six American cities had had populations over ten
thousand. It was therefore easy to exaggerate the alarming vice and squalor found
even in smaller cities such as Rochester. And again, it was the purpose of such
urban exposés to warn, or titillate, readers (or maybe both) with both the highs and
lows of city life. Stuart Blumin has argued that such writers offered "the big city
as a shockingly abnormal collection of the very rich and the very poor, and to
emphasize the difference between the big city and more traditional communities
by exaggerating the polarization of urban society."[30]

We can question the accuracy of positing an idyllic, harmonious rural community of rough equality in which all shared common interests and outlooks. Indeed,
even the most popular retailer of the fictional frontier, James Fenimore Cooper,
noted the rapid imposition of class hierarchies in the villages of his Mohawk
Valley, not that he allowed Natty Bumpo to approve of this process.[31] But Cooper
himself was the scion of privilege, and elsewhere in colonial and early republican America, such as in Virginia, the ideal of egalitarianism masked a reality
riven with deference by the lower class to the elite, who expected to rule, a situation periodically violently contested by outbreaks such as Bacon's Rebellion of
the 1670s, Shays' Rebellion in 1780s western Massachusetts, and the Whiskey
Rebellion on the western Pennsylvania frontier a decade later. Small-town artisans erupted in enraged job actions when their prerogatives were challenged

in towns, not just large cities, throughout the nineteenth century's first half. Nevertheless, for all this occasionally uncomfortable evidence to the contrary, the myth of agrarian harmony was still a powerful trope in the early nineteenth century.[32]

This idyllic dream was increasingly disrupted by messy urbanism, however, which helps explain why these city mysteries seemed to resonate with a reading public that increasingly sensed that something was wrong with the American Dream, or at least that the old goal of artisan self-sufficiency was no longer quite so easily attainable in the mid nineteenth century. But if the dream had mutated into a nightmare, it was somehow impossible to blame the Founding Fathers, or to imagine that this promise of easy egalitarianism (at least for native-born white Protestant men) was a chimera from the beginning. The Founding Fathers could not be accused of having sold the nation a bill of goods; a scapegoat needed to be found.

Like Lippard, succeeding "city mystery" authors wrote guidebooks that sought out the dens of iniquity polluting otherwise virtuous America. The glaring, tangible symbols that something was wrong with the classless egalitarian dream of the country had to be exposed as the reapers of their own improvidence, in no small part because their very presence reminded Americans of a nagging suspicion that the country's reality was not living up to its advance billing, that the promise just maybe had been predicated on a lie.[33] Not for the last time gate-crashers of the great big American party, the poor, were put in their place. And it was not pretty.

City mysteries' story lines often contained a credulous man—or better yet, woman—who arrived in Manhattan (or Rochester) and trusted a quickly made friend who seemingly bent over backward to aid the newcomer and then robbed her blind or greased her slide into some gutter or house of ill repute. New York and other cities might have been more exciting than whatever small town one was living in, but the excitement came at a heavy price. Of course, if these fictionalized words of warning didn't always dissuade readers from visiting the big, bad city, semifictionalized guidebooks to various cities also often contained a Baedeker of metropolitan whorehouses, for the intrepid traveler's convenience. And then once these "resorts" became popular with the sons of the idle rich, they were condemned by novelists, too. The city, then, was condemned for the sins of both the idle rich and the shiftless poor; the reader, authors presumed, identified with the virtuous middle, the producing class of real Americans.

These novels of urban despair, disguised as travel guides to sin city, reflect a nagging disappointment, already by the 1840s and 1850s, in the promise of the American Dream itself. The old ideal of becoming a self-sufficient artisan, someone capable of earning a moderate degree of prosperity, a "competence," died hard in the national psyche. As scholars such as Bruce Laurie and Sean Wilentz have pointed out, workers resisted the evidence all around them in Philadelphia, Boston, New York, and smaller cities, too, that the artisan ideal of moving up and out of dependency was a fading relic of an earlier time. Workers attempted to restore the artisan republic to its glory days by organizing the nation's first trade unions and workingmen's parties in the 1830s, but the Panic of 1837 swept away this early effort at self-help, and what remained by the time Lippard began writing was a rhetorical salute to the noble mechanic that masked an increasing degradation of his status.[34]

The artisan's republic would endure as a powerful political myth for decades. In 1860, Abe Lincoln would run for the presidency as the humble man who had started in a log cabin and made it to the heights of respectability. Perhaps because he embodied the kind of vertical social mobility that had almost been promised as a birth right to all white males, perhaps because they had to believe that such useful national myths were realizable, enough "mudsills and greasy mechanics" of New York, Philadelphia, Chicago, and dozens of other places voted for Lincoln to put him in the White House. Yet, as the slur *mudsill* bestowed on the lowly mechanics indicates, not all urbanites approved of the antebellum workingman. And when native-born artisans cheered on their man Lincoln in torchlight parades that defiantly embraced their status as "mudsills and greasy mechanics," they were only continuing the contestation for legitimacy and claims to represent themselves as respectable, albeit rougher, Americans that had set the theater ablaze—at least once, literally.[35]

Antebellum stages often featured depictions of "Mose" and his "Bowery B'hoys," working-class toughs who were streetwise and jaunty in asserting their place in "the Republic of the Bowery," that jumble of workingmen's saloons, dime museums, cheap theaters, and music halls in Lower Manhattan. First depicted in Benjamin Baker's 1848 play, *A Glance at New York,* Mose became a folk hero for the young, single tough guys of Manhattan and other urban places. The Bowery B'hoys dressed in outlandish manner with slicked-down forelocks, gaudily colored suits, expensive walking sticks, high working boots, and tall beaver hats set at a jaunty, defiant angle. Avid drinkers, carousers, and battlers with rival gangs, the Bowery toughs comically asserted their place in the urban landscape, with stage plays devoted to their exploits and their aggressive aping of their betters. George G. Foster, prolific tour guide to the shadows of New York, characterized Mose's best girl, Lize, as strutting down the Bowery with "a swing of mischief and defiance," like her paramour dressing "high," in "startling contrasts which Lize considers 'some pumpkins' and Mose swears is 'gallus!'" Often members of a patriotic nativist volunteer fire company, "Mose" and his gang defiantly take on all comers, whether Fifth Avenue dandies or threatening Irish immigrants encroaching on their turf.[36]

Life imitates art, and many young native-born New York working toughs emulated the look of their theatrical hero, and for a time the Bowery B'hoy could be seen in his multicolored dandy outfits in many cities. Respectable New Yorkers gawked at the B'hoys' conspicuous consumption and rowdy carousals with dismay; thoughts of the nineteenth-century equivalent of gangsta bling perhaps crossed their minds. For their part, lower-class dandies, just like Foster and Lippard, may have regarded the wealthy of an industrializing society, whose tastes and fashions they satirically inverted into their own urban style, as threats to a self-respecting Protestant artisan's independent standing.[37]

The feel of the Bowery B'hoy and his haunts in and near New York's notorious Five Points slum is vividly portrayed in Martin Scorsese's loose adaptation of Herbert Asbury's *Gangs of New York*. Daniel Day Lewis's Butcher is an over-the-top, albeit accurate, depiction of the kind of defiant Five Points dandy who graced Bowery theaters to the cheers of working-class audiences. With his high fireman's boots and artisan butcher tools (and sadistic readiness to use them against rival gangs, especially of hated papist foreigners whom he blames for the decline of the republic his father fought for alongside Washington), Butcher is a type who would have been embraced by 1850s Bowery theatergoers.[38]

The violence of Scorsese's fight scenes would have resonated, too, with New Yorkers, for workers knew from their own personal experience that the Five Points was a dangerous place, and that volunteer fire companies were only a slightly more refined name for ethnically defined fighting gangs. Moreover, the repugnance Butcher inspires in his Fifth Avenue collaborators in keeping down the Irish echoes the alarm the Bowery B'hoy inspired when this tough dandy of Lower Manhattan strutted out onto the street, a fear that was mirrored in stage portrayals of the day. While working-class audiences embraced "Mose, the Bowery B'hoy," as one of their own, upper-class New Yorkers viewed Bowery toughs on both sides of the footlights with increasing alarm; at least the lower-class threat that Foster, Lippard, Buntline, and others luridly predicted in their novels seemed to be all too apparent to Fifth Avenue in the antebellum theater.[39]

In 1849, stage violence spilled over onto the streets. When some of the Bowery theatergoers objected to the perceived slights that America's favorite homegrown Shakespearean actor, Edwin Forrest, received from uptown snobs who preferred the performance of visiting Englishman William Macready, the B'hoys decided to infiltrate the hated elite Astor Place Opera House and give the actor a downtown welcome; eggs, dung, and other souvenirs were hurled at the stage. When Macready tried to take the stage three days later, a mob of twenty thousand assaulted the opera house. The National Guard from the Seventh Regiment intervened to save the "civilized community" from the "mob" of "the baser sort," firing into the crowd and killing twenty-two and injuring thirty-eight. The "better class of the community" had been avenged, and an uneasy truce reigned in class-ridden New York, not to be broken for another fourteen years.[40]

Other Bowery B'hoys, even self-confessed "participants" in the 1849 Astor Place Riot, would later look back on their time in the gangs of New York with a more indulgent, wistful attitude. Writing forty-eight years after the pitched battles at the elite theater, John W. Ripley's account recalled:

I was at that time what was known as a "Bowery Boy," a distinct 'gang' from either the "know nothing" or "Native American" parties. The gang had no regular organization, but were a crowd of young men of different nationalities, mostly American born, who were always ready for excitement, generally of an innocent nature.

Whether society types fleeing the opera melee would have characterized Ripley and his friends as "generally of an innocent nature" is questionable. Foster had characterized the B'hoys in generally sympathetic tones but noted that these toughs spent a lot of time loitering on Manhattan street corners or in taverns, a constant worry to New York's better sort, who liked their opera going without the dung. The B'hoy "thinks little of his future destiny, and seems unconscious of any powers other than those brought into play by a race for a fire plug or a scamper on the avenue." Was this a young man "ready for excitement" or a well-dressed (if gaudy) bum with no gumption or ability to find a good-paying place in rapidly industrializing America?

Like the stage depiction of the Bowery B'hoy, accounts of the 1849 Astor Place Riot were contested images, with working-class New Yorkers seeing the brawl as defense of their favorite's honor against slights by foreign (and homegrown) aristocrats, while elite Astor Place residents read into the battles urban disorder and cataclysm of the kind George Wallace, Frank Rizzo, and Tough Tony Imperiale would see in the urban disturbances of 1967.[41]

As in the 1960s, a series of "tough on crime" measures arose to put the city's lawless millions back in their supposed place; even though mid-nineteenth-century rioters shared race and often even native-born Protestant status with Philadelphia and New York elites, city fathers were not reassured that peace and harmony could prevail without a gloved fist of restraint. As Stuart Blumin has documented, Philadelphia blue bloods increasingly came to fear rowdy urban mechanics, who often lived only a few streets away from the best Philadelphia addresses. Workers' often assertive attempts to reclaim their former prerogatives led to the establishment of a professionalized police force to supplement the old elite militia companies and restrain the urban mob. Similar moves establishing police forces gained ground in other American cities, as the new urban masses, especially those who were Catholic, foreign-born, and alarmingly Celtic, led to fears that the old voluntary town watches and gentlemen's militia companies were not up to the task. After all, it was only a short walk from Five Points to elite Astor Place; the poor were uncomfortably, assertively close at hand, as the Astor Place Riot and 1863's rampaging Irish draft rioters made alarmingly clear.[42]

Indeed, in the middle of the Civil War, America experienced its first "long, hot summer," although here it was not New York's minuscule free black population that instigated the riot. Rather, blacks suffered as targets of Irish working-class rage at the imposition of a military draft that ensured the poor and friendless would fight to free their supposed rivals for jobs on the docks of the city. In July 1863, Irish New Yorkers lashed out in the aftermath of the new draft law that allowed the wealthy to pay three hundred dollars (more than the annual wages of many immigrant workers) to buy a substitute. The mob attacked Yankee patricians, black rivals, and city police alike. As Joe Feagin and Harlan Hahn make clear, the draft was merely "a precipitating event" that allowed the Irish stevedores, enraged at the use of black strikebreakers, to vent their frustration, in an urban riot that had similar parallels among the actions of Baltimore dockworkers and boat builders enraged at the use by some businessmen of cheaper free black work gangs that well-connected Baltimore businessmen sometimes protected from white workers' wrath. In New York, for better than a week the Irish rioters ruled the streets, and the respectably staid and Republican *New York Times* covered this "urban disturbance" with uncharacteristically apocalyptic alarm.[43]

The enormity of patrician New Yorkers' alarm at the rampaging Irish, characterized by the *New York Times* as "barbarian hordes," should be clear from the brutal, swift, officially sanctioned reprisal. State militia troops were brought in to put down the riots and fought pitched battles with the ghetto hordes. More than four hundred civilians were killed by the police and militia, with hundreds of others injured and millions of dollars in property damage assessed. The rioters themselves extracted a toll on elite New Yorkers, pillaging Fifth Avenue before the forces of law and order could come in and do their brutal work.

But the draft rioters also extracted "vengeance" on New York's freedmen, killing eighteen people and burning a colored orphanage. To Irish New Yorkers the city was perceived as a conspiracy of high and low: the patricians who exploited them and the black New Yorkers who they feared would take their jobs and whom they were now expected to fight and die for in "a rich man's war and a poor man's fight." The point remains, though, that while the Draft Riots have largely been forgotten by popular-culture purveyors (at least until Scorsese featured them in the climax of *Gangs of New York*), in their own time the draft rioters inspired just as much dread and urban loathing as the Detroit and Newark rioters 104 Julys later. With more than four hundred deaths, largely at the hands of the forces of city and state authority, it is hard to disagree with Feagin and Hahn in concluding, "It is clear that no American riot, before or since, was of greater seriousness." Certainly in 1863 Hibernian New York elicited just as much dread in the upper classes as black Newark and Detroit would in 1967.[44]

As a result, it's not surprising that at least some novelists found their solution to the menace of the city in scapegoating the foreigners in their midst. Ned Buntline, popular author of city mysteries, would join the Native American Party, which blamed the Catholic immigrants for much of America's fractious nature in the 1850s. Buntline was not alone, for New York for a time had a Nativist mayor, publishing magnate James Harper, whose magazine gave much of the country its impression of the state of dangerous, unruly New York. Massachusetts, too, in the 1850s elected a Nativist governor to put Boston's wild urban horde in its place.[45]

While circa 1900 the urban menace would assume a Jewish, Italian, or Slavic character, already just before and during the Civil War some old stock Americans looked with alarm at the cities' violent immigrants. Fifth Avenue or Rittenhouse Square residents read their Foster and nervously glanced at the "lower depths" in the city's ominous "shadows" seemingly right around the corner. Working-class city residents had a different take. In their own daily lives in South Philly or Lower Manhattan, some sort of sinister conspiracy seemed to be blocking their chance to earn a "competency," and in their leisure hours such urban workingmen turned to the "city mysteries" with tales of secret cabals of high and low to see if they could figure out what had gone wrong with their towns.

Even a cursory look at the Philadelphia of Lippard indicates that many Americans often received a view of the country's cities that was unflattering or brutal. Around 1880, though, the dangerous city began to be conceptualized as positively exotic, as slums filled with newcomers who scared many old-stock Americans more than a thousand Devil Bugs.

Talk of urban blight began to reach a crescendo of alarm in the closing decades of the century as ever larger waves of non-Nordic immigrants inundated the cities. Progressive authors peddled The City as the site of danger, thrills, and exotic ethnic difference, and they explored the political impact that such urban safaris had on America. Cities began to be rethought of as dangerously foreign places as they filled with Italians, Slavs, and Jews, alien "races" who many nativists believed could never adapt to the American way of life. Italians' supposedly innate criminality was not just dangerous to the unwary pedestrian who might wander into Mulberry Bend after dark; rather, Mediterraneans' unfamiliarity with or incapacity for self-government threatened to rob the nation of its republican birthright, too.[46]

In the closing decades of the nineteenth century, and into the new century, the immigrant ghetto was a popular place. And new technologies of mass communication made it easier to convey messages of urban alarm in the mass-circulation magazines and newspapers that brought the sights and sounds of the ghetto to a middle-class readership far quicker than pre–Civil War novelists and writers for the broadsheets. Writers for gentlemen's magazines such as *The Century, Harper's, McClure's,* and *Scribner's,* as well as daily newspapers, sought to explain the "new immigrant" to native Americans. Yet, while the characterizations of immigrants often appeared in magazines that ostensibly were nonfiction, the boundary between the genres of fact and fiction still remained porous. The same writers who worked as journalists also published literature, often in the same magazines or serialized in newspapers, too.

The war correspondent and big-city journalist Stephen Crane is only the most celebrated of these genre straddlers. Crane also published the fictional exposé of city poverty *Maggie: A Girl of the Streets*, as well as his other "Bowery Tales," in general-interest magazines and newspapers. Before he realistically captured the complexities of the Civil War in *The Red Badge of Courage,* Crane depicted the life of poor Bowery girls reduced to prostitution *(Maggie);* an Irish son who is his adoring mother's favorite but falls in with whiskey-guzzling companions ("George's Mother") while his disillusioned, broken mother slips into a state of delirium and melodramatically dies before she can convince her son to return to the Church; and the grim vigil of an amalgam of Germans, Irish, and native Americans who have lost the race of life and glumly wait for a Bowery soup kitchen and flophouse to open its doors so they can escape a roaring blizzard and claim a bit of charity ("The Men in the Storm").[47] Written in the depth of the Panic of 1893, "The Men in the Storm" offers a vignette of quietly desperate homeless men huddled beneath the elevated tracks. They are waiting for a flophouse to open and offer at least one evening's relief from the snowfall, and also from the depression engulfing New York, Chicago, and much of the rest of the country:

In this half-darkness, the men began to come from their shelter-places and mass in front of the doors of charity. They were all types, but the nationalities were mostly American, German, and Irish. Many were strong, healthy, clear-skinned fellows, . . . who, in times of ill-fortune, do not habitually turn to rail at the state of society, snarling at the arrogance of the rich and bemoaning the cowardice of the poor, but who at these times are apt to wear a sudden and singular meekness, as if they saw the world's progress marching from them, and were trying to perceive where they had failed, what they had lacked, to be thus vanquished in the race. Then there were others, of the shifting Bowery element, who were used to paying ten cents for a place to sleep, but who now came there because it was cheaper.[48]

Crane was sympathetic to this desperate Bowery throng, but in a time when virtually no social support was available to those trampled by the march of "the world's progress," those reading the story of a flophouse mob were likely as alarmed as they were sympathetic. In 1893 it was too uncomfortably possible for many New Yorkers or Chicagoans to imagine themselves in the same position, and other journalists, such as Helen Campbell and Jacob Riis, were simultaneously presenting ominous accounts of the city's myriad ten-cent dives, black and tans, and police station makeshift shelters, where hundreds of thousands spent night after hopeless night. Charity contended with revulsion in those who read of these flophouses.

Another of Crane's "Bowery Tales" takes this act of imaginative sympathy with despairing slum dwellers even further. "An Experiment in Misery," which first appeared in the *New York Press* in 1894, begins with two young friends regarding a tramp. "I wonder how he feels," one comments. "I suppose he is homeless, friendless, and has, at the most, only a few cents in his pocket. And if this is so, I wonder how he feels." The other friend encourages him to try an experiment by disguising himself as a tramp to find out the answer himself. In Chatham Square, gateway to the old Five Points slum, the disguised young man finds a horde of tramps in tatters like his. He follows one of them to a seedy dive that promises "Free Soup Tonight!" although the gruel is barely worth the price of the beer he must buy as well. He quickly leaves the dive, "following a man whose wondrous seediness promised that he would have a knowledge of cheap lodging-houses." The guide does know of such lodgings but will only help the disguised tramp if he gives him three cents so he can afford the price of a room. The disguised man is appalled by the stench that greets them as they climb the stairs to the flophouse. "Shortly after the beginning of this journey the young man felt his liver turn white, for from the dark and secret places of the building there suddenly came to his nostrils strange and unspeakable odours, that assailed him like malignant diseases with wings, . . . the fumes from a thousand bygone debauches; the expression of a thousand present miseries."

That's not all that assaults the impersonator's senses. In the night, packed in among the other tramps on tiny cots, he is awakened by the shrieks of a tramp

who in his dreams was oppressed by some frightful calamity, for of a sudden he began to utter long wails that went almost like yells from a hound, echoing wailfully . . . through this chill place of tombstones where men lay like the dead. . . . To the youth they were not merely the shrieks of a vision-pierced man; they were an utterance of the meaning of the room and its occupants. It was to him the protest of the wretch who feels the touch of the imperturbable granite wheels, and who then cries with an impersonal eloquence, with a strength not from him, giving voice to the wail of a whole section, a class, a people.

In the morning he discovers his comrade scratching at the lice bites on his neck. "Hully Jee, dis is a new breed. They've got can openers on their feet," his comrade curses the vermin who've shared his lodgings without forking over their ten cents.[49]

The readers of Crane's "Bowery Tales" would likely have been unsurprised to find such filthy conditions in Manhattan dives, for magazine writers had been exposing the tenement evil, the flophouse scourge, and the vices of gambling and liquor dens with increasing fervor in the 1880s and 1890s. Jacob Riis made his career exposing the pathological state of the slums. And Helen Campbell, who exposed New York's *Darkness and Daylight* with her pen and camera in 1895, flatly declared, "The city is the natural gathering place of all the carrion birds" before she gave hundreds of pages of more graphic vignettes of "tenements where, in defiance of every law, moral and sanitary, men, women and children are crowded together like maggots in a cheese."[50]

Tenements, and their tenants, alarmed Progressives. Even when catchy Tin Pan Alley songs ostensibly celebrated the polyglot diversity of noisy, chaotic immigrant Manhattan, some notes indicated all was not well. "McNally's Row of Flats," by celebrated vaudevillian Ned Harrigan, listed "Irish, German, Jewish, Italian, Chinese, African," and other exotic types in this tenement but also sneered at this "paradise for rats!," which "the Tower of Babylonia couldn't equal that,/ A peculiar institution, for brogues without dilution,/ They rattled on together in McNally's row of flats." While on the East Side humor might be a needed form of self-defense, some Victorian slumologists perhaps were not amused.[51]

The human rats often alarmed affluent urbanites even more than tenement rodents, as Campbell's telling comparison of tenement dwellers to "maggots in a cheese" suggests. When Campbell elaborated, without a Tin Pan Alley accompaniment, the situation didn't improve. Campbell offered vignettes titled "Up Slaughter Alley . . . A Tour through Homes of Misery, Want, and Woe—Drink's Doings," illustrated with line drawings supposedly taken from photographs snapped in the dank alleys and courtyards in which filth, sloth, and criminality were regarded as equally to blame on slumlords and slum dwellers alike. Social Darwinism had already inculcated a notion that those losing the race to the bottom in Rockefeller's and Carnegie's America had only themselves to blame. Magazine writers, too, shared Herbert Spencer and William Graham Sumner's suspicion that especially when it came to non-Nordic types, there was likely a genetic factor at work explaining the filth of the tenements, and that ameliorative social legislation was futile at best, counterproductive in prolonging the lives of the "unfit" at worst.[52]

Campbell seems to have shared this conclusion. A further chapter of *Darkness and Daylight* is titled "Human Beasts in Filthy Dens." Here she visits a tenement inhabited by longshoremen with a female doctor, who takes care to point out the sink at the end of each floor's hall, a result of Progressive reformers' housing crusades. The doctor says:

That is a concession to popular prejudice. At first there was water only in the yard, and I am not certain but that they were as well off, since the sink is always stopped with filth; and the waterclosets fare the same, all the refuse going down there. . . . What could the Board of Health do in a house like this? . . . What good, when these human beasts flock here, with no chance of being anything but beasts so long as they have no desire to improve? It is a case of reflex action. The tenement pulls them down, but they also pull down the tenement.

Boardinghouse visits are grouped under a heading, "Where Criminals Are Bred," and Campbell sniffs, "Chiefest of all sources of misery and infamy . . . is the fact that well nigh every family harbor from two to eight or ten additional inmates, and that life is as promiscuous as that of brutes. The saloon is a perpetual invitation to spend earnings, and the atmosphere of the ward is one not only of wretchedness but of crime of every order."

Drunkenness, crime, sexual looseness, thievery, wanton slovenliness, and destruction of sinks and other benevolent improvements offered by enlightened reformers—the nineteenth-century immigrant slum dweller was guilty (in the eyes of Progressives) of virtually every sin that African-American residents of public housing would be accused of seventy years later. The popular conception of New York retailed by magazine writers, whether of short stories or "true" slum exposés, was not one to cheer Gotham's civic boosters.[53]

Crane's story of "An Experiment in Misery" ends with the tramps released from their flophouse into the tedium of a new day. The impersonator follows his flea-bitten colleague to yet another dive, but after they've lingered over a stale roll and greasy coffee as long as they can, there is nothing to do but shuffle into City Hall Park and camp on the benches: "They huddled in their old garments, slumbrously conscious of the march of the hours which for them had no meaning." As they lounge in the park, middle-class New Yorkers hurry by, avoiding eye contact with the wretches. Realizing he is in fact a bum, not just an impersonator, the masquerader settles in for the long, idle vigil as respectable New York continues "ignoring the wretches who may founder at its feet." The shamed tramp/impersonator "confessed himself an outcast, and his eyes from under the lowered rim of his hat began to glance guiltily, wearing the criminal expression that comes with certain convictions."[54]

Crane likewise dealt with the outcasts of Lower Manhattan in *Maggie,* in which all the urban pathologies of the popular press's accounts—drunken Irish fathers; rival gangs of fighting, thieving alley dwellers (Maggie's brother Jimmy is the leader of the Rum Alley gang, hated rivals of Devil's Row hooligans); con men; and fallen women seduced into brief, sorrowful lives in the white slave trade as "a woman of brilliance and audacity"—are concentrated in one awful tale of ruin. While Crane's account expresses some sympathy for the victims of the slums, he was already writing in a well-trodden template of shocking slum vignettes and in a time that frequently blamed the poor sufferer of virtually any misfortunes as a victim of his or her own moral failings. Social Darwinism's tenets required that the "undeserving poor" be so readily dismissed; otherwise the state might be required to step in and do something for the millions for whom any glimmer of attaining the American Dream of self-sufficiency receded year by year into a mirage of fantasy. In the Gilded Age any such suggestion that the poor might be in need of positive government action to smooth the rougher edges of capitalism lost out to the great gods of laissez-faire, a situation that would prevail for another forty years, until an even more severe depression. As a result the chasm between the lucky few who escaped New York's or Chicago's poverty and despair and the idle millions loomed ever wider as the nineteenth century came to a close, and working-class cities were again viewed with alarm.[55]

While Crane's language is staid and Victorian to our ears, his description of a busy downtown of rushing businessmen stepping over and around the thousands of wretches in rags parked right at City Hall's doorstep is evocative of our own day and age. Moreover, while Crane's depictions may seem genteel to post-Tarantino eyes, they were in the 1890s sometimes condemned as immoral, and Richard Watson Gilder, editor of the respectable *Century* magazine, rejected his "Bowery Tales" as unsuitable for a family readership.

Other writers of great power took up the theme of the poverty of toilers in great cities, and they were similarly condemned as immoral. Theodore Dreiser's *Sister Carrie* was refused publication in 1900 until Dreiser significantly altered some of his story's "immoral" content, and still the story of Carrie Meeker's travails in Chicago, and then triumphs in becoming a celebrity in New York, appalled many. As with Crane's misery experimenter, *Sister Carrie* also contains an account of a successful man brought low, not as a lark but by a string of misfortunes common to far too many Gilded Age Americans only a Panic away from disaster. The dandyish Hurstwood seduces Carrie but then becomes obsessed with her and loses his standing as a restaurant manager, only to end his days in a flophouse, where he commits suicide. Such an account may have cut too close to the bone in an America that knew the ease with which even a respectable man could fall through the wide cracks in Chicago's or New York's industrial economy.[56]

So, too, Frank Norris published *McTeague: A Story of San Francisco,* in which the working-class Polk Street district figures prominently as a skid row of broken dreams. Here some of 1899 America's most vivid nightmares were brought to life: McTeague, a simian Irish brute, somehow for a time passes himself off as a dentist, until his baser nature and greed spur him on to kill his wife when she refuses to hand over a small fortune she has won in a lottery. Zerkow is a Jewish ragpicker who is almost primordially filthy and greedy, with all the stereotypical, almost animal traits of cunning that cartoonists poured into their portraits of big-city Jews. There are also German-Swiss radicals in exile who condemn capitalism in their idle reveries in Scheutzen Park. As in Crane, Dreiser, and other naturalists, sympathetic accounts are given of the struggles of working-class immigrants battling against the odds in San Francisco's tougher neighborhoods, but the picture that emerges is of a city and city dwellers very much overwhelmed by the enormity of pathologies and poverty.[57]

If Norris, Dreiser, and Crane, too, at first were regarded as slightly immoral writers, at least in their frank portraits of Chicago, New York, and San Francisco as cities that barely worked, perhaps this was because surveyors of city life were uncomfortable with too much illumination on this nagging problem, and it was easier to condemn writers of homeless tales or novels of working men driven to suicide or murder than to find ways to solve the myriad urban problems in robber baron America. Indeed, Jacob Riis and other reformers warned New York that it was facing a homeless crisis, and in the depths of the nineteenth century's most ruinous depression, many feared the idle outcasts of industrial America no less than today's homeless are sometimes criminalized as a threat to the city's order.

During her voyeuristic tour of New York's slums in their *Darkness and Daylight,* Helen Campbell frequently broke her reporter's dispassion and expressed repugnance not so much for the conditions of poverty she found but for the poor themselves. Crime was the inevitable by-product of the combination of bad housing stock and bad "racial" stock, with "race" referring to the Irish, Italian, and other newcomers who were found wanting in comparison to earlier native-born workers. Campbell promised that "the tenement-houses . . . are making of the generation now coming up a terror in the present and a promise of future evil beyond man's power to reckon." Ironically, the earlier Bowery B'hoy who terrorized George Templeton Strong and other respectable Astor Place or Fifth Avenue New Yorkers was by 1895 held up by Campbell as a far superior form of urban working man than the newcomer. Campbell admitted that in the "Bloody Sixth Ward" of the notorious Five Points the Bowery B'hoys once made a "name of terror" for themselves, but that now the hoodlums of Irish parentage presented a "type far beyond it in evil," "knowing liberty only as the extremity of license."[58] She offered Lower Manhattan's Bayard Street as a den of iniquity in which young thugs who'd read of the evil deeds of bad role models in "dime novels" now practiced their crimes on unsuspecting real-life New Yorkers. In a vicious circle, it was thus popular culture once again to blame, for portraying all too accurately the crime and immorality of city thugs that writers had already learned to read as "a swarm of cockroaches," "street rats," and "happy barbarians," in Campbell's own gleefully contemptuous phrases for young street arabs of the urban poor.[59]

Further wanderings through Five Points and the Fourth Ward introduced the reader to the drunken Irish denizens of black and tans (dives where black New Yorkers could consort with immigrant drunks insufficiently self-respecting to shun them); a whorehouse kept by Italian Rosa; Chinese opium dens, and a school for young Italian thieves and organ grinders run by a demanding padrone. Indeed, Campbell argued that as the least American of big cities, New York was especially susceptible to child abuse, as no real American would beat his children with the severity used by Italian and Irish brute-fathers.

True, Campbell noted that "a generation ago it was the 'Bowery Bhoy' who filled this role, and who was the terror of all old ladies who found themselves in this once green and shaded thoroughfare of old New York." Still, she argued, there was a significant difference, and things had severely declined:

The Bowery Bhoy knew naught of the heroes of the cheap story papers, and was often at heart a very good sort of fellow, appraising every virtuous sentiment heard at the theatre, and settling at last into a decent citizen. He was usually American, and here lies the principal difference between the rowdy of then and now. It is chiefly the children of the lowest order of emigrants who grow into the young ruffians without sense of citizenship, . . . sell their first vote, and who know liberty only as license.[60]

While respectable 1840s society crossed the street when it saw the Bowery B'hoy Mose and his tough street gang approaching, by the 1890s he didn't look so bad by comparison to Irish or Italian paupers and had already become an object of wistful admiration. And while he didn't have the dime novel or a cheap newspaper story as a handbook for thieving, fighting, and carousing, the plays that glorified the B'hoys prior to the Civil War were condemned as vociferously as any rap song; likewise the B'hoy was known as a prodigious vote buyer and seller and brawler for his party every election day in 1840s New York. The transformative power of nostalgia had whitewashed an earlier era's dirty streets and recast a bygone city as functional and carefree. This pattern should be kept in mind when, in coming chapters, we see the transformative power of nostalgia at work yet again, this time reworking the black and tans, whorehouses, thieves' dens, and clip joints on the Lower East Side of Jews, Italians, and other wretched refuse into a hardworking paradise of immigrant strivers.

My point is not that there wasn't a substantial amount of hard work and thrifty living in 1890s New York, Chicago, and other immigrant enclaves, merely that popular culture purveyors by and large chose not to see it. It was the lurid detail of dysfunctional poverty that broke through the "shadows" of Lower Manhattan or the West Side immigrant area of Chicago and illuminated the exposés of magazine writers, novelists, composers, and cartoonists of the Gilded Age. Although some writers, such as Hutchins Hapgood in 1902, were already arguing that there was much of value in the associational life and self-help organizations of the Jewish immigrant area of the Lower East Side, Hapgood's treatment of this area in its workability was an exception. The valorizing of immigrant New York and other cities had to await the work of a later generation.[61]

In the 1890s the urban poor by and large were demonized, and even any initiative they showed was greeted with alarm. Indeed, it may have worried Campbell's and Crane's potential middle-class readers quite a bit that not everyone was as stoic in the face of despair as the fictional tramps in "An Experiment in Misery." Jacob Coxey led an army of thousands of tramps (we'd call them homeless) to Washington to demand relief, and the National Guard and army were employed to roust striking steelworkers and railway men in Homestead and Chicago. In the 1890s, too, memories of the Haymarket Square disaster were still strong. At a May Day strike rally in 1886 Chicago, shots were fired at policemen, and although no conclusive proof as to who had shot whom was ever offered, a celebrated trial ended in the conviction and execution of supposed anarchists. That some of those convicted were Germans, nineteenth-century America's stand-in for foreign radicals, fed the fervor of an antiforeigner, antiradical backlash in America. *Puck* cartoons of bomb-throwing, wild-bearded German anarchists may have been intended as satire, but they influenced a public that already suspected the immigrant beer gardens of Chicago's, San Francisco's, or New York's "Kleindeutschland" of harboring "terrorists."[62]

In the years after 1886 city after city erected monumental, medieval-style National Guard Armories and courthouse jails. Such structures can still be viewed in Philadelphia, Pittsburgh, and on New York's Park Avenue, among other places, and the grand, imposing stone edifices of these bastions of armed might leave little doubt that the ruling elite in Gilded Age America was expecting an assault on its parapets sometime soon. The assault was likely to come from the foreigners— Irish "dynamiters," Italian Black Hand, and German anarchists—already swarming within the nation's cities, and "law and order" Americans wanted to be ready. Other Irish were hopelessly slovenly shanty dwellers, as in a *Puck* cartoon, "A Gala Occasion," in which a woman asks her neighbor, "Mrs. MacGinty, wud yez lind me the loan iv yer father's false teeth fur the ould 'ooman? We are goin' to have mate fur dinner this day." Any way you sliced it, the cities' immigrant poor were a threat.[63]

Crane's Irish street urchin *Maggie* likewise simultaneously tugged at the public's heartstrings but called to mind the strident journalistic warnings of "the white slave trade." Many readers would have already recognized the misery and violence of Irish New York from the magazines that offered "truthful" looks at the slum and its pitiable residents that were no less fabrications than the characters of a novel. Moreover, Crane's "Bowery Tales" were first printed in newspapers like the *New York Press,* which on some pages fictionalized the squalor of the Bowery while on others ostensibly gave the news "straight." Journalists studying and explaining immigrants to white middle-class readers often worked for organs that had agendas they were hoping to further: immigration restriction, political reform of big-city machines, slum clearance, and tenement reforms, to name a few. Consequently the portraits they presented were often no less fictionalized than any presented by a novelist, and on other occasions working journalists like Crane did become novelists. As they sought to convince readers of the urgency of their causes, they therefore often played up the most despairing or dangerous elements of the immigrant quarters of America's cities, no matter whether a particular piece was supposedly fiction or nonfiction. Helpless wretches stared out at the reader from the pages of the reforming journals, beings seemingly without the means to assist themselves.

Of course, the popular press also was in business to sell magazines or papers, and when writers for these journals took readers for a stroll through immigrant areas, it was more often to delight than to instruct, to titillate "mainstream" readers with tours of ethnic exotica. Slum reporters were trained to pick out the colorfully destitute to populate their foreign landscapes; all that didn't fit the preconceived grid of immigrant squalor was airbrushed out.

Magazines such as *Harper's, Scribner's,* and *Century* began touring the slum in the early 1880s, and by and large writers didn't like what they discovered. What today would be called the "tangle of pathology" or elements of the urban underclass (thieves, peddlers, drunks, single mothers, and the like) of the immigrant neighborhoods was emphasized, while, with a few exceptions, the functioning elements of immigrant fraternal societies, churches, and building-and loan-associations were deemphasized or ignored entirely. Ironically, the same cities are now often dismissed as the site of a "culture of pathology" shamelessly peddled as distinctly African-American. From roughly 1880 to 1920, however, it was Irish, Jewish, Italian, and Slavic newcomers' disorder that more frequently raised reformers' blood pressure.

The chaos in the working-class streets of New York, Chicago, and other cities was the tangible evidence for many writers of the newcomers' genetic disorder. As early as 1881 a report on "Italian Life in New York" appearing in *Harper's* magazine set the template for the treatment of south and east European newcomers. "The more recently arrived [Italians] herd together in colonies," the reporter noted. ". . . It is no uncommon thing to see at noon some swarthy Italian, engaged on a building in process of erection, resting and dining from his tin kettle, while his brown-skinned wife sits by his side, brave in her gold earrings and beads, with a red flower in her hair, all of which at home were kept for feast days." But the author argued that, for Italians in America, "increasing wages make every day a feast day." Other writers argued that this was the problem with Italians, as well as the other new immigrants flooding into New York, Philadelphia, and elsewhere: They were too spendthrift and improvident on weekends or any one of innumerable feast days, indeed treating every day like a feast day and then being broke and neglectful of their children, their future, their city streets, the other six days of the week.

The author of this 1881 *Harper's* study visited the "herds" of Italians and seemed surprised to discover that "Teresa from the Ligurian mountains is certainly a more picturesque object than Bridget from Cork, and quite as worthy of incorporation in our new civilization." This may have been a kind of left-handed compliment, considering the contempt with which many native-born Protestant Americans regarded the Hibernian influx that was already establishing a toehold in the police forces, fire departments, and Democratic ward political clubs by 1881. And although the author of this article reassured his readers that the "superstition" that "the Italians are an idle and thriftless people" would be removed from the American mind in time, elsewhere he himself seemed not so sure. Teresa might be a "picturesque" addition to the city, but the author asserted that many Italians who had made multiple trips to New York out of greed proved all too susceptible to disease or ill fortune, ending up "in some damp and unwholesome den." While he admitted that the fruit seller from all parts of Italy "adds much to the picturesqueness of our streets," he also noted that frequently the fruit stalls were places where "the men lounge in the lazy, happy ways of the peninsula." In general, the prospect for Italian success in New York was qualified by the author, despite his reassurances that "a little kindly guidance can mould them into any form." He nevertheless concluded, "The idyllic life of an Italian hillside or a dreaming mediaeval town is but poor preparation for the hand-to-hand struggle for bread of an overcrowded city."[64]

Even compliments to the new immigrants often contained qualifiers that admitted some immigrants were rightly a cause for alarm. "It is much to be regretted that the sins of a few turbulent and quarrelsome Neapolitans and Calabrians should be visited upon the heads of their quiet, gentle, hard-working compatriots," the author commented, adding, "All Italians are proud and high-spirited, but yield easily to kindness, and are only defiant and revengeful when ill-treated." As in Italy itself, a distinction seems to have been made in America by reformers between northerners and southerners, with even the Dillingham Immigration Commission of 1909 classifying the two "races" separately. Already, in this 1881 article, compliments are handed out to artificial-flower makers from Pavia and fruit sellers from Venice, while cautionary caveats are delivered about "turbulent and quarrelsome" southerners by no means representing all Italians. Indeed, this tour guide through Italian New York says of "Ligurians" (Genoese) running a trade school for Italians, they "repudiate indignantly all kinship with the Neapolitans and Calabrians, whom they refuse to recognize as Italians."[65]

After a tour of Baxter Street, the author reports that "we passed through courts and alleys where swarthy Neapolitans were carting bales of rags, and up dark stairs where women and children were sorting them." Lewis Hine, too, would document the squalor of the tenement apartments in which immigrants engaged in piecework for garment and artificial-flower factories, and exposés of the invisible misery of homeworkers engaged in these industries frequently appeared in the Progressive Era reformist magazines. The writer for *Harper's* noted that "some homes were low, dark rooms, neglected and squalid," but that others were tidy and had been spruced up by their occupants with prints of the saints, flowers, and "rows of gay plates on shelves against the walls." However, in a tenement dedicated to outfitting organ grinders with monkeys and hurdy-gurdies, the scene was occupied by "unkempt" Neapolitans "swarming about the windows in all their brown shapeliness," suggesting that for all a magazine writer's attempts at objective reporting and comforting words about the nation's ability to absorb the "swarthy" newcomers, at times he, like his readers, saw his city as under threat of invasion by some barely human occupiers. Even the English language needed new terms of alarm ("brown shapeliness"?) to describe the menace. Terms evocative of science fiction were invoked to describe the threat that newcomers, invariably "swarming" throughout cities, posed to the normal. More than thirty years later, at a time when hundreds of thousands of migrants from the Mezzogiorno had joined these pioneers on Baxter Street, sociologist Edward Alsworth Ross advocated a halt to the influx of southeastern Europeans, singling out the Italian with his "backless skull" as a particularly pernicious threat to the country. Walking the streets of New York could be an adventure indeed when journalists and academics alike peopled it with such fanciful migrants.[66]

The words are reassuring, but the images are alarming. The line drawings that accompany this article in *Harper's* portray wretched poverty and, yes, "swarthy" women and tough young men ominously idling in front of tenement stoops, as well as dark-skinned "truants from school," not the industrious women "quite as worthy of incorporation in our new civilization." Even the picture of an "Italian fete day" scene on a New York street is balanced by "the monkey training school" where hurdy-gurdy operators learn how to run their scam, and all in attendance are depicted as "brown" or "swarthy" and unkempt.[67]

The most successful practitioner of the slum tour vignette was Jacob Riis, who first serialized his *How the Other Half Lives* in *Scribner's* magazine. In ostensibly seeking to reform inadequate housing laws that allowed slumlords to turn their tenements into hovels of despair, Riis established the template of city reporting that other journalists and fictionalizers followed when writing of the city.

Riis's occasional expression of sympathy for ghetto dwellers was often overwhelmed by his revulsion at the unclean places they lived, for if New Yorkers of the "other half" were trapped in Old Law tenements, Riis was a prisoner of the social Darwinist thought so prevalent in his day, as well as the ecological theories of city living that bestowed great corrupting powers on the ghetto. Referring to the Italians and Polish Jews, he declared, "The two races, differing hopelessly in much, have this much in common: They carry their slums with them wherever they go, if allowed to do it." While the "Teuton" "knows how to drag even the barracks upward a part of the way at least toward the ideal plane of the home, . . . the Italian and the poor Jew rises [*sic*] only by compulsion."[68] While Riis and other reformers sometimes targeted the slumlords who profited from the rents of tenement dwellers, within this declaration of slum-bearing newcomers is an implicit fear that immigrants were incapable of republicanism or even "civilized" living and would drag all other Americans down to their lower level. To prevent this, a little "compulsion" was needed, and this is where Riis's exposés came in.

While touring the crowded, disordered streets of Lower Manhattan, Riis frequently condemned both the slum dweller and the slumlord. Unclean immigrants exhibited almost axiomatic proof of moral laxity. "The true line to be drawn between pauperism and honest poverty is the clothes-line," he declared. "With it begins the effort to be clean, and that is the first and best evidence of a desire to be honest."[69] Other reformers, too, worried about this clothesline, but it was slum children's propensity to steal coal and firewood, and even their neighbors' wash off fire escape lines, that alarmed readers of Progressive magazines like *Survey*. Rent strikes organized by Lower East Side mothers in 1907 and kosher food "riots" protesting high prices during World War I were often read as evidence of foreigners' innate "violence" rather than signs of grassroots campaigns to solve immigrants' problems. Around the turn of the century, immigrants, using the clothesline or not, couldn't seem to win.[70]

Certainly within *How the Other Half Lives* there's a lurking suspicion that the new urban immigrant would never be able to achieve much on his own, no matter how much guidance Progressive reformers offered or how much soap the settlement house gave them. In New York, Riis wrote, the Italian "promptly reproduces conditions of destitution and disorder which, set in the framework of Mediterranean exuberance, are the delight of the artist, but in a matter-of-fact American community become its danger and reproach. . . . He soon reduces what he finds down to his own level, if allowed to follow his natural bent." The Italian, he concludes, "is content to live in a pig-sty." Not even William Julius Wilson, a century later, could have so succinctly set out the case for an "urban underclass."

As the allusion to "Mediterranean exuberance" makes clear, Riis couldn't help indulging in some "local color" when touring Manhattan's slums. The Italians' "vivid and picturesque costume gave a tinge of color to the dull monotony of the slums they inhabit," he admitted; at another point the Italian neighborhood's streets are transformed into an open-air carnival. For all its squalor, Riis portrays the Italian area around Mulberry Bend as practically a zoo, where exotic human types can be visited in their colorful native habitat. Edward Said has written on the manner in which western European travel writers depicted Middle Eastern locales and their inhabitants as exotic, licentious, and indolent, deserving of colonization and improvement by supposedly superior Europeans.[71] Much the same portrayal was presented of exotic Mediterranean interlopers in the Anglo-Saxon republic; the magazine writer allowed one to go on armchair safari to the Lower East Side or Little Italy. "When the sun shines the entire population seeks the street, carrying on its household work, its bargaining, its lovemaking on street or sidewalk." Mulberry Bend is a place tourists can vicariously come to see exotic poverty.

The carnivalesque atmosphere of Little Italy was further emphasized by other writers. H. C. Brunner's "Jersey and Mulberry" noted that spring and fall "are the seasons of processions and religious festivals. . . . Sometimes half a dozen times in a day, . . . some Italian society parad[es] through the street. Fourteen proud sons of Italy, clad in magnificent new uniforms, bearing aloft huge silk banners, strut magnificently in the rear of a German band of twenty-four pieces." He noted the immigrants' religious processions, too: "Six sturdy Italians struggle along under the weight of a mighty temple or pavilion, all made of colored candles, . . . the great big candles of the Romish Church (a church which, you may remember, is much affected of the mob, especially in times of suffering, sickness, or death); mighty candles, six and eight feet tall, . . . around a statue of the Virgin. . . . And before and behind them are bands and drum-corps and societies with banners, and it is all a blare of martial music and primary colors the whole length of the street."[72]

Of course, not every reporter of the immigrant scene saw these marching societies or oompah bands as civic improvements. When *Puck,* the premier political satire magazine of the late nineteenth and early twentieth centuries, presented cartoons of Italians, they invariably mocked the Italian monopoly on noisy, cater-wauling organ grinders, street musicians, and seedy fruit-vending stalls alike as urban nuisances that might cause the republic's degeneracy, if not deafness and stomach cramps. Indeed, Irish "marching societies," Italian organ grinders, and German oompah bands were all mocked as violent, noisy, and disorderly menaces to the public streets. *Puck* cartoonists mocked the "O'Donovan Rossa Dynamiters and Marching Society" in the case of the Irish, the gaudy and elaborate Italian "music masters," and the cacophonous German oompah bands and disheveled Italian organ grinders and ragpickers; and lurking behind each of these musical manglers was an invariable threat of more overt violence: the German anarchist, the hard-drinking, simian Irishman intent on blowing up all traces of civilization on behalf of the Clan na Gael, and other secretive sects.[73]

While immigrants themselves published glowing accounts of their fraternal societies' parades and festivals, unless one was a member of these organizations and subscribed to their journals, often in some inscrutable tongue like Italian or Slovak or Ruthenian, this picture of immigrant culture went unreported. Even from fellow Catholics, the immigrant's street *festa* often suffered a mischaracterization. Italian parades were mocked as pagan rites by chiefly Irish bishops and respectable Catholics worried they would be tarred by association as barbaric if they didn't get their coreligionists to behave genteelly. When Italian parishioners paraded through the streets behind bands, and often cannons, to announce the saints' days, and honored church ushers lofted high brightly painted, elaborate saints' statues bedecked with dollar bills supplicating an intervention, immigrants saw this as a colorful homage to the prestige of their patron. Robert Orsi has argued these processions were attempts by immigrants to adapt the Sicilian and Mezzo-giorno village processions to new locales such as East Harlem and Brooklyn, a claiming of city streets as the immigrants' own turf. Outside observers, though, saw something entirely different: chaos and disorder in need of severe control by the city's "better sorts."[74]

Even fellow Catholics a little more acculturated to American life, especially Irish bishops, were often alarmed by what they took to be pagan or at best unseemly displays of license on the public streets. Immigrants carrying saints' statues, shooting off little cannons as a sign of their veneration, or penitently pinning dollar bills to the Madonna's robes were often taken as proof of the barbarism southern Italians were delivering to Manhattan's shores. Bishops likewise sought to rein in Slovak and Polish rowdiness in Minneapolis, Pennsylvania's coal and steel towns, and elsewhere. Immigrant city street life would not become an icon of warm and fuzzy safe streets until another two generations had passed and city neighborhoods underwent a racial transformation.[75]

When these immigrant neighborhoods were forming, though, a different view prevailed. H. C. Brunner's account of the Italian slum around Jersey Street in *Scribner's* begins with the stereotypical organ grinder disturbing the neighborhood. Brunner defends the Italians but, as was usually the case with newspaper and magazine writers of his day, in a patronizing way. "If she had sent [her maid] down to the street with a dime, and told her to say: 'Sicka lady, no playa,' poor Pedro would have swung his box of whistles over his shoulder and trudged contentedly on." Instead, the maid was told to threaten the organ grinder with arrest, "and so Pedro just grinned at her in his exasperating furrin way, and played on until he got good and ready to go." Brunner went on to say that from his office window he observed the Italians of "the Jersey Street slum" and very likely even knew this particular organ grinder. After observing the Italians who dwell near him, Brunner comes to identify with them, but not perhaps in a way that would comfort some of his middle-class readers. "And do you know," he writes, "as we look out of those windows, year after year, we find ourselves growing to have a fellow-feeling of vulgarity with that same mob."[76]

Immigration restrictionists similarly argued that the hordes of non-Nordics settling in Jersey Street and dozens of other Little Italys throughout the nation might be spreading their "vulgarity" to the rest of the country, but it was not with as much complacency as Brunner that they watched this process in operation. A kind of Gresham's law of ethnic pollution was ironically at work, with the supposedly superior Anglo-Saxon culture perpetually in danger of dilution from too much contact with southeastern Europeans. Paradoxically, though, some of the same people who saw the United States as under assault also nervously asserted that if immigrants could be educated in American ways, all was not lost. Yet the difficulty of reaching newcomers, who were often referred to as "swarming" or "invading" the country, made for an anxiety-ridden dialogue for these writers. Could a Sicilian really and truly be turned into an American? No one seemed sure, but since so many hundreds of thousands of non-Nordics already by the 1890s were arriving in the metropolis, the professional class of Americans had better make a concerted effort to do so, if only for the nation's self-preservation.[77]

But how to reach the newcomers remained a problem. It was immigrants' tendency to segregate themselves in ghettos, away from the healing touch of American education and culture, not immigrants per se, that some writers bemoaned. H. C. Brunner noted that even in one narrow Manhattan alley, immigrant children kept to themselves. "My side of the street swarms with Italian children, most of them from Jersey Street. . . . Judge Phoenix's side is peopled with small Germans and Irish. I have noticed one peculiar thing about these children: they never change sides. They play together most amicably in the middle of the street or the gutter, but neither ventures beyond its neutral ground."[78]

Italian Mulberry Bend, then, was by turns a thrilling place to see the odd and colorful habits of its residents, a zoo of "outdoor lovemaking," and also an infection

in need of a cure. Jacob Riis became maybe the most famous champion of tenement housing reform, sanitation, and overall slum improvement projects in Progressive Era America. However, in his zeal to improve *How the Other Half Lives,*
he often came perilously close to condemning the immigrant poor themselves.
Riis was himself born abroad, but as a Danish-American police reporter for the
staid *New York Sun,* not the kind likely to cause Henry Cabot Lodge to lose any
sleep. Although Riis stressed the truth of everything on which he reported, there
is some strong evidence that he altered his articles and books for dramatic effect.
Maren Stenge and Bill Hug have demonstrated that the photographs and line
drawings based on these photos that accompanied Riis's writings often were
doctored and posed to remove any signs that "the other half's" lives had any
resiliency, cheer, or value. They also were sometimes posed to deliberately summon up images of earlier slum tours such as an 1846 *National Police Gazette*
illustration of "The New York Dives, or Street Thieves at Work."

Moreover, before he began publishing his slum tours, Riis conducted a popular
lantern-slide lecture of his slum tours, a lecture that he presented before dozens of
civic and reformist groups throughout the country. His popular traveling slumology
tour projected his selective ghetto images before audiences eager to "visit" the
darker half of New York and glean the "truth" of the destitute new immigrants.
Indeed, in Riis's "Flashes From the Slums," an 1888 illustrated article in *The Sun,*
the lecturer described his role as "guide and conductor" to the netherworld of
"Gotham's crime and misery by night and day." Also in 1888, Riis reassured an
interviewer, "The beauty of looking into these places without actually being
present there is that the excursionist is spared the vulgar sounds and odious scents
and repulsive exhibitions attendant upon such a personal examination." Is it any
wonder that the writer Harry Golden, who grew up on the Lower East Side, remembers as a child "performing" the role of street urchin for gawking bus-tourists
on safari to the Lower East Side?[79]

Riis was writing, and lecturing, in order to sway New York and other cities to
enact tenement reform laws, build city playgrounds, and rid the Lower East Side
and similar city neighborhoods of the worst sweatshop abuses. Therefore he presented the scene in "Mulberry Bend" or primarily Jewish Ludlow Street as one of
unrelenting misery and cropped his photos in ways that severely overemphasized
sorrow. In this way Riis fictionalized the city and its citizens no less than if he had
set out to write a novel.

Indeed, there is no mention of the dozens of *Landsmanshaften* (regional fraternal associations), literary cafés, and workmen's libraries and union halls that
cushioned the shocks of life on Ludlow and the surrounding streets for Jewish
immigrants. When Hutchins Hapgood and the artist Jacob Epstein set out to document the Jewish community of New York in 1902, they suggested that the rich
associational life of these immigrants allowed them to create a functioning neighborhood, even if its signposts were unquestionably foreign to the country's Protestant mainstream. By focusing their sights on the immigrants' own organizations, Hapgood and his artist collaborator present a portrait that might have been

on a different planet from the places Riis wrote of with such pathos, even though they were walking the very streets down which the police reporter had strolled. For Hapgood, "the spirit of the ghetto" was one of vibrant self-help and cultural life; for Riis, the city was strung together with rags.[80]

The photographs Riis used in his books, magazine pieces, and traveling slide lectures dramatically demonstrate the squalor of Lower Manhattan. When, like Crane's experimenter, he visited a flophouse for his "How the Other Half Lives" (an article first published in *Scribner's* magazine), Riis included a drawing of "Lodgers in a crowded Bayard Street tenement—'Five Cents a Spot'": "It was photographed by flashlight on just such a visit. In a room not thirteen feet either way slept twelve men and women, two or three in bunks set in a sort of alcove, the rest on the floor." In subsequent articles for magazines such as *Century*, Riis continued to offer "Light in Dark Places" just as Foster had supposedly done forty years before, but this time the exposé of the slum was aided with photographic evidence of the squalor and dysfunction of "The Mott Street Barracks" and "Bone Alley." Riis optimistically told his middle-class readers a better day was coming in New York, for Bone Alley was "to be removed to make way for a new East Side small park, under the Tenement House Laws of 1895."

However, the illustrations belie the optimism. The little alley is crowded with surly immigrant men and women loitering with vacant stares, as well as unattended infants taunting a cat and young toughs shooting marbles. Overhead the sky is blocked out by fire escapes and hanging laundry. The main focus of the camera is the human flotsam and jetsam, and it's not clear by the end of this short article if "to be removed" refers to Bone Alley or, perhaps wishfully, to its foreign inhabitants. In these and other Riis articles the pathetic expressions of the barely-above-homeless lodgers and impoverished, exotically ethnic city dwellers offered documentary proof of the force of Riis's accounts of a city spinning out of middle-class control, for already his Progressive Era readers were convinced the camera didn't lie.[81]

The places Riis aimed his camera, however, were not the artisans' lyceums, the Hebrew Immigrant Aid Society, or the vibrant worker cafés that dotted the East Broadway that Hapgood visited. Nor were Italian marionette theaters, syndicalist union halls (although these might have alarmed WASP readers, too!), or functioning Catholic parishes the subject matter he chose to highlight.

His reforming mission mandated that his camera must find the seamiest parts of an admittedly impoverished immigrant city, and find it he did. Referring to a dirty alley between two tenements just under the Brooklyn Bridge, Riis directed his reader's attention to "a horde of dirty children [at] play on the broken flags about the dripping hydrant, the only thing in the alley that thinks enough of its chance to make the most of it. . . . These are the children of the tenements, the growing generation of the slums." Accompanying this grim travelogue were pictures of absolute poverty, somber-faced, dirty urchin-children playing in a narrow "Double-alley, Gotham Court," and an even more disheveled "Italian rag-picker, Jersey Street." There is nothing of H. C. Brunner's even tentative optimism or admiration of "vulgar" Italians in Riis.

The flophouses and squalid gin joints were not the whole of 1890s immigrant Manhattan, but this was the part of the city that most middle-class Americans saw, courtesy of cultural producers like Riis. The template of a dangerous, desperately poor and helpless immigrant city within a city was established in Riis's "How the Other Half Lives: Studies Among the Tenements."[82]

Like Foster, Lippard, and Buntline before him Riis served as a tour guide to the nether reaches of Manhattan's destitute, and like Crane he visited the flophouses that dotted the Bowery, Chatham Square, and other streets of the bad wards. In a flophouse, he tells his readers, "Some sort of an apology for a bed, with mattress and blanket, represents the aristocratic purchase of the tramp who, by a lucky stroke of beggary, has exchanged the chance of an empty box or ash-barrel for shelter on the quality floor of one of these 'hotels.'" Riis describes the fights that frequently break out in these flophouses but reassures that "the commotion that ensues is speedily quieted by the boss and his club."

The immigrant flophouse of New York (as well as Chicago, Brooklyn, and other Gilded Age cities) was for some an apt metaphor for the chaotic charnel house the entire country was in danger of becoming. In a *Puck* cartoon from 1882, Uncle Sam desperately tries to keep the peace in the flophouse that America has already become! In this cartoon from America's premier satirical journal, ethnic flotsam and jetsam—not just mere "tramps," but Italian, German, Japanese, Russian, Chinese, and, especially. Irish refuse—are disturbing the peace, reducing America to the status of a two-cent "black and tan." Uncle Sam demands of the Irishman, who's hurling bricks marked "The Chinese must go," "Recall Lowell," and "Irish independence," "Look here, you, everybody else is quiet and peaceable, and you're all the time a-kicking up a row!"[83]

Elsewhere on Mulberry Bend the prospect of a good night's sleep for a native-born American was not much better. "I have spoken of the stale-beer dive," Riis writes.

As a thief never owns to his calling, however devoid of moral scruples, . . . so this real home-product of the slums is known about The Bend by the more dignified name of the two-cent restaurant. . . . The beer is fresh from the barrels put on the sidewalk by saloon-keepers to simmer in the sun until collected by the brewer's cart, and is touched up with drugs to put a froth on it. The privilege to sit all night in a chair, or sleep on a table or in a barrel, goes with each purchase. Generally an Italian, sometimes a negro, occasionally a woman, "runs" the dive. Men and women, alike homeless and hopeless in their utter wretchedness, mingle there together.

The mingling of non-Nordic types, suspect southern Italians, and "negroes" at these dives was as alarming as the other promiscuous and illicit activities that occurred in the flophouse's shadows. Fortunately, the tramps of the Bowery had at least one commodity they could exchange once a year for a few dollars: "But if they have nothing else to call their own, even tramps have a 'pull'—about election time at all events. They have votes, and votes that are for sale cheap for cash." Corrupt big-city machines like New York's Tammany could be counted upon to count each and every bum's vote for the ticket, Riis and other reformers alleged; this was another black mark against the city, and even staid Philadelphia was targeted by muckraker Lincoln Steffens as a paragon of big-city political corruption in *The Shame of the Cities*. And even a quaint 1882 magazine tour of the Quaker City was accompanied by line drawings of the fetid slums that the old colonial row house areas had become.[84]

Even if Riis's intention was to reform and improve the city (and often its inhabitants in spite of themselves) his choice of focus invariably reflected the seamier side of urban living and reinforced the predilections of WASP urbanites to view the other side of the tracks as dangerous, semicivilized places. This portrait was avidly embraced and carried forth by other, less reform-minded writers. Riis noted the proximity of respectability, prosperity, and "civilization" (modernity) to squalor and "barbarism" (or so it was conceived), with Riis taking his readers on a tour of "the other half's" city, noting it's just a short step from affluent, fashionable Fifth Avenue or Broadway to the slums. Also worrisome to many writers was the degeneration of a formerly fashionable quarter of the city, where George Washington once lived in presidential grandeur, into an overcrowded ghetto. This descent of a particular part of the city seemed to foreshadow the decline of the republic at large. "Turn but a dozen steps from the rush and roar of the Elevated Railroad, where it dives under the Brooklyn Bridge," Riis wrote, "and you have turned the corner from prosperity to poverty."

The miracles of industrial America, which inspired such confidence in civic boosters, were uncomfortably close to the warrens of those cast aside by the country's march to a brilliant future, and it made for some anxiety. David Hammack has noted that New York's civic elite tried to outgrow their problems by pushing for incorporation of the five boroughs into one city of "Greater New York" in 1898, with the "greater" offering vague hopes that slums might melt away in a bigger, better city. Then, too, the miracles of industrial America such as the elevated railway and the streetcar were celebrated for uniting a disparate city, but some alarm remained, too, since this facilitated an even easier mixing and mingling of people of all classes. Maybe the other half couldn't be contained in their slums.[85]

The poor were everywhere in the city, it seemed, using the technological wonders of progress for their own rapid movement beyond East Broadway or Canal Street, and so at least some of the affluent began a long, slow process of abandoning the city. After 1880, many middle-class urbanites therefore availed themselves of the transit revolution to divorce their residences from cities that were becoming too Catholic, foreign, and dirty for their tastes, hopping the first streetcar to newly fashionable suburbs an easy commute from the downtowns in Boston, Philadelphia, New York, and even Los Angeles. Of course, mayors desirous of working-class votes vowed to keep transit costs low, and the streetcar and (after 1901) subway fares were often within the means of lower-class urbanites, too, who used mass transit to establish a far-ranging network of shopping, worship, and social arrangements across the face of metropolises as different as Los Angeles and

Philadelphia. To the chagrin of middle-class nativists, it proved impossible to contain the "foreigner" within his or her ghetto.[86]

Within that ghetto Riis asked the rhetorical question of life in the tenements: Is life worth living? And then cited an excerpt from the last report of the Association for the Improvement of the Condition of the Poor:

In the depth of winter, the attention of the Association was called to a Protestant family living in a garret in a miserable tenement on Cherry Street [on the Lower East Side]. The family's condition was most deplorable. The man, his wife, and three small children shivering in one room, through the roof of which the pitiless winds of winter whistled. The room was almost barren of furniture, the parents slept on the floor, the elder children in boxes, and the baby was swung in an old shawl attached to the rafters by cords by way of a hammock. The father, a seaman, had been obliged to give up that calling because he was in consumption and was unable to provide either bread or fire for his little ones.

Again, while such scenes were accurate depictions of the severity of poverty in America prior to the New Deal, their repeated invocation built up sympathy in some but repugnance in others, who dismissed New York, Chicago, and other increasingly "foreign cities" as beyond help.

Unwittingly or not, Riis and other magazine writers contributed to the second conclusion, first, by dwelling on the "racial" and ethnic mélange of the city, where promiscuous mixing of non-Nordics of strange parts came in for much attention, and second, by dwelling on scenes of vice and dissipation where the poor, it was argued, wasted their paychecks. Both quarrels with the poor came into play in Riis's depiction of "A 'black and tan dive' in Thompson Street." This was the one of the centers of the city's still-minuscule black population, but already white ethnic groups were encroaching on this area of Lower Manhattan and frequenting the same disreputable bars as blacks. Such indiscriminate mixing of races as well as classes appalled Riis and other Progressives, and throughout "How the Other Half Lives" Jews, Irish, Italians, and (only as an afterthought) blacks come in for condemnation for their chaotic habits, poor housekeeping, and general failure to keep order in industrializing New York. In the decade in which Jim Crow solidified its hold on much of America, "race" mingling appalled magazine writers, but immigration restrictionists often referred to east European Jews as Orientals or Asiatics, it should be kept in mind, so that the jostling crowds mingling, arguing, and bargaining on Hester Street were often characterized as exotic and threatening interlopers on a formerly orderly city. Italian Mulberry Bend was likewise likened to a primitive village of pseudo-African Sicilians.[87] But whites fraternizing with blacks and the Chinese of Lower Manhattan came in for much condemnation, too, with the black and tans and Chinese opium dens singled out as municipal scourges by Riis.[88]

While Riis's language is predictably decorous for someone writing in the era of Anthony Comstock's "moral" code, his tour of New York's depths takes in enough prostitution, drug use, murder, and miscegenation to fill any Hollywood summer blockbuster. "Out of the tenements of The Bend and its feeders come the white slaves of the Chinese dens of vice and their infernal drug, that have infused into the 'Bloody Sixth' Ward of old a subtler poison than ever the stale-beer dives knew," he warned. Worse than drug addicts awaited. Riis claims that in Mott and Pell Streets are found the houses of "fallen women," or as he calls them, "these hapless victims of a passion which, once acquired, demands the sacrifice of every instinct of decency to its insatiate desire." On Pell Street, all "the men [are] worshipers of Joss; the women all white, girls nearly always of tender age, worshipping nothing save the pipe that has enslaved them body and soul. Easily tempted from homes that have no claim to the name, they rarely or never return." Prostitution in and of itself is bad enough, but the biggest sin, perhaps, is that white women (even if suspect white women such as Italians, Irish, or Jews) are found living with Chinese men, and yet many, Riis says, continue to "insist illogically upon the fiction of a marriage that deceives no one."

Riis was not alone in worrying about "white slavery" in the nineteenth-century city, as Timothy Gilfoyle makes clear in his study of New York City prostitution, *City of Eros*. Allen Street on the Jewish Lower East Side was the vice district of the day, which is perhaps part of the reason Police Commissioner Theodore Bingham labeled the city's Jewish immigrants the biggest contributors to Gotham's high crime rate. As we saw, slightly earlier the oldest profession plagued Philadelphia as well.[89]

Wherever he went, whether he encountered prostitutes, junkies, or merely the hardworking poor, an air of unsettled disgust underlies what Riis wrote. He continues his tour of the desperate side of New York and, with his readers, "invade[s] the Hebrew quarter." Riis laments,

One may find in New York, for the asking, an Italian, a German, French, African, Spanish, Scandinavian, Russian, Jewish and Chinese colony. . . . The one thing you shall vainly ask for in the chief city of America is a distinctive American community. There is none, certainly not among the tenements. No need of asking here on the east side where we are. The jargon of the street, the signs of the sidewalk, the manner and dress of the people, betray their race at every step. Men with queer skull-caps, venerable beard, and the outlandish long-skirted kaftan of the Russian Jew, elbow the ugliest and the handsomest women in the land. The contrast is startling. The old women are hags; the young, houries.

The "Orientalism" of this tour guide to the exotic, oversexed Lower East Side is evocative of the exotification of many subaltern peoples convincingly documented by Edward Said. In 1890s America Jews were regarded as Asiatic, alluring, but nevertheless threatening in their supposedly oversexed nature. Jewish duplicity in business, as well as a supposed innate propensity toward arson on behalf of stereotyped cartoon Jewish characters named Burnupsky, graced the pages of *Puck* for years. Perhaps expressing the fears of WASP Americans at the encroachment of newcomers on the country's republican traditions, a cartoon in the hundredth year of the republic also showed a peddler Rosenbaum dressed in colonial garb, "doin' de Lineal Descendant ofh Cheneral Lafayette racket, durin' der celebration!" And the Danish immigrant Riis's querulous complaint of being unable to locate an "American" neighborhood calls to mind, too, cartoons of the era that showed a bewildered American losing his way in the Lower East Side, where all the signs are either German or Yiddish. Circa 1890, Uncle Sam was getting shunted aside by hordes of outlandishly foreign immigrants on the sidewalks of New York.[90]

Indeed, Riis completes the thought by noting that the "houries" certainly led to over-breeding among the slum dwellers. He refers disparagingly to the large families of Lower East Side immigrants, that the women are "mothers at 16, at 30 they are old." The same arguments were made in countless settlement house and social work reports on the profligate nature of Catholic and Jewish immigrants; Edward Alsworth Ross, too, in 1914, urged his countrymen to restrict the arrival of "the super-fecund Slav." Of course, similar arguments would by the 1970s increasingly be heard by the children, or grandchildren, of southern and eastern Europeans about welfare cheating and overbreeding among blacks and "illegal aliens," but in the late nineteenth century Jews, Slavs, and Mediterraneans were on the receiving end of complaints. They bred prodigiously, reformers shrieked, and were outproducing the "better" races, and thereby becoming a drain on the public treasury. And they didn't speak English![91]

By the end of his slum safari Riis saw chaos everywhere, and even a few remarks on immigrant "color" and spectacle in the streets could not conceal the overall tone of hysteria. He is particularly alarmed that the chaos and disorder of the tenement spills over, too, into the public spaces of the city, especially in the summer months, when "the tenement expands, reckless of all restraint." Public courting by young immigrant men and women on rooftops, fire escapes, and even the carts in the streets, and "passing the growler" (drinking in public from pails of beer)—all this signified the collapse of a rational, orderly republic that Riis and his readers felt was under assault by Italians and "Oriental" Jews heedless of decorum. "Then every truck in the street, every crowded fire-escape, becomes a bedroom, infinitely preferable to any the house affords."

The "picturesqueness" of immigrants claiming the streets of Lower Manhattan as their own seems to have alarmed rather than delighted Riis, and in this he was not alone. "Friday brings out all the latent color and picturesqueness of the Italians, as it does of these Orientals [i.e., Jews]. . . . The Pigmarket is in Hester Street, extending either way from Ludlow Street, up and down the side-streets, two or three blocks, as the state of trade demands." But this is *not* the happy disorder of the "good old" vibrant immigrant neighborhood that will be remembered in rich sepia tones in later memoirs, novels and films such as 1975's *Hester Street* (a film adaptation of Abraham Cahan's novella, *Yekl and the Imported Bridegroom*). Rather, Riis and other Progressives were distressed at the loss of a rational city. Progressives' attempts to restore order to the unruly city often involved slighting dismissals of the new immigrants, so "reckless of all restraint," even if a quick glance at "Gaslight" Foster's novels reminds us that even the 1840s city was regarded as a sinful and lawless place.[92]

By 1900 it was the "idyllic" pre–Civil War city that was missed. Henry James and Henry Adams both similarly lamented the foreign intrusion into their vanished cities and saw Babel where later generations would recall warm and fuzzy

Jewish, Italian, and Slavic immigrant neighborhoods where "no one ever locked their doors." Adams, James, and Riis—and their sympathetic readers—instead saw a scene of biblical catastrophe invading their cities. "And the crowds that jostle each other at the wagons and about the sidewalk shops, where a gutter-plank on two ash-barrels does duty for a counter!—pushing, struggling, screaming, and shouting in foreign tongues, a veritable Babel of confusion." Of courser, even if James, Adams, or Riis couldn't understand this Babel, the conversations in Italian or Yiddish were certainly not confusing to the buyers and sellers of produce. Nevertheless, foreign live poultry markets and open-air vegetable stalls were the bane, too, of Progressive reformers, as Riis also comments that the bulk of the produce being sold is confiscated when a health inspector causes the immigrant "swarm" to scatter, leaving behind their pitiful "musty bread, rotten fish, and stale vegetables."[93]

In his condemnation of immigrant food ways Riis was not alone. Social worker Udetta Brown asserted that selling live poultry annoyed the neighbors in the heavily Slavic Dundee section of Passaic, New Jersey. Now, many people nostalgic for an imagined immigrant past revere live chicken markets as a marker of appealing white ethnic authenticity. But in 1915 Passaic; Johnstown, Pennsylvania; Tampa, Florida; Philadelphia; and Chicago, urban Italian and Slavic keepers of live poultry were roundly condemned as "bad investments for the country to make." It is only by waiting until 2006 that Italian live poultry markets can be redeemed as good and a symbol of a stable, working ethnic neighborhood in Tony Soprano's North Newark, for in this highly popular cable television show, nearly a century later chicken-market authenticity lends an air of a warm and comforting ethnic old neighborhood to scenes in the gangster's Italian neighborhood, as we shall see. But when immigrants first arrived in America their food ways and aggressive marketing conducted in "confusing Babel" languages was further proof of their unfitness for modern city life and their threat to America.[94]

Indeed, to reformers, often the slums of New York were plagued not just by bad housing, but by bad ethnic stock, which alarmed Riis just as much. "It is upon 'The Bend,' in Mulberry Street, that this Italian blight has fallen chiefly," he writes. Here the tenement house blight has been replaced by "the Italian blight," and in the face of this dilemma, "The reformer gives up his task in despair. Where Mulberry Street crooks like an elbow, within hail of the old depravity of the Five Points, are the miserable homes of the ragpickers." It is "the swarthy, stunted emigrant from southern Italy" who Riis notes is in

exclusive possession of this field, just as his black-eyed boy has monopolized the bootblack's trade, the Chinaman the laundry, and the negro the razor for purposes of honest industry as well as anatomical research. Here is the back alley in its foulest development—naturally enough, for there is scarcely a lot that has not two, three or four tenements upon it, swarming with unwholesome crowds. What squalor and degradation inhabit these dens the health officers know. Through the long summer days their carts patrol The Bend, scattering disinfectants in streets and lanes, in sinks and cellars, and hidden hovels where the tramp burrows.

As in so much Progressive writing, social Darwinism influences the tone here, with the city's poor referred to in rapid succession as "a blight," "miserable," "swarthy and stunted" semihumans who "swarm" and "burrow" among respectable New Yorkers. While the immigrant playwright Israel Zangwill would in 1908 optimistically predict that "The Melting Pot" would weld this amalgam into a stronger, healthier nation, his was a minority voice, and in the same year that his play appeared New York City Police Commissioner Bingham caused an uproar by asserting that the vast majority of the city's criminals were Jewish immigrants. As we shall see in the following chapter, fears of the immigrant and ethnic gangster pervaded popular culture into the 1940s, but already in the first years of the "new immigration" he was depicted as a problem, not an asset.[95]

Riis was not alone in presenting a bestiary of ethnic types. Criminologists embracing the phrenological work of Cesare Lombroso told middle-class Progressives that it was possible to tell at a glance which city dwellers were atavistically of the criminal type. The development of police mug shots came about in part in a "scientific" attempt to document and classify criminal types that neatly corresponded to eastern and southern European immigrant types. The development of "scientific" IQ tests to weed out the "unfit" from officer training school during World War I likewise led many social scientists to believe that those who had done poorly on the notoriously culturally biased tests were overwhelmingly from Slavic and Mediterranean "races," giving further strength to the growing immigration-restriction movement. Other tests measured the supposedly smaller cranial cavities of non-Nordics, while the thriving new sciences of IQ testing and criminal classification by facial and skull type only reinforced the cultural biases that had developed against "new immigrant" "races" through the works of Riis and other popular writers. Even Frank Norris's sometimes sympathetic portrayal of the hulking, dull-witted dentist *McTeague* made much of the symmetry between his physical appearance and his innate atavistic violence. Other characters in the skid row Polk Street area were similarly typed by their revealing physiognomies.[96]

Riis further speaks of the futile efforts of the Society for the Prevention of Cruelty to Children to rein in truancy and delinquency, "but neither these nor the truant officer can prevent ever-increasing herds of the boys and girls from growing up, to all intents and purposes, young savages, to recruit the army of paupers and criminals." The inevitability of criminal gangs swarming out of The Bend to invade the rest of the city alarms Riis, too, and the ecology of the slums is only partly to blame, for the police reporter is not sure that reforming institutions can compete with the destitute immigrants' almost natural predilection for flophouses and gin joints. "The step from these to trampdom, that owns the tenements in The Bend as its proper home, is short and easy. . . . The ten-cent lodging-houses more than counterbalance the good done by the free reading-room, lectures, and all other agencies of reform. . . . Reading-rooms and lectures are not indigenous to the soil of Mulberry Street; but the ten-cent and seven-cent lodging houses, usually different grades of one and the same abomination, abound," he says.[97]

Michael Miller Topp has recently documented the degree to which radical newspapers, reading rooms, syndicalist activists, and lecturers permeated the southern Italian communities in places such as Paterson, New Jersey; Boston and New York—and also Italy itself and South America. Other immigrant groups such as the Slovaks created a similarly vibrant world of radical lecturers, theater groups, and halls, even supporting a socialist mandolin society in Paterson! It is therefore doubtful that Mulberry Street's "soil" even in 1889 was entirely devoid of immigrant self-help societies, although whether such radical alternatives to the top-down reforms Progressives such as Riis were determined to impose upon southern and eastern Europeans would have pleased or alarmed the police reporter is difficult to say. Nevertheless, Riis ignored any of the institutions of self-help that proliferated in Italian, Jewish, and Slavic neighborhoods of New York, Philadelphia, Chicago, and many other cities and instead presented Chinese opium dens and white slave trades; criminal gangs violent and desperate enough to make Herbert Asbury blush; homeless children; and interracial gin joints.[98]

Riis ranged far afield in his searches for the colorfully destitute. In a West Twenty-eighth Street tenement, he found an English coal heaver's home that had been the scene of tragedy. "Suspicions of murder, in the case of a woman who was found dead, covered with bruises, after a day's running fight with her husband, in which the beer-jug had been the bone of contention, brought me to this house, a ramshackle tenement on the tail-end of a lot over near the North River docks. The family in the picture lived above the rooms where the dead woman lay on a bed of straw, overrun by rats, and had been uninterested witnesses of the affray that was an everyday occurrence in the house. . . . A heap of old rags, in which the baby slept serenely, served as the common sleeping bunk of father, mother and children."[99]

Riis predated New York's screaming tabloids such as the *Daily News, The Mirror,* and the *Daily Graphic* by about twenty years, and he beat *Fox News* and *Cops* to the grisly murder scene by almost a century. And to be sure, he may have been attempting to achieve something nobler than mere titillation or entertainment. But by focusing his attention on the scandalous side of working-class life, rather than its prosaic, uninteresting aspects, he created a portrait of the city that greatly exaggerated its level of mayhem. All in all the picture was of a tangle of pathologies that, correcting for late-twentieth-century notions of race, Daniel P. Moynihan might have recognized. Of course, here it was Irish, Italian, and Jewish New Yorkers who were dragging down the city.[100]

This portrait would by and large hold for the next forty years. Even a later novel by an Italian-American author like *Christ in Concrete* paints an often grim portrait of Italian immigrant life in the city; so, too, Henry Roth's *Call It Sleep* presents little of the immigrant entrepreneurial activity or self-help fraternal associations that became legendary engines of socioeconomic mobility once the third generation had long left the ghetto behind. Instead, Roth's Schearl family is mired in impotent rage, pathological violence, and furtive sexual dalliances in a desperate attempt to escape the grinding poverty and instability of their lives. The Schearls are utterly incapable of making sense of the Lower East Side slum to which they have moved, and the physically and mentally abused child David teeters on the brink of mental breakdown. Likewise, the communist-proletarian writer Mike Gold presented a portrait of *Jews without Money* that, for his own purposes, emphasized the exploitation, poverty, and dysfunctional lives Lower East Side immigrants faced.[101]

It was only later, in the 1950s, that some of these images were sepia-toned, or at least made room for immigrant agency and valorization. Emerging out of a radical milieu in the Italian neighborhoods of the Bronx, Ralph Fasanella's fanciful paintings of lively radical and trade union activity offered a different view of immigrants than Riis, one that allowed agency by Italians actively working through their unions, social clubs, and parishes to improve their communities. The template established by Riis, as well as sociologists such as Robert Foerster, created a picture of Italians and other new immigrants as primordially mired in poverty and pathology. Riis concluded in 1889, "The philosophy of the slums is too apt to be of the kind that readily recognizes the saloon, always handy, as the refuge from every trouble, and shapes its practices according to the discovery." The immigrants are predisposed to be drunks, Riis hints, and that may explain a good deal of their predicament. Whether Fasanella's garment workers were already meeting in these saloons, slumologists such as Riis neglected to find them.[102]

Of course, the immigrant saloon was also the center of many ethnic social worlds, the immigrant's fraternal society or lecture series meeting place, as well as the conference room of the alderman or ward boss, as James T. Farrell's *Studs Lonigan* would document in looking back at life in Irish Chicago's Bridgeport area. Drinking certainly went on, and Lonigan and his pals in the Fifty-eighth Street gang might have confirmed a social worker's most pessimistic assessment of the innate Irish propensity for brawling, both among themselves and to keep "the niggers" from invading their neighborhood. Bridgeport had indeed been one of the main recruiting areas for white ethnic gangs during the notorious antiblack riots of 1919, and the fictional Studs Lonigan had many real-life counterparts in Chicago, Philadelphia, East Saint Louis, and other cities only too willing to battle against aliens encroaching on their turf. Likewise, like many another teen gang member in Chicago, Studs rises in the world through his ability to provide muscle for rival Irish racketeers during Prohibition. But in Lonigan's Bridgeport the saloon was also the place in which the immigrant (or often the second-generation American) could make an important connection with City Hall and begin to rise a bit in the world by other, at least somewhat more legitimate, means.[103]

Of course, New York's Tammany Hall and similar political clubs in Irish Chicago were satirized by cartoonists like Thomas Nast, with his scathing apelike caricatures of Boss Tweed, and condemned by reformers like Jane Addams of Hull House. Whether native-born Americans would have regarded Lonigan's Chicago of bootleggers, teen gangs, and larcenous ward bosses as much better than the encroaching "Negroes" who so obsessed Studs is doubtful. In any event, Farrell accurately depicted the saloon as the nerve center of ward political life, but by

1932 even the Irish were alarmed at what "their" city had become. After returning from a visit to the ward leader at his headquarters, Studs's father tells him,

Barney did nothing but cry all the time I saw him. He was crying about the Polacks and the Bohunks. He says that they just almost cleaned out the Irish. He kept saying to me, "Paddy, if you want to get anything down at the Hall, you better put a *sky* on your name before you go down there." And he made one funny crack. He said that these days, down at the Hall, they only speak English from one to two in the afternoon. . . . Well, Bill, tell you, you know for years all these foreigners have been let into America, and now they've just about damn near taken the country over. Why, from the looks of things, pretty soon a white man won't feel at home here. What with the Jew international bankers holding all the money here, and the Polacks and Bohunks squeezing the Irish out of politics, it's getting to be no place for a white man to live.[104]

Earlier Lonigan and his brick-wielding pals have kept the "niggers" from invading their Fifty-eighth Street turf, as countless white ethnics would continue to battle into the 1950s and beyond. But now they were helpless as another provisional white group stood ready to capture the graft-ridden coffers of City Hall. And ironically, as earlier Chicagoans and New Yorkers had concluded the Irish had made the city no fit place for a "white man," now some similar conclusions were being reached about newer arrivals.

Ward leaders named McKenna and their lieutenants named Lonigan in the early 1930s were indeed worrying in Chicago that a "Slavic invasion" was threatening their bailiwicks, for in 1931 Anton "Pushcart Tony" Cermak, Bohemian-born ward boss, entered the mayor's office, and it might have seemed that the Hibernian ascendancy was entering a long, slow decline (ironically, after Cermak's assassination in 1933, another fifty-four years of Chicago mayors named Kelly, Kennelly, Daley, and Byrne would begin, but Farrell had no way of knowing that when his novel was published in 1932). Even Bridgeport's Irish evidently had read their Riis and Madison Grant and worried that urban America was going to the Slavic dogs.

In 1930, as in 1889, most writers assessing the city either accepted Riis's frustration at immigrants' unwillingness to be "helped" or "improved," or were equally alarmed that corrupt ward bosses of dubious ethnicity were helping themselves all too readily. "The indifference of those they would help is the most puzzling," Riis lamented. "They will not be helped. Dragged by main force out of their misery, they slip back again on the first opportunity, seemingly content only in the old rut." By 1932 James T. Farrell presented an Irish world of street thugs seizing the main chance through service to corrupt aldermen, and Chicago's image was still in the gutter. After all, as early as the 1880s and 1890s, *Puck* had made the grafting Irish ward boss and his thuggish followers a stock figure in its cartoon assault on the various interlopers in the Mugwumps' middle-class city. In "The Bugaboo of Congress," a giant, simian Irish ward boss lords it over a Congress of pygmies too timid to act on "the dynamite question"; *Puck*'s "Hint to Irish Modesty" suggested Hibernian ward bosses redesign New York City's coat of arms to reflect grafting realities (with boodling Irish aldermen, robber barons, and shamrocks woven into a design that showed the new political powers in the city). Now even an Irish-American novelist confirmed native Americans' suspicions.[105]

By the time Farrell's *Studs Lonigan* appeared, American readers had been told for better than forty years that their cities were in critical condition, and that their immigrant residents were "a bad investment for the country to make," as Henry Cabot Lodge asserted regarding Slovak newcomers. Graft and corruption were "the shame of the cities," Lincoln Steffens said in referring to Philadelphia, but even less serious-minded writers frequently conveyed an image of Manhattan, Chicago, and even Baltimore as exotic and somewhat entertaining, but at bottom primordially dangerous, dirty, and slipping beyond control of society's educated middle class. Many magazine writers, not just Lonigan's ward leader, had for decades been "crying about the Polacks and the Bohunks" invading urban America. Progressive writers embraced both Riis's mantle of reform and social-scientific truth, but also his distaste for the poverty-stricken new urban masses. Whether as entertainers or serious essayists arguing for reform of housing stock, slum clearance, better factory conditions, or immigration restriction, writers often shared a myopic vision of immigrants that saw little of worth in urbanites' own communities and self-help organizations.[106]

Peter Roberts, observer of "the Sclavs" of Mahanoy City, Pennsylvania, was typical in wondering of the newcomer, "Has he the power to appreciate adequately the advantages offered by democratic institutions and will he improve them?" Paddy Lonigan would have had a ready answer, and judging by Roberts's fixation on the drinking habits of immigrant miners, he, too, doubts if eastern Europeans can ever contribute much to the country. "The Sclav never had a good time unless there is plenty of beer and whiskey flowing," he sniffs, adding, "The Sclav does not know how to enjoy himself save by getting drunk; he does not know how to show kindness to his friends save by making them drink."[107]

Such accounts were common. In *The Slav Invasion and the Mine Workers* (a book that wears its agenda on its dust jacket with images of an Eastern horde descending on honest American workingmen), Frank Julian Warne argues that it is the Slavs' inability to organize and willingness to work at slave wages that are ruining the country's mine workers. In assessing immigrants in mine towns, all Warne notices is the Slav's tendency to reach for a bottle or a brick. Rather than appreciating the benefit of collective bargaining, Warne writes, Slavs are prone to congregate around a beer keg:

On Saturday evenings and Sundays, at weddings, christenings, funerals, and other celebrations and observances, drinking among the Slavs is carried to excess, the occasion ending not infrequently in a free-for-all fight, and sometimes in a small riot, in which participants are shot and stabbed and not infrequently killed.[108]

One has to wonder if every wedding or Sunday get-together ended in such carnage. Victor Greene long ago demonstrated Polish, Slovak, and other Slavic miners' dedication to the United Mine Workers during the 1903 anthracite strike, and the riots Warne denigrates were often the result of paramilitary suppression by coal company private armies or the Pennsylvania Constabulary, whose own official history argued, "A Polack only understands an argument that comes at the end of a knout." This may be why *Slovak v Amerike*, *Rovnost L'udu* (*Equality for the People*) and other immigrant papers often referred to the state police as "the Cossacks," but of course "mainstream" Americans received far more of their impressions regarding Slavs from Warne, Riis, and their like than from foreign-language newspapers. And Slovaks and Poles might think they were putting their best foot forward during Sunday celebrations or union demonstrations, but native-born writers continued to see what they wanted to see. Indeed, the image of Slovak drunkenness proved hard to dispel, although P. V. Rovnianek, leader of the National Slovak Society, tried to correct this impression "spread by the daily press that Slovak weddings and christenings are usually occasions for disorder and riot" in a 1904 article in *Charities and the Commons*. "If left alone," Rovnianek argued, "this merry-making would be harmless, but it usually happens that when the celebration is at its height, some emissary of a constable or alderman, with fees and costs in sight, appears among them and starts a disturbance."[109]

Yet it is difficult to argue with a Progressive reformer when he is armed with the facts. Warne reports that, since the influx of the Slavs, there has been an increase of crime in coal country. Of course, the same argument had been made thirty years before regarding Irish Molly Maguires, but now these were the "American" miners Warne regarded under threat by innately criminal Slavs. To prove beyond a shadow of a doubt that Poles, Slovaks, and Ruthenians accounted for the upswing in crime, Warne offered the example of Lackawanna, Pennsylvania. "In the alphabetical file of cases the M's have increased to three boxes, the S's to three boxes, and the R's to two boxes, when formerly they had but one box each. These letters largely predominate among the initials of the surnames of the Slavs."[110]

Even writers sympathetic to the Slavic immigrants emphasized the newcomers' helplessness. Edward Steiner, himself an immigrant who made good, compared the plight of the Slovaks of ramshackle Whiskey Hill, Pennsylvania, to the peacefulness of the nearby German Pietist community of Ephrata: "'*Friedsam*.' No one would be called this in Whiskey Hill. Weather-beaten wooden buildings there are, scaffolded structures, shaken by the vibration of coal-crushing machinery within."[111]

One cannot deny that such miserable dwellings were a large part of the Slovak experience in coal, steel, and textile cities in Pennsylvania and elsewhere. Yet, by focusing on the miners' misery to the exclusion of all else, Steiner creates a straw Slav to be used by those less sympathetic to the newcomers.

Edward Alsworth Ross, sociologist of the University of Wisconsin, was one such ethnographer of immigrant dysfunction who first serialized his "The Old World in the New" in the mass-circulation, general-interest magazine *Century*. Ross fixated on "the low standards of cleanliness and comfort" of the Slavs, and also their drinking habits. "The Saturday brewery-wagon makes the rounds," Ross writes, "and on a pleasant Sunday one sees in the yard of every boarding-house a knot of broad-shouldered, big-faced men about a keg of liquid comfort. . . . It is at celebrations that the worst excesses show themselves."[112]

A different picture—of desperate poverty, grinding work in steel mills, and early death by accident and disease, but also resilience and eventually successful union organizing during the Great Depression—was written by the proletarian writer (and Slovak-American steelworker) Thomas Bell in the 1941 novel *Out of This Furnace*. Here the "Hunkies" of Braddock and Homestead, Pennsylvania, get to answer Ross and other immigration restrictionists, and suggest that a shot and a beer on the one half day off might not have seemed like the worst sin to a furnace tender. Sadly, it was only during the Great Depression that such counternarratives began to break through to the "mainstream," courtesy of second- and third-generation white ethnics like Bell. Earlier in the century, native-born Americans by and large saw what they wanted to see, and discounted the functional communities Slavs and other immigrants built in the shadow of the steel mills or factories. Ross's 1914 book-length study, *The Old World in the New*, offered one expert's opinion on east Europeans: "Large of body, hard-muscled, and inexpert in making his head save his heels, the Slav inevitably becomes the unskilled laborer in the basic industries." Whether some of this had to do with native-born prejudice toward Slavs, or whether life in the steel mills fueled Slavs' own life goals (often back in *stara krajina*, the Old Country), as scholars such as Ewa Morawska and novelists such as Bell have evocatively argued, Ross fails to consider.

Instead, he sums up the reason for the Slavs' poverty and squalor in a succinct report:

Without calling in question the worth of the Slavic race, one may note that the immigrant Slavs have a small reputation for capacity. Many observers, after allowing for their illiteracy and lack of opportunity, still insist that they have little to contribute to our people. "These people haven't any natural ability to transmit," said a large employer of Slavs. "You may grind and polish dull minds all you want to in the public schools, but you never will get a keen edge on them because the steel is poor."

In Bell's *Out of This Furnace*, even a third-generation Slovak chafed at the ethnocentrism of Americans who assumed no Slav could really learn anything, and "poor steel" or not, he leaves school as soon as he can rather than waste his time. Many new immigrants likewise concluded they would invariably be pegged as hopeless, and went into the factories, steel mills, and coal mines, which, for all their problems, at least offered some "opportunity structure" enabling blue-collar cities to provide some possibility for a family wage for the new immigrants, especially after the Wagner Act sanctioned collective bargaining after 1935. In this regard, for all the ethnocentrism they faced, "white ethnics" had at least a leg up on residents of postindustrial cities in the decades after the 1960s.[113]

Still, at least in the first decades of the twentieth century, the biases against southern and eastern Europeans caused many Progressives to view them as blights on America's cities. In one steel city, Ross writes, the school superintendent reports that "the percentage of retardation for the children of Bohemian fathers was only 35.6 per cent.; but for Poles, the retardation was 58.1 per cent., and for Slovaks, 54.5 per cent." The reputation of Pittsburgh, Cleveland, and Chicago suffered as they filled with such stigmatized newcomers.[114]

Similar "scientific" tracts were employed by like-minded writers to prove that the Jews, the Italians, and even the Irish contributed nothing that the Anglo-Saxon republic very much needed. The tenor of the pieces that looked at the threat southern and eastern Europeans posed to America's cities is easily summed up by the subtitle of Lothrop Stoddard's 1922 screed: *The Menace of the Under Man.*[115]

There is only so much statistical science one can take. The lighter side of the slum, in which the immigrant was not so much a peril to the nation's pure racial gene pool, but a figure of derision and fun, was presented by voyeuristic magazine travelogues, with thrill-seeking glimpses of the city's diverting, exotic, colorful—but also more than a little decadent—ethnic residents.

"In the New York Ghetto," Katherine Hoffman discovers for her *Munsey's Magazine* readers in 1900 an entirely separate and exotic country a streetcar ride away. Striking east from Broadway,

and crossing the dividing line of the Bowery, in the neighborhood of Grand Street, the average New Yorker comes upon a country whose habits he probably knows less, and with whose inhabitants he certainly has much less in common, than if he had crossed the Atlantic and found himself in Piccadilly or Pall Mall.[116]

At a time when more than 45 percent of New Yorkers were foreign-born, it's doubtful that each and every Brooklyn or Manhattan resident would have agreed with Hoffman, but the normative face of what middle-class magazine readers wanted their city to remain was an English-speaking, respectable, Protestant city, even if, as early as 1850, many Bowery B'hoys could have told writers this was no longer the case. The neighborhoods Hoffman visits are, though, to her audience, indeed foreign climes. Of "Little Russia," she reports, "Its feasts and fasts, its great personages and its common folk, its markets, its restaurants, its ceremonies, the very language it uses, are as strange . . . as if the Bowery, with the shadow of the elevated forever darkening it, were some impassable stream." As she guides the reader through the warrens of the Lower East Side, Hoffman seems to have sailed not just across the Atlantic, but off the edge of some medieval map to a place populated by mythological creatures with odd skin conditions and misshapen bodies:

Fish, which proclaims itself before one reaches Hester Street, is cheapened wordily by dark eyed, parchment faced women, and as wordily defended against cheapening by bearded hucksters with heads thrust forward between their shoulders and dark eyes fiercely gleaming.[117]

The noxious smells and the exotic, semihuman features conjure up a place of equal parts danger and excitement. In the end, the danger is containable, because the readers are reassured they have not left New York, after all. Indeed, as they are reading this in the latest issue of *Munsey's,* they very likely haven't left their easy chairs, learning all they need know about the immigrant masses from the safety of their homes.

In "The Island of Desire," by Robert Haven Schauffler, this tour of the exotic is carried to comical extremes. A young college graduate, bored with his life, plans to leave New York for a tour of "my beloved Slavic countries." Instead, a friend proposes to cure him of his wanderlust with a dose of exotic Manhattan.

Like the reformers who professed to depict the truth of the immigrant neighborhoods they visited, the "slummer" in "The Island of Desire" peeks at genuine ethnic types in their tribal settings. The slummer becomes a fly on the wall; not only can he vicariously enjoy the exotic without ever leaving his home city, but he also surreptitiously enjoys the genuine ethnics in his midst without their ever knowing he is there. Perfect middle-class voyeurism!

The final stop on his tour is East Seventy-fourth Street, "the country of Dvorak and Smetana and Huss." Here he meets up with an "a Bohemian funeral . . . coming up Second Avenue, . . . filled with the lustrous melancholy of Slavonic lands." But real gold is struck when he stumbles into "the famous Bohemian Ball!" and loses himself in the whirl of ethnic types enjoying a simulated village green. Like the narrator, readers were edified and titillated by their trip to the haunts of exotic Yorkville Slavs.[118]

Judging by the frequency of these magazine slum tours, native-born America was obsessed with a desire to gaze on ethnic oddities. E. S. Martin's "East Side Considerations" breathlessly describes the delightful socializing along Delancey Street, full of "easy fellowship, and also of many pleasant social opportunities." The reader is again with Riis, seeing the outdoor, promiscuous immigrants as a carnival for the enjoyment of their "betters."

"The East Side is especially convenient for the observation of people because there are such shoals of them always in sight," Martin adds, "and because their habits of life and manners are frank, and favorable to a certain degree of intimacy at sight." In his commentary on Hutchins Hapgood's 1902 study of the ghetto, Harry Golden described the tour buses that brought gawkers to his boyhood Lower East Side; perhaps the tourists he and his friends taunted in their teens had themselves been egged on by Martin and other slumologists to visit the colorful, plentiful Jewish immigrants in their "oriental" native habitat.[119]

Such gawking had far from harmless political implications. Stephen Greenblatt has written of the wonder cabinets of medieval aristocrats, rooms full of "resonance and wonder" that showed off the oddities the noblemen had collected and catalogued in their world travels, and here there seems to be some of the same drive to collect and label the immigrant noble savage. Collectors possess the power to order and name their collections, and to shape the narratives around the caged items, human or not, in their collections. Zoo beasts or museum displays, after all, don't get to argue with their keepers. In the late nineteenth century, too, the U.S. underwent a mania for world's fairs, which presented supposed "savage" cultures to the view of more civilized Americans. Pacific Islanders fresh from Borneo, the Philippines, and elsewhere shared billing with the technological wonders of the new world in Chicago's Columbian Exposition, Saint Louis's World's Fair, and others. At a time when the U.S. was beginning its colonial ventures, turn-of-the-century fairs classified the "primitive types," those "little brown brothers" that William McKinley's and Teddy Roosevelt's America was sure would be improved by the Big Stick of U.S. intervention.[120]

Ironically the stigmatized urban newcomers, who were themselves the objects of slumologists' haughty classificatory gaze, often heartily embraced America's imperial expeditions against even more slighted groups. Slovak papers cheered Admiral George Dewey on, and warned of a "Yellow Peril" if the Japanese and Filipinos weren't put in their place. A Slovak-American soldier serving in the Philippines wrote a series of letters to *Národné Noviny* explaining how he taught civilization to "the Mohammedans" with a Bible in one hand and a pistol in the other.

Elsewhere, Finley Peter Dunne's Irish Chicago bartender character, Mr. Dooley, claimed Admiral Dewey as a long-lost cousin who might bring ward boss efficiency to the benighted Philippines. "I'll bet ye, whin we comes to find out about him, we'll hear hes' illicted himself king iv th' F'lip-ine Islands," the bartender tells his favorite customer, Hennessy. "Dooley th' Wanst. He'll be settin' up there undher a pa'm-three with naygurs fannin' him an' a dhrop iv licker in th' hollow iv his ar-rm, an' hootchy-kootchy girls dancin' before him." Perhaps Mr. Dooley had seen just such "hootchy-kootchy girls" from Hawaii or Mindanao performing for the crowd at the Columbian Exposition.[121]

While no one suggested marketing a midway exposition for the next world's fair of "colorful" Irish Chicagoans or Jewish and Italian New Yorkers, the immigrant was set alongside the technological wonders of the city as a fit subject for the middle-class gaze in *Harper's, Munsey's,* and other general-interest magazines. And as we've seen, the immigrant savage was thought often enough to need a great deal of civilizing, too. Indeed, *Puck* conflated the wonder of the Asiatic or African savage with WASP disdain for the only slightly less savage Irish in a cartoon that had Mr. Patsy O'Rourke taking a break from his midway carnival job masquerading as the Fiji Chief, while Tooley plays the Wild Man of Borneo. Elsewhere in *Puck* Irish zoo goers gawk before a gorilla cage: "Sure, it's a longin' fur liberty these poor monkeys are," Mr. Mulhooley observes. His daughter asks, "Is that what makes thim look so Irish?"[122]

Just as a World's Fair entrepreneur or "natural science" museum curator might show off Pacific Islanders or Fiji men, E. S. Martin informed his readers that a mother nursing her young "in Mott or Mulberry or Cherry Street . . . is a common sight and always interesting to the respectful observer." Just how respectful the gaze was may be assessed by Martin's addition of an illustration of an exotic immigrant girl, "An Oriental Type." Although even immigrants themselves embraced the anti-Asian biases, and antiblack racism, sadly all too quickly, as when the Slovak newspaper *Jednota* warned its readers of an imminent "Yellow Peril" should

Japan defeat Russia in their 1905 war, or should Chinese be allowed to emigrate to the U.S., the new immigrants themselves were racialized as others, fit for gazes, respectful or not, but hardly worthy additions to the city.

While Slavs might worry about "Asian invasions," WASPs saw the new immigrants themselves as the Asiatic threat, as Martin's reference to an "Oriental type" makes clear. Burton J. Hendrick, too, in 1907 warned in *McClure's* of "The Great Jewish Invasion," in language more apocalyptic than the lighthearted Martin: "The New Yorker constantly rubs elbows with Israel. The thoroughfares are almost impassably clogged with Jewish pushcarts. . . . In a word, New York is not only largely, and probably destined to be overwhelmingly, a city of Hebrews, but a city of Asiatics."[123]

Progressive reformers regarded such cataloging as necessary to create order out of chaos (and to native-born Americans, the immigrant quarters were nothing if not chaotic.) A taxonomy of wild, exotic Italians, Jews, and Slavs was created for magazine readers, and even if the slumologists by and large were only interested in amusing, such articles also reinforced the agenda of those who wished to exclude the immigrants altogether. Zoo creatures, after all, were hardly deserving of citizenship, and a comical zoo is only a step away from a dangerous one full of creatures that must forever remain behind bars. Nor did animals organize for self-improvement; they had to be sorted and ordered by people of a higher civilization. Of course, if WASP readers had cared to look, there was plenty of evidence of immigrant self-help and organization, and some of the same cities visited by magazine writers peddling an image of urban decay and helpless immigrant squalor also bore witness to public displays by ethnic marching societies, church groups, and public fraternal pageants on American and ethnic holidays, when tuxedoed or otherwise grandly costumed fraternalists paraded and Slovak "queens" were crowned, as in San Francisco in 1916, in regal medieval splendor. The pages of Slovak journals such as *Národné Noviny* and *Národný Kalendár* bore witness to the vibrancy of immigrant neighborhoods in Passaic, Homestead, San Francisco, Chicago, and other cities. These accounts, though, were published in one of the "Babel" languages Jacob Riis had dismissed on his tour of Lower Manhattan, so Slavic, Jewish, or Italian communities' vibrancy remained buried under a weight of popular presentations telling a different story. The stories stressed the horrors of poverty-stricken neighborhoods—and destitution and danger there certainly were in pre–New Deal America's steel, textile, and factory cities—but left the daylight out of these updated shadow narratives.[124]

Few horrified readers of urban nightmares were willing to take the cognitive leap necessary to support union wages for workingmen, or even more broad-ranging, systemic reforms of industrial capitalism, as Lincoln Steffens found out after he'd exposed municipal corruption in Philadelphia. Likewise, Upton Sinclair's *The Jungle* did more for reform of unhealthy meat-processing plants than for the immigrants such as the fictional Lithuanian Chicagoans. "I aimed for America's heart but instead I hit her in the stomach," Sinclair is supposed to have sardonically stated after his novel of Chicago's Back of the Yards led to the 1906 Pure

Food and Drug Act, but not much improvement in the Windy City's slums along hyperpolluted "Bubbly Creek"; nor did a groundswell develop in favor of improved working conditions for meatpackers. Reform fiction only took Americans' sympathies so far, and may have sometimes reinforced native Americans' revulsion at the slum dwellers who toiled in noxious slaughterhouses, steel mills, and the like. Since slum safari leaders like Riis lumped blind pigs, slumlords, tenement firetraps, and Irish drunkenness, and "Mediterranean exuberance" all together as urban maladies in need of reform, it is small wonder the city dwellers met with so little sympathy and so much contempt.[125]

Immigrants themselves contested these portrayals of their quarters as unrelentingly grim. Substandard housing and numbing poverty there certainly were in the ghetto, but novelists such as Anzia Yeszierska and Abraham Cahan sought to explain their communities and send a message of self-worth. Cahan's *David Levinsky* rises to become a respectable garment factory owner, but even as he succeeds in the eyes of others, this "all-rightnik" realizes he has abandoned the observance of strict Orthodox Judaism, with its emphasis on benevolence and charity. Although he is a success by American standards, Levinsky ruefully regards himself as a failure.[126]

Other characters in ghetto fiction, while presented by Jewish writers with more sympathy than magazine writers usually could muster, also ironically conformed to, or at least may have reinforced, stereotypes of immigrant helplessness and dysfunction. Cahan's *Yekl* deals with an immigrant sweatshop worker who fancies himself a "regular Yankee," the darling of the Lower East Side's dancing academies. When he sends for his wife and son from the old country, however, he's embarrassed by his bride's "greenhorn" ways and continues his philandering with a girl from the dancing academy.

Yekl brings to life problems of the modern city very much on the minds of social reformers seeking to improve the city circa 1900. The dance halls, vaudeville theaters, and, within a few years, nickelodeons of the city may seem to our age harmless, even charming, places of entertainment. However, the reformers of the age worried greatly about what Kathy Peiss has called "cheap amusements," which would ruin the morals of the new working class, rather than offer them moral uplift. Men and women of varying classes and "races" (for so the prevailing social sciences regarded the new immigrants, as different species from the country's Nordic founders) rubbing shoulders together in dance halls and cheap theaters would only degrade each others' habits, learning the most vicious lessons from too much easy urban mixing. The ease with which Cahan's "regular Yankee" Jake falls into the arms of a woman other than his wife at a Lower East Side dance hall may have confirmed the prevalent middle-class view that halls offering "ten cents a dance" were little better than houses of assignation. Long before the rise of MTV, urban entertainment raised fears of immorality, and for Progressive Era reformers, Cahan's Jake and Mamie might have been prime examples of the city's dance hall danger.[127]

Then, too, in a time when the problem of immigrant wives' abandonment was very much on the minds of reformers, this story may not have been the most

flattering picture the Lower East Side could have afforded of itself; when the
young wife is rescued by the couple's boarder, it only highlighted another supposed
problem of the immigrant quarters. Riis and other journalists despaired of the
overcrowding in tenement apartments, in which immigrants rented out every spare
inch to boarders, and the promiscuous mixing of men and women unrelated to
each other in such tight quarters raised Victorian fears of immorality. The "boardinghouse problem" documented in Progressive magazines such as *The Charities
and the Commons* was brought to life, too, in Cahan's novel. Boarders evidently
did come between immigrant husbands and wives, and tenement overcrowding
worried more than just the housing inspector.[128]

For her part, Yezierska presents tales of ghetto woe, too, and even if she deals
sympathetically with her characters, the picture of poverty and failure would
have been a familiar one to readers of *Century* and the like. In *Hungry Hearts*, an
immigrant mother despairs on coming to New York, where she has been shunted
aside by her embarrassed children. "Oi veh!" another immigrant mother wails.
"'Where is the sunshine in America?' She went to the tenement window and
looked at the blank wall of the next house. Like a grave so dark. To greenhorns it
seemed as if the sunlight had faded from their lives and buildings like mountains
took its place." Other Yezierska mothers similarly lament the poverty and sights
and smells of the horrid slums that offer no promise of gold in the streets.[129]

Slovak immigrants were already satirizing this trope of gold in the streets with
mocking bitterness. In 1908, *Slovak v Amerike* published one immigrant's recollection of a dream he had that there was so much gold in the streets he had to stoop
down and scoop it up. Still he couldn't carry it all, so he took off his underpants
and shoveled the gold into this makeshift net. "But at this moment I awoke and
looked whether it was true or not? I looked at my underdrawers, they were tied,
but no dollars were in them. They were somewhat yellow, for sure enough the
gold must have melted in them. Thus does all the American gold melt just like all
the other dreams in America disappear!"[130]

More decorously, and in English so that mainstream Americans could learn of
the immigrants' often frustrated resentment of the New World's broken promise,
Yezierska detailed, most famously in her 1925 novel *Bread Givers*, the stultifying
world of the Lower East Side, where fathers and mothers grow nostalgic for "far-off
times in Russia" when faced with the poverty and squalor of New York.[131] The narrator Sara Smolinsky's father wins brief notoriety in his building as "the speaking
mouth of his block" who leads a rent strike against the slumlord that allows the
immigrants the "pleasure of getting even, once in their lives, with someone over
them that was always stepping on them." However, it's a Pyrrhic victory that
doesn't change the fundamentals of the rotten tenement district where they struggle
to survive. "I hate the landlord worse as a pawnbroker," a tenant washerwoman
declares. "Every month of your life, whether you're working or not working,
whether you're sick or dying, you got to squeeze out so much blood to give the
leech for black walls that walk away, alive with bedbugs and roaches and mice."
Vermin-infested apartments remain long after recollections of a brief tenement
uprising have faded, and Yezierska's readers may have nodded knowingly in

registering more evidence of the unsettling menageries of lice-ridden immigrants that infested America's cities.[132] For all his frustrations with the New World, Sarah's father refuses her attempts to strive for something better; it's only by moving away from the claustrophobic immigrant quarter that Sarah can take tentative steps to realize her dreams of becoming a teacher, much as Yezierska herself went to Hollywood to try to become an artistic interpreter of the immigrant masses to the rest of America. In her sympathetic assessments of the poverty, despair, and frustrations of immigrant city dwellers, Yezierska painted a portrait that realistically accorded with the view of New York that many readers had already formed at the hands of less caring writers.

Another Yezierska story in *Hungry Hearts* features an immigrant mother who desires to redecorate and paint her tenement apartment to surprise her son, coming home from the army. "I'm sick of living like a pig with my nose to the earth, all the time only pinching and saving for bread and rent. So long as my Aby is with America, I want to make myself an American." While her neighbors admire the "gold shining in every corner" she has created, the landlord is unimpressed, but then tells her the now-improved apartment is worth more. "If you can't pay it someone else will." He has a contrasting view to his tenant as to what it means to be an American: Not paint but profit. "In America everybody looks out for himself." He raises her rent by such an exorbitant amount that she can no longer afford to live there. Enraged, she hacks at the walls and ceiling of her little apartment, railing at "the dogs, the blood-sucking landlords. They are the new Czars in America." If she can't live there she'll make sure her improvements will not be left behind for some other greenhorn family to enjoy. When her son arrives on the block, he sees a familiar sight: His mother at the curb with all her meager possessions in the gutter. Evicted. The frequent rent strikes, evictions, and prevalent homelessness on the Lower East Side were likewise captured in Mike Gold's *Jews without Money*.[133]

Other Yezierska stories feature enraged and jealous husbands suspicious of their wives' and daughters' newfound independence in the garment shops and streets of New York, with daughters likewise caught between the Old and New Worlds. In *Arrogant Beggar,* Yezierska even bit the hand of condescending settlement house charity that ostensibly catered to the needy of the slums but often reinforced the class inequities of the system. Adele Lindner returns to the ghetto, seeking to incorporate the best communitarian impulses of the immigrants themselves with the entrepreneurial and social work knowledge she has learned from Uptown "all-rightniks." Mostly, though, Adele rejects the paternalism that keeps the clients passive and in the ghetto-zoo as objects of others' gaze, benevolent or not. "Why should they have the glory of giving and we the shame of taking like beggars the bare necessities of life?" Adele demands.

As Katherine Stubbs has noted, too, many Yezierska stories feature an attraction between a cold-blooded representative of WASP America and a hot-blooded, exotic, "oriental" Jewish immigrant woman, a pairing that may have reinforced the prevalent notion the new immigrants were exotic representatives of different "races" not fully capable of the self-discipline and rationality necessary to make it in America.[134] The fear of women's rejection of their assigned roles came back in other immigrant narratives, with boisterous aunts arriving from the old country to meddle in family affairs, but also realizing with anxiety that the New World was too much for them to comprehend. In Henry Roth's *Call It Sleep*, David's Aunt Bertha arrives to boss her brother-in-law around, driving him into one of his frequent fits of murderous rage. But flamboyant Bertha with her flippant ways and untamed red hair proves no match for the daunting city, either. On a visit to Central Park and the museum there, Aunt Bertha gets hopelessly lost on the subway and only with the greatest of efforts manages to make it back to the family's squalid, but manageable, Lower East Side flat.

While these characters have more humanity than the stock figures of magazine slum tours, they often reinforced the picture of city vices the "serious press" presented. What we have, then, is an unequal contestation to interpret this puzzling text, the "new immigrants" and their city neighborhoods, in which many critics fabricated glosses that fit their agendas, ignoring other authors' readings of immigrant worth. And realistic accounts of the hurdles immigrants faced could all too easily be interpreted as proof of the dysfunctionality of the American city and its threateningly exotic new residents. While some visitors to the Lower East Side could write sympathetically of the vast array of intellectual, trade union, and self-help organizations that had developed on the Lower East Side, as well as appreciatively of Yiddish literary and theater artists along East Broadway and Second Avenue, the more usual popular-culture face of the Jewish immigrant was of Albert Schearl, the homicidally angry and incompetent father of Henry Roth's 1934 novel of immigrant Jews, *Call It Sleep*. If even the picture coming from within the immigrant community was often so grim, Hapgood's sympathetic portrait was destined to be a minority interpretation of the immigrant city, at least until sons and daughters of the ghetto began to leave it and tentatively enter the middle class.[135]

Even humorous depictions of the city drew attention to dark and ominous days to come if something weren't quickly done to check the newcomers' advance. In 1889, the illustrator and editor of *Life* magazine, J. A. Mitchell, published his dystopic look at the fate he feared awaited the Hibernian metropolis of Manhattan. *The Last American* tells of the exploits of a Persian admiral, a visitor from the year 2951 who stumbles upon the ruins of Manhattan and marvels at the crumbling "Two Monuments in the River" (the Brooklyn Bridge) and odd, green statue of a woman, overgrown with trees and weeds. Shades of *The Planet of the Apes!* However, in Mitchell's dystopic future, Lady Liberty doesn't suffer the indignity of burial up to her neck in sand, and it isn't the apes who cause the downfall of America.

Well, not exactly. The book is a cautionary tale from the future, a look back at the collapse sometime in the twentieth century of "the Merikahn people." A prefatory "few words by Hedful, surnamed 'the Axis of Wisdom,'" tells of this culture's demise according to the best understanding of Persian archaeologists. (Hedful himself is probably eminently qualified to recount this tale of decline and fall, as he is the author of "The Celestial Conquest of Kaly-phorn-ya" and "Northern Mehrika under the Hy-Bernyan Rulers.") He notes that the republic founded by George-wash-yn-tun ceased to exist in 1990, although records after "the massacre of the Protestants in 1907, and the overthrow of the Murfey dynasty in 1930" grow fuzzy.

The history of the Mehrikans makes clear, though, that they "were a mongrel race, with little or no patriotism, and were purely imitative; simply an enlarged copy of other nationalities extant at the time. . . . A shallow, nervous, extravagant people." Mitchell had perhaps tipped his hand already in his dedication, which offered his cautionary tale "To the American, who is more than satisfied with Himself and His Country." Were the Catholic newcomers leaving this American very "satisfied"? It seems unlikely. Not if the slaughter of the Protestants was a mere eighteen years away. If that was the fate Mitchell's dystopic novel foresaw for the next generation of Americans, perhaps, like another wildly popular 1880s writer, he was also "looking backward." While Edward Bellamy was alarmed at the misery hyperindividualism had caused the industrial poor in the 1880s robber baron era, and proposed a future of cooperationist planned communities in which all could excel in a scientifically ordered Boston of the year 2000, Mitchell perhaps looked back to 1863, the year of Irish rioters run amok in Lower Manhattan, and speculated—satirically humorously, granted—that the future held only further, more ruinous Hibernian revolts.[136]

Bellamy's *Looking Backward* offered a scientifically planned city that could overcome the chaos of industry ruining the many at the service of the few, and inspired a countrywide movement of Nationalist Clubs that could save the country from the gross inequalities of the Gilded Age. Although *The Last American* might have found many sympathetic readers in the Immigration Restriction League, it inspired no mass movement. But like Bellamy, Mitchell also worried that the plutocrats of his own age might be leading the republic to ruin no less than the Irish. When Mitchell's futuristic Persian admiral stumbles upon "the ruins of an endless city," he and his expedition are at first at a loss as to where they are. The mystery is revealed, though, when they stumble upon a crumbling "NEW YORK STOCK EXC," which tips off one of the scholars accompanying the admiral that they are in the legendary vanished city of Nhu-Yok. The scholar tells his admiral that many are surprised that this city of "four millions," and the entire republic of which it was the metropolis, should "vanish from the earth like a mist," but counters that the decline was not all that puzzling, really. Rather, "there was nothing to leave," he says. "The Mehrikans possessed neither literature nor art, or music of their own. Everything was borrowed. The very clothes they wore were copied with ludicrous precision from the models of other nations. They were a sharp, restless, quick-witted, greedy race, given body and soul to the gathering of riches. Their chiefest passion was to buy and sell."

Earlier, the Persian scholar speculates on the meaning of a decaying cornice marked "Astor House": "It was probably the name of a deity, and here was his temple." Like Lippard, Progressive writers such as Mitchell seem to have worried plutocrats no less than street urchins were threatening the health of the republic. And just as murder and rapine delighted the readers of "city mysteries," the Persians distastefully note that Manhattanites seemingly couldn't live without their daily dose of crime and scandal. While the yellow press of Hearst and Pulitzer was in its infancy, already in 1889 the "future visitors" to New York note of the daily press, "The more revolting the deed, the more minute the description. Horrors were their chief delight. Scandals were drunk in with thirstful eyes. These chronicles of crime and filth were issued by hundreds of thousands." That Mitchell, a working journalist, tarred the daily press with such a black brush smacks a little bit of ingratitude, but he was echoing a frequent critique of the yellow press and its lurid treatment of urban crime and decadence. Monitors of supposed glorifications of violence and immorality by Hollywood, television studios, and Internet posters can point to a venerable genealogy.

Greed, luxury, slavish imitation of European fashion, even the popularity of crime rags, only partially explain the decline of the city, however. We can't forget the immigrant menace. The explorers stumble upon a cache of silver and copper coins, the latest a "half doll" coin from 1937 bearing the stereotypically Celtic visage of Dennis Murfey; just so the point isn't lost on Mitchell's readers, an Irish harp decorates the coin's back. "It bears the head of Dennis," the scholar explains, "the last of the Hy-Burnyan dictators. The race is supposed to have become extinct before 1990 of their era." He then adds that although the original Mehrikans were of English origin, those who came later were less vigorous, and not suited for the country's climate. Enter the Murfeys, who must have found the "mongrel race" easy to subjugate. By the late twentieth century, the scholar notes, hundreds of ruined cities dotted the former republic. On a side trip to the ruins of Washington, the Persians encounter the last three surviving Americans, but a friendly toast in the ruins of the Capitol (held, conveniently enough, on July Fourth) degenerates into a brawl, and "the last of the Mehrikans" perishes before a mournful statue of Washington.[137]

The alarming tale of immigrant "invasions" seriously treated in magazine ghetto safaris was here given a comic, surreal, and futuristic bent. Did Mitchell really fear for his Protestant neck when he witnessed the hundreds of thousands of Irish Catholics milling—or is that swarming?—about Manhattan below Fourteenth Street? Who can say? He did, however, feed into a fear of the non-Nordic newcomers that increasingly reached crescendos of alarm, even if the objects of nativist immigrant phobia in the next few decades moved to southern and eastern Europeans. After all, Burton J. Hendrick in 1907 warned in *McClure's* of a "Jewish Invasion" that threatened to subject Manhattan to an "Asiatic" rule. Henry Cabot Lodge asserted Slovaks were too much like the Chinese and therefore should be barred, and *Puck* in 1913 suggested that if only southern and eastern Europeans could be outfitted in kimonos (like the barred Japanese), then the *real* undesirables could be kept out of America. Ross's and Warne's language was no less apocalyptic than the "Persian admiral's." In his national menagerie of alarm, Ross cataloged "Sicilians with backless foreheads," and "super-fecund Slavs."

Frank Julian Warne, for his part, warned the country that by 1903 it was under siege from a "Slavic invasion" that threatened the economic, social, and political well-being of the nation. Perhaps harps and Hibernian dictators' faces on "half doll" coins were not so far-fetched, after all.[138]

While cities increasingly were depicted as even more menacingly foreign places, as Hendrick's warning of oddly Asiatic-Jewish New York makes clear, popular culture never entirely forgot the Irish threat, either. *Puck* cartoons continued to feature Irish brawlers, saloonkeepers, and dynamiters as threats to the republic because of the very fact that the Irish were aping their betters all too successfully, already in the decade before 1900 entering positions of influence up to and including aldermen, mayors, sheriffs, and legislators in city halls from Albany to New York to Chicago to Philadelphia. *Puck* also was notorious for its cartoons mocking Jewish storekeepers almost genetically predisposed to overcharging customers, dreaming of arson for insurance money, and attempting to put on airs of arriviste gentility that they couldn't possibly pull off. A Jewish couple attempts to crash a "Hibernian masqued ball." "Dey won't let us in," the wife says, but her husband reassures her. Even though he is dressed in an elaborate medieval suit of armor, his nose protrudes from his helmeted visor. However, he is confident: "Ef dot disguise don't fool dem Irish, I'll go out of der peesness!" It's clear the newcomers don't fit in, even though *Puck* on another occasion, offers "A Hint to the Hebrews" on how to outsmart restricted bathing beaches: A tenement full of garish Lower East Siders pulls up to the beach on a homemade raft. Likewise, Irish politicians march in one *Puck* cartoon on the Fourth of July behind the banner for the Donovan O'Rossa dynamite Society, and every elite "Sons of Shamrock" gala ends in a stereotypical Irish brawl, and all the marchers in cartoon St. Patrick's Day parades have bandaged heads, arms, and legs, badges of honor from their presumably frequent barroom brawls.[139]

Not every comic depiction of the Irish city dweller was quite as apocalyptic as that presented by Mitchell, then, but the image of the Irish as uneducated gate-crashers in America's cities persisted. In the 1890s Chicago newspaperman Finley Peter Dunne related the wisdom of an Irish bartender from the Bridgeport section's "Archey Road" (Archer Avenue). Mr. Dooley has opinions "on ivrything and ivry-body," but in between his philosophizing with his favorite customer, Hennessy, on war, politics, and high finance, a squalid picture of the working-class clientele of his Bridgeport saloon often emerges. Like Studs Lonigan's father, the saloonkeeper already at the turn of the century worries that "the Huns, turned back from the Adriatic and the stock-yards and overrunning Archey Road," are driving the Irish from their community of cabbage gardens and shanties near the city's noxious industries. The Huns have "edged out" the Irish "with the more biting weapons of modern civilization—overworked and under-eaten them into more languid sur-roundings remote from the tanks of the gas-house and the blast furnaces of the rolling mill."[140]

In hearing of a gold rush in Alaska, Dooley recalls that he'd been told the same thing about New York when he set out for America, "where all ye had to do was to hold ye'er hat an' th' goold guineas'd dhrop into it. . . . But faith, whin I'd been here a week, I sen that there was nawthin' but mud under th' pavement—I larned that be means iv a pick-axe at tin shillings th' day."[141] In Chicago it was the same story and, on Archey Road in particular, mud, not gold, prevailed. Dooley reads in the paper of a criminal named Scanlan sentenced to a life in jail, and recalls his hardworking father, "worked fr'm morn till night in th' mills, was at early Mass Sundah mornin'" and his law-abiding brothers and sisters. And yet the cherubic Peter Scanlan is now serving a life sentence, the philosophical bartender muses. Dooley remembers coming upon Scanlan running up the alley behind his bar and later hearing a grocer was nearly clubbed to death during a robbery in his Halsted Street shop. When the police chased him back to his mother's house, Scanlan barricaded himself behind the door "with th' big gun in his hand; an' though they was manny a good lad there, they was none that cared f'r that short odds. . . . Sometimes I think they'se poison in th' life iv a big city," Dooley concludes. "Th' flowers don't grow here no more thin they wud in a tannery, an' th' bur-rds have no song; an th' childher iv dacint men an' women come up hard in th' mouth an' with their hands raised again their kind."[142]

Scanlan is not alone. In his reminiscences on Bridgeport's shady luminaries, Mr. Dooley recounts stories of battling rival brass bands at election time (with mobs clubbing the opposing candidates' drummers with spare trombones and Mr. Dooley's victorious mob proudly casting "2,100 votes f'r Duggan, an' they was only 500 votes in th' precinct"); a canal man so handy with his fists, clubs, and bricks that he rises to become a wealthy real estate contractor and power in the ward ("he got so pop'lar fr'm lickin' all his friends that he opened up a liquor store beyant the bridge, and wan night he shot some la'ads from the yards that come over for to run him"), and finally the ward leader with a diamond as big as your fist and a brick house, even though he has no visible means of support (his wife claims the alderman is in real estate, although in Bridgeport Mr. Dooley observes, "Th' real-estate business includes near ivrything fr'm vagrancy to man-slaugh-ter"); and further murderers and robbers, including the notorious robber and grudge holder Carey, who began their careers breaking into freight cars and ended in a murderous shoot-out with the police "within twinty yards iv me store." While today Mr. Dooley is remembered, if he's remembered, as a satiric commentator on the politicians of the 1890s and early twentieth century, in his own era he often offered graphic commentary on the dirty side of life in Chicago, too.[143]

The idea of The City has played a significant part in American pop culture throughout our country's history. As early as the 1840s Americans alarmed at the growing inequality of industrial America sought explanations for the country's problems in novels and guidebooks that spelled out the secret cabals of high and low that polluted the cities. But with the rise of mass culture coinciding with the mass migration of southern and eastern Europeans, and particularly with the development of illustrated newspapers and magazines at the turn of the urbanizing twentieth century, the image of cities such as New York has played a central role in the nation's imagined landscape. Around 1900, writers for *Harper's, Century, Munsey's, Puck,* and other magazines toured the exotic, foreign locales of New York's Jewish Lower East Side or its Little Italy. Armchair slumologists enabled middle-class Americans to go on "safari" and vicariously enjoy the sights and sounds of a foreign climate. Other, more serious authors warned that these colorful primitives on Hester Street were polluting the American republic, and the popular depiction of entertaining immigrant cities had a more sinister effect in reinforcing anti-immigrant, antiurban biases among the middle class.

When the talking motion picture emerged in America, it coincided with a further wave of urban phobia. Prohibition made the New York, Chicago, or Detroit speakeasy glamorous and thrilling, but also brought with it a further stigmatization of urban ethnic criminality. The exploits of Jewish, Irish, and Italian bootleggers and gangsters such as Meyer Lansky, Owney Madden, Al Capone, and Dutch Schultz filled the tabloid press, but now a new medium, the motion picture, captured a further chapter in cities' demonization. The gangster film took cities to new heights of thrilling spectacle, too.

—— 3 ——

"A Problem That We, the Public, Must Solve": The Gangster Film

Almost from the beginning, American cinema has had a love affair with the gangster. Before Jolson sang, or Cagney or Bogart barked orders to gun-toting henchmen, several one-reelers fed the moviegoing public stories of murder, extortion, and mayhem in the urban cesspool. Perhaps this was inevitable, for many Progressive Era reformers regarded the motion pictures themselves as a disreputable new medium, with the dreaded nickelodeon perceived as a threat to urbanites' morality. These cheaper movie venues catered in many cities to a poor, foreign-born population, which as we've seen were themselves viewed with skepticism, but even many early films depicted ethnic criminals in broad-brush stereotypes that would have been approved by the Immigration Restriction League.[1]

With the advent of Prohibition, however, new story lines on gangland violence proliferated that provided the copy for the new, sensationalist tabloid press in New York, Chicago, and other cities. These stories were appropriated by the talking movies in some of the first Hollywood blockbusters of the new sound era. James Cagney, Edward G. Robinson, and Paul Muni established their careers with *The Public Enemy*, *Little Caesar,* and *Scarface, The Shame of a Nation*. In the latter two cases, the portrayals were thinly veiled depictions of Al Capone, who had solidified his rule in Chicago—and place in the tabloid headlines—with the 1929 Valentine's Day Massacre. But even Cagney's portrayal in *The Public Enemy* adapted elements from the exploits of real-life criminals who may today be obscure but would have been recognizable to readers of the *New York Mirror* or *Chicago Herald and Examiner*.[2]

Whether fictionalized or adaptations of real-life criminals, the early gangster films furthered the depiction of the American city as a lawless place, full of violently threatening characters of suspiciously non-Nordic blood. The graphic depictions of their exploits, too, led to the imposition in 1934 of the Hays Production Code, but even this measure, designed to ensure that crime would never be glorified or depicted with too much gory realism, was frequently evaded by Hollywood producers, who knew what a lucrative franchise they had in the gangster genre. As with the nineteenth-century novels that ostensibly deplored the filth, moral disease, and violence of the nation's urban underworlds and masqueraded as moral uplift or travelogue to aid the uninitiated traveler in "avoiding" the worst vice districts, Hollywood producers often tacked on opening title cards that warned the public that the film they were about to see was exposing a real menace—the rackets, the bootlegger—that the public had to address. No doubt some good-government types took these somber warnings to heart, but for every reformer in the audience there were likely many more moviegoers there to enjoy the action.[3]

Other movies began with assurances that the gangland violence depicted was based on real-life cases in ongoing antiracketeering investigations. By such means producers sold the thrilling mob movies as moral uplift (or at least such an argument could be made to the Hays Office), while still reaping the box office receipts of a public eager to see cinematic hoods. By just such methods "Gaslight" Foster had grown wealthy in the 1850s "exposing" the heart of darkness in New York.[4]

Moreover, in many films of the 1930s, the thugs who are the overt face of the rackets are merely doing the bidding of secretive, wealthy big men who speak in Ivy League tones and dine at luxurious clubs, but nevertheless control the rackets that pollute the cities. In this respect many gangster films mirrored the penny dreadfuls and city mysteries of the nineteenth century, asserting that a secretive cabal of the high and the low was fleecing honest middle Americans of their livelihood and corrupting their hometowns. In gangster films such as *Bullets or Ballots* the city suffered from a rot from above and a rot from below.[5]

By the 1930s it proved harder to depict that rot as exclusively the result of unhealthy immigrant stock. Southern and eastern European Americans were poised on the brink of becoming important constituents in the New Deal coalition, and in any event second-generation Italian, Jewish, and Slavic Americans were avid patrons of the movies, unlikely to appreciate an unequivocal dismissal of immigrant backwardness like Riis's forty years before. Many films beginning in the 1930s differentiated between good and bad ethnics, with films such as *Little Caesar* and *The Last Gangster* offering subplots of ethnic Americans who resist the lure of criminal activity and aspire to assimilate into the American mainstream. Geography and genetics, then, are not destiny, and the raffish, "other half" of the city by the end of the classic gangster period also was capable of producing a brasher, hybrid urban-ethnic culture of the kind that George Gershwin made popular and that was mirrored in *City for Conquest* by the character of composer Eddie Kenny (portrayed by Arthur Kennedy as Jimmy Cagney's kid brother).[6]

After World War II, the somber tone continued with many film noir works to which an anxiety-ridden, post–World War II public could relate. Shady foreigners, criminals, petty conmen the city still had in droves. But to these were now added communist cabals, rampant disease, and other menaces. In any event, the city did not come off in a flattering light in films such as *Kiss of Death, Panic in the Streets,* and *Pickup on South Street.* Nor were the suburbs all that safe from a menace that, for all the best efforts of redlining, the Federal Housing Adminis-tration, and "neighborhood improvement associations," could not be contained by the old inner city.[7]

Crime films, then, contributed in a variety of ways to the well-established con-ception of New York, Chicago, and other cities as national problems in need of drastic reordering. The new medium reflected its era's ambivalent stance toward the nation's cities no less than earlier popular culture mirrored Progressive reformers' dread of foreign Five Points and Mulberry Bend.

In photographs and magazine illustrations the immigrant had been a frequent target of fear, as social Darwinist thinking warned that these new "races" were dragging the republic down, and now, as still images gave way to moving pic-tures, Mulberry Bend came menacingly to life. In a deft analysis of the early stereotypes of Italian criminality in silent movies, Giorgio Bertellini situates the first silent films firmly within the sociological and pop cultural othering of the new immigrant. As in Jacob Riis's treatments of Italian city dwellers, early silent films often drew on stock images of immigrant indolence, love of drink, violent tempers, and almost preternatural filthiness. Still, early films were playing simul-taneously to the immigrant audience in the nickelodeons, as well as appealing to the phrenological proclivities of the nativist middle-class reformers who regarded all southern and eastern European newcomers as prone to Black Hand violence; therefore filmmakers had to engage in some nimble straddling to reach both audiences, presenting and refuting ethnic stereotypes in one and the same work.

Such multivocal "Mafia" pictures date back as far as 1906, when Biograph re-leased a one-reeler called *The Black Hand*. Like Riis the new medium exposed the darker side of the city, and just like the lantern slide lecturer, the filmmaker argued for the unvarnished truth of what was depicted. Already this movie asserted that it was the "true story of a recent occurrence in the Italian quarter of New York," a threatened kidnapping of an immigrant's daughter if he didn't pay a thousand dol-lars in protection money to the Black Hand. While Bertellini argues this short film contrasts an honest, law-abiding immigrant (the Italian butcher, who immediately goes to the police when the ransomers threaten his daughter) and the ferociously brutal, drunken criminal band, when the film was screened outside Italian quarters in New York, Philadelphia, or Chicago, it is likely that, in concert with newspaper and magazine treatments of supposed innate Italian violent lawlessness, these fine distinctions were lost. To be sure, the short film ends with the Mafiosi vanquished, and such theatrical elements may have appealed to urban audiences, bearing not a little resemblance to the broad melodramas presented in the immigrant theaters of Manhattan.[8]

Indeed, Bertellini may be correct that "the distinction between 'good' and 'bad' Italians was a profitable narrative compromise," in which narrative arcs depicting honest immigrants overcoming hardships and resisting the threats of criminals "pleased the self-contention of Italians and, generally, immigrant spectators." Outside the cities, however, audiences may have registered the Black Hand as just one more piece of cultural evidence that southern Europeans threatened the republic, or at least Lower Manhattan.[9]

Other early films dramatized real-life attempts to destroy the Mafia in both Italy and the United States. In 1906 the New York City Police established a special squad to deal with the supposedly growing menace of Italian criminality, and in time this unit was led by Lieutenant Joseph Petrosino. Evidently the New York Police operated under the assumption that it took an Italian to catch an Italian, and so, evidently, did early filmmakers. In January 1909 Kalem released *The Detectives of the Italian Bureau*, which was publicized in *Moving Picture World* as a thriller demonstrating that "only courageous and honest men of Italian birth" had the capacity to thwart the Black Hand.

Unfortunately Petrosino was not up to the task Kalem's publicists, and race thinking, required. While investigating transatlantic criminal ties, he was murdered in Palermo in March 1909. An outcry of anti-Italian sentiment arose in New York and elsewhere in America, but several further films parlayed the Mafia hysteria and notoriety of Petrosino's murder into box office success. Feature Photoplay released *The Adventure of Lieutenant Petrosino* in 1912, promising "blood-curdling scenes . . . showing the workings of that mysterious band of the underworld," while in 1915 Neutral Film offered *The Last of the Mafia*, which presented a fictionalized comeuppance for the murderers of the New York detective.[10]

These films all posited good Italians battling criminal Italians but also operated on the racialized assumption that only the Mediterranean mind could penetrate, and defeat, an alien criminal menace to American cities. The implication here is that there is something genetic, or at least cultural, that puts even the ethnic crime fighter on a different wavelength from "regular" Americans. Therefore early crime dramas were unlikely to instill comfort in non-Italian viewers of cinematic depictions of the foreign city. Indeed, reliance on ethnic empathy to restore law and order has rarely served to reassure viewers of fictively chaotic cities. Petrosino's ethnic abilities to catch Mafiosi are a premise that resonates with urban crime dramas of nearly a century later, in which only a savvy black police officer (of the sort invariably played by Denzel Washington) can rein in urban lawlessness and gang violence. Ethnoracial stereotyping has presented even police officers (first Italian and then African-American) as seemingly primordially in tune with the criminal mind, hardly anything but a left-handed compliment. Then, too, often there was a fine line between law officer and lawbreaker, in both silent films of immigrant exploits and African-American crime dramas ninety years later. Washington's triumphs in *Training Day, Inside Man,* and *The Siege* have hardly created a positive image for New York or Los Angeles on the contemporary big screen.[11]

Other early films avoided explicit scenes of criminality but nevertheless conveyed the message that poor southern Italian immigrants were prone to jealousy, rage, drunkenness, or mule-headed stubbornness. In films such as the 1909 feature *Little Italy* or D. W. Griffith's *The Italian Blood* two years later, the hyperemotionalism of these urban newcomers leads to tragedies and near-tragedies. While Bertellini argues that some films, especially those starring the "Italian impersonator par excellence," George Beban, were somewhat sympathetic treatments of wronged newcomers overcoming a mountain of adversity, the tenor of some of these films may be gauged by titles such as *The Wop* (1913) and the original working title of Beban's own 1915 nine-reeler, *The Italian.* This film was first produced as *The Dago.*

Although Bertellini argues that Beban presents characters' misfortunes as the result of a poverty-stricken tenement environment and nativist prejudice, the lead character nevertheless plots a vendetta against his heartless boss and comes close to killing his daughter, an echo of the numerous newspaper articles and sociological treatises that asserted an innate Italian propensity to violent knifings and crime. All the negative characteristics on display in early films could have been lifted from the pages of Lombroso or Madison Grant.[12] As in Riis's photographs and the journalistic exposés, early films served as travelogues to the problematic, foreign parts of Manhattan and other cities.

To be sure, in these films immigrant lawbreakers or violent, vengeance-minded characters, Bertellini notes, are often juxtaposed to hardworking strivers. In many of these films an Italian is trying to become (or masquerade as?) a real American, and these characters, he argues, are depicted more favorably. It's difficult, though, to see these masquerades as anything more than tentative, nor was the disguise likely to have pleased or fooled nativist Americans, who in 1921 would succeed in passing severely restrictive immigration quotas drastically curtailing the influx of southern and eastern Europeans. Northern-European-descent Americans might have reacted to the efforts by Beban's characters to Americanize similarly to Lothrop Stoddard, who dismissed anthropologist Franz Boas's attempts to disprove "racial" differences among European groups as "the desperate attempt of a Jew to pass himself off as 'white.'"[13]

It would only be in the 1940s that Italian film characters such as Nick Bianco (tellingly named), a gangster trying to go straight in *Kiss of Death*, would make tentative moves into respectable suburbs, but only incognito, and only briefly and tragically. Then, too, Bianco is solicited as a government witness by an assistant district attorney named D'Angelo. Earlier cinematic Italians had the odds—and their gene pool—working against them.[14]

Even without the titillating feature of Italians' supposedly ethnically determined lawlessness, crime on the streets of New York and Chicago remained a popular topic for early film. Indeed, directors who would later become celebrated practitioners of the gangster genre were already experimenting with crime film tropes prior to World War I. Raoul Walsh in 1915 offered *Regeneration*, a story of a New York orphan who is exploited by a drunken couple after his parents' death. In this environment, the young Owen Conway rapidly learns the Darwinian law of survival of the fittest and develops his skills at robbery and street brawling. By the time he's twenty-five Conway is leading his own New York gang. Meanwhile, a crusading district attorney consents to escort Marie, a society social worker, on a slumming tour of the ganglands of Manhattan. Marie hopes to see a real gangster, as they seem to her to be interesting specimens. In this respect *Regeneration* follows the well-trod path of magazine slumologist tours that by 1915 had been offering cultural consumers vicarious thrills on the Lower East Side for decades.[15]

When the ghetto safari gets a little too exciting—Owen is about to rob and assault the district attorney when they naively blunder into the gangsters' hideout in a skid row dance hall—Marie's pleas save the day. After she establishes a settlement house in the neighborhood, she eventually persuades Owen with appeals to his better nature, and the gangster is reformed.

While *Regeneration* offers a sentimental, perhaps even pat, ending when judged by the later demise of filmic good-bad hoods such as Tom Powers in *The Public Enemy* or Eddie Bartlett in *The Roaring Twenties*, Owen's reform was an example of middle-class reformers' belief (or hope) in the triumph of social science over the noxious urban streetscape. In this respect, Walsh was operating in the settlement house school of Progressive reform, which firmly believed that the ecology of the slums rather than genetic predisposition fitted urban residents for lives of crime or pauperism. If one could improve the environment and train city dwellers in useful trades, as the settlements attempted to do, all might not be lost. When Marie saves Owen from his upbringing, the middle-class members of the audience breathed a sigh of relief. Nevertheless, prior to this conversion experience on the road to Delancey Street, viewers had been treated to seventy-two minutes of vicarious thrills in Lower Manhattan's urban dysfunction.[16]

Some of the ancillary gang members were portrayed by slum dwellers Walsh recruited to serve as extras while he was filming *Regeneration* on the streets of New York, legitimizing the public's tendency to regard the film as an unvarnished, documentary peek into the pervasiveness of metropolitan crime. The posing techniques employed by Riis in his photographs, designed to achieve maximum squalor for his camera, evidently could be adapted to the big screen as well. To be sure, prosaic city life likely would have been of little interest to a nickelodeon audience, but the genuine New Yorkers Walsh paid to portray pickpockets, murderers, and thieves may just as likely have been milkmen, dockworkers, and factory hands.[17]

Other early ghetto films likewise offered the hope that "street arabs" could be reformed, for in the years prior to the Hays Code, it was not yet foreordained that every cinematic hoodlum had to end as a cautionary corpse. Before he enthralled audiences with his heroic Klansmen in *The Birth of a Nation*, D. W. Griffith's *The Musketeers of Pig Alley* offered one of the earliest gangster films. This 1912 film was evocative of *Maggie: A Girl of the Streets* and Crane's other lurid Bowery tales, as well as Riis's celebrated magazine piece on the conquest of the slums, "The Passing of Cat Alley." The film captures the interactions of larcenous street urchins and contending gangs in the slums. One gang leader, Snapper Kid (played by Elmer Booth), robs a struggling musician, but he turns out to be not all bad, for in a cinematic case of extraordinary coincidence, he saves the musician's fiancée from disaster when a rival crook drugs her drink. The young woman, played by silent star Lillian Gish, is later grateful for this act of ghetto chivalry and provides Snapper with an alibi when the police seek to pin a gun charge on him. As we fade to black there is hope that, with the right companions, Snapper can be weaned away from crime.[18]

Like *Regeneration*, Griffith's film contains elements of Progressive Era redemption of slum dwellers who, while virtuous at heart, have been tainted by the ecology of the inner city. When Gish's character spies the good qualities hidden behind Snapper Kid's tough-guy exterior, she—and the audience—accept him as an essentially decent person who can be cleansed of the sins the slums have imposed on him. This trope of good-bad guys would endure in the gangster film, as even such later Hollywood tough guys as those portrayed by James Cagney in *The Public Enemy* and *The Roaring Twenties* exhibit loyalty to friends and a code of honor that only metes out violence to those who deserve it. As Christopher Shannon notes, the Irish gangsters played by Cagney in these and other films, such as *Angels with Dirty Faces,* uphold a neighborhood code that prizes family, friends, and not squealing to the police. Snapper Kid paved the way for this gangster morality, even if the fine nuances of robber ethics might be viewed less sympathetically the further the viewer was from Pig Alley. The city, however, was already presented as rife with moral ambiguities; when the camera captured the streets of New York, it was not entirely clear who was a thief and who a chivalrous Musketeer.[19]

Another element that carried forth the city mystery habit of alluding to wealthy urbanites' collusion with criminality appears here, too. When the Kid begins brawling with rival hoodlums in a blind pig, he is warned the "Big Boss" will retaliate for any fighting in his bar. As in *Quaker City* and other city mysteries, secretive, wealthy big bosses stand behind the more wretchedly visible lawbreakers; into the 1950s, they continue to reap the rewards of lower-class criminality in American films.[20]

Such connections seemed only too plausible, for already in 1909 muckraking journalist George Kibbe Turner exposed Tammany Hall's close ties to the Lower East Side's pimps, thieves, and murderers. In his *McClure's Magazine* article, "Tammany's Control of New York by Professional Criminals," Turner asserted that Jewish gang leaders Monk Eastman, Kid Twist, and Silver Dollar Smith relied on the three to four thousand women of the evening engaged in "fifty cent prostitution" to provide them with the funds necessary to supply Tammany with an army of bought votes each and every election. "The government of the second largest city in the world," Turner declared, "when the system is in full working order, depends at bottom upon the will of the criminal population—principally thieves and pimps." In the 1920s, Herbert Asbury's lurid *The Gangs of New York* carried forward the story of gangster-politician connivance. Asbury detailed the murderous careers of Eastman and other Lower East Side gang leaders in the pay of Tammany, and also discussed their Italian and Irish rivals in the Five Points slum, painting a picture of ongoing municipal pestilence designed to thrill and appall respectable middle-class Americans into writing off the nation's largest city.[21]

The city continued to be portrayed as a national cesspool of municipal corruption as America began its experiment with Prohibition. Even though many urban Americans initially were unconcerned by violations of the Volstead Act, violent turf wars for control of the liquor trade provoked calls for a crackdown on the gangster menace. In cities such as Chicago, editorial writers had good reason to suspect that city politicians were aiding and abetting the bootleggers in return for cash payoffs. The roguish ward bosses so vividly celebrated by Finley Peter Dunne and later James T. Farrell seemed like no laughing matter to the city's newspaper reporters.[22]

The murder of North Side crime boss Dion O'Bannion on November 10, 1924, inaugurated a five-year-long war for control of Chicago's liquor trade, and also began a chorus of newspaper editorials demanding that official complicity with the rackets had to end. *The Tribune* editorial writer expressed indignation, but little surprise, when no one was arrested for this murder, labeling O'Bannion "almost the political essence of this city," echoing Turner's wail at New York's capture by the prostitution rackets fifteen years before. *The Tribune* suggested that the broad cabal of public-official–gangster collaboration went far beyond this one bootlegger: "He was part of the Mafia, the lawlessness, the superlaw, the Camorra, which corrupts the processes of law, defeats the ends of justice, nullifies the protection of decent men and women, . . . and gets away with it because the political system is so rotten that it but gains by such procedure and the citizenship is so apathetic that it does not know what is going on."[23]

The editorial writer evidently had read enough Jacob Riis—or had attended a screening of *The Dago* at his nickelodeon—to be convinced that even an O'Bannion had to be "part of the Mafia"; as the slain gangster was soon supplanted by Al Capone, alarmed tales of the Black Hand continued to sell papers. Indeed, *The Tribune* persistently advocated the deportation of Sicilian and Italian criminals, blaming the proliferation of gangs on a "small army" representing a "deliberate, persistent alienism." Editorial cartoons advocated more rigorous enforcement of alien deportation laws, while an elaborate street-festa funeral for mobster Angelo Genna in 1925 was denounced by *The Tribune*, which suggested a racialized chasm between American morality and Sicilian values:

The funeral of Angelo Genna provides an interesting commentary on our city. This crude yet costly glorification of a man of blood is a straight transplantation from Sicily or Sardinia, where to a simple folk the bandit leader is the prince of heroes. The American of native or northern European traditions must observe such a pageant with a new realization of the gulf which lies between his mind and moral system and those of Genna's colony.

In the decade in which Stoddard, Foerster and others warned of "The Menace of the Underman," many middle-class readers likely nodded in agreement. Whether they agreed or not, however, such newspaper accounts were quickly mirrored in gangster films. Six years later, the gaudy sendoff that "Little Caesar" cynically grants to the slain Tony Passa may have resonated in the minds of some Chicagoans as an image of Sicilian lawlessness and misplaced, foreign values.[24]

Evidence of Chicago's lawlessness continued to accrue. In 1926, when an assistant district attorney was murdered while in the company of several Irish gangsters, editorialists suggested this was evidence of official complicity in the mob's activities. And Mayor Big Bill Thompson's advocacy of a "wide-open town" with lax enforcement of Prohibition was all the evidence writers needed that City Hall was in bed with the mob. Other cities had similar powerful criminal syndicates, such as Detroit's Purple Gang, run by vicious bootlegger and extortionist Abe Bernstein, and Cleveland's Mayfield Road mob. In the east, Newark's Abner "Longy" Zwillman and Mayor Meyer Ellenstein both emerged from the same Third Ward Democratic Club, controlling the city's rackets and City Hall, respectively. Nevertheless, Chicago, "the wide-open city," served as a template for the defiantly corrupt Jazz Age, with a reputation that reached across the Atlantic. When the Weimar playwright-composer team of Bertolt Brecht and Kurt Weill required a paradigm for gangster control of a wide-open city, they looked to Chicago as a pattern for *The Rise and Fall of the City of Mahagonny*.[25]

German filmmakers also portrayed cities of their own that were teetering on the brink of dysfunction. Fritz Lang offered, in succession, a dystopian *Metropolis,* in which thinkers rule in the skies while slavelike workers toil beneath ground; a criminal mastermind named *Doctor Mabuse*, based on the popular novel series featuring an erudite lawbreaker who uses his hypnotic powers to bilk aristocratic gamblers; and in *M,* a powerful conglomerate of "honest" robbers, pickpockets, and beggars determined to apprehend a sociopathic child murderer (played by Peter Lorre) who is bringing unwanted police attention to their operations. In these films, as in Chicago, not just the lower-class thieves but the ostensibly respectable wealthy come in for condemnation for their decadent ways. Upper-class gamblers upon whom Mabuse preys, it is implied, get what they deserve, and Inspector von Wenk himself dons a myriad of disguises that make him indistinguishable (physically but also perhaps morally) from the criminals he pursues. In *M,* the municipal officials are hopelessly ineffectual in the face of murder and mayhem— either incompetent or on the payroll of the criminals, who derisively whistle "Lohmann, Lohmann," when the police inspector pays them a visit. They clearly regard Berlin's finest as only a trivial annoyance.[26]

Quick cuts between the authorities and gangsters in their simultaneous delibera-tions about the fate of the fiend suggest a moral symmetry between officials and lawbreakers, and call to mind George Grosz's scathing cartoons and paintings exposing the moral bankruptcy of the Weimar Republic. Nevertheless, the conflu-ence of underworld corruption and city authorities also evokes well-ingrained images of the American urban jungle; by the Prohibition era, American gang lore influenced nearly every depiction of the city.[27]

Likewise, the futuristic affluence/decadence/squalor mixed together in *Me-tropolis* is modeled on the Manhattan of skyscrapers and fast-paced rapid transit, with workers reduced to mere machines. Scientific time-and-motion efficiency experts championing the tenets of Frederick Taylor attempted to achieve this feat in the steel mills, textile centers, and factories of America in these very de-cades. Such managerial plans to turn workers into more efficient (that is, produc-tive and quiescent) machines were more satirically presented in Charlie Chaplin's

Modern Times, in which a worker is subjected to the rationality of the Beddows Feeding Machine ("Save time!" the recorded sales pitch tells the factory owner. "Cut down on workers' lunch break!"), loses his race against the conveyor belt speedup, and ultimately perseveres against nervous breakdown, jail, and shuttered factory gates in a city's waterfront slums. For all its satire, *Modern Times* highlights the frustration of many urban residents that machinery, not people, were already calling the shots in the American city.[28]

Indeed, throughout *Modern Times*, workers are voiceless, and it is only machinery that gets to speak. In Chaplin's classic film, we see angry pickets, strikes, and police suppression of unruly workers demanding bread and relief, as well as other individual acts of rebellion, as when the "gamin" (played by Paulette Goddard) steals bread for her starving orphan siblings. The comic revolt here is only the flip side of a more angry urban proletariat in *Metropolis*, and whether Lang's megacity is explicitly New York or a 1920s guess at the dystopian trajectory the modern city might take, it nevertheless belongs to a tradition that sees urbanism as leading to a chaotic mix of hyperaffluence and angry resentment on the part of the degraded majority in the not-too-distant future. This genre calls to mind Karel Čapek's play *R.U.R.,* in which the scientific solution to the class struggle—workers fabricated of steel who are programmed to be efficient and obedient factory hands—ends in failure when even metal workers rebel at this raw deal and go out on strike. (This play imported the Slavic word *robotník*—"worker"—into the English language, where it would be shortened to *robot* and available ever after to imaginers of a cyborg future of untrustworthy mad scientists and their progeny.) Detective Deckard of *Bladerunner*, running after the mechanized-humanized drones and sex workers of Off-World in a nightmarish Los Angeles of the near future, is perhaps the most famous hunter after rebellious technoproles.[29]

In the main, though, back in the 1920s and 1930s America's urban ills were still placed at the doorstep of the gangster and only peripherally blamed on dehumanizing industry or the class struggle. Newspaper denunciations of corruption and the rackets made good copy, and one team of Chicago reporters, Ben Hecht and Charles McArthur, would soon go on to fame on Broadway with *The Front Page*. Hecht continued to mine the material of his journalistic days covering wide-open Chicago, garnering screenwriting credits on celebrated crime dramas such as *Scarface, The Beast of the City, Crime without Passion, Angels with Dirty Faces* (although uncredited), and *Kiss of Death*.[30]

Even before the sound era, though, almost simultaneously with newspaper exposés of gang rule in Chicago, several movies purported to reveal the true story of the criminal rot eating away at America's cities. Émigré director Joseph Sternberg presented *Underworld* in 1927, in which the blustering gang boss Bull Weed lords it over his city. Like Genna, O'Bannion, and Capone in the real Chicago, Weed (portrayed by George Bancroft) for a time wins the allegiance of his admiring neighbors through his flashy generosity. "Nobody helps me, I help them!" is Bull Weed's motto, and when he rehabilitates a down-and-out lawyer who has descended into skid row alcoholism after becoming crooked, he exemplifies the second half of his motto. Bull rechristens the disgraced lawyer Rolls Royce and takes him into the gang. Rolls Royce, played by Clive Brook, is only the first of film's lawyers to present a respectable, legal front for gangland rackets, with lawyer Frazier (played by Humphrey Bogart) in *Angels with Dirty Faces* and Lloyd Hart (played by Jeffrey Lynn) in *The Roaring Twenties* coming in the following decade.[31]

Underworld also introduced another staple of later gang films, the tough, beautiful gun moll who aids and abets (or at least profits from) the gang leader's crimes. In Von Sternberg's film the character of Feathers is played by Evelyn Brent, who had already honed the role of a shady urban lady in other crime sagas such as *Silk Stocking Sal* (1924) and *Three Wise Crooks* (1925). Streetwise movie flappers and jazz babies updated the part of the Bowery B'hoy's partner, Lize.[32]

While not as graphically violent as other films that would soon follow, *Underworld* nevertheless offers some vignettes of urban mayhem that were taken from the real city turf wars then taking place. When Weed rubs out his rival he sends elaborate floral arrangements of the sort that accompanied Genna on his way to a Chicago cemetery. And when Weed's protégé begins to grow into his underworld role as "Rolls Royce," he and Feathers are both tempted to betray their boss to the law or to a rival gang, as frequently occurred in the Machiavellian world of Prohibition era Chicago.[33]

The chemistry between sultry Evelyn Brent and tough-guy George Bancroft was reprised in Von Sternberg's 1928 film, *The Dragnet*, which similarly presented an amoral city of hoods and molls. The short stories of Damon Runyon humorously presented an immoral Times Square underworld of conmen and gangsters with colorful nicknames like "Nicely Nicely" Johnson and "Sky" Masterson (although the short stories also depict a world more violent than that seen in the later Broadway musical, *Guys and Dolls*). *The Dragnet* is indicative of this tendency to embellish the underworld's flashier aspects as well, featuring characters such as "Two-Gun" Nolan (Bancroft), "The Magpie" (Brent), "Dapper Dan" Trent (William Powell), "Sniper" Dawson, and "Shakespeare." In the movies and short stories of the Jazz Age, every city dweller has an angle, and a colorful alias to go along with it.[34]

Of course, real-life criminals in Chicago and New York were identified by aliases such as "Greasy Thumb" Guzik, Arnold "The Brain" Rothstein, Samuel "Nails" Morton, and Otto "Abbadabba" Berman, so Runyon and screenwriters could plead that their creations merely took their cue from real life in this regard, too.[35]

The year following *Underworld* Von Sternberg also directed *The Docks of New York*, again with the winning combination of Brent and Bancroft. While not explicitly a gangster drama, with its tale of a destitute woman rescued from a suicide attempt by a maritime worker, who then "marries" the prostitute, it was hardly a picture postcard designed to present New York in a flattering, morally sanctioned light. As in the city mysteries of Foster, Lippard, Campbell, and their imitators, here the boundaries between virtuous womanhood and white slavery are porous indeed.[36]

In *The Docks of New York*, Betty Compson gave her prostitute a tender side, which enabled the pre–Hays Code audience to empathize with this fallen woman. Still, the scenes in the raucous harbor-front tavern in which she and her rescuer (played by Bancroft) are "married" are evocative of the illicit black and tans Riis and other reformers condemned three decades before. The film also likely reinforced George Kibbe Turner's alarmist condemnation of New York as politically controlled by a secretive international gang of pimps and white slavers. Since Turner asserted that dance halls and taverns were where prostitutes were recruited, *The Docks of New York*'s lower-class bar is as full of menace as it is of matrimonial joy. New York might be fun to view at a distance, but many viewers of this film were perhaps grateful that they could gape at a down-and-out waterfront dive voyeuristically, and not risk getting rolled for their troubles.[37]

The year 1928 saw two more gangster classics add to the visual iconography of a city of unrelenting mean streets, introducing tropes to which Cagney, Bogart, Muni, and Robinson would give convincing voice only a few years later. Raoul Walsh directed *Me, Gangster*, which again served as an early experimental laboratory for some of the gangster tropes he would use in later films. At a time when real-life politicos such as Chicago's Big Bill Thompson and New York's Jimmy Walker were taking municipal corruption to new heights, *Me, Gangster*, told a tale of the temptations of the crooked ward boss that no doubt resonated with moviegoers.[38]

A dock worker struggling to get by decides that maybe crime pays after all when he sees his neighborhood's corrupt political boss, Bill Kane, getting ahead. The worker (played by Anders Randolf) agrees to serve as a ward heeler for the Kane machine, and finally has money to spare. His impressionable son, Jimmy, concludes that his father is correct in abandoning the honest, sucker's route, and turns crooked, too. When Jimmy robs a factory payroll, however, he is caught and sent to jail. The prison sequences were perhaps stored in Walsh's memory bank, for some prefigure the big-house scenes in his more well-known *White Heat*. With its mix of crime, political corruption, and prison sequences, *Me, Gangster*, has a semidocumentary look, bringing a "ripped from the headlines" breathlessness to its task of exposing urban iniquities, a tactic that would be frequently employed in gangster films for the next two decades. Then, too, in linking the amoral grafting of the city ward bosses to a street criminal's demise, the film takes tentative steps to suggest that the larger sociology of the city, with its failed institutions, bears responsibility for individuals' turn to robbery and other violent acts. This theme would also be more fully developed in later films such as *The Public Enemy* and *Angels with Dirty Faces*.[39]

Another cinematic gang story even more closely tied to journalistic accounts of freewheeling, blood-soaked cities was *The Racket*, which in 1928 was nominated for best picture in the new Oscars. A timelier film couldn't have been imagined, for this exposé of the Chicago gangster world followed close on the heels of the celebrated murder of a prosecutor in the Windy City, and two years into Big Bill Thompson's second stint as mayor, middle-class reformers were loudly asserting that City Hall gave bootleggers and racketeers all the cover they needed to conduct business as usual.[40]

The Racket tells the story of an honest Chicago police captain who hasn't learned that when it comes to the syndicate, his superiors (both on and off the force) prefer that crime fighting be perfunctory. Captain McQuigg so exasperates bootlegging king Nick Scarsi that the boss orders a hit man to take the captain out. The gunman deliberately misses, but the head of the bootleggers himself warns McQuigg that he'll be after him to finish the job himself. In an echo of *The Tribune* and other Chicago newspapers' complaints, McQuigg is repeatedly frustrated in his efforts to defeat Scarsi. Time after time, with one telephone call Scarsi's lawyer clears everything with "the Old Man," and wins the immediate release of his client. Here is established the motion picture trope of gangsters reaching higher up the urban food chain to be rescued by mysterious and unstoppable patrons. Wealthy, well-connected men, powerful and outwardly respectable, are portrayed as the real protectors of and powers behind organized crime. Whether Little Caesar likes it, he is ultimately answerable to "the Big Boy," who "Little Arnie" Lorch assures him "can fix anything—that's why he's the Big Boy!" while in *Bullets or Ballots* Bugs Fenner and Al Kruger obey the whims of a clique of tuxedoed, Ivy League bankers who remain out of the limelight, but nevertheless imperiously lay down their decrees with one phone call.[41]

As we've seen, this belief that a well-off cabal preyed on honest urbanites dates back to the 1840s, at least, but here, too, one wonders if these scenes reflect some disbelief in the ability of lower-class Italian, Jewish, and even Irish criminals to run the seemingly monolithic rackets that controlled New York and Chicago. Surely an Anglo-Saxon brain had to sit behind these operations.

Of course, the real "brain" of New York's bootlegging, gambling, and protections racket was Arnold Rothstein, model for F. Scott Fitzgerald's Meyer Wolfsheim in *The Great Gatsby*, and the man who indeed had played a large role in fixing the 1919 World Series and much else until his violent death in 1928. Rothstein was the son of middle-class Uptown Jews, well spoken and a shunner of the limelight who in no way fit the uncouth depiction of Wolfsheim that Fitzgerald imagines (no human molars for cufflinks, to say the least) or the crudities of cinematic gangsters such as *Little Caesar*'s "Little Arnie" Lorch. These fictional Jewish kingpins owed not a little of their mangled English and amiable sociopathy to the anti-immigrant sentiment prevailing among native-born Americans of Fitzgerald's set in the 1920s and 1930s.[42]

Rothstein's connections to Tammany Hall were firm, though, and these links were continued by his successors, such as Meyer Lansky, Lucky Luciano, and Frank Costello well into the 1940s, giving at least some credence to the cinema's well-attached gangster who could squash an indictment by calling the right penthouse.[43]

In the coming decade, filmdom's honest DA's and policemen repeatedly contended with similar frustrations, watching politically well-connected racketeers evade justice. This scenario played out in *Bullets or Ballots*, *Racket Busters*, *The Roaring Twenties,* and even 1947's *Kiss of Death*. In an era of frequent investigation of officials in the administrations of New York Mayors Jimmy Walker and William O'Dwyer, Newark's Meyer Ellenstein, and Chicago's Thompson for suspected ties to organized crime, popular culture offered a mirror world in which both the well-heeled high and the violent low were busy fleecing the honest workers of middle America.[44]

In *The Racket*, the crime boss Scarsi played to the broadly aired nativist sentiment that southern Italians, with their lawbreaking genes or immoral culture, were driving a stake into law-abiding America. It is perhaps no coincidence Scarsi's name calls to mind the nickname of Chicago's most prominent Italian bootlegger, Al Capone; in any case, *The Racket* debuted only months before the Valentine's Day Massacre solidified Chicago in the public's imagination as the most crime-ridden city in America, courtesy of "Scarface's" machine gunners.

While Michael Corleone had to convince his brother that a corrupt police captain could indeed be targeted by New York's fictional crime family, Scarsi has no such qualms, for he operates in a city that has already seen gangsters kill several reformers and authorities who got in their way. Hoping that a change of administrations at city hall might bring honest governance and an end to mobster influence, however, required extraordinary faith in the system, and Thompson's successor, Anton Cermak, was also suspected of walking perilously close to the edge of the moral abyss. In 1931, a crime reporter, Jake Lingle, was assassinated by mobsters, but the brazenness of Chicago's real mobsters may have gone even further. In February 1933, Cermak was killed by Giuseppe Zangara while riding in Miami with president-elect Franklin D. Roosevelt. While most contemporary commentators assumed Cermak had been hit by a bullet meant for Roosevelt, some evidence has recently come to light Zangara may have been acting on behalf of Frank Nitti, Al Capone's successor, since this gang felt that Cermak (who before becoming mayor had somehow amassed a $2-million fortune as the $10,000-a-year president of the county board) was favoring the Moran gang and was not sufficiently cooperative with their enterprises. The real-life city gave popular culture plenty of lively material with which to work. In Chicago one didn't need to go to the movies to find gangsters targeting uncooperative police captains, and maybe higher officials, for elimination.[45]

After yet another unsuccessful attempt to put Scarsi permanently behind bars, McQuigg the honest Irish cop questions whether the law can ever disarm the mob. As if to answer his question, Scarsi celebrates the murder of a rival bootlegger by calling in his political chits and having McQuigg transferred to the boondocks, where the captain ineffectually tries to rally a few crusading reporters in his futile war on the mob. Director Lewis Milestone twins gangland violence with cynical political corruption, conveying the message of the enormity of the rot facing Jazz Age cities.

Politically powerful protectors of criminals, though, have continued to punish naive, or determined, police officers into our own era. When *The Wire*'s Lieutenant Daniels persists in trying to charge a mighty senator's aide with drug running in the West Baltimore projects, the thoroughly dirty Senator Clay Davis howls, "I'm gonna have him walking a beat so far out there that he'll see the Philadelphia cops walking towards him!" In the late 1920s it was Italian bootleggers who terrorized Chicagoans with their bloody turf wars, alien cultures of pathology, and kickbacks to crooked politicos. By the twenty-first century the backroom wheelers and dealers and the gang members they shield are invariably African-American, but they walk in Scarsi's and his ward boss's shoes.[46]

Only a coincidence begins unraveling Scarsi's hold on the city. His kid brother and a flapper (played by Helen Hayes) accidentally run over a pedestrian in McQuigg's new precinct, and when The Organization's lawyer tries to kill the scandal before an important upcoming election, the captain takes the battle to the public via the crusading press. McQuigg suggests it is up to honest citizens to stand up to the corruptors at the ballot box and on the streets, for passivity has handed city hall over to the gangsters.[47]

With the advent of sound pictures, the crusade continued, with characters lecturing the audience it was up to them to take back control of a country in peril. In at least one case, however, *The Public Enemy*, this strident call was combined with an earlier tradition, the Progressive Era reformers' repeated advocacy of ecological reform as the cure to criminality and deviancy. Improve the slums and the slum dweller would follow, the more optimistic middle-class professionals believed; the gangster menace might be averted if a scrub brush of reform were applied to the alleys of Bridgeport, Back of the Yards, and the like.[48]

The producers of *The Public Enemy* added several title cards to their finished film to give the picture the veneer of a call to arms, one that other films would take up, too, either out of a conscientious civic duty or as a way to avoid charges that their films were graphically exploiting the violent deeds of real criminals with little concern as to whether such messages would corrupt impressionable youthful viewers.

It was up to the better element of the public, even in the movie theater, to do something about this real-life menace, which, it was argued, was only thinly veiled behind the stories of Tom Powers, Rico Bandello, and Tony Camonte. If the viewer left only entertained, not aroused to action, the producers asserted, their mission would have failed. The introduction to *The Public Enemy* and *Little Caesar* said these films "had a great affect on public opinion. They brought home violently the evils associated with Prohibition and suggested the necessity of a nationwide house cleaning. Tom Powers . . . and Rico . . . are not two men, nor are they merely characters—they are a problem that sooner or later, we, the public, must solve."

If this message didn't convince the viewer that *The Public Enemy* was out to condemn, not celebrate, the life of crime, a second title card opened the film. "It is the ambition of the authors of *The Public Enemy* to honestly depict an environment that exists today in a certain stratum of American life, rather than glorify the hoodlum or the criminal. While the story of *The Public Enemy* is essentially a true story, all names and characters appearing herein are purely fictional."[49]

These title cards were maybe only boilerplate, but in the overheated atmosphere of the times Hollywood needed to reassure censors such as the Reverend William

Short and his Motion Picture Research Council that gangster films were not
hell-bent on corrupting the youth of America. Cautionary title cards and other
devices were an inoculation against moralist outcries already building against the
gangster genre, and an effective way of evading charges these films would lead to
copycat crimes and corrupt America's impressionable youth. John Springhall has
demonstrated that pressure had been building on Hollywood directors throughout
the 1920s and early 1930s to tone down the violence of gangster films, which, it
was asserted by many alarmed reformers, was glorifying crime and spurring a rise
in juvenile delinquency. A series of gangster films featuring Lon Chaney and
directed by Tod Browning (perhaps most famous as the director of *Dracula*) and
Von Sternberg's crime pictures came in for particular condemnation, so that by
1930 a formal Motion Picture Production Code was written for the industry's self-
regulating agency, the Motion Pictures Producers and Distributors of America.
This office, under the leadership of former U.S. Postmaster General Will Hays,
formally adopted the so-called Hays Production Code in 1934, but already by the
time *The Public Enemy* and *Little Caesar* debuted filmmakers had been warned:
Crime could not be made to appear too attractive, nor could the wrongdoer triumph
in the end. Criminal acts "were never to be presented in such a way as to throw
sympathy with the crime as against law and justice or to inspire others with a desire
for imitation."[50]

Popular culture has often been regarded as immoral, and the gangster movie was
one link on this chain of supposed seduction reaching back to the city mysteries,
music halls, and nickelodeons and extending ahead to MP3s full of hip-hop and rap.
For all the cautionary words and plot devices that made it clear that Tom Powers
would end up a trussed-up bloody corpse, delivered teetering onto his mother's
living room doorstep, it was perhaps still easy to cheer, if not exactly emulate, the
hypercharismatic James Cagney. The gangster proved just too attractive, and
therefore, to many, a threat.

Consequently in the early to mid-1930s a cascade of newspaper editorials
warned of the role crime films played in exaggerating juvenile delinquency. The
Newark Ledger, for example, claimed that cinematic gangsters were "poisoning
the minds of the youth of this country," conveniently avoiding the paper's own
reputation for being notoriously uninquisitive about the shenanigans of the city's
wrongdoers in and out of office, a situation of uninvestigative reporting that would
endure for decades.[51] It was far easier to pick on popular culture than to clean up
the real city, and in 1934 an alarmist book, *Our Movie Made Children* by Henry
James Forman, leaped from the cautionary, reasoned social science of Ohio State
University educators to an alarmist exposé of the ruinous effects gangster films
were having on young Americans. Juveniles' reports that they "identified" with film
gangsters were taken at face value, and Forman concluded that such dark portraits
of the city were corrupting the country. The image violence-plagued cities had
in the films of the Great Depression was not always flattering, or viewed with
complacency by self-appointed moral watchdogs.[52]

Even though there was much to condemn in Tom Powers, *The Public Enemy* presents the gangster as a product of his sociological context. From the opening street montage, it is strongly suggested the public enemy is not necessarily born bad but is made that way, shaped to some extent by the dangerous and morally ambiguous environment in which he grows up. A title card situates the viewer in "1909," where we see a bustling slum scene in Chicago's Back of the Yards neighborhood. For the moment, the movies' attention was still riveted on Chicago, not New York, with the talkies' first three notorious gangsters ruthlessly ruling there in Al Capone's stead (desperately trying to clean up his city's tarnished reputation, Mayor Cermak furiously threatened to ban all crime films from exhibition in his city unless Hollywood stopped picking on Chicago!).[53]

In this ramshackle neighborhood of stockyards, poor shanties, and factories, there seem to be two or three saloons on every corner, and even the men coming home from the dirty factories carry pails of beer. Another man "rushes the growler" with several beer cans suspended on a long pole; all the slum's residents ignore a Salvation Army band that parades past the crowded saloons. Later, at a wake for a neighborhood boy, policemen, priests, and funeral directors all generously help themselves to huge mugs of beer, all the while sanctimoniously declaring, "Larry got what he asked for! I warned him!" before the beer-swilling priest flatly declares, "He was a no-good boy!" These Chicago characters may be oblivious of the saloon menace and the tragedies reformers were certain it all too often caused, but many of the viewers of the film no doubt drew the proper, middle-class reformer's message on the dangers the city posed.

For their part, young Tom Powers and his pal, Matt Doyle, are already stealing swigs from the pails of beer they are carrying home outside a saloon's "family entrance," and shoplifting from a downtown department store, probably out of sheer boredom and a desire for some thrills their squalid neighborhood can't provide. Cagney's later film *Angels with Dirty Faces* reprises this suggestion that slum children often begin lives of crime out of frustration with the limited opportunities available in their tenement districts. Rocky Sullivan and his pal, Jerry, head to the freight yards to break into boxcars simply because they are bored with hanging out on the tenement fire escape overlooking their bleak corner of the city. Geography locked many movie hoodlums into their crooked paths.[54]

Still, Chicago's mean streets don't foredoom its children to lives of crime, and *The Public Enemy* is more nuanced than the earlier magazine slum safaris. Here the slum can produce prosaically hardworking characters like Tom's brother, Mike ("He's working on the ding-ding in the daytime" and "goes to school at night," Tom sneers about his trolley-conductor brother), but its many temptations are the unindicted conspirators that make the gangster. Matt's sister already predicts that Tom will wind up in jail, because "everybody who belongs there ain't there. And that's where you'll be someday, Tom Powers." When Tom's policeman father hears him boasting that "if I do go it won't be for swiping pigeons," he takes him into the house for a beating with the strap, a scene we are to understand has already occurred often enough. Tom is defiant, asking his father if he should take the beating with his pants on or off, but the suggestion has already been planted in the viewer's mind that Back of the Yards is at least partly responsible for Tom's later life of crime.

It is one of the other menaces of the slum that steers Tom and Matt into lives of crime. Progressive reformers frequently warned city dwellers of the evil of the pool hall, and as in *Angels with Dirty Faces,* slum kids are tempted to advance from petty larceny into more serious crime by hanging out in the seedy dives of their neighborhoods. The criminal Putty Nose, who fences stolen watches for the boys at the Red Oaks Club, puts Tom and Matt up to robbing a fur warehouse. "Ya gotta grow up sometime," he tells the boys, before giving them guns as a "Christmas present from Santa Claus. With best wishes for a prosperous New Year."[55]

While there is nothing inevitable about Tom and Matt's descent into crime, and a twenty-first-century viewer might regard the Red Oaks Club as innocent enough, the visual iconography of the reformist press had already coded the pool hall, saloon, and other ghetto menaces as the incubators of worse crimes to come, and viewers who had been served such warnings by Progressives for decades likely read these scenes as such. Journalist George Kibbe Turner sounded the alarm at the dancing-academy menace, warning respectable Americans that immigrant-filled dance halls were really only fronts where pimps lured unsuspecting young women into the white slave trade. Turner asserted that, in New York, Jews were the vast majority of both the procurers and the prostitutes, and that this disease of pestilential Manhattan was infecting the rest of the nation. "About one half of all the women now in the business throughout the United States started their career . . . in New York," Turner asserts. While offering no evidence for this alarm, he claimed a pimp-political stranglehold on Newark, Philadelphia, and Chicago was ultimately controlled by itinerant procurers swarming out of Manhattan. Turner found many willing believers in healthful small-town America, as he cataloged the number of smaller cities and towns to which Jewish prostitutes had spread, raising another cry against Sodom on the Hudson.

This alarmist screed and others like it caused many nativists to suspect that immigrants at play in pool halls or dancing academies were after more than just a brief respite from miserable lives in the sweatshops. In the first decades of the twentieth century, sin was suspected to lurk everywhere in the immigrant city, and it is ironic to view *Hester Street*, a nostalgic 1975 movie of the supposedly more innocent Jewish Lower East Side that is based on Abraham Cahan's short stories—but is largely set in a dancing academy! Native Americans would not have viewed the film's characters as "regular Yankees," but as suspected white slavers.[56]

In *The Public Enemy*, it turns out that the pool hall is a front for petty thieves, and in this the movie continues earlier reformers' well-established tradition of viewing ethnic urbanites' recreation venues with suspicion. Settlement houses such as Jane Addams's Hull House offered night schools, recreation centers, and other healthy alternatives to pool halls, dancing academies, and other such supposedly immoral urban haunts, and in *The Public Enemy*, we hear that Tom's somber brother, Mike, is attending one such night school and is likely bypassing the seedy Red Oaks for just such a settlement. Although Tom can only see the world as full of conmen and angles—he dismisses his brother as a "sucker," who by going to school is only "learning how to be poor," and is sure Mike "got fired for snatching too many nickels" when he sees him walking on the street in the middle of the day—Mike points to some of the other choices working-class urbanites made. As in the Italian one-reelers, a virtuous ghetto type is contrasted with his brother in order to signal that at least some hope of betterment resided in the American city.[57]

After the botched warehouse robbery, Tom and Matt are abandoned by the shady fence Putty Nose, but instead of going straight, they merely find a more reliable patron in lawbreaking, until they wear fancy suits, drive huge limousines, and are addressed as "Mr. Powers" and "Mr. Doyle" when they visit their elite nightclub. Throughout their meteoric rise, however, Tom remains almost gleefully dedicated to the violent aspects of his enforcement of Paddy Ryan's bootlegging routes, and as in other films of the era, the fun and hedonism of Jazz Age night life are inextricably tied to crime. Those jazz bands at night clubs, whether belonging to Sam Vettori and Little Arnie Lorch, Panama Smith, or Tom Powers and Matt Doyle, are supplied and ultimately controlled by gangsters. Pleasure, sin, and lawbreaking are tightly intertwined in the cinematic city, just as the real Stork Club was where Walter Winchell often rubbed shoulders with George Gershwin and Frank Costello, all on the same night. In the Jazz Age, real-world, high-toned nightclubs such as the El Fay (which featured wisecracking Texas Guinan, the model for *The Roaring Twenties*' Panama Smith), Harlem's Cotton Club, or Dutch Schultz's Embassy Club were mob-controlled. This tradition continued when "Bugsy" Siegel, Cleveland's Moe Dalitz, and other hoods discovered a sleepy desert way station named Las Vegas. Part of the pleasure of the city, both onscreen and in real time, was its illicit nature and knowing one might be consorting, even vicariously, with the "big boys" of the mob.[58]

While Tom and Matt do "find out Paddy Ryan's your friend" in the course of their criminal careers, it's hard to read their neighborhood loyalties as entirely positive. Christopher Shannon has argued that Paddy Ryan's assertion that "nobody can do much of anything without somebody else. . . . You've gotta have friends" is evidence that Irish mob figures in the movies expressed a communal morality of loyalty to one's neighborhood and family, an ethos of solidarity that resonated with moviegoers traumatized by the effects of the Great Depression and the atomizing effects of mass culture and consumer society itself. While Tom Powers expresses greater loyalty to his patron, Paddy Ryan, and his friend, Matt Doyle, than the Italian gangster Rico in *Little Caesar*, we might do well to remember the kind of condemnation that clannish hoodlums with their own codes of honor superseding federal laws came in for in the 1920s and early 1930s. Even those who by 1931 felt Prohibition was a failed, rather than noble, experiment wasted little sympathy on Dion O'Bannion, Vincent "Mad Dog" Coll, and other Hibernian gangsters. In the era in which *The Public Enemy* debuted, local neighborhoods with their own particular codes of silence and supralegal allegiances were more often regarded as amoral than moral.

Even within the context of the film itself, friends cannot shield Tom and Matt from the violent ends that punctuated many bootleggers' turf wars. The film is saturated with violence, even if the Production Code and technological limitations of early 1930s film dictated the blood be more discreetly doled out than would be the case sixty years later. When Tom and Matt catch up with Putty Nose many years after he betrayed them, Tom makes good on his earlier vow to "give it to [him] right in the head the first time I see him!" Tom tells Putty Nose, "You taught us how to cheat, steal and kill," and while it's hard to believe either Matt or Tom would have been content with a job "on the level" driving a trolley car like Mike, the indictment of bad neighborhood influences in leading them into a life of crime is clear. Putty Nose must die perhaps not only for abandoning them in the warehouse heist, but for introducing them to crime in the first place. His murder is quite graphic—as he plays his slightly bawdy song at the piano for his "pals," Tom shoots him, and the horrible clash as he falls on the keys, together with Matt's grimace as he (and not the audience) sees the murder, tells us everything we need to know. Without spelling it out, director William A. Wellman's quick cutting between the piano and Tom's and Matt's reactions conveys that this hood's death is quite grisly.

Likewise, "Nails" Nathan, the "rather remarkable man from the West Side," is quite gleeful in spelling out to his respectable and squeamish bootlegging partner that he "has got some pretty handy boys with their gloves all oiled" as well as Tom and Matt, "the trouble squad," to convince saloonkeepers to take their beer and their beer only. This character was modeled on the real-life Jewish Chicago gangster Samuel "Nails" Morton, whose demise did indeed come about, as in the film, through a horse-riding accident, even though in actuality, no one put a contract out on his horse. Before that, though, his violent intimidation of saloonkeepers and rival bootleggers was amply covered in the Chicago press,[59] and the film's exploding bars and gun battles likely seemed almost documentary in light of the gang wars that were ongoing in the year of this film's release. When Nails complains that a "Pete over on Kedzie Avenue" has stiffed him for some beer, he orders Tom to bring him "cash or his heart," and Tom laughingly promises, "I'll bring them both!"

Nails also uses connections to both aristocratic businessmen and his political clients (these latter are unseen but alluded to as very much missed by Paddy Ryan after his death, when political protection disappears). Tom, too, tells his mother he has a job in politics, but his brother, Mike, is disgusted with this lie and overturns the beer keg Tom has supplied for his homecoming party. "You murderers! There's not only beer in that keg, there's beer and blood! Blood of men!" he cries as he throws the keg off the kitchen table. Tom points out, however, that few in his city neighborhood, not even his straight-arrow brother, are all that different from his crew. "Your hands ain't so clean!" he tells his brother. "You killed and liked it! You didn't get them medals by holding hands with the Germans!" In *The Roaring Twenties*, too, government-sanctioned killers Eddie Bartlett and George Hally (played by Cagney and Humphrey Bogart, respectively) return from the trenches of the Great War to resume violent careers—this time as bootlegging gangsters in New York.[60]

This moral ambiguity is expressed, too, in the case of Lehman, a dandified brewery owner with a derby, walking stick, and vaguely English accent, who asserts "that my desire is merely to furnish a better grade of beer than the working man can now obtain." Lehman is shocked, *shocked,* to find Nails using violence to line up his customers. Nails cuts him off: "If you're in it, you're in it for the coin the same as the rest of us."

Once again, the high and the low are uneasily allied in a conspiracy against the respectable middle, but at least here the gangsters know all assertions of respectability are merely so much "north wind blow." At a time when certain bootleggers entered Murder Inc., while another from Newark who moved to Canada gained a knighthood, the genteel figure insisting that "my name is not to appear" may have seemed only too real. In the Jazz Age city, the only difference between a gangster and an entrepreneur is the size of his bank book or his degree of delusion.[61]

The most brutal feature of *The Public Enemy* is Tom's grisly end, and even allowing for the greater restraint 1930s filmmakers showed, this ending rivals anything Scorsese or Tarantino later brought to the screen. After Schemer Burns ambushes Matt Doyle in a hail of machine gun bullets, Tom robs a pawnshop of an arsenal of guns to go and kill Burns. Arriving at Burns's headquarters in a torrential rainstorm, Tom is instead ambushed. As he collapses into the gutter, coughing up blood, Tom futilely throws his gun through Burns's window, sputtering, "I ain't so tough."

We next see an invalid Tom all bandaged up, immobile in a hospital bed. "You're coming home, ain't you, Tommy, to stay?" his mother asks, and when he nods, she is elated to have "both my boys back! All of us together again!" But Paddy Ryan secretly informs Mike that Burns has "kidnapped him [Tom] from the hospital this afternoon. . . . First they give it to him in the back, then they take him when he's helpless." Paddy vows, "I'll bring Tom back if it's the last thing I do."

Of course, Tom's homecoming is not what his mother expects. As she prepares his bedroom upstairs, Mike answers the knock on the door, only to have his brother's mummy-wrapped corpse totter and fall onto the family's living room floor. As we see Tommy's mother continue her happy preparations, Mike slowly walks away from the bandaged dead body of his brother; the Victrola record ends, and all that remains is for Mike to break the news to their mother in that eternal moment just after this end. No more violent filmic image comes readily to mind of the homicidal lengths city criminals go to when eliminating their rivals.[62]

In the same year of 1931, Mervyn LeRoy directed Edward G. Robinson as the ruthless Rico Bandello, *Little Caesar*. Rico and his partner, Joe Massara, begin as provincial gas-station robbers, but from the start they are both enamored of the "big city" back East, where their particular ambitions can be realized. Rico reads in the newspaper about a banquet the "underworld" has thrown for its leader, Diamond Pete Montana, and his envy is palpable. "Diamond Pete Montana. He don't have to waste his time on cheap gas stations. He's somebody. He's in the big town doing big things in a big way. Yeah, and look at us. Just a couple of nobodies. Nothing." Joe feeds his partner's dreams of glory, asking, "Is that what you want, Rico? A party like that for you? 'Caesar Enrico Bandello. Honored by his friends.'"

Following Rico's meteoric rise in the rackets, his cronies do throw him a gala, which is also elaborately covered by the press. No amount of opulent window dressing can conceal the gangsters' boorishness, and the dinner degenerates into a lower-class food fight. Italian gangsters, like many other urban ethnics, are boorish interlopers at the American banquet, no matter how many fancy tuxedos they buy. More humorously, all of the Marx Brothers' pretensions are quickly unmasked, as when Chico arrives at another elegant banquet in *The Cocoanuts*. He is introduced as "Count," but Groucho puts him in his place by heckling, "Hey, Count, take out the trash!" For his part, Chico in *Animal Crackers* exposes an aristocratic pretender to respectability at a high-class party as "Abie the fish peddler! Abie the fish-man!" The telltale birthmark of boorish ethnicity is exposed under Roscoe W. Chandler's tuxedo shirt, proving he's merely Abie Kabibl (the main character in a popular comic strip of pretentious all-rightniks), another gate-crasher like Ravelli and Rico Bandello. The Italians and Jews in early sound films could still not fit in, for no matter what they appeared, at bottom they were ragmen or racketeers.[63]

Rico's gate-crashing entails more sinister implications than Chico and Harpo's boorishness, but even in *Little Caesar* other characters strive to escape the restraints of place or ethnicity. Joe Massara also dreams of making it big in the city. Joe dreamily gushes, "Yeah, there's money in the big town, all right. And the women! Good times, something doing all the time. Exciting things, you know. Gee, the clothes I could wear." Rico dismisses Joe's dreams of returning to a life of dancing, asserting, "I don't want no dancing! I'm figuring on making other people dance! . . . Have your own way or nothing! Be somebody!" The rest of *Little Caesar* is set in Chicago, the "big town" back "East" "where things break big!" For both Rico and Joe the city has almost mythical connotations of sin, hedonism, and opportunity in the film. The metropolis represents the conflation of glamour and crime, violence and amusement. Joe Massara has one tap shoe in each world, just as entertainment and crime syndicates overlapped in the persons of George Raft, Ben "Bugsy" Siegel, and many other Jazz Age figures.

Joe Massara takes a dancing job at an elite nightclub, the Bronze Peacock, but this high-class venue is really only a front for the mob. When the straightlaced Crime Commissioner McClure later finds out the club is really owned by "the man they call Little Arnie," he sputters, "I didn't understand that a man of this type was connected with this place" as he and his blue bloods rapidly leave. To paraphrase "Nails" Nathan, if McClure didn't know of the club's unsavory connections, then he was the only one in Chicago. While New York's Special Prosecutor Thomas E. Dewey would later personify the role of the straight-arrow, good-government crusader against the mob, such moral rectitude and blindness to the interconnection of entertainment and crime in Cermak's Chicago or Jimmy Walker's New York was dubious at best. We have to wonder if the respectable Mr. McClure was also surprised to find alcohol in the "lemonade" served at this opulent nightclub. McClure could have walked into any one of a hundred nightclubs and found well-connected but shady owners paying protection to their superiors in the machine.[64]

Rico takes another path to the top, offering his services to Sam Vettori, a cigar-chewing mob boss who holds court at his own front. The other members of Vettori's gang are rapidly introduced, and they are a rogues' gallery of swarthy, cunning, and violent Italian stereotypes. With the real-life model of Al Capone fresh in the public's mind, it is the Italian menace this movie is warning us about, although "Little Arnie" Lorch likely called to mind in 1931's audience *shtarkers* such as Arnold "The Brain" Rothstein, who had only been murdered three years before. In any case, all of Vettori and Lorch's hangers-on have thick eastern and southern European accents to accompany their violent streaks and glowering stares.

And yet, as in so many nineteenth-century city mystery novels, as well as later gangster films and even HBO's *The Wire*, criminal enterprises that at first seem the domain of wild street thugs are orchestrated from the penthouse. While Rico thinks that Diamond Pete Montana runs the rackets, it turns out that behind him and Arnie Lorch sits a larger, more powerful crime lord—one who can "pass" as white, or may not even be Italian: "the Big Boy." When Montana warns his mob that "the Big Boy" wants them to lie low because "McClure, what's head of the new crime commission," is turning up the heat, Little Arnie isn't worried. "I never seen nobody the Big Boy couldn't get to. That's why he's the Big Boy! This boy McClure will be pie for him—he'll twist him around his little finger!"[65]

When Rico eventually gets to meet the Big Boy, at his extravagant Lakeshore Drive mansion, complete with a butler, Louis XV desk, and portrait of a king that cost him $15,000, this power behind the mob appears to be a born and bred aristocratic type, suggesting that Italian and Jewish underworld leaders were pawns under the control of bigger, "respectable" gangsters. The Big Boy has earlier admitted to Arnie Lorch that he pays protection to powerful politicians to shield the gangsters from prosecution, but when Rico dons a tuxedo in preparation for his first meeting with the Big Boy, an admiring Otero says, "You're getting up in the world, Rico! Y'know, there ain't none of us ever invited to eat up at the Big Boy's dump! And nobody ever crashed the gate except Pete Montana. See what I mean? Now you don't want the Big Boy to think you ain't got no class."

The violence of Rico and his henchmen is useful to the Big Boy, just as Kruger serves a coterie of scheming bankers in *Bullets or Ballots*. But the Italian and Jewish underworld leaders haven't yet been invited up into the mansions where the real rackets are run or the fate of America's cities is ultimately decided. For all the pretensions of Rico and later Robinson gangsters, such as Joe Krozac in *The Last Gangster,* to be Napoleons in the making, hoodlums remain peripheral figures. The real menace, it seems, to which "we, the public" must be alert is the degree to which gangsters are only the tip of a wider, more well-connected problem.[66]

Within his own world of ruthless ethnic gangsters, though, Little Caesar's rise is meteoric, just as Tony Camonte ascends in the criminal hierarchy in *Scarface* by murdering his superiors. The amoral gangster rises to the top by stepping over others who no longer have "what it takes," or are "slipping." First, Rico replaces Sam Vettori, sneering, "Sam, ya can dish it out but you're getting so you can't take it no more. You're through!" Next, Little Arnie is convinced to leave Chicago after his hit on Rico is unsuccessful. Even after the Big Boy replaces Pete Montana with Rico as "the new boss of the North Side," Little Caesar isn't through. "Let me tell you something, Otero," he tells his fawning henchman. "It's not only Pete Montana that's through, but the Big Boy himself. He's not what he used to be." In the mob, and by implication the city itself, a Darwinian world of red claw and fang prevails.

While it may be easy for Rico to push aside ethnic gangsters who get in his way, the secretive Big Boy, who stands above the immigrant hoodlums, is more enduring. Even at the movie's end, after Sam Vettori has gone to the gallows, Little Arnie has been driven from the city, and Rico has been slaughtered by a machine-gun wielding policeman, no mention is made of the need to rid Chicago of the Big Boy. Either he can, as Little Arnie is sure, "fix anything" and Sergeant Flaherty has been instructed by paid-off superiors to leave him alone, or he is so well shielded behind his mansion and other trappings of respectability that the police are oblivious of who really controls the rackets. This theme returns in *Bullets or Ballots*, *Racket Busters,* and other crime films, but in either case the law-abiding city is the loser.[67]

While in *Little Caesar* the gangster is a figure of unrelenting menace, very quickly Hollywood learned to play on these tropes and suggest that "respectable" swindlers were the bigger frauds and menaces, and that even a bootlegger attempting to enter straight society had better watch his wallet when talking to a stockbroker. Such sentiments were understandable in the depths of the Great Depression, and later Edward G. Robinson comedies, such as *The Little Giant* (1933, directed by Roy Del Ruth) and *A Slight Case of Murder* (1938, directed by Lloyd Bacon), present a world of dual morality, in which street codes of tough-guy honor actually prove superior to high society's hypocrisy. In the first, a Chicago bootlegger realizes that the coming repeal of Prohibition is going to put him out of business and uses this excuse to retire from the rackets and buy his way into California high society. When he rescues Polly Cass from a tumble from her horse, he's introduced to her stockbroker dad, who promptly sells him some phony stock. Other well-bred shysters prey on the out-of-his-element gangster, who must call in the boys from the old neighborhood to help him out of the jam he has gotten into by trying to play according to the rules.

In the second film, whose screenplay is by Damon Runyon, Remy Marco (again played by Robinson) likewise uses the end of Prohibition to announce his retirement, but circumstances conspire to keep this from occurring. First, his legitimate brewery flops when it turns out his beer is appallingly undrinkable, and then a series of unwanted corpses turns up to ruin his idyllic retreat to the country with his daughter and her boyfriend—annoyingly (for Marco), a state trooper![68]

Serious gangster films also suggested the futility of criminal urbanites' trying to go straight. *The Doorway to Hell* tells the story of Louie Ricarno (played by Lew

Ayres, who was nominated for an Oscar), a genius mob boss who has organized the various crime lords into a conglomerate that honors each hood's territory, thus keeping the peace and maximizing the profits for all concerned. Once his business is solidified and the gang wars end, Ricarno retires to a life of gentlemanly ease. It is only when the greedy hoods start feuding among themselves that they lure him back to Chicago. A plot to kidnap his straight-arrow younger brother to blackmail Ricarno into returning to his life of crime goes horribly awry when the boy is inadvertently killed, and now Lou is only too happy to return and settle some scores. Jimmy Cagney appears as one of Ricarno's menacing henchmen, already working on the tough-guy mannerisms that he'd perfect a year later in *The Public Enemy*. It is hard for the boys from the old neighborhood to escape the stigma of their origins, or to succeed among more gentlemanly crooks, and many early gangster films suggest it is futile for a city boy to try.[69]

Within the ghettos from which they emerged, fictional gangsters, like their real-life counterparts, are urban folk heroes. Rico is celebrated by his mob associates at his own banquet at the Palermo Club. A banner proclaims the club's motto, "friendship, loyalty," even though we've already seen that Rico rises in the rackets not through faithful service to Sam Vettori, but by shoving aside his patrons the minute he perceives their weakness. At the banquet the boys carry on like animals, causing one to complain, "What's a matter with you birds? Don't youse know how to behave at a banket?" The gang is further stigmatized as *gavones* when Scabby stands to give a mangled tribute to his chief: "Well, folks, you all know what we're here fer. So what's the good of me tellin' ya about it? Rico here is a great guy!" After the cheers die down, he struggles to continue: "Sure. And, uh, well, aw, say, Rico, I don't know how to talk fancy. But this here watch is for you! From the boys! Come on, everybody! Clap like!" The festivities are dampened, though, by news the testimonial watch has been stolen, which leaves the boys slightly embarrassed. Still, newspaper photographers are eager to publicize the festivities, and a beamingly proud Rico buys ten copies of the paper covering his banquet from a fawning newsstand owner. In their ethnic neighborhoods gangsters rise to become folk heroes to their people, even if they can't fully penetrate the upper reaches of society or replace the Big Boys of the world.

In other ways *Little Caesar* depicts the degree to which gangsters were already achieving legendary status, much to the disgust of nativist middle-class Americans. When Rico shoots the repentant Tony Passa before he can return to church and confess his sins, the slain mobster's funeral turns into an elaborate street parade in which bands, candle- and flower-bearing pallbearers, and costumed fraternal society members march in his honor. In his limousine, Sam Vettori reasons, "Well, this was no time to be tight with money. Tony deserved a swell sendoff." While this scene may strike contemporary viewers as merely ethnic color, it should be recalled that Italian street festa were often viewed as gaudy displays of barbarism, even by Irish Catholic prelates; when the festivities commemorated a mobster's passing, viewers from outside the immigrant community often reacted with horror.[70]

It's clear, though, that Rico's neighbors regard him as something of a Robin Hood, for when Little Arnie tries to assassinate him on the street, the entire city rallies around their hero as he mocks the would-be killer, "Fine shot you are!" Waiters rush out of the Palermo Club and passersby embrace Rico; when the police show up and Sergeant Flaherty says, "So, somebody finally put one in you!" it's clear the crowd is on Rico's side. Flaherty sarcastically says, "The old man will be glad" Rico was just grazed, to which the mobster retorts, "You tell him the cops couldn't get me no other way, so they hired a couple of gunmen!" The crowd laughs appreciatively at Rico's defiant attitude, and considering the tight collaboration between elements of the Chicago police and various criminal gangs in the 1920s and early 1930s, their suspicions that the police might just be another well-armed gang aren't entirely unwarranted.

Flaherty will later prove to be an even bigger gangster than Rico, taunting him to come out of hiding and then brutally machine-gunning him on the street—by a billboard advertising his old partner in crime, now a celebrity dancer. The sadistic glee with which Flaherty machine-guns Rico, who by this point has been reduced to a bitter bum living in a Riis-like flophouse, poses the question as to just who is the bigger gangster. At a time when gangsters disguised as Chicago policemen were able to convince many that they were indeed members of the police force working for one or another of the city's rival gangs, the suggestion that Flaherty is perhaps acting at the behest of rival gangsters in his homicidal vendetta against Rico is not all that implausible. In the filmic city, even the forces of supposed law and order rule by the tommy gun, and Flaherty is not such a moral pillar when hunting his foes.[71]

Yet it was not zealous policemen who alarmed middle-class students of the city. Teens' emulation of criminals worried reformers throughout this era, and *Angels with Dirty Faces'* depiction of a Catholic priest battling teens' hero worship of Rocky resonated with many real-life efforts to turn neighbors against their own public enemies. Brownsville, Brooklyn, home to many of the associates of Murder Inc., was also home to the precinct with the largest number of juvenile delinquency cases in the 1930s, a fact police hastened to link to teens' wrongheaded emulation of the neighborhood's flashy heroes. In spite of later sepia-tinged depictions of Brownsville's fictional gangsters like *Goodfellas'* Paulie Cicero, Richard Gambino has demonstrated that before World War II many Italian-Americans fought hard to battle the image of gangsters as representing all of their compatriots. Only after many Italians and Jews moved away from Brooklyn, Newark, and the blue-collar lives they had led there could a glamorous mobster image be celebrated in *The Godfather* and its successor productions. In the 1920s and 1930s, campaigns to put distance between law-abiding citizens and the Capones and Lucianos were all the more vital since contemporary accounts in film and other media condemned how urban ethnics allegedly lionized the mobsters in their midst, as Rico's veneration by his neighborhood and the *Chicago Tribune's* account of Angelo Genna's funeral make clear.[72]

Movie producers already recognized that a large part of their audience was composed of white ethnic southern and eastern Europeans, and thus films such as

Little Caesar often continued twinning good ethnics with violent gangsters, just as the early silent one-reelers gave at least some play to honest Italians. Unlike Rico, Joe Massara has some reservations about ever getting involved in gang activity, and as soon as they make it to Chicago he tries to go straight. He is the repentant, "good" ethnic, and since he is played by Douglas Fairbanks, Jr., and not the Romanian-born Jewish Edward G. Robinson, he exhibits barely any traces of his foreignness, with no *gavone*-like traits, discernible accent, or other Italian signifier. He appears to have assimilated to a far greater degree than Rico or the other gangsters seen fighting at their garish banquet.

Joe is the good city ethnic, too, in knowing his place—doubting if he can ever escape his past or his genetically coded destiny. He aspires to become an entertainer, and not to a more mainstream profession. This was a role native Americans could comfortably see ethnic urbanites fulfilling, for from Irish performers in blackface to dialect comics in vaudeville to the slum safari tours of popular magazines, the immigrant had been a source of amusement at least since the 1840s. But even here Joe is repentant and doubts whether he can escape his sordid past. When his girl-friend, who also bears a non-Nordic name and background, asks if he can give up his formerly shady associations, he replies, "What'd be the good of you asking, kid? Once in the gang . . . you know the rest." Olga cuts him off. "I don't wanna know!" she says, adding, "Only, maybe—maybe it could be different this time. If we try." But Joe doubts he can ever escape what both descent and personal choice have branded him: "I've never seen a guy that could get away with it yet." Still, we are to understand that Joe is a moral character, both for wanting out of the rackets and nevertheless trying to tip off Rico when Arnie Lorch is gunning for him. Unlike the immoral ethnic, Rico, Joe Massara does not abandon his friends when he sees a chance for personal advancement.

Other Italian characters are twinned in a duality of nurturing loyalty and rapa-ciousness at the expense of friends or associates. *Little Caesar*'s guilt-tormented gangster Tony Passa is urged by his mother, who stereotypically embodies immi-grant simplicity and piety, to stop staying "out late nights, you drink lotta wine." Instead, she urges him to stay home and return to the immigrant verities of family and faith. "I have some spaghetti for you on the stove. If you feel better, eat-a something, yes? It do you good. You used to be a good boy, Antonio. Remember when you sing in the church? In the choir with Father McNeill. You in white. Remember? . . . The church was beautiful. You little boy with long hair. The tall big candle. . . . Remember, Antonio?" The paradigmatic sainted mother gets Tony to repent, even though he is cut short on his way to church and Father McNeill's con-fessional, and will only receive his "tall big candle" in his funeral procession.

A less flattering stereotype is presented in Ma Magdalena, a cunning thief as demonic as any "innately criminal" Sicilian conjured by the *Chicago Tribune*'s editorial page. When a desperate Rico runs to her "fruit store" to hide from the police, Ma cackles, "Well, ya got yourself in a nice fix!" She agrees to hide him in a secret room in the back of the store—evidently every Italian fruit store is indeed a Mafia front—but will only give him $150 of the loot his gang has hidden. She defiantly tells Rico she can get away with this, "'Cause I'm the only one who knows where the money is hid! Kill me and you won't get a cent! I'll give you $150, if you be a good boy!" Ma Magdalena is the flip side of Ma Passa's sainted Italian motherhood, a cunning brigand crone who demands obedience from her "children" while preying on her own kind. There is no honor among thieves, and just like Rico, Ma is only interested in what she can get from a vulnerable fellow Italian. This was the image of Mediterranean "racial types" most prevalent in the early 1930s, and the film again feeds off nativist slurs against immigrant culture. Because of Ma's cruelty, Rico rapidly ends up back in the flophouse pit from which Flaherty lures him to his doom.[73]

Later cultural productions paint the immigrant bootlegger as a harmless figure of fun, maybe even a pillar of ethnic initiative who merely supplies his people with something they want and need that Puritan blue bloods have denied them. This is the subtext already in *The Roaring Twenties* and it is embraced in later comedies such as *Some Like it Hot*, or novels nostalgically looking back on the 1920s from an even longer, sepia-tinged time frame, such as *Middlesex*. Yet during Prohibition itself, bootleggers were often figures of menace, a "problem that we, the public, had to solve." Jeffrey Eugenides's Greek immigrant bootleggers of 1920s Detroit stand as a reproach to the later, supposedly more violent and dysfunctional, city the narrator argues black Detroit after 1967 has become. But novelists and the reading public need only check contemporary accounts of the Purple Gang and other white ethnic mobsters to see that urban nightmares come in many ethnicities. Rico, Tom Powers, and real Detroit's notorious Bernstein brothers were in their day regarded as a menace to society, too.[74]

Scarface further reinforces the image of ruthlessness and psychotic violence lurking in the heart of the immigrant city. Tony Camonte rises to the heights of the mob in the film, but throughout he is portrayed as a man whose violent outbursts and irrationality lead to his downfall. The gangster portrait mirrors much of the "racial" social science of the film's era. Mathew Frye Jacobson has demonstrated that writers such as Lothrop Stoddard and Madison Grant argued that violence and rage were intrinsic characteristics of all southern Italians; the "race's" supposed lack of self-control, intellect, and rationality was the reason immigration restrictionists argued the gates had to be shut tight, for this lack of self-control endangered the republic. Popular culture often took its cue from these stereotypes, although influence was often a matter of cross-pollination, for every magazine or movie slur on Italians gave social scientists something else to footnote.

Even in the late 1930s a supposedly flattering puff piece in the *New Yorker* on director Frank Capra noted that his doctor attributed Capra's surviving a burst appendix to "the fact that Sicilians, conditioned by generations of knifings, have very hardy interiors." *Life* similarly weighed in, reporting with surprise about Joe DiMaggio, "Instead of olive oil or smelly bear grease he keeps his hair slick with water. He never reeks of garlic and prefers chicken chow mein to spaghetti."[75]

Whatever one might think of this line of reasoning, a fictional gangster could hardly be expected to escape such slighting depictions if even the Yankee Clipper couldn't steer clear of them. *Scarface* certainly captures the saga of a man of irrational appetites and simian violence, closer on the evolutionary scale to the bear grease end. Tony Camonte begins the movie as a bodyguard to gang leader Big Lou Costillo, last of the old "Moustache Pete" gang bosses, but already his outsized ambition is on display. Violent and erratic, childlike in the best of circumstances, and easily roused to anger, Tony (as portrayed by the Yiddish theater star Paul Muni) continues a tradition of presenting the foreigner in America's midst, and by implication the city he dominates, as out of control. When he sits down to eat a plate of spaghetti he doesn't so much eat as inhale his food, embodying nativist stereotypes of "uncivilized" Italian food ways.[76]

More troublesome passions come to the fore when Costillo is slain. The police suspect Camonte, who is in fact paid by rival gangster Johnny Lovo to remove Costillo, but since no body has turned up, they have to let their prime suspect go. Once Camonte sees how easy it is to remove other gangsters, he begins terrorizing his former superiors, forcing Lovo and Chicago's other gangsters to pay tribute to him. As Tony rises to the top, his megalomania and outsized violence grow, too, and at a time when the public was still riveted by the exploits of the real Scarface and his successors.

Other members of Tony's gang are depicted as practically illiterate, a further slight on supposedly ignorant Italians. Similar depictions recur in later movies, as in *The Last Gangster*, in which foreign-born gang boss Joe Krozac (Edward G. Robinson) reassures his henchman, Curly, that his old-country bride can't understand what they're talking about. "Exactly how much English does this doll understand?" Curly asks. "Oh, just enough," Krozac replies, but Curly says, "Pretty soon I'll have to spell out things to you." "Yeah, if you could spell," Krozac replies. But when the police show up, Curly sarcastically tells his boss, "There's a couple of storks for you here. C-O-P-S. Did I spell it right?"[77]

Gangsters, though, can be both illiterate and pathologically violent, and in other capacities Curly is useful to Krozac in gunning down rival gangsters at a family wedding. Later he indeed spells things out for his old boss when he kidnaps and tortures him into giving up a fortune in stolen loot. This quite horrific scene shows how even supposed "idiot" gangsters were capable of pathological violence when motivated by greed or other base emotions. The simpler-minded gangster continues to be a figure of menace to respectable middle-class urbanites into the post–World War II era, as in *The Desperate Hours*, where the gorilla-like Sam Kobish smashes apart the upscale living room of the Hilliard family, destroying what he cannot possibly hope to understand or possess.[78]

In *Scarface* Camonte's rise to the top sets off a violent gang war, as even Tony's compatriots realize the menace he poses. Lovo and the other mob bosses begin worrying at the oversized ambitions of Camonte, and a major confrontation builds. The police close in on him, too, but ultimately, Italian gangsters are portrayed here and in *Little Caesar* as turning on themselves—and perhaps champions of immigration restriction took some cold comfort in that. Once the mob wars run their course, the city has been cleansed, although not by the forces of law and order or through the hysterical urgings to "Deport them! Deport them all!"

Rather, the violent, tommy-gun-wielding Tonys and Big Louies exterminate each other, and in a roundabout way, the social Darwinist principle of survival of the fittest saves the city.[79]

As in earlier silent films featuring Italian criminality, one reading of the mob movie allowed nativists to indulge restrictionist fantasies of the foreigner as implacably criminal, a genetic and cultural threat to the republic. Yet the best films of this genre are multivocal, and in *Scarface* there appears a "good ethnic," Inspector Ben Guarino, relentlessly chasing Tony Camonte across the city. It is important to remember that by 1932 a good part of the moviegoing audience was made up of immigrant and second-generation southern and eastern Europeans. Even if for some middle-class WASPs a Jewish immigrant portraying an Italian gangster (Muni or Robinson) was a frightening dream personified, some filmgoers had to be given a qualifier, a good ethnic for whom to root, or someone to counter the negative ethnic stereotypes associated with Rico or Tony. With Inspector Guarino (played by C. Henry Gordon) we have returned again, as in the early one-reelers extolling Lieutenant Petrosino, to a duality in the Italian community, where crafty Mediterranean crime fighters more in tune to their compatriots' violent minds and cultures can help the Anglo-Saxon authorities vanquish the unrepentant, unassimilable foreigner unwilling to rise in America through patient endurance and honest hard work.

The few "good ethnic" characters in these films nevertheless offer at best an afterthought, a passing nod to other possibilities in the foreigner-filled city, and their appearances in such early gangster films are at best an added coda to the main tune of violence. It is doubtful that their appearance alone can serve to redeem the picture of Chicago; the character of an Italian inspector pursuing Camonte seems like a hasty addition to reassure Italian moviegoers the producers realized not each and every one of them was a potential Scarface.

If so, this was not the only last-minute addition to *Scarface*. While the cinematic Chicago presented here is indeed a bleak urban landscape, this picture of irrationally violent gangsters is also an entertaining one. Self-appointed moral censors again worried that the cinematic gangster would be a little too attractive to impressionable audience members who might imitate the career of Tony Camonte. Such fears demonstrated once again the city could be simultaneously menacing and thrilling, a duality of attractive repugnance. To make sure that a moralistic censor such as Will Hays or Reverend Short didn't condemn the picture, additional elements were added to the movie to make it clear its producers came to bury, not praise, the mobster.

First, the title was changed so that *Scarface* became the "shame of a nation." The release of the film was delayed—it actually should have debuted at about the same time as Tom Powers and Rico Bandello were thrilling/repulsing a nation—so that new footage could be added that thoroughly condemned the exciting yet violent career of this foreign gangster. Civic reformers now preached directly at the camera, as if giving an updated version of Riis's magic lantern slide shows on the evils the supposedly "respectable" moviegoer was seeing. The reformers roused the moviegoing public by preaching, "You can end it! Fight!" Another new scene was shot so that now the police don't fatally shoot Camonte on the street, gangland-style (mirroring "the end of Rico"); now the "shame of a nation" is brought to trial and sentenced to hang. The system is thus made to be seen to function, and in a legalistic, "civilized" manner.

Other scenes were added so that the gangster menace was broadened into a foreign threat, with a reformer character arguing, "Put teeth in the Deportation Act. These gangsters don't belong in this country. Half of them aren't even citizens." An anonymous Italian character timorously agrees, saying, "That's true. They bring nothing but disgrace to my people." Good ethnics and reformers could agree on the threat the city faced, and cinematic moralizing reassured the censors, too, that *Scarface* was wholesome entertainment, or at least on the right side of the gangster menace.[80]

The Last Gangster likewise subtly suggests that the "foreign" menace of the gangster should be expelled from the country. The film's opening shot is of an ocean liner passing the Manhattan skyline. Gangster Joe Krozac (movingly portrayed by Edward G. Robinson) is returning from his unnamed European homeland with his new bride, and although we don't see the earlier, first ship's voyage that brought Krozac to America, he is still a "foreigner," someone the viewer understands is exploiting and preying on American communities. The threat of the foreign gangster is somewhat humorously first alluded to in this powerful movie, as reporters comment on the well-known gangster's reasons for going back to his homeland. "He's gone to his old country to find a wife," one reporter says, to which the second adds, "Joe's smart, he knows his eugenics." "Onions, you mean," the first wryly answers. Americans in the 1930s, too, knew their eugenics, and the foreign gangster polluting the city was still regarded as a non-Nordic blot on the nation by many citizens.

Krozac later is deported from America, after a fashion. Following his conviction for income tax evasion—again a bit of real-life mob history adapted to the screen, since this was the way the government finally shut down Al Capone—Krozac and other inmates are shipped to Alcatraz in a prison railcar loaded on a tugboat. Krozac is again the steerage-class immigrant—this time jettisoned from, not welcomed to, America. The wretched refuse desperately peer out of the cattle-car slats at another island (not Liberty, not Ellis) to see where they're going. This scene mirrors Joe's earlier boat ride, when the swarthy immigrant who's made good by preying on regular Americans returns to New York in triumph. But this scene also evokes the hundreds of Lewis Hine images photographed twenty-five years earlier on Ellis Island as huddled refuse similarly gazed in awe and fear at their destination. In the film we don't see Krozac's arrival as an immigrant, but no doubt at least a few WASPs after the restrictionist 1920s saw the scene of his going to Alcatraz, supposedly set in 1927, as a matter of good riddance to "bad eugenics," the Krozac and Sicilian gangster who has infested the nation's cities. If, as the reporter at the beginning of the movie notes, "Joe knows his eugenics," so did many "real" Americans, who didn't necessarily like what they were seeing. *The Last Gangster*

pays graphic visual obedience to the commands shrieked at the camera by reformers in *Scarface*—"Deport them all!"[81]

Still, *The Last Gangster* is marvelously ambivalent on where criminality arises,
and offers a suggestion that foreign genes cannot be blamed entirely. On the ocean
liner reporters accost a dignified ambassador, telling him, "There's an ex-fellow
countryman aboard. Joe Krozac." The ambassador sniffs, "We are not proud of
him," and even when the reporter argues, "Some people think there's a lot of
glamour about a big shot racketeer," the diplomat sticks to his guns. "I do not," he
counters. "I regard him as an enemy of the public. A blot upon your civilization."
The ambassador gets his—or the screenwriter's?—digs in at nativist America.
Croatia cannot be blamed for this public enemy; he is a product of the rot at the
heart of *your* cities, not a supposedly deficient foreign gene pool. Increasingly by
the late 1930s, it was tenable to argue it was time for America to get its house in
order and do something to eradicate the deficiencies in the industrial order, rather
than scapegoat "foreigners."[82]

"Good" foreigners, though, were a mere grace note; the foreign menace remained
an important trope in gangster films. Cinematic denunciations of foreign criminals
bore fruit in congressional proposals such as the 1937 Dempsey and Hobbes bills
to deport all foreigners believing in a change of U.S. government; the first chair of
the House Un-American Activities Committee, the rabid anticommunist Martin
Dies, also offered a suggestion that six-million foreign-born Americans should be
deported to provide jobs for "real" Americans. These measures were vociferously
protested by the National Slovak Society and other ethnic fraternal organizations,
but at least one by-product of fictional portrayals of the gangster menace was to
lend support to the cry to "deport them all!"[83]

In a less xenophobic vein, such moralist framing devices were in later years
expanded to lend a documentary legitimacy to the genre. But these tropes were
also soon slyly and self-referentially remarked on by gangster characters themselves. In the very beginning of *Bullets or Ballots*, mobsters Bugs Fenner and
Al Kruger enter a movie theater to catch the start of "the crime picture." Bugs
(Humphrey Bogart) asks the cashier, "What time does the crime picture start?" in
the movie's first, brilliant line. The two gangsters then enter the theater and for the
movie's first five minutes watch this film-within-a-film expose the "real" menace
the rackets pose to America's cities.

On screen, an announcer proclaims, "This is William Kennedy bringing you
the second of a series of short pictures exposing the rackets of America, . . . the
syndicate of crime to arouse them to a national menace, the modern racketeer."
Fenner then leans over to his boss and whispers, "Wait'll you see the actor that
takes you off." In the years to come, one has to wonder if real mobsters such as
Lucky Luciano similarly checked out their cinematic counterparts, such as crime
boss Eddie Vanning in the gang film of 1937, *Marked Woman*, featuring the brutal
assault on a woman about to testify against the Italian crime boss.[84]

Such framing devices allowed films simultaneously to depict violence and
corruption and make claims they were merely aiming to expose, not celebrate, the

racketeering virus. In *Bullets or Ballots* Fenner and Kruger continue to watch scenes of shakedowns and gambling operations as Kennedy announces, "The crime syndicates of America entrenched in 88 American cities of more than 100,000 population and reaching into thousands of surrounding towns rob the American people of 15 billion dollars. Huge sums. . . . Across the street from 100,000 American schools attractive games are installed in stores, shops and restaurants. And in one American city $85,000 is extracted." On the screen, ominous tentacles of the "mob" stretch across the map of America.[85]

Pseudodocumentary touches similarly framed *Racket Busters*, which leads with a title card promising the film is "based upon official court records of the special rackets prosecution of the trucking racket in New York City." As in so many films, too, newspaper headlines blare the sad story of urban corruption. "Martin Machine Wins Again," and "Racket Rule to Continue," the newspapers exclaim in the beginning of the film, giving another piece of verisimilitude to the film in an era when tabloids sold quite a few papers recounting the exploits of Luciano, Costello, and other hoods.[86]

The Roaring Twenties likewise uses an announcer to trace Eddie Bartlett's bootlegging career. The voice sounds suspiciously like Walter Winchell's; already by 1939 he was famous as a chronicler of big-city celebrities on both sides of the divide between law and the rackets, and the man who famously arranged for Louis "Lepke" Buchalter to end his flight from justice and turn himself in to Special Prosecutor Thomas Dewey.[87]

In the movies, crusading crime commissioners mirror the real-life efforts of Dewey, and in many films a character with a striking resemblance to the fastidious, mustachioed prosecutor stands in for the racket buster. Even a postwar film like *Kiss of Death* features an assistant DA who resembles the then New York governor, although he is given the Italian name of Lou D'Angelo, again playing to the good/bad ethnic duality familiar from *Scarface*. Earlier, in fact in the very era when Dewey was first gaining national fame, *Racket Busters*, the film that promises it is based on official proceedings against New York's crime kings, features a Dewey-esque special prosecutor. Hugh Allison not only looks but sounds like the straightlaced Dewey. After he has been sworn in by a lame duck governor as a special prosecutor, Allison downplays his earlier career fighting the mob, saying he's "done nothing but throw a few racketeers in jail. The rackets went on with new men at their head. Gentlemen, you don't seem to realize that racketeering is a national institution. The public takes it as much for granted as its radio and its moving picture. It's attached itself to our system like an ugly sore."

Indeed, crime's "Czar" Martin (Humphrey Bogart) has already bragged to his henchmen, all passably attired in tuxedos as "respectable" politicos, celebrating their election night victory, "I got plans and I got organization. I'm gonna make this whole town pay off to me, from bootblacks to bankers." How this is possible is suggested when a crony comments on the cheering election-night throng, "Boy, listen to that mob!" To which Martin adds, "Yeah, listen. Holler, suckers! When I get through with you you'll holler even louder."[88]

Crusaders bucking the menacing confluence of gangsters and bought-off politicians often faced threats of physical retaliation. In *The Roaring Twenties* gangsters
worried about the zeal of assistant prosecutor Lloyd Hart, Eddie Bartlett's former
bootlegging partner, pay his wife a threatening visit at her Long Island home. In
Bullets or Ballots a crusading publisher is gunned down before the mob can be
brought to heel. In real life, in 1935, Dutch Schultz plotted to follow Dewey on his
predictable morning path to a neighborhood drugstore and bump off the prosecutor.
Before the Dutchman could follow through on his plans, associates in Murder Inc.
who were worried about the backlash ordered Schultz's murder, which occurred
at Newark's Palace Chop House.[89]

If these crime commissioners and special prosecutors prevailed, it was often an
uphill battle, for mysterious wealthy vice overlords were always lurking in the
background, and these men, viewers were informed, were often capable of paying
off or otherwise controlling the political system. In its promotional shorts (which
in themselves were an art form celebrating the violence and voyeuristic thrills to
come in the gangster film promoted, as well as the supposed "factual" basis that
sat behind the promoted film), films such as *Bullets or Ballots* promised, "Who
rules the rackets? This picture puts the finger on the political higher-ups!" Other
promos for this film lectured, "Every citizen should see it!" and "The producers of
'G-Men' and 'Special Agent' raid the headlines for another dramatic scoop!"

In *Bullets or Ballots* itself, Al Kruger and Bugs Fenner are only the surface of a
larger, more well-connected syndicate of vice. The big bosses and their bought-
and-paid-for politicians have grown tired of the city's seemingly sole honest cop,
Detective Blake (played by Edward G. Robinson), and exile him to a beat in the
far-off Bronx as punishment. Blake gets his second chance when an old friend is
appointed crime commissioner after Bugs Fenner murders publisher Ward Bryant.
A furious Al Kruger tells him, "Someday you're gonna get wise to the fact that that
strong-arm gangster stuff went out with Prohibition! You're not running liquor
anymore, you're in big business! I pulled you out of the gutter! And you take a
chance on ruining a $200 million gold mine to satisfy a grudge! Well, it's a fine
way to pay me back!"

Kruger's tirade is interrupted by a phone call from "the bosses," who, he tells
Bugs, are "liable to knock the props right out from under me on account of this
Bryant mess. If they do it'll be the last thing that'll ever happen to me. You know
that. Swell, having to cover up for you to save my own neck." Bugs asks, "Who
are they, Al?" but Kruger ominously answers, "If you knew you wouldn't sleep
much tonight."

It turns out vice in Kruger's New York is run not from some Brooklyn social club,
but from a huge, colonnaded bank, the Oceanic Bank and Trust Company. The real
bosses of crime are tuxedoed financiers who sip scotch in well-appointed board-
rooms, speak in vaguely aristocratic tones, and calmly warn their hireling mobster,
"I think you're beginning to slip, Mr. Kruger." Another says, "And if you make
one more mistake, you're through. . . . There's just one way to interpret it. That's
all, Mr. Kruger." Unlike Little Caesar, when these captains of industry (and the

rackets) sense weakness in their underlings they do not machine-gun them, merely quietly arrange for a "personnel change" (probably at the hands of other hired goons who can't be traced back to Wall Street). The implications are clear: The city faces difficult odds in loosening the racketeers' grip when the power behind them rules from the nation's Oceanic Trusts.

In New Deal America, ethnic gangsters might still inspire animus, but by 1938, the public had been well primed to direct its venom at those whom President Roosevelt termed "economic royalists." To be sure, such affluent cabals were on display a century earlier, and continue to control the rackets in *The Wire*'s Baltimore, where a secretive "Greek" (who laughs, "And then again, I'm not even Greek!") can rapidly fold up his drug, prostitution, and hijacking operations and jet out of the country first-class as others face the music. But in the context of the Great Depression, the moviegoing public was primed to lend credence to a boardroom full of respectable gangsters wearing Harvard ties.[90]

The big bankers control things from behind the scenes, and this cabal is corrupting urban America. Later, when Blake goes undercover and pretends to join the rackets, he meets these banker/gangsters and learns the identity of these affluent heads of the rackets. "You're the heads, huh?" he says. "No wonder the organization has been so well protected." A banker tells him, "Incidentally, Mr. Blake, you are the only one who will know who we are." "I understand that," Blake replies. The odds of cleansing the city of its vice are long indeed when no one knows where the real infection lies.

Similarly, Joe Krozac is furious when he is convicted for income tax evasion, and asks his lawyer, "Well, how about that ex-governor?" It's apparent Krozac's reach extends to some pretty high and mighty places. Likewise, Eddie Bartlett in *The Roaring Twenties* is initially astonished that Panama Smith can get him out of jail so quickly. Afterward, Eddie watches in amazement as a policeman enters a speakeasy and happily knocks back a beer. "See, buster, it's easy," Panama tells Eddie. "All you gotta do is pay off. . . . With sucker money. Ever since Prohibition it's been floating around waiting to get picked up."

Eddie soon realizes how right she is. After he begins running the Panama Club as an elegant front, he tells his gang how easy it will be to continue running the city, provided they divide it among an amiable syndicate. "Now look, now that we've got things fixed with the right people in office, we can sort of arrange things among ourselves, y'hear? Which means instead of shooting things out, we'll talk things out. We'll get a setup where we can all work together." Meyer Lansky, Lucky Luciano, Longy Zwillman, and their associates in Prohibition America might have agreed. A few payoffs to Tammany, Newark's Third Ward Democratic Club, and similar organizations kept the mob in business. In many gangster films such as *Bullets or Ballots*, as in many 1850s novels, the high and mighty are thoroughly corrupt and in bed with the down and dirty.[91]

Secretive operatives continue to fix things so the real criminals escape unscathed in post–World War II urban movies. One need only think of master lawyer Howser in *Kiss of Death*, who springs Nick Bianco and Tommy Udo with only a phone call to the right connected official. Likewise, in *On the Waterfront*, Hoboken's corrupt longshoreman union boss Johnny Friendly may go down for the long count after Terry Malloy's testimony before the Waterfront Crime Commission. Still, in one brief scene a well-spoken rich man in his mansion, far, far from the gin joints and docks of Hudson County, instructs his butler, "I am not at home for Mister Friendly—ever." Behind the public face of the mob sits an aristocratic conspiracy preying on the republic, a threat that is harder to defeat since it can weather the downfall of its mobster front men with relative ease. The public face of corruption may eventually face justice, but those who control and reap millions through the rackets merely move on. Can we ever clean up the city if we catch only the briefest glimpse of who's really in control?[92]

Yet all was not hopeless, for by the 1930s a more sophisticated depiction of the urban lawbreaker emerged. Often in the same films that condemn the violent mobster there appear characters who recognize it is the ecology of the slum that breeds crime, not necessarily something innate in the ethnic gangster. The slum itself is the real public enemy number one all Americans should be active in combating. The leftist writer Lillian Hellman served as screenwriter for 1937's *Dead End*, based on a play by Sidney Kingsley, who was later blacklisted for leftist sympathies. It therefore is perhaps not surprising an architect from the Lower East Side slums explains that local gangster Baby Face Martin is the logical outcome of such vast inequalities of wealth, and that unless the slums are cleaned up and better opportunities provided for the Dead End Kids who idolize Martin, more gangsters will be formed. Once on his soapbox, architect Dave Connell continues, blaming capitalist slumlords and those who prevent honest workers from striking for higher wages and better working conditions with perpetuating the conditions in which gangsterism thrives. The point is graphically rendered by placing a luxurious, doorman-equipped apartment building right across the street from the docks and slums of this dead end. But at the height of the New Deal, and the New York reign of city planner par excellence Robert Moses, such optimistic faith in architecture, social planning, the Wagner Act, and government programs to overcome the gangster-breeding slums resonated with many moviegoers.[93]

A more thoroughgoing condemnation of the gangster-producing slum occurs in *Angels with Dirty Faces*. Even as he battles his boyhood friend, Father Jerry Connelly is consistently sympathetic with him. The priest argues it is a combination of poverty and bad breaks that has caused Rocky to follow a life of crime. In its famous opening scene, the bored slum kids head to the rail yards to see what they can swipe. Young Rocky points to one boxcar, telling young Jerry, "Looka here. Rueleen Coal Company, Pittsburgh, Pa. Too bad it's not winter. We could grab some bags of coal." What they find instead is a freight car full of fountain pens, which Rocky argues they can sell to buy food. Jerry isn't so sure, however: "Maybe we shouldn't, Rocky. We don't need those pens. It ain't like stealing coal to keep warm."

To the New York, Philadelphia, and other city poor, such pilferage wasn't necessarily regarded as theft or juvenile delinquency, but part of the moral economy that ensured survival. Many such boxcar strippers may have regarded the coal companies and slumlords as the real thieves in life. Among the working poor of the early twentieth century, pilferage was an accepted part of the moral economy, even if Progressive Era magazine writers were not so forgiving. But hints are given that mere survival necessitates some of the acts of Rocky, and later even Father Jerry fondly laughs when recalling the stores from which he and Rocky used to steal.[94]

Rocky is caught and sent to reform school, and he begins his trajectory to a life of crime. Jerry suggests he confess so the authorities might show leniency to Rocky. But Rocky won't hear of it: "Now listen. Just 'cause you can run a little faster than me is no reason you gotta go hating yourself." "But it ain't fair, Rocky," his friend argues, but Rocky is sure reform school won't be so bad, hinting poverty has already caused his family problems at home. "The old man's got troubles enough without me. Forget it, those are the breaks. You got away and I got caught. . . . Always remember, don't be a sucker."

The years rapidly pass in classic movie montage. When the movie's "present," 1938, arrives, the degree to which nothing has changed in the slum neighborhood that spawned Rocky is dramatized by an establishing shot that introduces us to the Dead End Kids. A montage of the Lower East Side shows the same tenements, the same laundry hanging off the fire escapes, and the same pushcarts as when Rocky and Jerry broke into boxcars. Nothing much has changed in the dirt-poor city streets. The Dead End Kids are hanging out on a stoop just as Rocky and Jerry were hanging out on the fire escape with nothing to do eighteen years before. Thus this movie is a condemnation of gangsters, but also an environmentalist/ecological denunciation of the slums. If we don't give these kids recreation centers and social work, then in another eighteen years we'll have still more Rocky Sullivans on our hands.

Again it is suggested it's poverty that may lead to a new Rocky Sullivan emerging from the Dead End Kids. When the grown-up gangster Rocky hands out money to the adoring teens, one exclaims, "Fifty bucks! Boy, my old man never made that much dough in his whole life working for the Department of Sanitation!" Later, with the money Rocky has given them the young gang heads to Murphy's Pool Room, where, after winning at pool, Soapy remarks, "Eight bucks, not bad! My mother has to work almost all week for that much!" The poverty of the slums breeds criminals, the film suggests, and until street sweepers or maids are more fairly compensated, the racketeer will thrive.

For all the dysfunctionality, such neighborhoods breed a primitive code of honor, as when Rocky tells the Dead End Kids who've lifted his wallet, "Never bother anybody in your own neighborhood." In this regard, Rocky exhibits traits of the social bandit, a criminal by outside authorities' lights, but someone who wins the allegiances of his local people by preying on those perceived to be bigger bandits and parasites—the government, the banks, the idle rich—and distributing enough of the booty to his people to become their protector. Such social bandits in the context of 1890s Sicily and other regions have been documented by

Eric Hobsbawm, and the ghetto boy who made good in the rackets might also be regarded as a form of social bandit. (Of course, this is just what moral reformers feared, worrying that gangster films might lead to an unhealthy emulation by impressionable ghetto children. Rocky had to perish in order to satisfy the moralists).[95]

In their own ways, Rocky and Father Jerry both adhere to a complicated code of loyalty to their streets, too. The gangster remains loyal to his boyhood friend, even after the priest begins a vice crusade and goes on the radio denouncing "the cesspool of official and near-official corruption," urging his listeners, "We must rid ourselves of the criminal parasites that feed on us. We must wipe out those we have ignorantly elected." The individual mobster once more is only the tip of an iceberg that descends to grafting politicians and seemingly respectable lawyers such as Humphrey Bogart's Frazier. With coded language Jerry indicts Tammany Hall and the rackets that Dewey in these very years was tying to the political clubhouse.[96]

Father Jerry tries to explain to Rocky's girlfriend that he remains essentially loyal to his friend. He agrees with her that Rocky is "just a kid who made a mistake and got sent to reform school. . . . But he's not bad, not really bad." It is amazing to hear such sympathy in our present era of mandatory minimum sentencing and three strikes, but Father Jerry, even though sympathetic, explains that a higher loyalty makes it imperative he continue his crusade against Rocky and all his works. "You see, Laurie, there's all those other kids, hundreds of them, in the streets and bad environment. Who I don't want to see grow up like Rocky did." In his own way, Father Jerry adheres to a code of honor and allegiance to his old neighborhood, too.

This code, though, is a complicated one, often at odds with upper-class WASP society, but there are rules one doesn't transgress. Adherence to the code leads to difficult decisions and acts that mix the best of consequences with impure motives. Rocky is bad, but the crime for which he is sent to the electric chair is killing Frazier and Keefer because he overhears them plotting to murder Father Jerry. As Rocky has already reminded us, "Never bother anybody in your own neighborhood," and this precept must be applied to well-dressed hypocrites like Frazier, too. Rocky also welcomes the "honest competition" of Father Jerry's good-government league, and allows reformers to try to beat him fair and square, even if real-life mobsters such as Dutch Schultz hadn't quite seen the "competition" this way. Rocky, the product of Lower Manhattan, has a code of honor, even if this ultimately leads to the hot seat.

A later movie, *A Bronx Tale*, has a young Italian-American boy in 1960 stay silent after he witnesses a mob hit, and his bus driver father tells him that he's "done a good thing for a bad man." Here Rocky does a bad thing for a good man, saving Father Jerry, then doubling down on his good act by famously and publicly dying a bad man in the impressionable gang's eyes, turning yellow at the moment of his execution. Father Jerry pays back this debt to a friend from the old neighborhood, closing the movie by saying, "All right, fellas. Let's go and say a prayer for a boy who couldn't run as fast as I could." As in *Dead End* and *The*

Roaring Twenties, it's the problem of the slum that leads to the gangster, whether because Eddie Bartlett can't find honest work after the war, or because poverty and a punitive prison system churn out an army of Rockys and Baby Face Martins. At least some gangster films of the late 1930s argue that essentially good men are driven into lives of crime by desperate circumstances.[97]

Moreover, in the city good characters flourish, too. They demonstrate through their talent and will that it is possible to overcome the menace of the slums. In *City for Conquest*, Jimmy Cagney plays boxer Danny Kenny, and his composer brother, Eddie (Arthur Kennedy), calls to mind George Gershwin. Dozens of athletes and entertainers emerged from the mean streets of Chicago, New York, and other cities to become national celebrities by 1940, although even in this film, classical composers consort with their mob friends from Forsyth Street. The Kenny brothers bump into their old friend, Googy, who sarcastically lists the number of prisons he's been in the last few years. "Yeah, I been a lotta places and no place," he tells them, perhaps indicting the limited opportunities in the slum.

But Googy's ambitions lead him to the top of the rackets, and it's clear he isn't alone among the products of Forsyth Street (the Lower East Side) in cutting corners to get what he wants. Eddie remarks that "the old bunch. Every one of them, they keep turning up like bad pennies. First Pete, now Googy. And the other day I heard that Mushy Kelly finished his stretch for burglary. What a bunch!" By 1940 popular culture presents a sociological view, and an indulgent one at that, to explain the choices slum dwellers make. The slums cultivate burglars, but also classical composers, dancers, men of talent. And not all slum denizens are completely evil. Googy proves his loyalty to an old Forsyth Street pal when he avenges Danny by rubbing out a rival gangster who had arranged for a boxer to blind him in the ring with "resin rubbed in his eyes by the tip of their gloves." Once again a bad man does a good thing for a pal.

Depending on their ambitions, characters struggle to leave the slums by varying means. Peggy, Danny's "best girl," dreams of escaping the slums as a Broadway dancer. On a boat ride back from Coney Island, she explains, "Don't you see, Danny, we're only hurting each other if we let ourselves in for the lives our families had. Always struggling, always trying to make a dime do for a dollar. I want to climb out of Forsyth Street." To which Danny replies, "We don't have to live down there. We can move up to the Bronx."[98]

One of the most underrated gangster movies offers a moving, remarkable suggestion that the right combination of proper aspirations and antiurbanist flight to a better neighborhood can overcome genetics and wean "good" foreigners away from a gangster past. *The Last Gangster* argues that those who try to assimilate and shun not just their criminality but their foreignness can be accepted into the national mosaic. Gangster Joe Krozac's wife from the old country abandons him when she realizes the extent of his criminal enterprises, and assumes a new identity in a streetcar suburb of Boston (compared to New York, Brooklyn, Chicago, and other "foreign" cities, this city barely registered on the national radar screen of urbanist alarm, instead evoking memories of patriots and Plymouth Rock).

Talya is "hand picked from my old hometown" so that Joe is sure he can "[keep] my private life private" and raise a family with her. But after Joe is imprisoned, Talya begins to have her doubts. She takes their baby, Joe, Jr., to Alcatraz, where a prison guard snaps "Talk English!" Talya is indeed eager to show her husband that "I talk English better now, don't you think?" Krozac, though, barely acknowledges his wife, and is far more delighted to see his infant son, gleefully calling "Joe!" through the dividing glass. However, Talya wants her husband to dispel the stories she's begun hearing about his career: "I read about you, Joe. Things I never knew. I show them to Curly and he only laughs. . . . The lady in the hotel where we stay. She stopped speaking to me and little Joe when she found out who I am." Krozac snaps at Talya and tells her he "wants to talk to my kid and look at him, see? We got plenty of time for all that baloney. Look, keep quiet, will ya?" Talya meekly acquiesces.

However, when a tabloid newspaper reporter (played by Jimmy Stewart) tricks her into getting a picture of her baby with a gun as "Public Enemy Number 1 Junior," Talya furiously confronts the paper's editor. She wants to know why Joe committed the crimes the paper says he did. "Maybe it was so his son, your baby, could grow up and go to college and be rich and have a big car and a raccoon coat," the editor says, adding, "Why it's just news, Mrs. Krozac. Why, your baby will be famous for a long time. Everybody will want to read about him for a long time!" After this frank paean to the tabloid press, which cynically glorified gangsters and scandal to sell papers, Talya realizes her baby will be hounded by the public unless she can escape her past. The editor's cynicism calls to mind that other famous baby of the 1930s, Charles Lindbergh, Jr., who had disappeared under much more tragic circumstances, but Talya flees clear across the country to give her son a chance of effacing his tainted roots.[99]

After a short time Talya is living with Paul, the repentant reporter, in a suburban house "out on a trolley line," with the requisite white picket fence. Talya's son in rapid succession refers to Paul as "Uncle Paul" and then "Daddy." The foreign past is left behind, and while Talya retains a hint of her eastern European accent, within the idyllic suburban setting, as she swings on a backyard swing, no less, it is only a charming hint of foreignness, not the threat it might appear if she were still married to the mob.

Her baby, though, makes an even more astounding metamorphosis, becoming "Little Paul," who, her new husband assures Talya, "will never know." Talya, though, protests to her husband that "it wouldn't be fair to you. No matter how hard we try to forget. Tried to hide. All that's been still is, Paul." The transformation of an ethnic, liminal woman into a regular "white" resident of the suburbs is still uncertain in 1937 America, and Talya, representing the "good" ethnic, submissive to the American Dream, still worries not about her own aspirations but what her taint might mean for Paul.

The next generation, however, achieves greater assimilation. Paul, Jr., speaks with no trace of an accent—at least nothing Croatian. Indeed, as he grows up he attains a trace of an aristocratic, pseudo-English accent, wears middle-class sailor suits, and engages in all-American pursuits like fishing, playing in his spacious backyard with his dog, and going camping with his newspaper editor "dad." Indeed, the Krozac about him has been entirely effaced, and Talya's little hint of an accent is no doubt an acceptable, amusing bit of local eccentricity to the neighbors.

When Talya discovers Krozac has been released from jail, Paul reassures her that her new status can't be taken away from her. "Darling, you're hidden, you're hidden by 10 years and me and this house. . . . And nobody and nothing's gonna change that." The attainment of an assimilated American status, won through geographic mobility into the suburbs, intermarriage, and cultural erasure, could not be rolled back or taken away, white ethnics already hoped, by 1937.

It is, I think, not a stretch to argue that Talya's "whiteness" and suburbanness trump her Slavic accent and immigrant past. Karen Brodkin has convincingly stated the case for suburbanization as a key component in Jews' ascension into full American "whiteness" and acceptance in the years just before and after World War II, and in *The Last Gangster* race is subtly on display, as well.[100]

In another telling way the Krozac in Paul/Joe, Jr., and Talya has disappeared, too. The family retain the services of a stereotypical black maid, who humorously (at least circa 1937 humorously) hollers at mischievous Paul/Joe, Jr., "Hey, you crazy chickadee! You stay out of my lard bucket!" By this point it is the African-American maid who is the perpetual other, here comically, but soon, and as needed, an urban threat. Paul/Joe, Jr., is the master's son, and in comparison to the Aunt Jemima servant is just another white child (Talya, so far as we know, won't even bother teaching him a word of her language). These immigrant ethnics have achieved the American Dream, moving out to the suburbs, covering over their otherness, but as scholars such as David Roediger, Matthew Frye Jacobson, and George Lipsitz remind us, southern and eastern Europeans' achievements came at the expense of, and the distancing from, African-Americans.[101]

In a final touching scene, Krozac rescues Paul/Joe, Jr., from kidnappers, returning the child to his home. Paul/Joe, Jr., reassures his "parents" that Krozac is all right, even though his assertions of parentage to this all-American boy are taken for insanity. Still, Paul/Joe, Jr., is enough of a tolerant New Deal American to attribute Krozac's strange ways to a sadly deficient upbringing. "Sometimes he doesn't realize what he's saying," he explains to his American "parents." "But it's all right, Joe. You can talk to Mother and Dad. They're wonderful. You probably never had anyone like them because you wouldn't have had all the trouble you've had." Again it is ecology, a sad lack of a good home life, that explains for sympathetic Americans like Paul/Joe, Jr., the Krozacs among us. At film's end, Krozac leaves the home, a good ethnic at last in realizing his son will have a better chance in his WASP surroundings. The Production Code demanded that ruthless Joe Krozac die in a hale of bullets, but as he does, he clutches the Abraham Lincoln medal that his assimilated son has given him. The immigrant problem fades; in dying he is an American at last.[102]

After World War II, *Kiss of Death* would offer another portrait of a good ethnic, Nick Bianco—tellingly, his name is a sign of his aspiring whiteness—attempting to start over in the suburbs. His murderous former colleague, Tommy Udo, who displays suspiciously Hollywood psychotic/latent homosexual tendencies, hunts him down and forestalls the possibility of the "big man" starting his life over. Unlike Paul/Joe, Jr., Nick Bianco is not yet ready, or permitted, to make the leap to full whiteness and the suburbs.

Other urban pathologies are on display in film noir classics of the immediate postwar era, reflecting American phobias about new urban menaces. Homicidal rage still resides in the city, as Tommy Udo visits the "rat" Rizzo at his apartment near the Third Avenue El only to push his wheelchair-bound mother to her death in one of the most brutal film murders ever.[103] But the new gangster displays signs of effeminate psychosis, perhaps fitting in an era when many during the McCarthy era were just as worried about the homosexual "menace" as the communist threat.[104] Film noir explored the diseased mind of men such as Udo, who continually and sycophantically refers to Nick as "my pal the big man here," but tells his gun moll—named Buster—to get lost because "you can't have any fun no-how with dames." Those Udo despises are "squirts," whom he will shoot in the belly. He takes pleasure in watching crippled Mrs. Rizzo suffer and die. And every time Nick enters a room where Udo has been, he catches a suspicious whiff of perfume. Gangsters might be one thing, but those with maladjusted gender roles were a new breed of urban menace. We can think here, too, of Coady Jarrett, shouting, "Made it, Ma! Top of the world!" as he expires in a post-Hiroshima fireball in 1949's *White Heat*.[105]

At a time when the country's anticommunist crusade was hurtling ahead, cinematic cities faced new foreign threats. An exchange between Nick (played by Victor Mature) and District Attorney D'Angelo comments on the need for ruthlessness when going after the enemy. About to become an informer, but for the team of supposed virtue, Nick comments, "Your side of the fence is almost as dirty as mine." To which D'Angelo replies, "With one big difference. We hurt bad people, not good ones." It is 1947, after all, and the House Un-American Activities Committee (HUAC) was already asking "squealers" to name names. Being a rat no longer carried the same opprobrium as it had earlier, not if "hurting bad people" was the result. Likewise, *On the Waterfront*'s Terry Malloy (famously directed by Elia Kazan, who had testified against several supposed communists he knew in Hollywood in congressional hearings) realizes that there are higher codes of honor than being "deaf and dumb" in the face of waterfront corruption, and proclaims, "I ain't no bum!" (or rat, either) after following Father Barry's demands that he come clean. Indeed, Lee Bernstein has argued, the anticommunist and antigangster menaces were conflated in 1950s America, and *On the Waterfront* deftly combines these threats to America, too.[106]

The new urban menace of communism was metaphorically tackled in New Orleans by another Richard Widmark character, Doctor Reed, in *Panic in the Streets*. Here it is "the foreigner," who brings a plague into a city already reeking with shady characters of suspicious origins, such as the gamblers Poldi and Fitch (played by Tommy Cook and Zero Mostel). Merely by looking at a tissue sample on a corpse, Reed can tell that it belongs to a "foreigner," who has unleashed an epidemic upon an American city. Reed tells New Orleans' ignorant officials, "One of the jobs of my department is to keep the plague out of this country!" In 1950, trusting government operatives to quarantine a foreign menace to the city once again became holy gospel, and not coincidentally, the plague that enters New Orleans is spread first by a man the medical examiner is certain is an "Armenian, Czech, or mixed blood." As it turns out, it is an eastern European from communist Czechoslovakia who spreads this menace among other foreign quarters of the city. Moviegoers in 1950 no doubt made the parallels between a medical service doctor dismissing arguments that he is "an alarmist" for cutting a few corners and a senator from Wisconsin doing the same thing about another foreign threat.[107]

By 1953, even old-fashioned pickpockets and conmen, who twenty years earlier would have raised an alarm, were enlisted in a battle against the communist menace. Widmark once again is the tough-talking protagonist in *Pickup on South Street*, although here he's an honest, red-blooded New York thief enlisted, at first unwillingly, to stop a nest of Soviet spies from shipping a secret formula out of the country. His character, McCoy, grabs the formula out of the pocketbook of an unsuspecting dupe of the communists riding the subway. When an FBI agent tries to get him to help them, McCoy is at first uninterested. "If you refuse to cooperate, you'll be as guilty as the traitors who gave Stalin the A-Bomb," Agent Zara snaps. "Are you waving the flag at me?" McCoy snarls, and when he's asked if he knows what treason means, he asks, "Is there a law now I gotta listen to lectures?"[108]

By 1953 many audience members were hearing from Senator Joseph McCarthy and his many accomplices that if there wasn't a law, there ought to be, since many were told, by people like *Kiss of Death*'s D'Angelo, that only "bad people" would be hurt. Thieves and con artists are here portrayed as all-American—at least all–New York—types who can be relied upon in the end to resist this new foreign menace. The snitch Moe is asked if she'd "sell [McCoy] to a commie?" To which she snarls, "What do you think I am, an informer?" Moe then lectures McCoy, "What's a matter with you, playing footsie with the commies! . . . Listen, I know you since you was a little kid. You was always a regular kind of crook. I never figured you for a louse! Even in our crummy kind of business you gotta draw the line somewheres." A new line is drawn, and again the city is perceived as under assault.[109]

And yet, by the 1950s virtue had abandoned the city altogether. Federally subsidized, fixed-rate mortgages, courtesy of the Federal Housing Authority (FHA), had allowed millions of white Americans to flee the cities for the Levittowns sprouting up on their edges. On such well-manicured streets, it was possible to ignore the dysfunctional city, save on television crime dramas such as *Naked City,* which from 1958 to 1963 promised, "There are eight million stories in the naked city. This has been one of them." Individuated home ownership allowed some of these urban ills already to become voyeuristic entertainment, something to be watched and judged, but matters that couldn't possibly invade one's own living room directly. The show was filmed on the mean streets of New York, and might be regarded as the slightly tamer grandfather of *Cops*.[110]

The silence these suburbs really concealed was that, courtesy of federally sanctioned redlining, new homes in "good school districts" were available only to white Americans. Blacks were denied FHA-approved mortgages well into the 1970s, and those few blacks who tried to move into white enclaves in cities such as Detroit, Philadelphia, and Chicago faced angry crowds, "neighborhood improvement associations" demanding they leave, fire bombings, and worse. Yet most of these devices—both the subsidization of white flight to the suburbs and the devices, both governmental and extralegal, by which blacks and Latinos were contained in ghettoized, older city neighborhoods—were ignored in the 1950s media. The national story line of individual success via hard work leading to home ownership in a little Levittown was rarely broken by discussion of such uncomfortable realities.[111]

Hollywood, too, was mostly silent and decidedly uninterested in matters of race throughout the 1950s. The menace to the suburbs is frequently portrayed, but rarely explicitly spelled out in racial terms. One such powerful cinematic threat to the suburbs wears the face of Humphrey Bogart. In his next to last film, *The Desperate Hours* (1955), he plays yet another savage criminal, Glen Griffin, who with his convict brother and the apelike, brutal Sam Kobish escapes from jail and takes a respectable middle-class family hostage in their own cul de sac home. Ominous music opens the movie as a limousine carrying the escaped convicts prowls the streets of neat, comfortable suburban Indianapolis. Something dangerous is afoot, and the American home is under threat.

After the gang takes the respectable Hilliards hostage in their own home, the apelike Kobish is amazed by but resentful of the opulence of this cul de sac castle, something he's never experienced. Its three bedrooms and two bathrooms delight him. "What a layout!" he gushes, but then sets about smashing the family's furniture in an angry search for their liquor cabinet. Kobish wrecks the house when he gets angry, resenting those who have achieved the American Dream on full display.

The housewife, Ellie, as well as Deputy Sheriff Bard, expresses the new suburbanites' belief that there are some people who clearly don't belong. "The house is crawling with them!" she complains to her husband, and the deputy sheriff begins his manhunt for the escapees by targeting a seedy, rundown part of Indianapolis. The menace, it is presumed, resides in the heart of the inner city, for evidently it is inconceivable to Bard that "the wrong sort" can already have infiltrated the suburbs. Later, Bard complains of Dan Hilliard's attempts to reason with the gang: "The idiot! Doesn't he know you can't play ball with savages like that?!"

Indeed, the gang know they don't fit in to this world of extra bedrooms and big backyards. They belch, break furniture, forget to use coasters, and express hostile resentment of the Hilliards' comfortable middle-class life. When Dan Hilliard objects to Glen's demands that his wife fix the gangsters' dinner, he sputters, "My wife's not your servant!" But of course African-Americans, we have already seen, were even serving Krozacs in disguise by 1937, and we might legitimately wonder just who keeps Dan's living room so immaculate. Griffin, though, reacts with class-based envy. "Listen, Hilliard, you ain't calling the tune!" he hollers. "I got my guts full of you shiny-shoed, down-your-nose wiseguys with white handkerchiefs in your pocket!" Griffin's younger brother, although he realizes they don't fit in, is less resentful of the family than his brother, who he agrees taught him "everything," "except how to live in a house like this." Glen Griffin again snarls at "Mr. Hilliard," one of the "smart-eyed, respectable suckers" who tell the convicts, "You ain't fit to live with decent folk. Decent!" At which he again smashes their furniture. It is only at film's end that Dan is able to regain the upper hand and expel the interlopers from his house. "Get out of my house!" he exultantly hollers, as suburban order is once more restored.[112]

American cinema still in the 1950s, as it had been in the 1930s, tiptoed around race, the color line that W.E.B. Du Bois had persuasively argued forty years earlier would define the twentieth century. But whether the brutal Kobish and sullen, resentful Glen Griffin are "whiteface" stand-ins for a racial threat or merely lower-class boors who don't belong in this idyllic subdivision, it is clear in 1955 America that such suburbs are built and marketed on exclusion. The unexpressed fear that the city and its pathologies—crime, ethnic others, lower-class problems of all kinds—might intrude into these minimum-acreage paradises is given vent in this film.[113]

The likelihood, though, is that by 1955 even someone named Kobish would be accepted into the new suburbs—much native-born resentment of Slavic, Jewish, and other white ethnics melting away, or at least taking a backseat to the white-black binary as new communities were created courtesy of redlining. While scholars going back at least to Will Herberg noted that Jewish, Catholic, and Protestant Americans often assimilated into separate, confessional communities, other writers have recently persuasively argued that post–World War II suburbanization powerfully effaced ethnic and confessional differences that only a few years earlier had seemed great. A Kobish would no doubt be acceptable, even in Dan Hilliard's part of Indianapolis—provided he remembered to use a coaster and not his gat.[114]

The problem of racialized exclusion, though, persisted. One of the few major films of the era to confront it was *A Raisin in the Sun*, which in 1961 adapted Lorraine Hansberry's powerful 1959 play to the screen. The Youngers aspire to escape Chicago's black ghetto and buy a little house, with a vegetable garden out back, in all-white Clyburn Park. Miss Ruth displays a moving faith that, in spite of all the troubles they face, their family, like her struggling little plant, will take root in its new home.

The white businessman who offers to buy them out so that the white residents of Clyburn Park can "have their community the way they want it" had his real-life analogues in postwar Chicago, and other cities, and they often used less gentle means than are on display here. During World War II white residents of Detroit neighborhoods erected flag-bedecked billboards proclaiming, "This is a WHITE neighborhood," and developers later built concrete barricades to separate white and black sections of the city so that white home buyers might still enjoy FHA-backed mortgages. In 1951 Slavic Philadelphians in the Point Breeze section, led by their priest, barricaded a work site to prevent public housing being built for "these undesirable outsiders." As early as 1943, and then again more explosively in 1946, 1951, and 1953, the white residents of areas such as South Chicago's Trumbull Park area firebombed the home of the first prospective African-American residents, and brutal resistance to open-housing ordinances would continue in Chicago and other cities through the 1960s. In the very week in 1954 that the U.S. Supreme Court declared "separate but equal" segregated schools unconstitutional, *The Nation* was denouncing the ongoing white assaults on blacks moving into South Chicago. Indeed, what Thomas Sugrue, Arnold Hirsch, Matthew Frye Jacobson, and others have identified as a white ethnic backlash to black advancement was already in full flower by the time the Youngers were moving in.[115]

By the latter part of the 1960s it was impossible to ignore the urban crisis, as blacks no longer accepted the easy ghettoization and brutal resistance by whites to their aspirations to live, work, and go to school where they chose. Deindustrialization, too, accompanied white flight, leaving cities poorer, more violent places (although an incredible amnesia developed among white Americans, who conveniently forgot the demonization of a Detroit full of murderous Jewish and Italian criminals in the Purple Gang, or the fear Brownsville, Brooklyn, with its Murder Inc., evoked in the hearts of native-born New Yorkers). In the comfortable era of Eisenhower's America, most white Americans were unaware of—or at least unconcerned by—the problems that were percolating in their cities, and this was reflected in most 1950s cinematic portraits of the city, where blacks were by and large absent. As the civil rights and later Black Power movements built to a crescendo, though, the popular depiction of the city changed yet again, and this time it was not a Krozac or Kobish who was perceived as a threat to the country, but a new type of urban American.

4

"Certain Sociological Realities There": A City for the 1960s and Beyond

In the fall of 1963 a television show debuted that promised to expose the ills of a city deep in crisis. *East Side/West Side* featured George C. Scott and Cicely Tyson as social workers in the slums of New York. Over the course of the series Neil Brock (Scott) and Jane Foster (Tyson) dealt with the problems of the Manhattan slums in a sophisticated and honest way quite unlike anything television viewers had hitherto seen. The show also gave Americans their first look at African-American actors who would go on to greater acclaim. In an episode titled "Who Do You Kill?" a frustrated ghetto father is played by James Earl Jones. The decaying tenements of Harlem seem to embody the frustration of Joe and Ruth, recent migrants from North Carolina who barely make ends meet through Ruth's evening bartending job at a grim neighborhood dive. Joe cares for their baby son, but the very built environment of the couple's apartment and neighborhood makes it evident they are falling through the cracks of Camelot's affluent America.

As would be the case throughout the series, shooting on this episode was done on the streets of New York, a rarity as yet in the sound stage era of television production, and the garbage-strewn lots, crumbling tenement ceilings, and dangerous hoodlums loitering on Joe and Ruth's corner offering unemployed men the escape of "the needles, the pipe jobs" lent an air of Harlem realism to the show.

Then there were the rats, insistently squealing in Joe and Ruth's walls. "Listen to them," Joe complains to his wife as they gnaw through the walls of his dream castle. "It's their house. Not ours." The rats echo the grim opening of Richard Wright's novel of Chicago ghetto life, *Native Son*, in which Bigger Thomas battles to keep the vermin from his child's crib. A proletarian novel of the late 1930s might be expected to expose such inequities of American society, but for television dramas such issues were as yet a rarity.[1]

When the couple's baby is attacked by rats, Joe rushes him to an emergency room, but he dies. Enraged, Joe acquires a weapon and roams the streets looking for someone—slumlord, politician, anyone—on whom to exact vengeance. In the end, the tension is resolved as social worker Brock agrees with the enraged father that no white man can really understand the ghetto residents' pain, while a black minister dubiously counsels patience and laughter as the best weapons for overcoming poverty and oppression. As on later episodes, some of the dynamite the series lit was defused rather than exploded. Joe suffers and endures; unlike Bigger Thomas he does not kill. Nevertheless, the powerful topic of slum inequities had been placed on the prime-time table, even if the show couldn't quite deliver a realistic conclusion to the dilemmas it had raised.

Subsequent episodes featured a black prostitute who is confronted by child welfare agencies when she is deemed an unfit mother; corrupt city politicians, and young, rebellious free spirits of an urban counterculture (although evidently television writers suffered from a time lag, for they still fretted, in an episode featuring a young Barbara Feldon, about a "beatnik" invasion). Another installment dealt with a middle-class black couple's attempts to flee the unpleasant city by purchasing a home in a Long Island suburb. However, they discover that for African-Americans, the FHA's redlining practices and the unwelcome mat of white homeowners' societies resisting integration as bitterly as any Alabama sheriff really do offer them "No Place to Hide."

The couple, played by Earle Hyman and Ruby Dee, are exemplary, middle-class residents in every way—the television forebears of Bill Cosby's Cliff and Claire Huxtable—but the episode nevertheless details the enraged reaction of white residents to the news the first black family is moving into their community. Cynical real estate agents are shown pouncing on the community, hoping to impel panic selling by the white residents and then turning around to offer the same modest homes to black families at obscenely inflated prices. The subject of blockbusting, racial steering, and whites-only vigilantes seeking to keep "outsiders" from entering the community were all subjects familiar to readers of *The Nation*, the *New York Times,* and other serious journals, for as we've seen, Detroit, Chicago, Philadelphia, and other cities had already exploded in white-on-black violence as the Great Migration brought nonwhites to these cities. But fiction programs had not yet approached anything as explosive as this topic. Not until Archie Bunker circulated a petition to keep the Jeffersons from moving into his Queens neighborhood would any show again broach this topic in such a realistic manner.[2]

If anything, *East Side/West Side* was still a few years ahead of its time. Viewers slowly adjusting their conception of what a city should be, and how much of that reality should seep into their living room, proved unreceptive to the series. By the following spring the series was dead, a casualty of indifferent viewers.

Such a disturbing view of the city disappeared—at least from prime time. Very few Americans, evidently, were much interested in having reality intrude into the time that had so far been set aside for entertainment of a more escapist variety. Then, too, an honest depiction of race relations, growing black civil rights demands, and urban poverty was more than many Americans wanted to see addressed. Twenty-six southern affiliates refused to carry the program, the show's depiction of an integrated workplace more than station managers could tolerate. The state of Georgia, too, absolutely banned the screening of the "Who Do You Kill?" episode over the Atlanta station; Shreveport, Louisiana, also declined to air this episode.[3]

But even in the North the show was more beloved by critics than viewers. While the *New York Times*'s Jack Gould praised the "Who Do You Kill?" episode in particular as one of television's rare successful forays into "the drama of protest," regular viewers didn't flock to a program with rat-infested apartments, white ethnics assaulting the first blacks on the block, and prostitutes battling child welfare agencies. In a programming year that saw Martin Luther King's "I Have a Dream" speech, a president's assassination, and then the nation's first major black disturbances in cities of the North, a show that dealt with racism, slumlords, prostitutes, blockbusting, and endemic ghetto poverty did not in the end find much of a receptive audience. Critics were mixed in their reviews, although most championed the show's bravery in presenting some of the thorny issues facing real social workers in places like New York.[4]

Perhaps the 1960s, though, had not yet begun in earnest, or maybe the public already wanted to put urban reality on permanent hold (nothing like *Cops* had yet created, or catered to, a voyeuristic thrill seeking among television viewers). Being labeled gritty was still a kiss of death, not yet a promise of winning the ratings jackpot, and after one season *East Side/West Side* faded to black.[5]

Indeed, if other television writers had wanted to, there was plenty of material readily on hand for a dozen spinoffs of this gritty urban drama, and most of the issues raised on the show were reflections of the transformation altering American cities in deleterious ways. Following World War II, demographic and economic tidal waves transformed cities into very different places than they had been at the dawn of the 1930s. The Great Migration of African-Americans from the rural South to midwestern and northeastern metropolises, interrupted by the Depression, proceeded apace, but the nonwhite newcomers were bitterly resented and resisted. Clashes between ethnic and racial groups grew fiercer as African-Americans began to demand the full benefits of citizenship so long denied them, and white ethnics in cities such as Chicago, Detroit, Boston, and Philadelphia violently resisted the attempts by nonwhites to move into their residential neighborhoods. The violently anti-integrationist mobs that greeted blacks attempting to move into South Chicago and other areas continued in many cities through the 1950s, 1960s, and even early 1970s, culminating in the antibusing movement in South Boston, Charlestown, East Boston, and other working-class neighborhoods.[6]

At the same time that urban demographics were changing a long, steady process of economic impoverishment through government action and inaction bled city mayors of needed resources to provide services for their constituents. To be sure, as we've seen, Chicago, New York, and other cities had always contained infamous slums, but they also contained a multiplicity of industrial job sites, churches, and other social institutions that offered at least the possibility of serving as engines of economic mobility. What Theodore Hershberg and his collaborators have termed "the opportunity structure"—the array of job sites, social-support agencies, and other human capital in a particular time and place—offered working-class city dwellers a greater number of options for attaining some level of security, especially after the gains of unionization and other programs of the New Deal were solidified.

But even earlier, what might seem a slum from outside the neighborhood was often a complex web of poverty, prosaic working-class residents, and small ethnic entrepreneurs, a much more nuanced city mosaic than ever emerged in contemporary popular culture, as Olivier Zunz demonstrates for Polish, German, and Irish enclaves in 1880–1900 Detroit.

Following World War II, increasingly these resources fled cities along with suburbanizing middle-class whites. The opportunity structure left to blacks in post-1945 Detroit, Chicago, and other cities was much more impoverished than it had been for white ethnics in previous decades.

Of course, in novels, magazine stories, and, later, films, such working-class entrepreneurship was often ignored even in the 1900 city, in favor of the flashier story line that criminality, poverty, and other urban ills offered to writers. But the point remains that after World War II black urbanites faced longer odds of making it, with even less likelihood that they might receive sympathetic treatment from fiction writers.[7]

Indeed, for Detroit, Chicago, and even New York, in the aftermath of World War II, the picture radically changed. Those who had made it into the middle class were encouraged through federal economic inducements to flee cities—increasingly identified with crime and nonwhite interlopers, in any case—for a monoclass suburban nirvana. Those who had benefited from the New Deal—primarily white, primarily male—were swayed by government policy, programs and tax codes, as well as newspaper and magazine editorials and advertising on radio and television—to transport their gains to the newly emerging suburbs and remove themselves from the cities. Madison Avenue encouraged the relatively affluent to "see the USA" in their Chevrolet. Driving that Chevrolet out of the nation's Newarks, Philadelphias, or Brooklyns and into a suburban Levittown driveway was a good start.

But it wasn't just a matter of new lifestyle choices, freely arrived at by individual consumers; government agencies simply made the new members of the white middle class an offer they couldn't refuse. Federal government policies on mortgage subsidies for new home buyers made all the sense in the world for individual consumers. But in the aggregate, and combined with other government policies and business trends, they amounted to a bad deal for the cities.

Uncle Sam doled out tax breaks for businesses investing in new plant construction in suburban locales (and eventually, starting in 1965, to Mexico and other countries); federal construction of freeways and defunding of interurban mass transit bled older cities of middle-class homeowners, ratables (taxable property), and industries that paid a living wage to those who remained in the inner city. Freeways, subsidized FHA mortgages, Pell Grants, and before that GI loans for college guaranteed to certain Americans (whites) a hasty exit from the city and all that urban Rorschach inkblots like Harlem, Newark, and the Bronx implied.

Manufacturing declines in cities such as Detroit, Chicago, and New York has-tened in the three decades following World War II, leaving behind lower-wage, nonunionized work sites for the increasingly nonwhite populations of these and other cities. Yet these discomforting economic realities by and large flew under the nation's radar screen, shielded from view as they were by the rising gross national product and the suburbanized prosperity of much of the nation. When Michael Harrington published his sociological exposé of the nation's hidden poverty, *The Other America*, in 1962 it was greeted by many Americans with surprise. The dis-covery that all boats were not rising in Eisenhower's reign, or the sunny Camelot that followed, came as a great shock to many Americans.[8]

How could they have been so deluded? Although newspapers sometimes duti-fully recorded the racial strife in white enclaves such as Chicago's Deering Park that felt besieged, they did so on the inside pages, and other urban ills only slowly percolated into the news cycle.[9] Yet increasingly Americans turned to their televi-sion sets to serve as arbiters of their social realities. And very little of this urban verity made it onto the small screen for at least the first fifteen years of the new medium's commercial operations. Cities may have been suffering a PR crisis just as television was coming into its own, but most programs chose to deal with the eroding stature of the city by ignoring it. Cities' increasing relative irrelevance to many American consumers' concerns had led by the early 1960s to either absence of accurate urban pictures or, later, after about 1966, a demonization of the dark and dysfunctional city.

Television had already fallen into a paradigm of an escapist entertainment- and consumer-driven model. Avoid controversy, seemed to be the industry's rule of thumb, at least so far as much of its nonnews programming was concerned, and a racialized, urban menace was the last thing that networks wished to present to their consumers/customers. When FCC Chairman Newton Minow complained that television had become a "great cultural wasteland," in spite of its early promise to inform, not just entertain, the public, he might have been thinking of the networks' sparse coverage of the accurate urban scene.[10]

The Eisenhower era may have contained far more discontent and unease with the status quo than consensus historiography has previously led scholars to believe. However, based on the nation's film, and especially its television, viewing habits, suburban homeowners of the 1950s, and even the first half of the 1960s, preferred not to examine too closely the accurate state of the cities they had left behind. A cityscape that at best was nostalgic and reassuring, at worst escapist and unin-formed, greeted the nightly viewer. The freeways, minimum-acreage zoning policies, and racial steering by real estate brokers that created self-contained bastions of consensus were reflected, too, in the programming decisions of the television networks for America's new medium in popular entertainment and urban masquerading. Little that emanated from the family's television set disturbed the class- and race-segregated Potemkin villages that were being created on the periphery of America's Eisenhower era cities.[11]

Marshall McLuhan has famously criticized television for being a cool medium, for the most part uninterested in disrupting its audiences' complacencies and predispositions. When it came to America's metropolises, little that troubled the viewer made its way on-screen. The voyeuristic pleasures of *Cops*, *CSI*, and *Homicide: Life on the Streets* were still three decades away. The insular Manichean view of television's cities as the absolute evil to be kept from the wholesome home with only minimal, rational policing prevailed.[12]

Rather than the nuanced portrayal offered on *East Side/West Side*, cities on television crime dramas were purely evil places that could be safely contained. Although the shabby inner-city exteriors (especially in shows such as *Naked City*, which like *East Side/West Side* was shot by cameraman Jack Priestly on location in Manhattan) provided graphic physical reminders of a landscape of despair, every week the dark crimes of the noir city were conquered by the detectives of *Naked City*'s Sixty-fifth Precinct. Moreover, even such a relatively high-quality show shied away from any in-depth coverage of urban issues, and the violence and ethnic strife—indeed, even the black presence—here were kept to a minimum. Still, the somber feel of the streets on which the series was filmed provided a weekly reminder of the proximity of decay or, for viewers tuning in from outside the cities, the unproximity of crumbling apartment buildings and all they connoted. If slum streets appalled earlier ethnographers like Riis, the very tenements' disarray standing in for moral chaos and criminality, by 1958 these dwellings and streets had had sixty more years of wear and tear, and the comparison was even more insidious for the new residents of cul de sacs. The "naked city" might have had six million stories, as its announcer promised, but many viewers may have concluded that ghetto streets were fine for one nightly cursory viewing, but not for too realistic or discomfiting an analysis of urban problems.[13]

Naked City at least made a stab at approaching a serious discussion of urban issues, and the fact it was filmed on location on New York's streets, where extras were recruited from among local residents, added some air of honest urban realism to the program. Much as D. W. Griffith availed himself of slum dwellers when finding extras for *The Musketeers of Pig Alley*, though, the portrait these later New Yorkers presented was not necessarily a flattering exhibit of the Big Apple. The show was, after all, a crime drama, so prosaic scenes of law-abiding inner-city denizens were by and large absent.[14]

Moreover, the role of institutionalized racism in turning cities into more impoverished places than they had otherwise previously been for the most part went unquestioned. Indeed, how could it be otherwise if even an otherwise gritty show such as *Naked City* offered few African-American actors? In both the evisceration of race matters and the foregrounding of crime matters, the show was indicative of the way television treated the city in the 1950s and early 1960s.

Other shows would provide even starker depictions of a city in need of an army of old-school policemen, without even *Naked City*'s occasional attempts to provide the context behind some of the urban lawlessness that it displayed. The original *Dragnet* in the 1950s, for example, represented a fairly monochromatic (white) Los Angeles, in which no-nonsense, "just the facts, ma'am" Sergeant Joe Friday almost effortlessly restored order to his city, which seemed to be very much in need of his cool expertise considering the array of harried and helpless eccentric crime witnesses he and his partner confronted.

In *Dragnet*, as in so many shows that followed, crime was presented as an individual pathology, something that had to be quarantined or defanged in a logical, dispassionate manner. It was not Joe Friday's job to comment on the larger sociological factors—poverty, deindustrialization, and white racism among them—that may have caused a particular episode's criminal to turn out the way he did. Then, too, Friday and Officer Frank Smith patrolled Los Angeles, a city that had already seen official complicity in the criminalization/demonization of its Mexican residents during World War II, when innocent residents were dragged into jails en masse in the Sleepy Lagoon murder case. Politicians likewise labeled all zoot suiters wild, rebellious, and oversexed criminals for their outlandish hipster outfits of tight-fitting, loud-colored pants and broad-brimmed hats, and then looked the other way when on-leave naval officers and other white Angelinos beat up Mexican city residents, and black sailors, too, indiscriminately. And just over the horizon, Watts was ready to erupt, and when it did in 1965, it caught Sergeant Friday, and the city power structure he represented, completely by surprise.

None of these uncomfortable, racialized features of "the city, Los Angeles, California," made it onto Joe Friday's radar screen or the small screen, even though the zoot suit riots were only twelve years in the past when *Dragnet* debuted, and surely at least some African-American or Hispanic viewers remembered and noticed this lacuna in the televised story. These demographic considerations and accurate depictions of the urban problems of postwar Los Angeles were for the most part missing from Joe Friday's beat.[15]

Indeed, the show's myopic depiction of Los Angeles was not an isolated event, either in television or in the real city. Friday and his partners—first Smith and then in the 1960s and early 1970s Bill Gannon—strode through a department that was monochromatically white, in both avatars, and even the city residents confronted by the partners were unreflective of a city that by 1970 was majority-minority. Although the announcer assured viewers that "the story you are about to see is true" and pulled from the files of the real-life Los Angeles Police Department, the stories seemed frozen in a film noir city of an earlier era.[16]

The same television myopia continued on *The Streets of San Francisco,* which in the mid-1970s had a twenty-year grizzled veteran (played by Karl Malden) still using detective methods seemingly first perfected by Sam Spade. Even his fedora harked back to another era, and while *Dragnet* and *The Streets of San Francisco* sometimes made reference to hippies, student radicals, and other signifiers of the late 1960s and 1970s, the paladins of law and order were almost anachronisms. Or maybe they were meant to serve as preservers of a supposed old-time moral order in an era when many viewers wondered what was becoming of the nation's cities. As Henry Taylor and Carol Dozier have argued, televised depictions of police and other forms of state-sanctioned violence from the 1950s and 1960s often had a conservative purpose, "legitimiz[ing] the use of violence—including deadly force—by those who defend the status quo, and reinforces the idea that the police are the good guys, altruistically dedicated to the protection of society from evildoers."[17]

While by the time of *San Francisco* other shows had made a more honest effort to look into some of the causes for supposed urban decline, *San Francisco* remained popular with many who preferred a Manichean city in which old-time hoodlums were vanquished by taciturn tough guys with a badge, G-men updated for a new era. As they strode through chaotic cities, such straight-arrow, no-nonsense older white cops as *San Francisco*'s Lieutenant Mike Stone seemed to be men out of their element, colonial administrators bent on keeping order among an unruly foreign populace.

Indeed, this was the way that many African-American urbanites saw the police forces in their real-life cities. Recruitment of black police officers lagged far behind the new demographics of cities such as Detroit, Newark, Philadelphia, and Los Angeles, so that when the first (at least as noticed by white Americans) race riots erupted beginning in 1964, one of the loudest complaints by blacks to the new city commissions on race relations established in the riots' wake was that police were viewed as occupying armies that shared little sympathy or understanding with ghetto residents of the dilemmas they faced. Since metropolitan police forces such as those of Los Angeles, Detroit, and Newark only had a handful of African-American police officers, virtually none promoted to officer or supervisor status until the late 1960s, ghetto residents may have been justified in condemning police departments as unsympathetic at best, predatory at worst.[18]

Dragnet boasted that it was assisted in its production by an official adviser from the Los Angeles Police Department, but since the decades of abrasive relations between that department under Chief Darryl Gates and his predecessors was a festering sore of resentment to many blacks in Watts, this boast perhaps only underscored the fabricated nature of *Dragnet*, so far as many real Los Angelinos were concerned. It wasn't until the savage, real-life beating of Rodney King in 1991 and the subsequent rioting that some of the shortcomings of Gates, and his law-and-order emulator Joe Friday, became apparent.[19]

Rodney King's unscheduled prime-time appearance, though, was a long way away, and whatever program one watched, save on certain news broadcasts, one could by and large avoid too unpleasant a picture of L.A., New York, and other cities. One way to deal with urban ills was to indulge in fits of laughter, pretending that nothing much to worry about was going on in places such as Brooklyn or the Bronx. *Car 54, Where Are You?* presented an almost ludicrously zany Bronx pair of policemen, who presided over a corner of this New York borough that already by 1961 bore little resemblance to the real city. While main characters Muldoon and Toody were joined in their precinct by two black officers, played by Nipsey Russell and Frederick O'Neal, they expressed few complaints about their treatment or status either in the department or the city at large. Little realistic city texture existed in this show, where the most accurate comment on the contemporary city came in the comedic theme song ("There's a holdup in the Bronx, Brooklyn's broken out in fights"). Unlike the far grittier *East Side/West Side*, the show virtually ignored the problems the real New York was tentatively handling at this time.[20]

To say the least, the Bronx in the early 1960s already was a more complex place than that patrolled by the buffoonish Muldoon and Toody. Within five years, the South Bronx would become a national symbol of urban disorder; a short time later, Jimmy Carter kicked off his presidential bid from Charlotte Street, promising not to ignore the plight of the Bronx and its peers in urban misfortune. By this point, one would have thought that light urban fairy-tale comedies were an endangered species, and indeed television and movie dramas had by this point promoted franker cityscapes.

Yet other shows followed in the vein of *Car 54*, and even throughout the 1970s and into the early 1980s urban crime was sometimes portrayed as a tame matter indeed. Reassuring a nation during a time the South Bronx became a national symbol of urban disorder, one brand of televised urban police show continued with strains of light comedy as a way of laughing past the urban graveyard; we might call this the *Barney Miller* approach. At the height of New York's fiscal meltdown, Son of Sam serial killings, and blackout-assisted record crime waves, Captain Miller and his multicultural precinct usually dealt with problems no more pressing than squabbling tenants and landlords, tourists victimized by purse snatchers, and such. The lockup at this precinct was surely, like Muldoon's early 1960s Bronx, a paradise of avoidance of real urban issues.[21]

In the wake of the urban disturbances of the late 1960s and early 1970s many more somber and violently graphic depictions of urban lawlessness and collapse appeared on television and especially in blaxploitation films and other movies such as *The French Connection, Death Wish, The Taking of Pelham One Two Three,* and *Taxi Driver*. These dramas might be regarded as lineal descendants of the blunt and voyeuristic magazine exposés and tours of ethnic exotica in the Progressive Era magazines and newspapers.

Yet perhaps because actually seeing filmed footage of such urban problems was more disturbing than merely reading about them as earlier generations had done in magazines such as *The Century* or *Harper's* (with at most an illustration or grainy staged slum photograph), many preferred the unrelenting urban film loop to be interrupted by something more akin to earlier vaudeville stagings of the city. Television comedies of urban ethnic clowns, whether in *Barney Miller's* precinct house or *Welcome Back, Kotter's* Brooklyn high school classroom, had an enduring history of assisting nonurbanites to laugh away the problems of the city. Teacher Gabe Kotter or Detective Dietrich could mention New York's pervasive crime or garbage-filled streets and be assured of a hearty chuckle on canned laugh tracks. The urban ills of New York, Chicago, Detroit, and other cities by the 1970s were for many Americans little more than punch lines.[22]

Earlier, other urban shows placed lawlessness safely in a nostalgic bubble, where it could be mythologized as something belonging to a distant past as viewers pretended all was well in the contemporary city they had fled. *The Untouchables*, by setting white criminality in Chicago's past, contains it as a historical oddity peculiar to the Prohibition mistake, something settled. Nostalgia and use of devices such as narrative and period setting and clothing create the illusion that for all of the violence in the 1920s city, this was a bygone problem. By focusing on gangland hits thirty-five years old, the show created a fictional case that such gangland mayhem no longer existed in the Eisenhower era city. Walter Winchell's voiceover breathlessly tells his public of the exploits of Elliot Ness, stories that already by 1960 might be recalled by viewers as tales their parents told them about a place long ago and already by now far away. Current-day Chicago and its problems, if any, need not concern the viewer.

These crime dramas, like the gangster films that followed about a decade later, functioned as nostalgic recollections of bygone eras. In imagined places in which the disruptions of a few lawbreakers could be quickly contained, nostalgic glimpses back at an earlier, more supposedly blood-soaked metropolis such as Ness's Chicago assured viewers all was right with the present. No purveyors of televised fiction during the Eisenhower era provided an honest look at 1950s Chicago, in which, as we noted at the end of the last chapter, white ethnic homeowners frequently rioted when blacks attempted to move into their neighborhoods.[23]

The approach paved by Ness, as portrayed by Robert Stack, was further developed a decade later as the first sophisticated historical gangster films, beginning with *The Godfather*, situated white ethnic criminality three or so decades removed from the moment of filming. By the early 1970s the point of reference was the supposedly more lawless ghetto of the post-civil-rights era, and now bygone white ethnic criminality, by comparison, looked explicable, even praiseworthy. In Don Corleone's immigrant Hell's Kitchen, crime could be explained away as part of immigrant striving after economic security and acceptance as full citizens in the republic. Perhaps because he had been defeated so long ago, the historical gangster now wasn't so much a threat, rather a fuzzy tintype of a supposedly better city, at least compared to the context of racialized and class-stratified angst the current, penurious New York was undergoing in the early 1970s. The silent signifier against which such films were measured remained contemporary majority-minority cities and their seemingly more intractable problems, and compared to all the long, hot summers the country had endured, Don Corleone didn't seem half bad.[24]

While gangland Chicago and New York had raised alarm bells as to a foreign menace threatening the nation during the real 1920s and 1930s, by now southern and eastern Europeans were well on the way to full suburban American citizenship, and already by 1960 new urban threats, which could not be so easily contained by Elliot Ness and Walter Winchell, were lurking in the background. Popular culture for the most part still preferred not to deal with these racial and urban dilemmas, and continued battling the ghost of Al Capone.

Mostly, though, McLuhan's "cool medium" preferred not to traffic in too great an examination of either crime or race and ethnicity. If it did address urban lawlessness, humor or a long lens of nostalgia was used, but even these forays into the heart of urban darkness were rare. Urban police shows such as *Naked City* or *East Side/West Side* were few and far between. And in the 1950s and early 1960s the easiest way, it seemed, for network programmers to deal with the contemporary city was to laugh it away, via ethnic comedy.[25]

In 1951 the radio comedy *Amos 'n' Andy* was transported to television. On radio the all-black characters had been performed by the series' white creators, Freeman Gosden and Charles Correll, and other white actors. The show was the culmination of the minstrel tradition of mocking supposedly lazy, conniving, sybaritic, and argumentative blacks. From the vaudeville stage to humble immigrant church halls to the Hollywood big screen, minstrelsy had proved enormously popular with white audiences, who, George Lipsitz argues, could "attribute to black people the characteristics that it feared most in itself." This process of what Eric Lott calls "love and theft" of white-imposed images of an imagined hedonistic black culture was especially prevalent, it seems, with immigrant groups such as Slavs and Jews, which even in the early 1950s had, as yet, only a tenuous hold on their "whiteness," and who on their arrival in America had been stigmatized as "Asiatic" or "Oriental" interlopers in the nation.

Many immigrants were new to the discipline of the industrial workforce in factories of the urban Northeast, and resented the strict work discipline necessary in the Victorian workplace, especially in America, the "land of the time clocks." By associating the repressed desire for psychic goods (leisure time, pleasure) that one could not have with the reviled black "underclass," white voyeurs at the minstrel show could both have their subversive fun and repress and mock it, too, as part of the shiftless American racial pariah's deviant culture. Such racial voyeurism and masquerade had pernicious consequences in the real world, as when Democratic senators during the New Deal justified relief payments that were lower for blacks than whites since blacks could live on less and were bad at managing money anyway. Such conclusions were perhaps drawn at least in part from the antics of *Amos 'n' Andy* and other blackface comics.[26]

Now the shiftless stereotypes came to television, and when they did, Gosden and Correll hired black actors to play the lazy Harlem cab driver of the Fresh Air Cab Co., his dim-witted pal, and the bombastic charlatan Kingfish and his loud, argumentative (thus "unfeminine" by the light of postwar America) wife, Sapphire. The Kingfish in particular seemed a throwback to the racial cartoons of the late nineteenth century and early twentieth century. A street hustler with elite pretensions and a highfalutin', malaprop-filled vocabulary, he wasted all his time at the Mystic Knights of the Sea lodge rather than work at any visible means of support. So far as the show was concerned life in Harlem was one big con game, with little redemptive value shown in this patch of the city.[27]

The show was a ratings success, but many black organizations objected to the caricatures on display. The New York branch of the NAACP threatened to call a boycott of the program's sponsor, Blatz Brewing Company, and the NAACP criticized the show at its 1951 national convention. The national organization later issued a paper, "Why the *Amos 'n' Andy* TV Show Should Be Taken off the Air." Among the points the group raised were:

- It tends to strengthen the conclusion among uninformed and prejudiced people that Negroes are inferior, lazy, dumb and dishonest.

- Every character in this one and only TV show with an all-Negro cast is either a clown or a crook.
- Negro women are shown as cackling, screaming shrews, in big-mouth close-ups, using street slang, just short of vulgarity.
- All Negroes are shown as dodging work of any kind.
- Since many whites never met any Negroes personally, never attend any lectures or read any books on the race problem, or belong to any clubs or organizations where intergroup relations are discussed, they accept the *Amos 'n'Andy* picture as the true one.

Other blacks accepted the show as reminiscent of the kind of broad satire night-club comics had performed before audiences at all-black venues such as Harlem's Apollo Theater. Most of the show's cast members were indeed veterans of the black burlesque circuit, where characters such as Kingfish were popular comic types. Donald Bogle has argued that "black audiences accepted the exaggeration as precisely that and not as anything real," while George Lipsitz has noted that some black viewers enjoyed seeing black actors who comically rejected the Protestant work ethic or Talented Tenth message of making it through hard work. The writer Julius Lester recalled that

in the character of Kingfish, the creators of Amos and Andy may have thought they were ridiculing blacks as lazy, shiftless, scheming and conniving, but to us Kingfish was a para-digm of virtue, an alternative to the work ethic. Kingfish lived: Amos made a living. It did not matter that my parents lived by and indoctrinated me with the Puritan work ethic; Kingfish had a joie de vivre no white person could poison, and we knew that whites ridi-culed us because they were incapable of such elan. I was proud to belong to the same race as Kingfish.[28]

Something of the same evocation of the subversive/liberating potential of hip-hop and gangsta rap would be expressed by some black commentators, even as others worried, like 1950s activists, about the bad image reinforcing white prejudices of lazy, or worse, black urbanites. In Lipsitz's evocative phrase, there certainly is the potential in television comedies and much other popular culture for the possibility of "sedimented contestations" to the normative messages of a text. In the 1950s urban ethnic comedies often preached the folly of anything but suburban conformity and aspiring to a middle-class, consumer-based life. Not everyone read these texts the same way, however. No doubt shows were interpreted in a variety of ways, some of them counterhegemonic. But when devoid of the context of other black voices in prime time, the mockery shone through far more than the Kingfish's subversive possibilities. Placing *Amos 'n'Andy* in a historical continuum of blacks' depictions for the consumption of whites that stretches back to the minstrel show, the wild, uncontrolled gourmandism and sexuality of unchained ex-slave legislators in D. W. Griffith's *The Birth of a Nation*, and continuing on into blaxploitation films and 1990s gang films such as *Boyz 'n the Hood* and the rap music that simultaneously arose, the image of black urbanites that emerged in white viewers' minds was not flattering.[29]

Nor was *Amos 'n' Andy* understood as broad-brush satire or escapism; rather, it reinforced antiurbanist predilections in many viewers. Throughout the 1960s and 1970s and beyond, TV dramas and films were in dialogue, or multivocal conversations, with the nightmarish images of real American cities presented on the news. "If it bleeds it leads" runs the old newsroom aphorism, so the verdict that emerged was often that majority-minority cities were beyond repair, and that minority city dwellers chiefly had themselves to blame for their plight. Whether the message came from Daniel Moynihan's infamous 1965 assessment that the female-headed black family was "a tangle of pathologies" or more "humorously" from the Kingfish and his pals, the result was the same. And if this show's comic antics were the only view of black life that made it onto television screens, as was the case in the early 1950s, the black city came off very poorly.[30]

In the late 1950s and into the mid-1960s commentators such as Albert Johnson decried the lack of accurate portrayals of black life on either television or movie screens. The contemporary city, at least the African-American portion of it, was by and large ignored. And while the NAACP's protests forced *Amos 'n' Andy* off the prime-time lineup in 1953, it remained available for viewing in syndication until 1966. As Bogle notes, any honest examination of the state of race relations was impossible on *Amos 'n' Andy*, for the characters moved in an all-black milieu, Harlem. In this respect, at least, the show was accurate, as black urbanites increasingly dwelled in inner-city neighborhoods abandoned by suburbanizing whites who didn't care to look behind at what remained in the older cities until they erupted more than a decade later.[31]

When they turned to urban communities such as Brooklyn or the Bronx, early television programs more often presented white ethnic families on shows such as *Life with Luigi, I Remember Mama, The Goldbergs,* and *The Honeymooners.* But ethnicity was itself a curio piece, either in shows set in the past such as the Norwegian neighborhood of bygone San Francisco on *I Remember Mama,* or in tales of 1950s families struggling to adjust to a new, middle-class consumer society in the contemporary city. Here immigrant particularisms were depicted as fast fading away.[32]

To be sure, the gains made by white ethnics during the New Deal were still tenuous enough so that families are still here shown stretching paychecks that barely cover the consumer desires Madison Avenue has newly manufactured for them, and older characters often question the modern, assimilationist ways of younger folks. Still, it is these ways that win the day by the end of every week's episode; the Jewish, Italian, and other ethnic urbanites are humorously well on the way to leaving the old neighborhood and its particularistic ethnic ways behind. Indeed, *The Goldbergs*—who do leave the Bronx in the show's final season (1955–1956), in favor of the middle-class suburbs—often have to convince the mother of the superiority of new ways of doing things, such as buying creature comforts on time. By series end, the immigrant characters' protestations in comic broken English were feebler as the superiority of a happier way of living courtesy of Madison Avenue prevailed.

But the family's upward path to middle-class assimilation is told in a way that masks the costs exacted on their old Bronx neighborhood, and with no suggestion that the racially biased federal programs that privileged Goldbergs, and not King-fishes, had anything to do with their success. The Goldbergs' move to a suburban home occurred in 1955, in the middle of the era in which thousands of white families availed themselves of the programs that were hastening white flight and locking minorities in inner cities where they were denied subsidized mortgages as "bad risks." As Kenneth Jackson has noted, cities such as Paterson and Newark (by the mid-1960s majority-minority) received zero FHA-backed mortgage loans in the 1950s and 1960s, while the suburbs surrounding these cities received thousands, as second-generation Jews, Italians, and Poles did as the Goldbergs did and moved to suburbs, where ethnicity faded and the black-white binary was the only salient dividing line between city and affluent town. Indeed, Karen Brodkin has argued that it was only the large-scale movement of Jews into the suburbs following World War II that fully solidified the group's position as "white" Americans, just as invested in maintaining residential boundaries against African-Americans as other white ethnics.[33]

Yet on the show, the Goldberg family's move is a happy individual, consumer's choice, not because of government policy or the result of white flight or panic buying when their neighborhood "changes." Just as the consumerist message of post–World War II magazines, advertisers, and television programmers would have it, this decision is conveyed as simply the decision of discrete individuals merely doing what is best for their families—purchasing a newly constructed home and some of the fabulous creature comforts available and on display in the kind of television show in which this Bronx Jewish family starred. Who was barred from making a similar trek to the suburbs and what the implications were for the real Bronx and other cities as thousands of white families fled for the suburbs on Uncle Sam's tab were matters these comedies didn't address.[34]

Rather, the Goldbergs conformed to, reflected, and (for white, newly suburban-izing viewers) contributed to the dominant amnesiac ideology of other suburban-izing, Eisenhower era Americans: One was making it on one's own, not as a result of structural factors and government policies that favored certain groups (white ethnics such as the Goldbergs most certainly) and restricted the socioeconomic mobility of others. Those who made it to the suburbs were to be congratulated for their personal, individual hard work, while those left behind in the cities were ignored (if quiescent) and condemned for supposed personal moral failings (after 1965, when they grew assertive and noisy).

The irony that just such rhetoric had been directed at working-class immi-grants and their city neighborhoods only a few decades previously, though, went unreflected. So, too, the often fractious and assertive labor, socialist, and tenant and consumer activism of immigrants, such as those who would have been familiar in the Jewish Bronx, for the most part was effaced from the show. In the real world, however, as George Lipsitz notes, the left-wing past of one of the program's stars, Philip Loeb (who played Uncle Jake), ran afoul of a right-wing watchdog group, which excoriated the actor for the political crimes of appearing at antifascist rallies before World War II and signing petitions advocating the integration of major league baseball. Since some telltale signs of alleged communist affiliation at the height of the McCarthy era were "premature antifascism" and advocacy of "race mingling," sponsors pressured the show's creator to drop Loeb in 1952. Although he received a severance package of forty-five thousand dollars, Loeb was barred from working as an actor and committed suicide in 1956.[35]

This off-screen tragedy might have resonated in a real-life milieu such as the Bronx, where many Jewish families no doubt knew of a rich institutional web of union, socialist, and consumer activism within the old neighborhood. Such counterhegemonic messages were at cross-purposes, though, to the networks' main agenda, and few signifiers of working-class culture survived the transfer to network television. While both *The Goldbergs* and Ralph Kramden on *The Honeymooners* organized rent strikes on occasional episodes, for the most part the rich institutional web of working-class activists, at most only fifteen years in the past, was already omitted from 1950s television programs.[36]

As Lipsitz astutely argues, "Television's most important economic function came from its role as an instrument of legitimation for transformations in values initiated by the new economic imperatives of postwar America." Personal consumer behavior was to be emphasized and granted normative values; collective activity on behalf of one's class-based mates and ethnic peers was preempted on the tube, and forgotten (conservative businessmen, politicians, and network executives hoped) off it. Discussion of the differential socioeconomic trajectories of Jewish and black Bronx residents, which might have led to honest exposure of redlining and racial steering, was attempted by the social worker characters played by George C. Scott and Cicely Tyson, but their show proved a ratings flop. The dominant television of the late 1950s and early 1960s featured working-class white ethnics like the Goldbergs or Chester Riley of *The Life of Riley* making it on their own, starry-eyed dreamers like Ralph Kramden flopping and staying stuck in a one-bedroom tenement flat in Bensonhurst, and the completely-beyond-redemption black urbanites of *Amos 'n'Andy*.[37]

Yet for all that the amnesia was incompletely realized, for in the 1950s, suburbanites' hold on the good life was tenuous, recent, and still not divorced from the urban school of hard knocks. Therefore shows such as *The Honeymooners,* Lipsitz notes, exposed the tensions between the televised suburban, middle-class consumers' ideal and urban reality and the historical record exposing just how difficult and recent the gains had been. The Kramdens' grim apartment overlooking the back of a Chinese restaurant, antediluvian ice box and Ralph's frustrated plans to impress his boss and win even a bus dispatcher's toehold on the middle class indicated how far from the affluent life many Americans in many Bensonhursts still were.[38]

While the show, like so many other 1950s comedies, presented a raceless Brooklyn, for Ralph and Ed their neighborhood certainly was not a classless Brooklyn. No matter how much the Kramdens and Nortons might wish their way into the affluent middle class in Levittown's America of Organization Men, the proof of "happier living through television" is never quite attainable.[39] During one argument Alice hollers in frustration that Ralph only makes "$52 a week!" "Do you want my salary to leak out?" he asks, to which she replies, "Your salary couldn't drip out!" When Alice takes a job to help make ends meet, Ralph insists they hire a maid to keep up appearances. Impersonating a big shot, Ralph chokes on his big cigar and harrumphs his way through an interview with prospective maids. The employment agency director asks if Alice will be home to supervise the maid, but Ralph says no, she's a "career girl." Alice then tells the agent she works at Kausmeier's Bakery, where "my career is stuffing jelly into donuts." The Brooklynites are clearly fooling no one with their attempt to masquerade as big shots.

In another episode Ralph indignantly organizes a one-man rent strike when his monthly rent is raised by five dollars. Evicted, Ralph and Alice stoically hold forth on the sidewalk with all their possessions until it begins to snow, and Ralph relents. Brooklyn and other cities had been the scene of scores of militant rent strikes and antieviction campaigns at the height of the Great Depression, but now on the heights of Eisenhower era affluence, which had supposedly lifted all boats, Ralph's defiant holdout over five dollars might have seemed absurd to middle-class viewers.[40]

Ed Norton, too, aspires to live as an affluent middle-class consumer, through the newly valorized mechanism of buying on time. The simple sewer worker says he has four accounts going at the local Brooklyn department store, but then corrects himself: "No, five. Last month I bought a water softener." Yet, for all this, Ed is doggedly blue-collar in his allegiances and tastes, a sewer worker with a connoisseur's eye for pipes and drains. When Ralph learns that Ed is an expert typist, he wants to know why his friend never became a secretary or similar white-collar worker. The answer: "I just couldn't stand the idea of being cooped up all day in some office."

Ed and Ralph have grand dreams and pretensions, certainly, but the show also succeeds at times in exposing in a comic fashion how far certain urban residents were from still attaining a consumerist lifestyle of endless ease and gadgets all bought on time or, very soon, the American Express Card. These myths of an entirely affluent society with the good life open to all were comically exposed, but the laughs may have been loudest from ex-Brooklynites who recognized in Ed's frequently expressed love of the wide-open sewers and Ralph's unrealistic schemes, perhaps, an older brother or cousin still back in the crumbling old neighborhood. Television's imposition of a hegemonic middle-class message was imperfectly imposed, poor ethnic cousins back in Brooklyn still peering out from the margins.

Still, as Ralph's own daydreaming and scheming seem to be what keeps the Kramdens stuck in a tenement flat much like those Jacob Riis had portrayed, perhaps it was possible for viewers to conclude that only the starry-eyed failures were still trapped in such places. Ralph endeavors to get ahead with the most quixotic schemes, and the bus driver might be laughed at for his harebrained plans to open a uranium mine in Asbury Park, New Jersey; invest in no-cal pizza; and sell the handy housewife helper, peddled disastrously on late-night television by the Chef of the Future. Only such misfits, it might be concluded, were left behind in the nation's Bensonhursts as the rest of "us" graduated to the suburbs.[41]

Locally based ethnic and class communities in television's Brooklyn or Bronx neighborhoods, then, were depicted as quaint relics, on the path to fading away as the *The Goldbergs* pack and head to the assimilationist suburbs and Ralph and Ed plot and scheme, year after year. Race, however, was just getting started.

Popular-culture producers in films, and especially the new medium of television, lagged behind in their accounts of the transformed city until urban disturbances, beginning in 1964 with outbreaks in Harlem and Philadelphia's Columbia Avenue riots, and then the 1965 Watts rebellion in Los Angeles, forced the city's agenda onto the attention of television producers. The most famous federal response to the urban disturbances—the 1968 National Advisory Commission on Civil Disorders, or the Kerner Commission—issued a report that lay some of the blame at television's door. The Kerner Commission joined earlier, localized commissions in calling for government to take proactive steps to bridge the nation's racial chasm, which, the report argued, was creating "two Americas, one black, one white, separate and unequal." Television, too, was faulted for its monochromatic, myopic refusal to treat honestly and accurately the nation's urban minorities.[42]

When television producers did catch up to urban reality in the mid to late 1960s, though, the depiction of cities, even if somewhat nuanced and sympathetic and certainly more honest than earlier fantasy cities, ultimately reinforced a message of despair that may have caused many Americans to write off the nation's cities as beyond repair.

Rather than leading to calls for Great Society programs to rescue the poor, such shows may have reinforced the impression of many Americans that, in the wake of Watts, Detroit, and Newark, cities were hopelessly out of control.[43]

In 1967 two of the first grittier urban dramas debuted on TV. *N.Y.P.D.* was, like the earlier *Naked City*, shot on location in the down-at-the-heels streets of New York, and boasted that it was made with the cooperation of the New York Police Department, and like *Dragnet*, it promised that some of the episodes were based on real case files. New York's beleaguered mayor, John V. Lindsay, who for some Americans was already becoming a symbol of liberal impotence in the face of perceived spiraling crime and other urban problems, gave the show his imprimatur. Whether this was the kiss of death or not, the show only lasted two seasons.[44]

Still, *N.Y.P.D.* was innovative in that it featured both black and white detectives, with actor Robert Hooks as Detective Jeff Ward joining white detectives played by Jack Warden and Frank Converse. While in 1963 Cicely Tyson's social worker on *East Side/West Side* caused some outrage, perhaps a black character was, by 1967, acceptable as a lead character on a show, provided he was cast as a detective, dedicated to buttressing the system and not burning it down. Other black detectives and police collaborators emerged in coming decades to serve as a continuing reassurance to white America that "ghetto cool" could be employed in the service of the status quo. Characters such as Linc of *The Mod Squad*, Detective Neal Washington on *Hill Street Blues*, Tubbs of *Miami Vice*, and *Starsky and Hutch*'s jive master informant, Huggy Bear, come to mind. The ghetto's threats could be made to work for the system, just as Lieutenant Petrosino, New Yorkers had hoped in 1909, could rein in his fellow Italians.[45]

A far longer-lasting show also debuted in 1967. Whether the show's hyperviolence had anything to do with its longevity, *Mannix*, the L.A. private eye, continued dispensing his brand of vigilante justice until 1975. Mannix had been a police officer, but by the series beginning, he has become a two-fisted private detective in the tradition of Sam Spade. With the assistance of his black secretary, Peggy Fair (who, we are told, is the widow of Mannix's slain police partner), Joe Mannix subdues Southern California's array of hoodlums with plenty of high-speed car chases, crashes, gun battles, fistfights, and other red-blooded mayhem. The harried citizens of the lawless City of Angels, the series implied, could not be too squeamish in choosing which sorts of paladins to rescue them; if Mannix has to kill two or three bad guys every week to protect the rest of the city, so be it.[46]

A contemporary series, *Adam-12*, was also set in Los Angeles, but this program centered on police officers still battling crime by the book. Series creator Jack Webb again publicized the cooperation he received from the LAPD, with real station houses, badges, weapons, and tactical units of the department featured in the series. Correcting for the less-sophisticated nature of late 1960s police technology, such cameo roles by authentic equipment and procedures foreshadows the popular *CSI* series, in which televised police forces in Las Vegas, Miami, New York, and other cities use forensic medicine, lab technology, and surveillance equipment to solve the lurid murders and other atrocities that have turned America's cities into a grand guignol. Now science and technology, it was hoped, might preserve the moral order (a similar leitmotif ran through even the 1949 James Cagney film, *White Heat*, where sophisticated surveillance devices enable the LAPD to keep tabs on Coady Jarrett).[47]

Featuring the procedures, gadgets, and special units of a law-enforcement agency was one way of receiving "good press" on television crime dramas. The opinions of those inner-city residents who complained, with some justice, that many big-city police departments behaved like occupying armies (complaints very much in evidence in the wake of the Detroit and Newark riots of July 1967) were unlikely to receive much play in crime dramas that were "assisted" by advisers from big-city police departments.[48]

Still, some nuanced coverage of the urban crisis made it onto the small screen. One *Adam-12* episode, "Pig Is a Four Letter Word," has Reed and Malloy defusing the inflammatory racial situation in L.A. after two black hoodlums shoot and kill an elderly, respectable black couple during a holdup. The officers negotiate the anger of the city's black and white residents, and in October 1969 (when the episode first aired), certainly Los Angeles, like many other American cities, was uncertain as to whether the nation's long, hot summers might persist into the coming decade.[49]

Other black characters were introduced into shows that sought to tame and harness the counterculture on behalf of respectable society. In 1968 *The Mod Squad* featured three young dropouts who had been recruited by the LAPD as undercover cops. The three were Julie, a runaway daughter of a San Francisco prostitute; Pete, the son of a wealthy couple who rebelled against his pampered, superficial lifestyle and goes on a crime spree; and Linc Hayes, the brooding, Afro-coiffed Watts resident plucked from the riot by an older cop and trained to serve and protect. The three—and especially the sullen, at times revolutionary Linc—were held up as emblematic of the nation's rebellious, disaffected younger urbanites. Amazingly, casting young rebels in the role of police snitches somehow worked, and the show, which ran from 1968 to 1973, was wildly popular. Whether it merely used the stylistics of counterculture as window dressing for a conventional police drama, as some critics argued, enough rhetorical homage was paid by Linc and his pals to the need to care for society's underdogs and build a more ethical society to appeal to some younger viewers.[50]

As Donald Bogle has noted, whether *The Mod Squad* actually worked for The Man, several episodes offered strong critiques of perceived inequities and rot in late-1960s–early-1970s American society. The My Lai massacre, as well as society's shabby treatment of a returning Vietnam veteran (played by Louis Gossett, Jr.) who still feels like "a third- class citizen" in Los Angeles, is commented upon quite scathingly in one episode. Slum landlords are condemned, and the young under-cover agents speak sympathetically of the problems of ghetto youths. Linc, after all, was supposedly rescued from a Watts family of thirteen. Clarence Williams III, the actor who portrayed Linc, also expresses racial solidarity with his people and sympathy for some of their law-bending actions. At one point he refuses to inform on black suspects, telling his white fellow snitches, "I don't fink on soul brothers." As Bogle notes, Williams somehow pulled off the delicate task of making a police snitch seem like a race-conscious radical.[51]

Los Angeles was yet again the urban-zoo setting for another television drama seeking to traffic in relevant contemporary urban problems. *Room 222* is set in L.A.'s Walt Whitman High, where earnest teachers grapple with the kinds of problems that had only grown exponentially since the 1955 film *The Blackboard Jungle*. Although some critics, such as black writer John Oliver Killens, dismissed the series as "a nice, liberal-oriented, interracial innocuous show," throughout its run the series endeavored to present serious analysis (albeit in a fictional framework reassuring enough to garner network approval and corporate sponsors) of such problems as drugs, abusive home life in the ghetto, school integration, and inad-equate school funding. The show mirrored the gritty feel of other contemporary dramas of city life by being shot in L.A.'s real-life Whitman High, where suburban viewers again were exposed to some of the few views they received of inner cities that, by 1970, many now avoided altogether.[52]

While the characters spoke earnestly of their idealistic efforts to solve urban dilemmas, the series visuals may have contributed to a configured landscape of urban despair. Graffiti on the walls, aging school facilities, and crumbling housing stock, not optimistic dialogue, may have been what viewers took away from the program and others like it. As in the slumology exclusives of Jacob Riis's day, exposing urban ills was no guarantee that middle-class cultural consumers would develop any great sympathy for the ghetto poor. This hadn't worked for Lower East Side Italians and Jews in 1900, and was equally problematic when the subject switched to Los Angeles Hispanics and blacks.[53]

Indeed, it may be that too much urban realism contributed in the viewing public to what would later be called *compassion fatigue*. Ghetto crime dramas such as *Adam-12, Baretta,* and *Starsky and Hutch* might be compared to those titillating ethnic safaris of the magazine slum tour, which did lead to some Progressive reforms but also a great deal of impatience with the helpless and unassimilable immigrant. Here, too, crime shows on TV blended into the white noise of news reporting on urban criminality, contributing not to understanding but rage and frustration with the city and its rebellious minorities. Roland Barthes has written of the inoculation effect played by crime reporting and coverage of municipal corruption in the metropolitan press. He has argued that exposés of the defeat of crime lead readers of tabloid newspapers to conclude the system works, because the bad guys have been apprehended.[54]

But to judge by the alarms raised from the Nixon years on into the present in favor of tough law-and-order solutions—which culminated in the restoration of the death penalty and more than two million young African-Americans incarcerated by the end of the Reagan administration—the cumulative effect of such urban crime dramas may have been not inoculation but a conviction that the metropolitan patient was a terminal case beyond redemption. Films and television portrayals of ghetto crime and its defeat at the hands of tough-guy cops like *Mannix* or *Starsky and Hutch*, rather than serving to reassure the public that law and order triumphed in the chaotic city, may have created the impression of an unrelenting wave of criminality that only barely was beaten back and contained.

Suburban viewers by now had little actual contact with inner cities, as these areas no longer served as shopping, cultural, or recreational hubs for metropolitan regions that now sported suburban shopping malls and sports stadiums in ex-urban areas adjacent to interstate highways. The city in real time could be bypassed, and instead sampled in weekly voyeuristic doses. The unrelenting picture of crime run rampant on television dramas led viewers to conclude the system was reaching a crisis. News reportage of bankrupt cities such as Abe Beame's New York, urban disturbances (Newark's and Detroit's 1967 riots, then the various riots and ghetto crises of 1968, as well as New York's 1977 blackout and subsequent looting binge), and crumbling municipal infrastructures only confirmed, for many, the lessons learned on *The Streets of San Francisco* or *Mannix*.[55]

A firm hand, then, was granted on TV dramas to many prime-time cops. Violence by the forces protecting the status quo was valorized, as when Reed and Malloy team up on *Adam-12* to capture a "socially conscious" sniper terrorizing L.A. In this instance the show features members of the Los Angeles Police Department's special weapons and tactics (SWAT) squad, which in real life had been tasked with subduing a feared uprising of black radicals after the urban disturbances of the mid to late-1960s.

At a time when San Francisco was terrorized by the real-life zodiac killer, a series of murders that inspired Clint Eastwood's snarling vigilante, Dirty Harry, to challenge "punks" to "make my day," *Adam-12*'s sniper might have seemed ripped from the headlines. Again, though, the city was portrayed as a chaotic place that should give its officially sanctioned forces wide leeway in using whatever state-backed violence they deemed necessary. For his work on *Adam-12*, Webb was honored with an honorary badge in the LAPD, but it would only be twenty years later, during the Rodney King affair, that a video very much unauthorized by the LAPD demonstrated just where this tolerance for "by any means necessary" policing might take a nation.[56]

Ironically, this was just the opposite tactic from what sociologists such as Hahn and Feagin and civil disturbance commissioners like Otto Kerner and New York Mayor John V. Lindsay had advocated. Of course, conservative Americans, such as the authors of a New Jersey State Patrolmen's Benevolent Association report, countered that any leniency or attempts to understand black militancy in its social context would lead the country inexorably down a "road to anarchy." Such views came to the fore, both in television, film, and the nation at large, as law-and-order politicians denounced the "coddling of criminals by judges, social workers and the rest of the permissive society." Through the 1970s and beyond, television cops who expressed sympathy for victims but wasted little breath on the "vermin" who preyed on them (and sometimes bent the rules to make sure such vermin were caught) were featured on shows such as *Kojack, Baretta, Starsky and Hutch,* and *Miami Vice*.[57]

This by-any-means-necessary style of police work was much in evidence on the big screen, too, particularly in the San Francisco policeman Harry Callahan in 1971's *Dirty Harry*. In the film the City by the Bay faces the threat of a serial sniper named Scorpio (based on the real zodiac murderer, who menaced San Francisco and was never apprehended). But the bigger problem Inspector Callahan faces is the ineptitude and liberal mollycoddle attitude his police superiors and the city's ineffectual mayor adapt toward the criminals in our midst. Dirty Harry is well known for his can-do, take-no-prisoners brand of policing, and he is assigned to hunt down the serial killer. When the killer is found, not surprisingly in 1971, he is a hippie strung out on any number of hallucinogenic drugs.

But a liberal judge turns the killer loose because Harry's search of his hideout is illegal, and the mayor gets in on the act by balling the inspector out. As the audience has seen, Harry does more than omit a search warrant, shooting the suspected killer in the leg and all but torturing him into revealing his kidnapped victim's whereabouts. In 1971, three decades before the methods of Jack Bauer of *24* were condoned both on- and off-screen, the mayor's reservations about such extrajudicial methods might be understandable. But the film's sentiments are with Harry all the way; we are to conclude that murderous madmen are the "logical" end result of hopelessly ineffectual bleeding-heart policies.

When the mayor urges conciliation as the way to stop the madman—who has now, upon his release, hijacked a busload of schoolkids—Dirty Harry gives up on the rules, which have handcuffed the police and allowed chaos to run rampant in his city. Using his own special methods, Dirty Harry Callahan saves his city, not that he's holding his breath waiting for an official citation or a tickertape parade.

Public enemy number one in this film seems to be the liberal nostrums of all those Great Society bureaucrats and bleeding-heart crime commissioners demanding more welfare programs. The subtext of *Dirty Harry* is that the New Jersey State Police were right after all: The road to anarchy is paved with weak-kneed intentions.[58]

By the early 1970s the cinematic and televised city was by almost universal consensus on its last legs, and even the cops are shown as brutalized and cynical beyond redemption. The beats they walk leave little hope for faith in the system. Cops can either choose the way of Harry's superior, Bressler, which is go through the motions, or throw out the rule book and let the .44 Magnum explode. Like his demoralized counterparts in the nation's bankrupt cities, Callahan is protecting "us" by brutalizing some other urbanites. And many viewers shrugged and accepted this compromised arrangement.[59]

Other police and vigilante figures from this bitter era of cities teetering on the brink of a fiscal abyss and supposed lawless anarchy were equally morally ambiguous, compromised figures. Charles Bronson's meek architect Paul Kersay in *Death Wish* goes on an urban revenge-fest when the justice system fails him miserably and allows his wife's savage killers to walk free. The former bleeding heart belatedly realizes the impossibility of relying on civilized procedures to rein in the criminals. Paul takes matters into his own hands after the NYPD is incapable of finding the murderers and rapists who have quite graphically shattered his illusions of a workable city. New York, it is implied, is facing a pernicious invasion. Although of course, by 1974, the predators aren't an earlier age's Italians and Jews, whom Theodore Bingham and magazine slumologists warned about; New York is said to be facing a new invasion, and it's up to Bronson/Kersay to restore law at the barrel of a gun.

The formerly milquetoasty architect is quite good at his vigilante avocation—and even enjoys blowing away all the street thugs he runs into, seemingly on every corner. The police at this point are faced with a dilemma: Do they vigorously pursue and rein in this freelance wrecking machine, who has become a municipal hero, and thereby earn the scorn of those for whom he is a folk hero? Or do they admit that their own tame methods are ineffectual and invite a bunch of Kersay admirers to head for the gun shops?[60]

Death Wish offered a primal scream with which many Americans could identify. Convinced that "soft on crime" liberals like New York's Judge Bruce Wright (dubbed "Turn 'Em Loose Bruce" by the tabloid press) were leaving them defenseless at the hands of urban gangs, many moviegoers cheered at Bronson's blunt response to city crime. Indeed, life imitated art ten years later, when a slight, bespectacled engineer named Bernie Goetz answered several African-Americans' queries for change with blasts from his concealed, unlicensed handgun. "Yes, I have a dollar for each of you," Goetz answered these subway panhandlers before firing away; looking at one of the teens he had severely wounded, Goetz snarled, "You don't look so bad; here's another." Just as if they were still at the movies, many New Yorkers cheered these "make my day" taglines.[61]

Other tough-guy models were offered to New Yorkers by mid-1970s movies. In *The French Connection*, Popeye Doyle knows the only way to get some information out of sullen Harlem barflies is to crack a few heads and ask questions later. And the inscrutable questions he asks—"Do you pick your teeth in Poughkeepsie?"—seem deliberately designed to evoke noncooperation, or "resisting arrest," from minorities whom the detective longs to beat up. Here, too, as Carlo Rotella notes, the gritty cinema verité of the film, shot on location in squalid, deindustrialized pockets of Harlem and Brooklyn with jumpy camera action and grainy film stock, lends the entire film an air of despair, as if all of New York civilization might collapse with one strong wind. In the years leading up to the city's fiscal meltdown, this seemed the only end game for New York and other metropolises.

Then, too, even the dogged, albeit sometimes dirty, police tactics of Popeye Doyle and Sonny Grosso can only collar the international drug ring's lower-echelon players. Compromised higher-ups allow the real French connections to walk, and the real criminal masterminds continue to sun themselves on balconies overlooking the Mediterranean, far from Popeye's perpetually slush-filled Brooklyn beat. As in the nineteenth-century city, well-connected criminals hold the political system in their pockets; the rest of us, in the 1970s, just as the 1870s, might conclude that the city needed protection from its swarming masses and aristocratic swindlers, and we'd take our protection from whatever quarter it came.[62]

Even some urban subalterns were talking back to The Man. Blaxploitation films of the early 1970s, such as *Shaft*, *Superfly*, *Sweet Sweetback's Baadasssss Song*, and *Coffy*, present strong black characters speaking back to power and asserting their sexuality and agency in ways never before seen on the big screen. Still, some of the ghetto-cool characters ultimately, it seems, reinforced white attitudes toward the worth of inner-city minorities, feeding off stereotypes of hustlers and sybarites running rampant in the ghetto, even as actors such as Richard Roundtree and Pam Grier gave black audiences heroes—or antiheroes—for whom to cheer. Finally, black characters didn't just suffer the ghetto silently, but acted.

African-American directors Melvin Van Peebles and Gordon Parks almost single-handedly created the new blaxploitation genre. Before he turned to explicit ghetto themes, Van Peebles had in 1970 debuted *Watermelon Man*, a scathing satire of the current explosive state of race relations. Black standup comic Godfrey Cambridge plays bigoted insurance salesman Jeff Gerber—in whiteface. In the first half of the movie he and his wife watch televised news reports of ghetto rioting in their unnamed city, puzzling over just what "those people" could want or hope to achieve through such violent tactics (here Cambridge ventriloquizes the myopic befuddlement of countless whites who, by 1970, had watched scenes from Newark, Detroit, and Watts). Jeff himself is an insouciant bigot, teasing an older black lunch-counter man that one of these days he's going to ask for fried chicken and watermelon. The counter man, played by Mantan Moreland, who had portrayed countless bug-eyed Negro servants in, among other films, the Charley Chan series, cackles and says, "Yessir, Mr. Gerber," to every one of the bigot's gibes.[63]

Jeff's world changes overnight when he awakens to find himself transformed into a black man. Angry phone calls in the night warn the "nigger" to get out of town, but more genteel bigots in the *Raisin in the Sun* tradition offer to buy Jeff's house so that their neighborhood will remain lily-white. At first, Jeff sees this as his new ticket to financial security—imagining he can travel the country, threatening to integrate cities nationwide, and cashing in as a real estate blockbuster in reverse. But after his marriage falls apart, he moves instead to a ratty apartment in some inner-city slum. There, at film's end, he is shown engaged in paramilitary training with a cadre of angry militant blacks—including the formerly benign lunch-counter man. The film ends in a freeze framing on Jeff's angry black face as he shouts his slogan and thrusts forward with his homemade weapon. The ghetto contains many such unknown revolutionaries masquerading as benign servants or middle-class salesmen.[64]

Now, though, the white face came off. The year after *Watermelon Man* Van Peebles directed *Sweet Sweetback's Baadasssss Song*, which unapologetically celebrated ghetto rage and fighting back against exploiters, albeit in a framework that may have reinforced some whites' negative stereotypes of black city culture. Although Van Peebles himself argued that his film was the story of "a bad nigger who opposes white oppression and wins, living life on his own terms," the film's hero seems destined to raise a white fear for every Black Power salute. Sweet Sweetback works as a stud in the Los Angeles ghetto, where a prostitute has given him his nickname because of his sexual prowess, even at the age of ten. When the film's hero is rousted from the whorehouse where he lives by two cops looking for a suspect in a crime that's enraged the ghetto, Sweetback witnesses their brutalization of a black revolutionary. This enrages the stud, who avenges the revolutionary leader by beating the cops senseless with their own handcuffs. As he flees through the ghetto we see Sweetback's further adventures, a series of violent assaults on ghetto oppressors real and imagined (as well as priapic adventures in sexual violence against women, black as well as white). Ghetto kids free Sweetback a second time by torching a police car. Perhaps Sweetback's high point occurs when he spears a racist cop with a pool cue. Eventually Sweetback escapes the ghetto, fleeing across the desert into Mexico. As he runs toward freedom, an ominous promise is flashed on the screen: "A BAADASSSS Nigger Is Coming to Collect Some Dues!"[65]

While such defiance played well among some minorities angry at inaction on the intractable poverty and problems of the ghetto, the message likely confirmed many whites in their alarm at the state of urban America. Every gibe at single-family black households and the tangle of pathology, from the Moynihan report on up, seemed borne out by this film's celebration of the baadasssss life.

Even a black critic such as Lerone Bennett, Jr., qualified his praise for the film by wondering what whites were making of so much dysfunctional behavior on display. Allowing that "after seeing it we can never again see black people in films (noble, suffering, losing) in the same way," Bennett also called the film "trivial and tasteless, neither revolutionary nor black," rejecting Van Peebles's assertion that he was attempting to work "toward the decolonization of black minds, reclaim the black spirit from centuries of manipulation by the power structure." Bennett argued that "nobody ever f****d his way to freedom. And it is mischievous and reactionary . . . for anyone to suggest to black people in 1971 that they are going to be able to screw their way across the Red Sea."[66]

Other blaxploitation films positioned their protagonists, at least ostensibly, on the side of the law. *Shaft* and *Shaft's Big Score* by director Gordon Parks initially pit black private detective John Shaft against Harlem black gangsters, as well as violent black nationalists, but eventually he teams up with them to defeat an even bigger menace, the Mafia, which is trying to muscle in on the black crime boss, Bumpy. The Shaft films featured an assertive, flashy ghetto male who expresses his cartoon manhood through violence, sexual conquests (with white as well as black women), and standing up to white oppressors. When a tough Mafioso calls Shaft a nigger he comes back with wop, then smashes a bottle against the bigot's face. Promotional material designed to sell tickets in Harlem, South Chicago, and other black enclaves championed Shaft as "a lone, black Superspade—a man of flair and flamboyance who has fun at the expense of the white establishment."[67]

Parks scored another hit in 1972 with *Superfly*, whose hero, Youngblood Priest, is a ghetto cocaine dealer looking to make one last big score so he can retire. Throughout the film we learn that well-connected white officials are after the dealer. But they are not seeking to save the city from this scourge, merely to rob him and kill him, for one of the city's biggest cocaine dealers, we learn, is one of the white police inspectors.[68]

As in Lippard's novels, it's the high and mighty who are the real drains on the system, but in the heightened racialized turmoil of the early 1970s, few white or black observers of *Superfly* likely made the connection. Youngblood triumphs over his adversaries, sticking it to The Man by violently beating up white cops and black thugs alike and conquering both black and white women with casual ease, before he drives off in his Rolls Royce, gleefully snorting one last hit before he retires to a life of ease. Superfly, like Shaft and Sweetback, triumphs over the dominant forces in society through a combination of sexual bravado and fighting prowess, and in both of these attributes these figures hark back to the blues' mythic tough guy and sexual libertine, Staggalee. Pam Grier added the superheroine to this trope in films such as *Coffy* and *Foxy Brown*.[69]

On the other hand, just as much as *Dirty Harry* and *Death Wish*, blaxploitation films flourished in an era when disinvestment and deindustrialization in New York, Los Angeles, and other cities continued apace, and trafficked in images that reinforced many Americans' decision to give up on the city. While the 1960s are often perceived as a liberal era, by their end law-and-order politicians from President

Nixon to George Wallace to Philadelphia's police commissioner and soon mayor, Frank Rizzo, were championing tough-on-crime and welfare-cheat policies to appeal to a "silent majority" in often racially coded language. These cries continued at full throat throughout the tough-on-crime 1970s, 1980s, and beyond. By the 1970s, though, a modified moral sensibility required that even critiques of civil rights programs, social spending, and other programs be couched in an anti-urban rhetoric, which, Robin Kelley and others have argued, has amounted to just a more polite form of the races' ghettoization.[70]

The kinds of television shows and movies that citizens watched shaped this widely held conception of cities circa the 1970s as hopelessly beyond redemption. Sociologist William Julius Wilson might write cogent arguments for the existence of an urban underclass; far more Americans derived their opinions of the South Bronx, Harlem, or Southside Chicago from *Shaft*, *Superfly*, or *Fort Apache, the Bronx*.[71]

In an era when fewer and fewer whites had direct contact with the inner cities, this process of accepting the simulacrum for the reality was only exacerbated. Cities that had only a few years previously been essential shopping, work, and entertainment destinations for their regions were increasingly becoming peripheral to the concerns of many middle-class suburbanites. Shopping had been given over to suburban malls from the late 1950s on, so that major downtown retail icons, whether Meyer Brothers of Paterson, Bamberger's in Newark, or the flagship Hudson's Department Store in downtown Detroit, fell by the wayside.

Suburban shopping malls had already siphoned retail wealth and activity, in many cases, away from the cities, further impoverishing inner-city neighborhoods. (In Detroit, for example, Hudson's flagship downtown store lagged behind the activity at its suburban locations and, even before the 1967 urban disturbances, had been abandoned by suburbanized white former patrons who now patronized closer mall outlets. After the riots, the city's downtown became something of a ghost town.)[72]

Sports stadiums in older city neighborhoods, such as Shibe Park in North Philadelphia and the Polo Grounds adjacent to Harlem, were likewise increasingly avoided, and when teams relocated they either headed west or, if they stayed in the older cities, built new stadiums conveniently located in quasi-suburban parts of the city, deliberately surrounded by huge parking lots and adjacent to freeways for easy entrance and exit from the game site, with minimal interaction with the older, nonwhite parts of the city. Suburban fans were increasingly shielded from interaction with the left-behind parts of the older cities from which many of them had fled only a short time before. Places such as Philadelphia, Brooklyn, and Detroit, then, which had into the 1950s been regional economic and entertainment hubs, were irrelevant to large numbers of ex-urbanites, save only as images of despair projected back onto whites' fevered fantasies courtesy of television and movie theater screens.[73]

Maybe blaxploitation films unintentionally furthered this trend even more than the films with white protagonists, since into the mix was added an evocation of potential racial revolution, the great fear that in 1968 had garnered 20 percent of white ethnics' votes for "law-and-order" third-party presidential candidate George Wallace in cities such as Newark. Now all these films contributed to the growing sense that American cities were somehow newly lawless places where only the strong survived. Whether *Death Wish* or *Superfly* was one's urban vigilante model perhaps depended on where one was positioned in America's racial divide. The part of the audience cheering for Bronson's *Death Wish* was unlikely to celebrate *Superfly* or *Shaft*, and vice versa. One man's urban cowboy was another man's hostile menace.[74]

In this era the city's cinematic end was never very good. *The Planet of the Apes* series warned that New York was destined to face an army of former slaves—the apes—rising up to enslave the mostly white humans. It is plausible that in 1968, the year of the first film's debut, this sci-fi ending mirrored the fears of those who saw anarchy in the urban disturbances, and that the apes, as in so many science fiction films, stood in for society's real oppressed subalterns. New York played a role in bringing this horrible possibility to pass, for recall that the buried Statue of Liberty at film's end indicates that Americans have gone and blown up the planet after all. In *Beneath the Planet of the Apes*, it's revealed that this came about due to an explosion triggered by an army of subway-dwelling mutants who worshiped nuclear bombs far beneath Manhattan. Many visitors to the nation's largest city likely agreed with this assessment after riding the subway. Less apocalyptically, the John Godey novel and 1974 film *The Taking of Pelham One Two Three* offered the terrorist seizure of New York's subway train as a metaphor for an entire city hurtling toward the end of the rails. It was only a short leap from the chaotic present to imagining a future mortgaged to the apes.[75]

These two ends for New York were perfectly embodied in two films of the Carter years of national malaise that offer different, yet equally bleak, possibilities for Manhattan. From the opening shots of Martin Scorsese's *Taxi Driver*, with a cab plowing through the steam of a festering New York manhole, Times Square and its environs conjure up the rot that many by 1976 had concluded was at the heart of the city. Travis Bickle's disturbed eyes as he scans the sleazy vice district from his rearview mirror, coupled with the ominous music (pounding bass lines giving way to a jazz-tune love poem to Manhattan, a very disturbed gal, indeed) tell us all about the psychosis embedded in Manhattan, not just this cabdriver. As his cab prowls by tawdry marquees—"*Texas Chainsaw Massacre,*" "*Fascination*"—the troubles to come are deftly foreshadowed. This vehicle and its insomniac driver are looking for trouble, and we know that they'll find it.

As in later Scorsese works, the past is subtly held up as preferable to what the city has become. When Travis takes Betsy on their first disastrous date, they walk past a Times Square street musician playing jazz drum riffs from a bygone era. "Now, a blast from the past, Gene Krupa!" he says, evoking an earlier, romantic city that's irretrievably lost in the Times Square of dime porn shows that Travis inhabits. Just as Mayor Lindsay's game campaign labeling New York "fun city" seemed like archaic wishful thinking in a city running out of cash, good humor, tolerance, and functionality, Travis's assertion to the dispatcher who hires him that his driving record is "real clean, like my conscience," convinces no one. As he drives the streets, Travis murmurs the country's real verdict on his city: "All the animals come out at night. Whores, skunks, pussies, buggers, fairies, queens, dopers, junkies. Sick, venal. Someday a real rain will come and wash all this scum off the streets." Earlier, in his lousy little apartment (the kind of place *Midnight Cowboy*'s Ratso Rizzo also calls home), Travis jots in his diary, "Thank God for the rain, which has helped wash the garbage and the trash off the sidewalks," but it's evident that the trash he detests walks Forty-second Street on two legs. And in 1976, the year of *Taxi Driver*'s release, many agreed. The previous year President Gerald Ford had issued his famous "Drop Dead" to a bankrupt New York, merely providing the final autopsy for a city on which Travis and 90 percent of the country had already given up.[76]

Even within the urban jungle, distinctions are made between dangerous and absolutely hopeless places, and it is race that once more marks the boundary. Travis tells the cabbie Wizard and his buddies, "I heard on the radio some fleet driver . . . just got all cut up. . . . Cut half his ear off." When Wizard hears it happened on 122nd Street, he mutters, "F*****g Mau Mau Land," and the camera pans to some stereotypical black pimps glowering in the Automat's corner. After *Superfly*, the urban menace is indelibly marked as black; considering the rage that simmers in Travis's mind, the irony is apparent. The cabbies discuss the "rough customers" they've encountered, and Travis admits he doesn't carry a "piece." Wizard comments, "I never use mine, I'm conservative, you know? But it's a good thing to have, just as a threat." Over this commentary on the "Mau Mau Land" New York has become hangs the campaign poster of the presidential hopeful Travis will later meet and stalk; its promised "return to greatness" is one more archaic Krupa jazz riff in a city of too many Travises.

Later, in a bodega, Travis shoots and kills a black robber with his unregistered gun. When the bodega owner and Travis realize that the robber's "eyes are still moving," the owner beats the robber's inert body repeatedly with an iron bar as Travis flees. "That's the fifth mother f****r this year!" the owner sputters. In another throwaway example of the chaos of this urban jungle, Travis spies from his cab two old men beating each other. As prostitutes watch, but do not intervene, one drags the other around the corner. All this is something prosaic, not worthy of further comment.

Travis, though, disagrees. When a presidential candidate takes an unscheduled ride in Travis's cab, he asks Travis "What's the one thing about this country that bugs you most?" "Well, whatever it is, you should clean up this city here," Travis replies. "Because this city here is like an open sewer, you know, it's full of filth and scum. 'Cause sometimes I can hardly take it. . . . I think the president should just clean up this whole mess here, he should just flush it right down the f*****g toilet." When the candidate tells Travis "we're going to have to make some radical changes," the cabbie replies "Damn straight!"

While *Taxi Driver* was loosely based on the diatribes contained in the diary of Arthur Bremer, the man who tried to kill Alabama Gov. George Wallace, ironically Wallace's own strident calls for flushing the "filth and scum" resonated with many beleaguered lower middle-class voters in the urban Northeast, too. When Travis watches TV in his squalid apartment, the candidate exults, "The people are beginning to rule," but considering the kinds of people we've met in New York this is a scary prospect.

Indeed, in the real-life 1970s, many other Americans responded with rage at the ballot box to the antibusing crusade in South Boston, Spiro Agnew's popular diatribes against effete liberals, and assaults on supposed moral promiscuity and liberal ineffectiveness by politicians from Wallace to Rizzo to Newark's Tough Tony Imperiale. As Travis does push-ups in his apartment and trains for his one-man assault on the system, he snarls, "Too much abuse has gone on for too long." He's talking about his own body and the junk food he's been eating, but the audience is also supposed to connect "too much abuse" of "regular" Americans (like himself?) to the city's "filth and scum" that he's already denounced.[77]

In the same year news anchor Howard K. Beale struck a chord in *Network* with his rant into the festering Manhattan ether, "I'm mad as hell and I'm not going to take it anymore!" (In this film, the television newscast playing in the background as Beale's inner world falls to pieces is the second failed assassination attempt on President Ford on the streets of San Francisco; fictional and factual cityscapes converge in their disintegration and mayhem.) In *Taxi Driver*, only a chance circumstance as thin as a knife's blade separates a vigilante hero from a deranged assassin, and in either case he articulates a backlash anger for many fed up with the city as cesspool. When Travis prepares for his final assault, he snarls, "Listen, you f*****s, you screw-heads, here is a man who would not take it anymore. . . . A man who stood up against the scum. . . . Here is someone who stood up." In 1971, *Dirty Harry* hunted the angry psycho. Now Scorpio isn't sniping at us, he's driving our cab. And the scariest thing about the city is that Travis is not alone.[78]

If the current city contains little to recommend it, the future city is even less inviting. In 1981 John Carpenter carried New York into the future with *Escape from New York*, where "the once-great city of New York" is "the one maximum security prison for the entire country" in 1997. This had become necessary, a narrator tells us, because "in 1988, the crime rate rises over 400 percent." Consequently, "a fifty-foot container wall is erected" around Manhattan, and "the United States Police Force, like an army, is encamped around the island. There are no guards inside the prison. Only prisoners and the worlds they have made."[79]

As we now know, Manhattan was not converted into a maximum-security prison in 1988, at least not literally. However, security barriers and procedures were implemented in a wide variety of formerly public places in Los Angeles, New York, and other cities even prior to September 2001. Many who now have to remove shoes or have bags, belt, and intentions inspected at an airport, mall, or subway stop might wonder if Liberty Island has indeed been converted into a "security control center," as in the film. Rudy Giuliani was elected mayor in the real New York in 1993, and promptly implemented his zero-tolerance policy toward all manner of so-called quality-of-life crimes. During his tenure Patrick Dorismond, Amadou Diallo, and other minority residents were subject to increasing assaults on their person by the "United States Police Force" (including, most infamously, Diallo's murder in a hail of forty-one police bullets in the lobby of his own Bronx apartment building). The number of Americans incarcerated in the growing colonies of private, for-profit prisons as well as state and federal facilities meant by 2000 that more young African-American men were in jail than in college. Such measures were extended elsewhere in America, as with the erection of concrete barricades to block off through streets leading from Cleveland into the surrounding affluent, mostly white suburbs, thus creating a dead-end containment wall around the ghetto. These measures seemed to take their cue from this film, in spirit if not in actual citation by lawmakers. While no fifty-foot concrete barrier and watchtowers surrounded minority neighborhoods in Manhattan or elsewhere, those victims of heavy-handed police techniques might be excused for wondering if they didn't already live in a "lockdown nation."[80]

But he who lives by the prison may get trapped in it. In *Escape from New York*, the president's plane crash lands somewhere in Manhattan, threatening a summit that hopes to end the perpetual warfare the world is enduring (in this, the film also seems prophetic). War hero Snake Pliskin is offered a reprieve from a life sentence he is serving for robbing the Federal Reserve if he'll rescue the president from the pit of New York, but the policeman who briefs Snake on his mission indicates that a commute to New York won't be as easy as invading Siberia: "The crazies, they live in the subways. Complete control of the underground. They're night raiders." As in *Pelham* or *Planet of the Apes*, the New York subway is the site of deviancy.[81]

Police Commissioner Hauck warns Snake the president must be found in time to salvage a nuclear summit conference, otherwise "life as we know it" will soon end. Snake's reaction tells us what we've already come to expect from more than a decade of modern urban nightmare films: Life as we know it already has ended; the crazies rule in the subways and pretty much everyplace else. The city Snake wanders through may still harbor ironic "I Love New York" graffiti and posters, but the armies of homeless crawling out of the sewers to assault him on the grimmest city streets are already familiar to us from a myriad of exposés of the garbage-strewn South Bronx, Newark, and Detroit. Such images had been established as representing the American city long before Snake begins his rescue mission, and sci-fi here, as elsewhere, merely provides the viewer with images of the urban future that one had already come to recognize as one's now. The future is merely the present disguised by a little more technology and dirt.[82]

New York will always be New York, though, and a cabbie (played by Ernest Borgnine) figures prominently. Like the Krupa drummer of *Taxi Driver*, he evokes a happier, seemingly more innocent urban era. Glenn Miller tapes continually play in his cab, and even though we've seen that in the 1930s not everyone was comfortable with the sidewalks of New York, he seems to be a throwback to the smart-talking, savvy blue-collar New Yorker of vintage screwball comedies. The cabbie is the kind of New Yorker who takes street mayhem in his stride. He's seen it all before and knows the city like the back of his hand, and like many a street-wise, working-class emissary, he sets the out-of-towner straight on where he can and cannot go in New York. "Where ya goin', buddy?" he asks as he rescues Snake from yet another jam. "Bad neighborhood, Snake. You don't wanna be walkin' from The Bowery to Forty-second Street at night. Hah! I been drivin' a cab here for 30 years, and I'm tellin' you, you don't *walk* around here at night! Hah! Yes, sir, kids'll kill you and strip you in 10 seconds flat!" It'd be nice to imagine that a fast-talking cabbie straight out of Preston Sturges could guide one through hell, but this cabbie is seemingly the one lone holdout in a New York run amok.

Similar urban dystopias were offered by sci-fi films of a future that is only a bit more of the predictable urban mayhem. In the not-too-distant future, Walter Hill's *The Warriors* postulates, gangs will control the five boroughs and hold summit conferences to divvy up the spoils. *RoboCop* presents a not-too-distant-future Detroit in which television ads peddle services that electrocute car thieves, and privatized police forces of Cyborg storm troopers stop whoever corporate moguls deem are the bad guys. Empathy monitors are designed to ensure the praetorian guard never turns on the innocent; the system works about as well as it did for Diallo. *Johnny Mnemonic* is mostly a sci-fi satire of information overload, in which by the year 2021 couriers with computer chips embedded in their heads literally explode from Nervous Attenuation Syndrome. Corporations have cannibalized most of what remains valuable in cities, but the film's main courier is racing to deliver his cure for the ailment to the dysfunctional Free City of Newark. New Jersey's largest city evidently has proven so irredeemable that the United States has given it away to minority gangsters.[83]

Carpenter also populates his gulag New York with a blaxploitation gang lord, Isaac Hayes's Duke of New York. He lords it over his fellow felons from the gutted New York Public Library, with his main squeeze, Maggie, by his side, and rides around the city in a Cadillac adorned with candelabra hood ornaments and a gaudy mirror ball on the roof. Hayes's portrayal is an exaggerated, nightmare vision of assertive Staggalee blackness. In the early 1980s climate of backlash against all manner of social spending, such fearful images rested near the top of the American mind. The Duke tortures the U.S. president into genuflecting before him and intoning, "You're the Duke of New York, you're A-Number One." Such images fit in neatly with contemporary nightmares of black criminality as the supposed culmination of too much bended knee by authority figures, and in the first year of the "morning in America" conservative revolution many seemed to believe that the White House had already been held hostage by New York and everything it represented for too many years. Once the authority figures have ceded control of Manhattan, a hypermasculinized black criminal has stepped into the void, naturally. *Shaft* and *Superfly* have nothing on the Duke, nor do Reagan era urban legends of the Cadillac-driving welfare cheat using food stamps for vodka.[84]

Of course, the city may have been ceded to *Superfly* black criminals, but the line must be drawn at the suburbs. When the Duke attempts to break through the concrete barricades separating his urban nightmare from suburban New Jersey on the fictitious Sixty-ninth Street Bridge, the president reacts with a vengeance. From atop the concrete walls reining in New York and its lawless minorities, the president cackles maniacally as he sprays his enemies with machine-gun fire. Black gang lords are permitted in 1997 to rule the chaos of abandoned city spaces, but any attempt to go beyond that triggers reaction, as real estate developers of gentrified, gated communities in Denton and Massey's apartheid America would no doubt approve.[85]

Moreover, the president's gleefully vicious reaction might cause one to wonder if state-sanctioned violence and brutalization of inmates of lockdown Manhattan have played any role in such people's turn to criminality. In 1997, within both the real-time version and its *Escape from New York* simulacrum, such musings were increasingly rare.

It should be noted that from the later 1970s on, another New York has reemerged, the gentrified, resilient city of artists and avant garde free spirits. Neurotic and insecure but nevertheless wittier than anything this side of Noel Coward, these New Yorkers have most famously been seen populating the Upper West Side of Woody Allen's films, such as *Annie Hall, Manhattan,* and *Hannah and Her Sisters*. These films, especially *Manhattan*, are visual love poems to the literary and cultural high points of the city, with homages to Riverside Drive, Brooklyn Heights, and the area around Columbia University. Allen's characters also often make pilgrimages back to their origins in Brooklyn's working-class areas, but these recollections, if quirky (recall the Singer family abode under the roller coaster at Coney Island in *Annie Hall*), are also warmly evoked memories of a bygone Jewish Brooklyn with nothing more threatening than an overbearing mother.[86]

Woody Allen's New York is the enclave of writers and musicians who have summer homes in the Hamptons. Allen characters such as Alvy Singer in *Annie Hall* might be struggling writers, but they always live in the smartest parts of Manhattan and spend their time at Elaine's. A more accurate depiction of the lives of most of New York's starving artists or even moderately successful novelists is found in the film *Smoke*, based on Paul Auster's *New York Trilogy*. Here the novelist Paul Benjamin lives in a decidedly unupscale part of Brooklyn, in a cramped, cluttered apartment with a broken intercom and easily penetrated front-door lock. For artists not blessed with a trust fund, the prewar brownstones of *Hannah and Her Sisters* are a nice escapist fantasy, a part of New York viewers walk through on a different kind of voyeuristic tour. For all of its challenges, New York reemerges in Allen's films and other upscale Manhattan idylls as a place where smart if neurotic artists and their set figure out their lives and loves over a six-dollar cappuccino.[87]

Still, since Manhattan's metamorphosis into a place where even Harlem and the Lower East Side have twenty-five-hundred-dollar-a-month studio apartments, most crime dramas have migrated to the far outer boroughs, as in Spike

Lee's *Clockers,* or even to cities such as Detroit in John Singleton's *Four Brothers* or L.A. in his *Boyz 'n the Hood.* In this spatialized nature, where ethnic neurotic comedies inhabit the trendy Manhattan areas, and African-American crime fetes push to the peripheries, cinema has again reflected, or maybe shaped, Americans' conceptions of a city hypersegregated by class and especially race.[88]

Indeed, throughout the 1980s and beyond, in another part of the city far from the bistros and jazz piano bars of Allen-land, television and film figures continued to wage war in ghettos out of control. On television, Steven Bochco's *Hill Street Blues* revolutionized the crime drama genre, with jerky handheld camera work, several subplots all going at once, and officers continually speaking over each other in a simulation of precinct house chaos unlike the placid zaniness seen on *Barney Miller* or even the previous perpetual level-headedness of Joe Friday and Bill Gannon. The show is set in an unnamed city on the brink, although visual clues and plot elements suggested the setting is Chicago. Wherever Captain Furillo presides over the Hill Street Precinct, however, this city is coming apart at the seams. Coinciding as it did with the Reagan era's massive scaleback in social services and hastening of the disinvestment in urban America by all manner of government and business actors, over its six-year run *Hill Street* offered the full range of 1980s urban nightmares. And save for the ineffectual whining of lone precinct liberal Lieutenant Henry Goldblume, the series "express[ed] the belief that liberal ideologies no longer worked for resolving the old tensions and problems," as Donald Bogle argued, "reflecting the era's resulting political conservatism."[89]

The show's main character seems to be the squalid streets of the Hill, where drug gangs, prostitution, and violent crime at times seem to drain the life blood and humanity out of the officers. Officers often express resentment and frustration with the dysfunctional city residents with whom they come into contact, frequently echoing the pronouncements of 1980s politicians, pop sociologists, and talk show hosts. When Officer Andy Renko lectures his African-American partner, Bobby Hill, on the ghetto mentality here, he sounds like Rush Limbaugh with a badge. As in the film *Fort Apache, the Bronx* (which was released the year *Hill Street* debuted), by the Reagan era it seemed fictional police were resigned to their role as an occupying army, punching a time clock and keeping a lid on the lawless urban frontier, but with little pretense that they could bring any real peace or improvement to their slum. The *Hill Street*'s first desk sergeant begins his morning briefings by admonishing, "People, let's be very careful out there." After actor Michael Conrad's death, the new sergeant, played by Robert Prosky, perhaps more deeply enmeshed in the 1980s culture of writing off larger and larger swatches of minority urban America, snarls, "Let's do it to them before they do it to us."[90]

Other characters respond to perceived urban pathologies in ways that mirror the increasingly militarized response to minority residents by the big-city mayors of this era. The SWAT team commander, Lieutenant Howard Hunter, is the kind of soldier of fortune who disastrously purchases a tank in which to patrol the streets where he serves (?) and protects. In another episode, one of Hunter's new SWAT paramilitary recruits shoots and kills a black suspect, but creates a minor furor when he's caught on TV news tape gleefully shouting, "Got you, you son of a bitch!"

While Howard Hunter's tanks may seem a stretch, recall that in 1985 the city of Philadelphia dropped gasoline-soaked bombs on the West Philadelphia home of MOVE activists and squatters, gutting dozens of homes on Osage Avenue in the process. And during the Giuliani administration in New York, this American mayor condoned the fatal shooting of Amadou Diallo, shot forty-one times by police officers while reaching for his wallet, as well as the sodomization of another black suspect, Abner Louima, by several officers within a precinct house bathroom. The "got you, you son of a bitch!" moment had arrived in American urban culture, on TV as well as in front of the screen.[91]

Throughout the 1980s and beyond, big-city mayors and police commissioners used quasi-militarized tactics and "zero-tolerance policies" to keep a tight lid on the ghetto. Mayors proved more interested in placating downtown business interests and projecting a tourist-friendly image of their cities than tackling underfunded schools, disinvestment by businesses that pay a living wage, and other issues that affect the minority neighborhoods. Whether *Hill Street* influenced, or reflected, such thinking is a difficult question of causal relations. But Howard Hunter certainly could have advised any number of Reagan era mayors that it was far easier to buy a tank or helicopter than fund a preschool breakfast program.

The show ran into some heat for the almost uniformly black and Hispanic criminals seen in the series. Creator Steven Bochco gamely defended this as just more gritty urban realism, arguing "The criminal element at this particular precinct was almost 100 percent Black or Chicano." He added, "We're not trying to make a specific comment about Blacks per se, though there is a very high incidence of abandonment within the Black community in ghettos. There are certain sociological realities there." Still, while the series presented black police officers, including the ghetto-savvy fashion plate Neal Washington, and occasionally indulged in examinations of serious issues such as substandard public housing, overworked single mothers, and a policeman's accidental shooting of a seven-year-old black boy playing with a toy gun, the larger "sociological realities" of public disinvestment in urban education, recreation, and infrastructure went largely unexamined.[92]

The show frequently places the city's racial animosities on raw display. A Hispanic gang leader is frequently called into Furillo's office to negotiate with the police for effective ways of pacifying the ghetto, creating for conservative viewers perhaps another picture of authority figures held hostage or blackmailed by minority criminals. Some such "blackmail" rhetoric had been thrown at advocates of social programs following the late 1960s urban disturbances and would be heard again in the wake of the Rodney King outbreaks in Los Angeles, and here came a ghetto gang leader demanding a share of decision-making authority in urban policing. That the gang leader later in the series goes back to school and becomes a lawyer working in the public defender's office only slightly blunts this image of a city held captive to intrinsically criminal minorities.[93]

Other times, resentments are expressed by white characters at the growing political clout of black urbanites in belittling ways that again mirrored some of the rhetoric aired on Reagan era talk radio. When a black police lieutenant, Ozzie Cleveland, runs and wins the mayor's office, white police officer J. D. LaRue dismisses him to his black partner, Washington: "Ozzie is a real nice guy. I just don't see him as mayor of the city." Washington snaps, "White man's job, right?"

Other characters certainly think this is "right." Howard Hunter rejects black mayors in Chicago and Los Angeles "with the last names of former generals and presidents" as "usurpers. They're trading on the names of our great dead heroes." That New York's David Dinkins (who at least had the good grace not to "usurp" a general's name) was indeed regarded as a usurper or, as comedian Jackie Mason called him, "an unemployed black male model," when Mason worked for Rudy Giuliani's election campaign, was likewise expressed by the Italian Brooklyn residents in Spike Lee's *Jungle Fever*.[94]

Lieutenant Hunter is set straight by Hispanic Lieutenant Ray Caetano. "They had their real names stolen from them," he reminds his conservative colleague. Ray's own efforts to advance in the department are repeatedly frustrated, as he is passed over for promotion. And when he is given the department's Hispanic Police Officer of the Year Award, he rightly calls out the wheeler-dealer police chief on this farce: "I look around this ballroom and ask myself, why are the only other Hispanic faces here busboys?" In an era when "minority set-asides," not persistent racism and enduring urban poverty, were the favorite whipping boys of politicians such as Jesse Helms, Chief Daniels has no answer for Ray or the viewer.[95]

The main picture that emerges of the fictional Hill Street ghetto is of a city of simmering ethnic resentments, a never-ending long, hot summer (or freezing winter) of crime, and ineffectual liberal policies and their legacies. In another reflection of actual events of the 1980s, the cynical mayoral aspirant Councilman Arnie Detweiler emulates Chicago Mayor Jane Byrne by living in the dilapidated housing projects of the Hill. Unlike Byrne's brief residence in Chicago's Cabrini Green (which was later dynamited to make way for five-hundred-thousand-dollar luxury condos, as gentrification, not urban rot, crept throughout the lakeshore area, displacing primarily African-American residents), Detweiler's photo-op goes horribly awry when he leans on a window grate and falls through the window, plummeting to his death.

In another episode a slumlord is sentenced to live in one of his own rat-infested buildings on the Hill. Precinct officers are shown apprehending him at his affluent suburban home. The complete divide between those who prey on the city and those who must pick up the pieces is demonstrated in this vignette; in another reflection of real-life dysfunction by affluent Reagan era urbanites, yuppies get the undercover cop Mick Belcher (masquerading as a homeless wino) drunk and take him up to the top of a building, where they encourage him to jump and end his sad life. In the real New York of the 1980s, a similar bunch of sadistic yuppies looking for kicks immolated homeless men, shocking a city that, one would have thought, had by the mayoralty of Ed Koch developed a thick skin of steel.[96]

It is black Mayor Ozzie Cleveland who inherits a city that has already been bled dry of resources, just as seemed to be the case in Detroit, Newark, and other cities in the 1970s and 1980s. At series end, Captain Furillo is being recruited as a reform candidate and "great white hope" for mayor. Only a policeman (or in the real New York of the early 1990s, an Italian-American federal prosecutor), the implication is, can save a city whose biggest problems are the lawless, primarily minority, hordes. The only answer white ethnics have to thwarting the encroaching tide of lawlessness is to pretend to be "connected," as when Officer Joe Coffee runs into an old friend of his Italian-American family who is posing as a Mafia boss. "Here the streets are safe, not like on the Hill," the fake mob boss tells Coffee. As we'll see, fictional white ethnic cities of the past and imagined, preferable Italian and Jewish neighborhoods, even with a little organized crime thrown in, had already by the late 1980s been established by popular culture as more desirable, workable bygone cities than the supposedly more chaotic and criminal black metropolitan sewer. In *Hill Street*'s garbage-strewn streetscape of human pathology, one might as well let the tanks roll.

NYPD Blue and *Homicide*, in New York and Baltimore, respectively, updated this morally ambiguous world of the urban ghetto as a colonial outpost over which police preside, but not so much offer hope. In *Homicide*, Detective Giardello, the half black, half Italian cop, supervises a unit that goes from grisly murder to grisly murder, not so much solving crimes as filing them away, shrugging, and moving on to the next disaster of the week. The jumpy camera work, hyperjazzy/urban rock sound track, and gritty streets when the show filmed on location, present a Baltimore continually on the verge of a nervous breakdown. Creator David Simon was a former police reporter for the *Baltimore Sun*, and like the screenwriter Ben Hecht from the earlier gangster film era he brought the jaded sensibilities of a big-city newsroom to his fiction. Without the restraints of the earlier era's Production Code, far more graphic depictions of violence and foul language permeated Simon's Baltimore than Hecht's Chicago, although this may be a matter of 1990s art's more realistically approximating a street life that even during Prohibition was blood- and profanity-laced. *Homicide*, like *Hill Street Blues* earlier and, as we'll see, Simon's later Baltimore series, *The Wire*, occasionally touched on sensitive issues of urban inequities, disinvestment, and urban-suburban mutual segregation.[97]

The resulting effect on viewers, though, who perhaps did not have the back story of Baltimore's savage history of hypersegregation—much of Baltimore's public housing remained strictly racially segregated until 1967, historian Rhonda Williams notes—and racial exclusion in key city industries, as well as savage white protests and vigilante action when blacks sought to move beyond their ghettoized "places," was to create an image of Baltimore as yet another city of violence, hopeless despair, black dysfunctionality, and official venality that was devoid of a larger context of how the city got this way.[98]

The very genre of a crime series guaranteed that the picture of Baltimore that emerged was one of savagery and danger, but viewers of the series might be excused if they vowed never to venture ten feet beyond the confines of Camden Yards or the Inner Harbor's Disney-esque urban simulacrum when visiting Baltimore.

On *NYPD Blue*, Detective Andy Sipowicz, like actor Dennis Franz's earlier character, Norman Bunz of *Hill Street Blues*, deals not just with efforts to recover from alcoholism but with his simmering resentment at a city where German- or Polish-Americans have to contend with African-Americans in positions of authority. His frequent racial epithets and strong-arm police tactics reflect the attitude of many in the 1990s as they looked at cities' outer neighborhoods.[99]

It might be an unfair burden to require of filmmakers or television artists subtle analyses of the sociological and historical reasons that disinvestment, redlining, and subjugation of blacks' aspirations by political, economic, and neighborhood actors had contributed to the cities' dilemma; this back story, as it were, was only sketchily provided on some shows, such as *The Mod Squad* and even *Hill Street Blues*, but a half-hour or hour show (leaving time, of course, for the all-important few words from laundry detergent, toothpaste, or diaper manufacturers) left little room for a sophisticated treatment of the root causes of urban decline stemming from federal actions and inactions, such as is more deftly treated by scholars such as Kenneth Jackson and Thomas Sugrue. A crime on *Mannix, The Rookies,* or *The Streets of San Francisco* for the most part stood devoid of its social context, as something that had to be defeated by grizzled police department veterans or vigilante private guns for hire who weren't always genteel in defeating wrongdoers, or too scrupulous in following the letter of the law, but who did rein in the chaos that supposedly had inexplicably overrun the cities depicted on the small screen.

And while police forces were slightly more multiracial on *Homicide* and other more recent shows than in the past, the crime they battle continues to be almost wholly the product of the black ghetto, a ghetto whose creation is rarely tied to the larger forces of fifty years of subsidized urban disinvestment and white flight. When these shows are coupled with similarly amnesiac political rhetoric demonizing the urban victims of such policies rather than honestly addressing possible cures, these cultural productions may be contributing to an ongoing antiurban mind-set that is sadly almost as old as the republic.[100]

Similarly, ghetto films of the early 1990s and the first years of the twenty-first century, even when well intentioned, sympathetic, and sophisticated productions by black filmmakers, often contain enough ammunition for those purporting to find a culture of violence and dysfunction among black urbanites. John Singleton's powerful debut film, *Boyz 'n the Hood*, opens with a sobering statistic on-screen, in emulation of the 1930s' gangster movies' use of pseudodocumentary title cards: "One out of every 21 black males will be murdered in their lifetime." Immediately the camera zooms in to a traffic sign: "STOP." Before we can even see any of the action in the film, we hear gunfire and police sirens, and when we do meet the young Trey Stiles and his friends on their way to school, they discuss the frequency with which shootings punctuate South Central L.A. "Both my brothers shot and they still alive," one kid mutters in dismissing Trey's discussion of "the shooting last night."

Yet the preteen Trey and his friends walk past campaign posters urging "Four More Years" for a cowboy-hat-wearing Ronald Reagan. The plight of the ghetto is perhaps linked to this and similar domestic budget-slashing administrations and similar decisions made out in the suburbs, far from the ghetto, Singleton suggests. Trey's father, Furious Stiles, will later make these points more explicitly.[101]

Singleton also presents plenty of characters who attempt to live exemplary lives in the ghetto's extremely difficult setting. Although he loses his temper when a bully taunts him, young Trey already intelligently leads his class—and clueless teacher, who fixates on rote recitation of the glory of "the Pilgrims"—in a detailed discussion of African history and culture. Both Trey's mother and, in more detail. his father, Furious Stiles, are shown instilling values and a work ethic in their son. "I don't wanna see you . . . a drunk standing in one of these liquor stores," his mother tells him, while Furious lectures his son on sexual restraint as well as self-respect as integral components in being a real man. Those residents of his neighborhood, his friends included, who don't have a strong male role model, however, end up fathering children for whom they can't possibly care, serve frequent stints in juvenile jail, and engage in other poor behavior that conforms to late-1980s–early-1990s conservative family-values preaching. Trey lectures a drug-addicted prostitute, "Just keep the baby out of the street. And change her diapers! They almost smell as bad as you!" In its valorization of strong male role models and portrayal of single mothers falling apart, their children heading straight into crime and drug use, *Boyz 'n the Hood* bolsters patriarchal, conservative moralizing in the ghetto and its minority residents almost as much as the Moynihan report and all the pop sociology on the tangle of pathology that became a small cottage industry by the late 1980s and early 1990s.[102]

To be sure, *Boyz 'n the Hood* also indicts the paramilitary occupation army that cordons off the ghetto, as helicopters ubiquitously hover over Trey and his neighborhood. The constant surveillance seems just as threatening as any real crime that may be lurking in South Central. Indicted along with this panopticon is the embittered African-American policeman who is quick to pull the trigger on black L.A. teens he finds out at night. As in Nathan Heard's furious novel of ghetto life in Newark, *Howard Street*, the black cop in Singleton's film is the bigger SOB of the two who patrol Trey's neighborhood.

When he demands, "Something wrong?" just itching for an excuse to use his gun on the model student, Trey mutters, "Something wrong? Yeah, it's just too bad you don't know what it is." After Trey deliberately leaves Crenshaw Boulevard, where a gunfight is imminent over rival gangs' macho posturing, this black cop pulls him over a second time, and exhibits sadistic glee at Trey's terror. "Oh, you're scared now, hey?" he rasps. "I like that! That's why I took this job, I hate little mother f*****s like you. Little niggers like shit." Without becoming pedantic, Singleton is able to suggest that the ghetto embitters certain black men into hating their peers and taking on a role as part of the ghetto's occupying army; very few other career paths seem to be open on Crenshaw.[103]

Furious also critiques the twin threats to his neighborhood: gentrification and the aggressive escalation of drug sales introduced into the ghetto by unnamed outside forces. "Well, how you think the crack rock gets into the country?" he reasons with an older black man in Compton who complains about drug use in his neighborhood. "We don't own any planes, we don't own no ships. Now we are not the people flying and floating the rock in here." Furious also notes drugs were not a national menace until they filtered out of the ghetto into "Iowa and Wall Street."

Yet for all the positive role models and nuanced treatment of the restricted life options open to South Central teens, the film ends with the violent, senseless murder of Ricky, a star athlete who, with a football scholarship to UCLA, seems poised to leave the ghetto. It is this negative image of black Los Angeles, and all the other ghettos with which this city is lumped, that many viewers likely took away from this film. The ghetto is a dangerous place; dysfunction reigns on Crenshaw. Likewise, Singleton's later *Four Brothers* may accurately reflect some parts of Detroit, and city councilmen complicit in illegal activity may mirror urban reality in some contemporary city halls. But the hail of machine-gun fire that destroys the Mercer Brothers' bungalow house is the kind of bad press the Motor City has been lamenting at least since July 1967. For all the adopted brothers' racial solidarity may offer some hope of a city that has moved beyond its LBJ era animosities, perpetual mayhem blankets the film and, by extension in many viewers' minds, perhaps the entire city in which the film takes place.[104]

Spike Lee's adaptation of *Clockers*, the Richard Price novel, also paints a grim image of the Brooklyn housing projects, where the quiet teen Strike works as a dope pusher. While his brother, Victor, also aspires, like Furious, to be an upright role model for his brother, it turns out that the ghetto offers few such options for its residents. Lee sensitively suggests that it is the claustrophobic world of high rise ghettos—in places cut off from other more legitimate options—that shapes if never quite determines the choices characters make. Strike is a teen who is already working on a second ulcer, and the pain eating away at his gut might be equated with the rot of a society that shrugs and relegates so many millions to places like this.[105]

But should the viewer choose to ignore the more empathetic conclusions, which (to his credit) Lee never didactically preaches, there is violence enough in the projects' courtyards to reinforce the image of the far reaches of Brooklyn as a place better written off and avoided altogether, save for voyeuristic pleasures. The project residents sardonically comment on the body chalk-marks that regularly appear in the projects, welcoming any respite from a tedious pace of severe under-employment and ennui. A dead body in the courtyards is at least some diversion, and for all of Lee's honest condemnation of the deadly influences at work steering kids into drug dealing, one of the few options open to them, the screen violence likely reinforces more dismissive narratives about the ghetto. While certainly Lee's *Clockers* is an honest approximation of the very desperation suffocating the real Brooklyn projects, the sympathy he endeavors to build for his character may get lost in the screened violence.[106]

Still, Lee captures some of the real desperation in places such as Brooklyn—just as his earlier *Jungle Fever* replicated the Italian-American rage expressed in Bensonhurst when African-Americans such as Yusef Hawkins ventured onto "their" turf. Recall that a young black man was beaten and chased to his death in the primarily white Brooklyn neighborhood for nothing more heinous than walking into these streets in search of a car to buy. In this respect the near race riot that ensues when Lee's architect, Flipper, has an affair with an Italian-American secretary is a grim reminder of the ugly salience of racism in still marketing "safe" and "dangerous" urban spaces. Bensonhurst is very unsafe—for a black man. And when cops put their guns to Flipper's head as he playfully wrestles with his girlfriend—assuming they have come upon the mythical black rapist in their midst—we see a plausible scenario in the New York of the film's era and beyond. Sadly, such slices of life may be more evidence of the city's racialized abyss.[107]

So, too, *Freedomland*, the Joe Roth adaptation of Richard Price's novel set in a thinly veiled Jersey City, centers on a single mother from Gannon, a neighboring working-class white city, who claims her baby was kidnapped by a black man in the housing projects of much-feared Dempsey/Jersey City. The border between white and black cities is already tensely patrolled, a replication of the real-life Detroit and Cleveland-Cleveland Heights concrete perimeter barriers, but now the projects are invaded like some high-rise Iraq, white police officers from the woman's neighborhood treating the projects' all-black residents as all equally worthy of contempt and brutalization until the child is produced.

The film/novel mirrors the real vigilante witch hunt that ensued when Charles Stuart fabricated black hijackers in Boston allegedly responsible for his wife's death (it later turned out that the white stockbroker had killed her himself). Likewise, Susan Smith, a white single mother, evaded responsibility for drowning her own children for several weeks by blaming it on a mythical black carjacker. And by the time of this film's release the militarization of the space around public housing (at least rental housing, not federally subsidized suburban homes) had already proceeded apace, so that real public housing residents had to run a gauntlet of security checks just to enter their own homes.[108]

Freedomland reports with little exaggeration the heightened policing of the black-white demarcation points in turn-of-the-century America. In Philadelphia, a primarily black and Latino neighborhood, Kensington, was cordoned off by police checkpoints in the late 1990s in an effort to end drug dealing. Even though the buyers were primarily white suburbanites entering the city, it was the minority residents of the neighborhood who had to show ID and otherwise justify their existence to police officers every time they sought to enter or exit Kensington's "security" zone. In such a climate the hysteria generated in *Freedomland*'s Dempsey is plausible indeed, and life and art are mutually reinforcing factors in the demonization of the American city.[109]

In our era the city and its minority residents are the blank screens onto which all too many Americans project their phobias and fantasies. The ultimate step in turning minority areas of desolate big cities into fantasy playgrounds of crime and mayhem, voyeuristically consumed, had, after all, already been taken with the introduction of reality television shows, particularly *Cops*, in which black suspects (at least ostensibly still granted the benefit of the doubt) "starred" in their own shows as the hunted quarry of big-city police forces out to serve and entertain the gawking television viewer. In earlier years voiceovers breathlessly announced a different kind of safari on *Mutual of Omaha's Wild Kingdom*; by the 1990s the prey was of the human, African-American variety.[110]

The city, as was demonstrated in the previous chapter, was always perceived as a dangerous place, but the level of brutalization of its occupants may be what had changed by the 1990s. To be sure, filmmakers and TV producers had greater freedom in the 1990s compared to the 1930s for conveying urban criminality in graphic detail. But any cursory glance at the newspaper depictions of gangland Brooklyn in the day of Murder Inc. gives the lie to the notion that Jewish and Italian criminals were more innocent and angelic than some of the present-day black and Latino gangsters. Nevertheless, in the here and now, it seems the mayhem of fictional Chicago, Los Angeles, Jersey City, and Brooklyn is presented in a framework where, compared to nostalgic films of bygone cities, the violence is always grimmer, and the end game is always more desperate.

Indeed, it is usually only in its past that the city of movies from the 1970s through the 1990s was largely seen to be functional, and in this respect the nostalgic gangster film set the groundwork for establishing a trope of a remembered, privileged white city of the past. Concurrent with demonizations of the present-day city in television and film came a new wave of gangster films that situated white (Italian/ Jewish) crime comfortably in the distant past, not a threat to the here-and-now city. *The Godfather* and its successor films evoked earlier mobsters with a backdrop of sepia-toned nostalgia, and family verities of honor and loyalty figure just as prominently in these films as murder and machine guns.

Nor are the depredations of the fictional Corleones implicated in any evils the city now faces (remember that Don Corleone declines "The Turk's" offer to deal in heroin, arguing that those who do so are animals preying on children in city schoolyards, something the crime patriarch will have no part of. "Leave it among the coloreds," the don sneers, for he is at least assimilated enough to the American way of life to know which group he can stigmatize and not be gainsaid. "They're animals anyway"). Still, heroin is indeed introduced into New York's black neighborhoods by the other white, Italian gangsters, and ironically, it is Sonny, the don's hotheaded son, who brings violence to Harlem when he beats up his brother-in-law on the uptown streets where he controls the numbers racket. Nevertheless, for all their street battles, these criminals are presented as part of movies in which white criminality is depicted in the nostalgic past, explicable, excusable, and never as dangerous, bloody, or morally reprehensible as the agonies that the city of the 1970s or 1980s suffers.[111]

The Godfather appeared the year after sociologist Michael Novak celebrated *The Rise of the Unmeltable Ethnics,* second- and third-generation whites of southern and eastern European descent who were very quickly valorized in comparison to black and Hispanic Americans disrupting polite civil discourse.[112] Other nostalgic glimpses back at a bygone city in 1970s–1990s film and television often efface urban crime or other pathologies and celebrate a golden cityscape of Jewish, Italian, or other white ethnic strivers, buttressing Novak and other conservative sociological writers' arguments that the white immigrant city of the past had worked, and suggesting that something in the present "underclass's" "culture" had led to a different, more persistently poor and dysfunctional city. The imagined immigrant narrative of arriving with ambition, a strong work ethic, and no disruptive or law-breaking tendencies quickly became a game of insidious comparison making. Since "we" had made it, the argument went, with no street demonstrations, special government programs, or minority set-asides, and since "we" had never ever broken the city's peace or threatened to riot, why can't "they" make it today the same way we did? This fable of self-help by European immigrants indulges more freely in amnesia regarding the militancy and activism of southern and eastern European newcomers, as well as the fear such behavior evoked in "real" white Americans from 1890 to 1940.

Gangster nostalgia has become something of a cottage industry, and for all the violence of white ethnic hoods and made men, the bygone cities they personify come off as more attractive places than the black ghetto. Martin Scorsese's breakthrough *Mean Streets*, shot in New York's Little Italy with jerky, handheld camera work, gives Little Italy the feel of an urban village where values are under siege by larger forces than the characters can understand. Charley, nephew of a mob boss, expresses his code of honor, in which you rely on the church and faith, but also "do it in the streets," where one wins the praise of coethnic friends. For all the small-time loan sharking and hustling of the characters, the neighborhood bars and Italian coffeehouses connote a place of values, friendships, and rootedness. As Charley's connected uncle regales him with past glories of "Charley Lucky" (Luciano), this world where neighbors sit on their stoops and still watch out for each other is evoked; archaic, certainly, but nonetheless inviting to the viewer.[113]

There are none of the visual icons of a city out of control—the garbage, ghetto drug dealers, and pimps so prominently on display in blaxploitation films. And while Johnny Boy (Robert De Niro) gets shot at film's end through his own stupidity in insulting a small-time hood, none of the real mobsters in the movie need display any overt violence or spectacular film firepower, as the black hoods of the contemporary blaxploitation films were doing. Uncle Giovanni is an acceptable gangster for the 1970s, given the other options on the table.

The feast of San Gennaro, with its street festa bands and operatic singers, also serves as the backdrop to the story of Charley and Johnny Boy; only these Mediterranean trappings are no longer the ethnic oddities and vulgarities that Progressive Era reformers were certain such Sicilian intrusions were, but rather signs of worthy immigrant culture. By 1973 and the rise of an ethnic backlash against black civil rights and perceived incursions into neighborhoods of "ethnic purity" (as Gerald Ford termed them in the 1976 presidential debates), such symbols now signify for the viewer that, however much Johnny Boy may firebomb a mailbox, or even get shot after he calls the local loan shark a "scumbag" once too often, Little Italy is a roguish, albeit valorized, space in the city, unlike other scarier parts of the mean streets this movie doesn't walk.

Then, too, the sound track, on which "Be My Little Baby" and other Motown tunes play as the action unfolds, serves as an auditory signifier of wistful nostalgia for the Little Italys of America that, by 1973, were already rapidly becoming archaic places, repositories of nostalgia. Rather than the Curtis Mayfield sound track of blaxploitation films or hip-hop reverberations and the much-maligned gangsta rappers featured in the ghetto movies of the 1990s, it is nostalgic doo-wop or early 1960s music that invariably underscores the scenes in white ethnic neighborhoods of nostalgic gangster films such as *Mean Streets, Goodfellas,* and *A Bronx Tale.* Such golden oldie sounds evoke a warmer Bronx or Brooklyn past; even if some of the hardworking white ethnics are here shown heisting trucks or fencing stolen goods, much is forgiven through such devices, which set up a musical sigh for bygone, happier times. How dangerous can these goodfellas be if they hang out at cool places like the Bamboo Lounge or play stickball or shoot craps to the Motown stylings of the Shirelles? Use of music sets this white ethnic criminality in a framework of "the good old days," a functioning city where everyone knew his or her place.[114]

Neighborhood hangouts, too, seem less threatening places—indeed, almost refuges from collapsing societies—in these films. The Chez Bippy, Sonny's bar in *A Bronx Tale,* keeps the turbulent 1960s at bay throughout this film, while the cab stand hangout of East New York's Brooklyn goodfellas is an inviting place where we, along with Henry Hill, are happy to run after the tedium of school. The rest of East New York (the real Brooklyn neighborhood of Murder Inc.) is shown as pretty squalid, as indicated by the Hills' cramped apartment, and Henry's gushing, "As far back as I can remember, all I ever wanted was to be a gangster," makes sense in such a milieu. As 1950s tunes play on the jukebox and Henry's nostalgic voiceover introduces us all around the Bamboo Lounge to Jimmy Two Times, Charley Eyes, Frankie Stabile, and the other colorful neighborhood types, we can understand. Who in 1955 Brooklyn would choose any other life?[115]

In these films, the unspoken comparison to "dysfunctional" blackness sometimes peers out. In *Mean Streets* Michael's love for his schoolteacher girlfriend rapidly fades when a pal identities her as someone he saw "kissing a nigger" over in Jersey. In *Goodfellas*, a truck driver who has collaborated with Henry and Tommy De Vito on a heist rushes into a diner feigning alarm. "Hey, you got a phone?" he shouts. "Two niggers just stole my truck; can you believe that?" In the outer boroughs of *Goodfellas* everyone can believe that, for already by the early 1960s (the film's fictional time), to say nothing of the early 1990s of its release, criminality is equated with blackness, and Irish and Italian hoods fly under the radar screen or are given a pass.

Characters' witty repartee, as well as their Robin Hood attitude toward what they are doing, stands in contrast to the more condemnatory tone taken regarding black criminality even in ghetto films. Here Henry and Tommy are likable, OK, maybe even "amusing" characters, and their criminal activity rarely results in violence or death. A few gangsters turn on each other, as when Tommy returns to a bar to kill Billy Bats for insulting him, or shoots the waiter Spider for bringing him his drink too slowly. But civilians or innocent bystanders never seem to be harmed by the enterprise of these white strivers. Their dips into the till of the local cash cow, the airport, indeed seem, compared to the drug deals and AK-47s of the black 'hood, to be victimless crimes.

In Henry's neighborhood, adjacent to Idlewild (later Kennedy) Airport, hijacking cargo from trucks is merely immigrant initiative, and since it seems 80 percent of the neighborhood (including truck drivers, cops, and bar owners) are cut in on the action, no wonder the gangster Jimmy Conway is, to his outer-borough neighbors, Jimmy the Gent. The *Goodfellas* milieu of small-time pilferers is argued away (at least by Henry and Karen Hill) as just "blue collar guys . . . showing a little initiative," and maybe helping their neighbors and extended kin, too.[116]

In other nostalgic gangster films, such as *A Bronx Tale*, we don't even see much criminal activity or violent score-settling by Sonny and the other made men who are the lords of 187th Street. Unlike in black-centered crime films, the illicit activity here is mostly off-screen. While the protagonist's father tells him to stay away from the Chez Bippy, "where all the guys hung out," we never see any of the extortion, protection rackets, or union skimming by which the real-life Sonnys of the Bronx made their living. What we do see is portrayed in a glow of nostalgic warmth for stickball, crap games, and hanging out. There is a numbers racket, which the straightlaced bus driver refuses to join, but even his wife says $150 a week to run a few numbers would not be such a terrible compromise. Overall, the gangsterism here is of a distanced, secondhand quality, courtesy of narrative voiceovers, musical effects, and period sets, cars, and clothing that evoke, for all the numbers rackets and loan sharking, "the good old days." As the protagonist Cee gushes, "What a time it was!"

This is not to say these films aren't masterful explorations of the white ethnic underworld of Brooklyn, the Bronx, and elsewhere; it is merely that they have not operated in a void. Other political debates, complaining of a supposedly more violent city, have been raging at least since the years of these films' release, and it is with political debates over just when the city (in the past so supposedly functional) went wrong that these films are in dialogue. *Goodfellas* may well be the most compelling movie of the 1990s, but it nonetheless sets up—in spite of itself, perhaps—a bygone hood land that still resonates powerfully with those longing for a rooted, functional past.

Other films engage in a fuller exploration of the connection between the functional good-old-days immigrant neighborhood and the street-corner politics of keeping the outsiders off our turf. Robert De Niro's directorial debut came with *A Bronx Tale*, which offers a sophisticated examination of the old Italian neighborhood of Fordham resisting the lapping tides of racial and cultural change throughout the 1960s. The doo-wop sound track lets us know that we will be traveling not just back in time, but to a place that, so far as the sophisticated, modern Manhattan is concerned, the young narrator tells us "might as well be 3,000 miles away." The scenes of the neighborhood signify again that it is a stable community, with Italian fruit vendors traveling by horse and wagon, old men playing *modra* (the "fingers" game), men in undershirts listening to the Yankees (the Mickey Mantle Yankees) on the stoop with a cold bottle of Ballantine, or playing stickball in the alley, all the icons of white ethnic old neighborhoods. Every boyhood trip to Orchard Beach (or other urban recreation spots of a bygone era) is evoked in the viewer in this film.

Nostalgia, though, is predicated on what is excluded, not just what is included. As Calogero (Cee) and his young friends watch in 1960, some blacks ride the bus through their neighborhood. "Those niggers got some balls, coming in our neighborhood," one young kid snarls, and even though Calogero reasons, "They don't live here, they're just passing through from school," his friend knows better, courtesy of the neighborhood's racist preaching. "Yeah, well, my father told me that's how it starts."

As the other kids chase after the bus, Calogero witnesses an attempted mob hit that the local don, Sonny, breaks up by killing the assailant. The neighborhood, all of it, watches as the young kid is taken by the police to identify the shooter. As he is paraded past the mobsters lined up along the Chez Bippy, the rest of the neighborhood are the real witnesses. Everyone's actions are witnessed and judged by the whole block, and when Calogero does "a good thing for a bad man" by refusing to rat, he earns a privileged place in the neighborhood's pantheon. As everyone knows, "A rat is the lowest thing anyone could be in my neighborhood. And I didn't rat."

The racial certainties of the neighborhood, though, are embraced less whole-heartedly by Cee. While he is skeptical of his pals' street logic, countering his friends' assertions of an imminent "threat" of black takeover, in voiceover Cee has already told us that in 1968 "there was change everywhere. But my neighborhood was still the same." And the film's visuals indicate quite clearly that this encroaching 1968 already angrily lapping at Fordham's doorsteps is not desirable. On the other side of the tracks—literally—a black ghetto straight out of *Sweetback* and *Superfly* is only a block beyond Calogero and Sonny's world. Bikers invade the neighborhood, and if not for JoJo the Whale, Sonny, and the other paisans, the misery of the rest of the Bronx, it is implied, would engulf this bastion of *modra* and stickball, unlocked doors, and safe naps on the fire escape.

Indeed, it is the gangsters who rule the streets, but by doing so they keep crime, black rebelliousness, and other symptoms of 1968 literally on the other side of the tracks. When mobsters take a young Cee to meet Sonny, they reassure the kid, "Come on, nobody's gonna take that bike." The streets are kept safe by the old-line gangsters. At least safe for some people.

Sonny lives in the neighborhood and protects it. There is no need for cops in this ghetto, unlike on the other side of the tracks. But the crime boss actually has more enlightened racial attitudes than Cee's hardworking father. While Cee's dad loves jazz artists such as Miles Davis, he nevertheless thinks that "blacks should stick with their own," and not mingle with whites. It's the gangster who tells his young protégé it makes no difference what race a girl is, provided she's "one of the great ones." Still, the young gangster wannabes hanging out at the Deuces Wild social club react with rage when blacks begin riding through their all-Italian neighborhood, first on the bus and then, by 1968, in cars and on bicycles. Cee's friends are enraged by this: "Today it's one car, next week two cars, then it's their neighborhood. And then they're f*****g our broads."

While Cee eventually does the right thing, these racial tribalisms are tightly bound with the nostalgic sense of connectedness to place; like the narrator, the viewer may find it hard to disentangle the barricades around outsiders, especially the nonwhite interlopers, and those parts of 187th Street that are recalled with fondness and longing.

One difference between the corner of the city represented by *A Bronx Tale* and ghetto films is the sparseness of violence on display. We don't see any of the muscle Sonny must employ to control his empire in the Bronx—and again, his illicit enterprises take a backseat in the film to his role as neighborhood benefactor and protector. Save for the execution of the attacker on Carmine (Joe Pesci) at the film's beginning, an argument that is *not* over a parking space, mob violence is implied, not splattered all over the streets. When violence is employed here it is to preserve neighborhood and family values—to keep the contemptuous, disrespectful bikers (in 1968, *Easy Rider* comes looking for trouble in the Bronx) out of the neighborhood—or to rescue a friend and patron from a hit. When it is to teach "those niggers" a lesson, the Italian-American hood wannabes who are resisting the onset of the inevitable new Bronx are themselves blown up. And Sonny tells young Cee to avoid these losers who act on their own to lash out at blacks.

The film aptly captures the moral ambiguity surrounding the gangster figure, as well as the problematic longing for a bygone city of certitudes and fixed identities. On the one hand we, like Calogero, may agree "what a time it was" as we regretfully must step away from 1968 and the last game of stickball. And yet, as much as we know the compromises with the shady characters at Chez Bippy that were required to keep those stickball games safe, and that other Bronxites were perpetually told to stay the hell out of "our neighborhood," the viewer has already been conditioned by a variety of cultural productions to regard *A Bronx Tale*'s city as far preferable to the city of *Fort Apache, the Bronx*, which would invade and overrun Calogero's city by 1981. In this respect such nostalgic gangster films have contributed to a national myth that "we have made it, and why can't they?" our streets are immaculate, why not theirs boosterism that once more leaves African-Americans barred from the promised land.[117]

Moreover, this national myth, for such it has become, ignores the systemic deindustrialization of cities just at the moment blacks were arriving in significant numbers in the North, as well as the more impermeable barriers of race faced by African-Americans encountering virulent racism as they strove to achieve full integration and equal participation in the American Dream. For all the animus immigrants inspired circa 1900, these antiblack barriers stood longer and higher, so that, as George Clinton observes, blacks inherited "chocolate cities surrounded by vanilla suburbs" circa 1970.[118]

Conveniently forgotten, too, in these evocations of a mythical, functioning city prior to supposed liberal excess and "welfare giveaways" is the well-documented history of just what Hobbesian places New York, Chicago, and other American cities were prior to the New Deal, and the venomous attacks launched at working-class immigrant neighborhoods by Progressive Era writers alarmed by Jewish and Italian criminal gangs. Such profound cultural amnesia and hardheaded "sink or swim like we did" moralizing have been greatly reinforced by cultural productions such as urban dramas and their nostalgic doppelgangers that celebrate an earlier, urban immigrant past.

These films' wistful privileging of the bygone mean streets over the imagined contemporary ghetto points to important ways in which nostalgia has furthered an insidious agenda in urban politics and popular culture. In the concluding chapters, I shall briefly look at some new popular genres that have continued the trajectory of privileging a city of the past, imagined as an Edenic place, that somehow was stolen from white ethnic Americans by the blacks who inhabit the feared ghetto portrayed in the films we have considered. First to consider are what I term the nostalgic urban memoir novels, exemplified by *Middlesex*, Jeffrey Eugenides's novel of Detroit, and *American Pastoral* and the other work of Newark's favorite white memoirist, Philip Roth. Novels of the turn of the twenty-first century, they look back with alternating longing and rage to imagine better places of functional, hardworking white ethnic immigrants, the trope embodied in so many Ellis Island stories, while reviling the current city.

Cable television series set in the contemporary city, particularly HBO's *The Sopranos* and *The Wire*, often indulge in nostalgic recollections of immigrant thrift and hard work, too, while cleverly commenting on the sad state of American apartheid in the 1990s and beyond. And finally, the Internet has recently proven the ultimate tool in creating imagined communities, virtual cities, where one can project whatever political agendas one wishes onto a wired "old neighborhood" of the past. These new genres, then, will briefly, tentatively, be examined as the final (so far) adaptations in the project in which cultural producers seem eternally engaged: building up the metropolis only to tear its lurid pieces down.

5

"All of Life Was There Before": The Urban Nostalgic Memoir

Popular culture's 1960s assaults on the city did not go unanswered, and some cultural producers, particularly African-American artists, sardonically commented on the deprivations that were visited on their cities in that decade and beyond. Novelists such as Nathan Heard *(Howard Street)* and Barbara Wilson Tinker *(When the Fire Reaches Us)* published searing indictments of the ghetto conditions in Newark and Detroit, respectively, in the aftermath of the urban disturbances of July 1967. Other black responses to the 1960s characterization of the city as a lawless, senseless place came as well from visual artists and musicians, but the reception from the public at large that greeted such protest art was decidedly in a minor key. It would be thirty years after the urban rebellions themselves that white novelists and others would create a consensus memoir of the city that lamented that supposed decline from an immigrant Eden that places such as Newark and Detroit had been. For all that minority city residents strove to speak back to power—in the political realm as well as the arts—it was these consensual nostalgic memoirs, particularly by Philip Roth and recently, for Detroit, Jeffrey Eugenides in his novel, *Middlesex*, that set the tone for explaining the decline of the city.

Black novels published right after the riots told a different story. Barbara Wilson Tinker's novel *When the Fire Reaches Us* is set in Detroit's Twelfth Street corridor before and during the riots, and presents a glimpse at a poverty-stricken but functioning black community. While there are prostitutes in the neighborhood, they are treated as human beings, not crime statistics. And other neighborhood characters endeavor to function in a climate of severe deprivation as best they can, and pitch in to help each other. An extended family, a community, emerges from Tinker's portrait.

In the aftermath of the riot, Tinker's main character, Danny Sands, reads a newspaper account of the events, and hardly recognizes his community:

How come that shitass reporter to write all that crap about us with no regard to our feelings or asking us permission? Ain't likely he done it for no humanitarian reasons, . . . because any damned fool knows, Mr. Charley don't want nothing else but to sweep the dirt under the rug and if he do run across a article like the one this reporter wrote he ain't going to make nothing of it but what he wants to. Same time I had to be fair and give that writer credit; he'd put down the facts, but the facts don't always add up to the truth. That cat just didn't know where it was at.[1]

"Where it was at," so far as Tinker was concerned, was a city in which Danny's Uncle Ambrose recalls the false promise made to black laborers like himself during World War I, as factory owners lured needed black workers with promises Detroit was racism-free. The quick realization that the northern ghettos were only marginally better sinks in as tales are related of slumlords refusing to fix plumbing in overpriced apartments, and racist white unions refusing to accept skilled black electricians ("Boy, don't you know we don't want any niggers fouling up our union?" a white union official in Detroit asks Mr. Winters, a neighbor of Danny's). As urban renewal, which a local black militant calls "nigger removal," slices pieces off their street to make room for parking lots for downtown office buildings, freeways to ease employees' exit to the security of Grosse Pointe every workday at 5 p.m., and high-rises in which no one in the neighborhood can afford an apartment, life gets grimmer as available jobs and city services—scarce for blacks even at the height of the Great Migration—dry up. Families look out for each other, and still social workers primly lecture a black woman on welfare not to "misuse her food money and buy you a new ribbon for your hair or a pair of secondhand skates instead of something useful. They never did seem to understand heart stuff like that or how humiliating it is to have the bare bones of your living laid open to the eyes of a stranger who is going to put it down on a piece of paper and make you a number."[2]

Danny doesn't deny there are many rough edges to the black ghetto. Seeing few other opportunities, or disgusted by low-wage, dead-end jobs, many of the older teens at his high school graduate to "hustling snow and coke or running after-hours joints or car theft and armed robbery." Danny doesn't take this path, nor does he approve it in others, but the tone is not a knee-jerk, condemnatory dismissal of ghetto pathology, such as was already building to a crescendo in many white commentators. Then, too, while Tinker doesn't mention it, it's curious to note that, forty years before, the Twelfth Street corridor had been an eastern European and Jewish immigrant slum, and at that time the Bernstein brothers and other white ethnic hoodlums of the Purple Gang had made their livelihoods by similar endeavors on these very same streets.[3]

For all that, Danny's Pine Street also includes many older neighbors who provide role models and who teach the neighborhood kids willing to learn about black history, stories of Nat Turner and Harriet Tubman and blacks fighting alongside Mr. Charley in the American Revolution. "We had some very different ideas about being black and the world in general from other Negro children," Danny says.[4]

Danny knows, too, some of the humiliations that have been visited on blacks in Detroit in the years leading up to the riots, as when Cynthia Scott, a black prostitute, was shot and killed by a policeman in 1963. Danny notes that the official exoneration of the policeman, which alleged that Scott had pulled a knife on the officer, rang hollow in the slums, as even the coroner's report noted that Scott was shot in the back. No punishment at all was meted out to the officer, and Danny notes, "So we ain't forgot—not that nor any of the injustices which has been perpetrated on us." The neighbors angrily recount, too, the June 1967 assault on a black Vietnam veteran and his pregnant wife by a gang of white teens. The Thomases had committed the "crime" of entering a park in a whites-only neighborhood for a picnic. When the white teens began assaulting Mrs. Thomas, the couple tried to flee, but their car wouldn't start. The husband then tried to scare off the gang with his gun, but when he dropped it in a struggle, one of the teens fired it at the black man and killed him. As historian Sidney Fine has noted, surveys conducted after the riot that occurred a month later indicated that the riot's ostensible cause—a police raid on a Twelfth Street "blind pig" illegal after-hours bar— was merely the proximate cause, and that many blacks cited the history of police brutality, white-on-black assaults, inadequate ghetto housing, and unresponsive city agencies as the dry tinder that had been building under this ghetto. All it took was one spark to cause Twelfth Street to explode.[5]

When rioting erupts, Danny notes that both blacks and whites opportunistically take part in looting, both in the ghetto area and in outlying areas of the city, facts confirmed by Fine in his *Violence in the Model City.* Danny recalls that after buildings began burning and looters threw "bottles and stones and pieces of glass and anything else they can lay hold of at the firemen," the police began firing back at the looters. "You better believe that at this point ain't no policemen grinning and good-natured; they is coming with clubs swinging. Well, you cannot hardly blame them for being upset, but they is beginning to knock folks around without no regard to just who is just standing by and who is throwing and looting."

Of the forty-three killed in the Detroit disturbances, Fine notes that the majority were black, but many were indeed not engaged in criminal activities when they were assaulted by the authorities. A similar indiscriminate firepower was leveled in Newark, where journalist Ron Porambo notes that all but one of the twenty-six deaths were of civilians (one was a fireman, who may have been killed by a panicky state trooper's fire), and many were fleeing or were otherwise not engaged in criminal activity. Tinker also has Danny note that "more than one head was split open" by police, "believe you me; they were not white heads, either." The biracial nature of looting, as well as the literal overkill of state authorities in Detroit and Newark both go unremarked in later urban memoirs.[6]

When the Fire Reaches Us presents a complex and nuanced portrait of the ghetto and its residents, in which older blacks lament the looting of black-owned businesses and residences, and white merchants, desperate to escape destruction, hastily cobble together "SOUL BROTHER" signs for their stores. The novel attempts to explain, not excuse, the causes for the riot and the intertwined rage/ elation/sadness that characters feel as the fire reaches their neighborhood after a long, long fuse has been lit. Danny recalls the glee that his Detroit neighbors felt as they saw news reports in 1965 of Watts burning in far-off L.A.:

Though on top they was all the time talking about what a dreadful thing all this looting and burning was, . . . underneath was a kind of gladness and pride. It didn't make no difference that these black people down in Watts had done a whole lot of unlawful things—what counted was that they had got right up and said by those acts: "We had it. We ain't going to stand for nothing more. You done shoved us just as far as we can be shoved and we will not tolerate it no longer and that is that."[7]

Nevertheless, at other points Danny laments the mutual suspicions that centuries of racism have bred in both black and white Americans, and the tone here is of regret that the same song keeps getting played over and over in this regard:

If you set down and really study on the United States of America you don't know whether to laugh or cry. It has got so bad here that black peoples nor white peoples can't never see each other or theirselves straight. Color always got to come between. This do twist the thinking of both parties up so they can't hardly iron out the difficulties which this problem has caused because they is so busy looking wall-eyed at each other trying to figure out what the other side is up to. . . . God knows where it is going to end.[8]

The newspaper exposé of the riots that sets off Danny's account of Twelfth Street likewise frustrates him in its inability to capture this complexity. A photograph captioned "The Paradox of Pine Street" shows the body of Laurie, a black prostitute who died trying to rescue a white friend who was in the line of fire of National Guard snipers. But Danny is struck by "the whole lots of things that camera did not see," ending with "the young white guardsman with his rifle on the ground where he had throwed it and his face turned away twisted with sudden crying." Danny can't help feeling that, if they had lived in the same neighborhood, they might have been friends.[9] With her recognition of the agonistic mutual segregation and misunderstanding endemic in 1967 Detroit, Tinker highlights the ways in which mainstream accounts of the ghetto, with their monochromatic characterization of all blacks as senseless rioters and whites as innocent victims, left much out of the picture. Tinker's novel gives expression to the inner city's urban pathologies but also the racism and mutual misunderstandings and recriminations that precluded an honest settlement of Detroit's problems; she presents a 1960s city in all its ambiguities, with more sympathy for the ghetto's many residents than later, more successful novelists would evoke.

Howard Street, which Nathan Heard wrote while in prison for armed robbery, features less redeeming characters, the hustlers, pimps, and prostitutes of Newark's destitute Central Ward. Although his novel features enough pathological behavior to fill twenty Moynihan reports, and does not specifically address the riots, nevertheless, the poverty and not-so-benign neglect that the slum faces are accurate portraits of some of the problems that exploded in a cauldron of rage in July 1967. If one reads the novel not as an indictment but as a warning cry, some of the proximate and long-festering reasons for Newark's eruption in July 1967, documented by Porambo, Nathan Wright, Joseph Conforti, and Tom Hayden, are present in the dysfunctional world of the Howard Street hustlers Hip and Cowboy.[10]

The forces that have created this ghetto are present in the only white characters seen or alluded to in *Howard Street:* the cops who shake the neighborhood hustlers down, the drug suppliers in the mob, and the Italian thrill seekers from the city's West Ward, who come to the vice zone in search of black prostitutes. Cowboy, the drug dealer, can't provide the Howard Street junkies with their fix until he gets his supply from "the wops"; regrettable Italian slurs aside, in the real Newark of the 1960s the Boiardo mob did indeed control the heroin trade, as well as the numbers rackets and protection "services," and they operated through a comfortably close payoff scheme with the city hall of Mayor Hugh Addonizio. Heard furiously indicts the conditions in which the main character "Lonnie . . . had been predicted to go far, which in the Third Ward of Newark—'the Hill,' as they called it—could mean that he would wind up being a pimp, or opening a tavern, or making it big in the numbers racket, fronting for a syndicate."

The black hustlers of Howard Street, though, are only the street-level face of the mob and corrupt city hall officials who rake in the big bucks, for "much of what they made found its way into the pockets of the big-time white gangsters and cops, lawyers and politicians." Indeed, a well-connected lawyer, Mr. Meyer, rakes in most of the money from the pimps and drug dealers and, through his connections to city hall, gets any legal problems wiped away. Such a novel—coming as it did when historians and sociologists picking over Newark's shell suggested that endemic municipal corruption, organized crime, police brutality, and white flight had played a large role in the city's immiseration—might have also served as a wakeup call to America, an urgent cry to do something to alleviate these festering sores.[11]

But if protests at what Detroit historian Jerry Herron has aptly called "the humiliation of history" registered with the larger public, the reception was muted. Cities such as Detroit and Newark became code words for urban pathology, and artists who tried to express some nuanced picture of how the ghettos had come to be the way they were, such as Heard and Tinker, found limited audiences.[12]

Other artists found it difficult to get beyond the images of violence and destruction in their midst. Juke Boy Bonner and John Lee Hooker both set protests over the riots to music, yet both only minimally tried to suggest that the poverty and hypersegregation of Detroit played a role in the uprisings. "Goin' Back to the Country," by Bonner, admitted that he didn't "want no sniper hanging 'round," and Hooker's "Motor City's Burning," written just days after the disturbances, gave a Detroit native's impressions of the sadness at seeing "my home town's burning down to the ground, worse than in Vietnam." Still, a politicized answer to the problems was more than Hooker could offer in a standard eight-bar format. He sings, "It started on 12th and Claremont this morning, but I just don't know what it's all about," and the answer to all the snipers and "fire bombs bustin' all around" is a personal one of flight. "I don't know what the trouble is, I just can't stay around to find out, Taking my wife and my family, and ole Johnny Lee's leavin 'town." By the 1960s this was the option many white ex-urbanites had already taken.[13]

Other artists who stayed in the inner city were determined to make a graphic statement on their abandonment by a society that no longer deemed their neighborhoods worthy of basic amenities. When Detroit artist Tyree Guyton grew tired of trash dumped in vacant lots on his Heidelberg Street, and could not convince a severely cash-strapped city to haul the refuse away, he began an artistic project affixing the trash—baby buggies, bath tubs, boots and shoes, and more—to the sides of vacant homes on the street. The elaborately colored and fanciful creations, such as an ark containing dolls and stuffed animals, at last attracted the attention of city officials, who previously couldn't quite locate Heidelberg Street on trash pickup maps, but now tried to remove the material. But after every bulldozing, the Heidelberg Project grew again, a phoenix from deindustrialized ashes. Eventually the Heidelberg Project attracted critical acclaim, and became something of a tourist attraction, so that at last certain city officials tolerated and sought to market it as a way of drawing consumers/spectators back to the dreaded inner city. For a time a piece of one of the houses was valorized as art by being invited into the halls of the elite Detroit Institute of the Arts—but not before the junk-based art was fumigated. Exotic inner-city types and their arts evidently needed delousing, not fully funded social services as in the suburbs from which arts spectators flocked to Heidelberg.[14]

So, too, as on the Lower East Side circa 1900, a ghetto was commodified and conceptualized as an urban safari, perhaps almost literally. When the present writer and a Detroit poet friend in 1996 visited the Heidelberg Project, which by that time had grown to cover several houses on Heidelberg and adjoining streets, it was noticeable that all the other whites driving slowly down the street kept their windows rolled up and doors tightly locked. As we cavorted on the houses' porches, the images of Lion Country Safari were hard to ignore. Keep your hands in the car and make no sudden moves; we are entering the ghetto.[15]

A similar sardonic commentary on the imprisoned, impoverished Newark ghetto was erected in that city's Central Ward (scene of the riots) in the 1980s by artist Kea Tawana. The three-story Newark Ark was built by Tawana out of construction material she salvaged from homes demolished on Hunterdon Street, a comment, perhaps, on the plea of Newark residents for someone to rescue them from the floodwaters of neglect and poverty lapping over the Central Ward. Built according to Noah-like specifications, the ark also had lights provided by a generator that Tawana installed, although suspicious city officials investigated to make sure she wasn't stealing power in the middle of her rubble-strewn vacant lot. Health inspectors, too, were ready to pounce—ironic, considering the not-so benign neglect that Central Ward landlords had allowed to accumulate in the neighborhood for decades before, during, and after 1967. The ark was not the kind of project to warm the hearts of the chamber of commerce, and the city ordered it destroyed after a short time.[16]

More enduring fabricated cities have been created by nostalgic urban novelists. And as chance would have it, the two cities that were most severely affected by the 1967 urban disturbances have each received their novelistic chronicler, but in the work of each a partial, white-privileged memoir emerges.

Novelist Philip Roth has neatly divided his native Newark into functioning then and nightmarish now. Compared to black artists, he has won far more consent for his version of the past, using as he does the popular mortar of selective memory, amnesia, and an angry nostalgia to erect a fictional Newark his characters often assert was stolen from them by violent, irrational blacks.

The past for Roth and for many readers remains an Edenic pastoral, even if, ironically, many outsiders viewing southern and eastern European urban communities might have seen only chaos and disorder, a dysfunctional intrusion into the previously WASP or Irish pastoral city. As Kenneth Jackson's *Crabgrass Frontier* makes clear, already by 1910 the native-born Protestant business elite of old Newark were fleeing the city in droves for streetcar suburbs like Short Hills, West Orange, and Maplewood, and they were fleeing the scary Jews and Italians![17] It is the selective optics of insider versus outsider, them and us, that must be kept in mind when we consider these white ethnic neighborhoods, and the same caveat should apply to considering the African-American city of 1967 or beyond in the work of Roth.

The novel that most fully expresses this rage at a stolen Garden of Eden, located somewhere along Chancellor Avenue in Newark's predominantly Jewish Weequahic, is *American Pastoral*, the 1997 work for which Roth won his Pulitzer Prize. The novel is divided into subsections that spell out immediately Roth's game of selective memory and mythologizing the city's past. First comes "Paradise Remembered," then "The Fall" (which will arrive in July 1967), and then "Paradise Lost." These benchmarks indicate that, Roth, like many aging white ethnic ex-urbanites, crankily knows for certain that he was robbed of his blissful patch of the city by Mephistophelean outsiders. This is a monologue not just of loss but of theft. But as Larry Schwartz has accurately argued, vis-à-vis Roth's entire historiography of Newark, New Jersey's favorite white novelist "offers a very blinkered view of Newark and its racial politics."[18]

The novel tells of writer Nathan Zuckerman's encounter with a high school hero, Swede Levov, who was a star athlete and, for Jewish Weequahic, "a boy as close to a *goy* as we were going to get." He is the son of Lou Levov, a self-made man who'd risen from the fetid tannery floors where he'd gone to work at age fourteen to become president of Newark Maid Gloves, a paragon of hard-nosed, immigrant success. The difficult conditions by which some (and only some) immigrants overcame industrial dangers and noxious slums to become success stories are valorized here, but along with success comes an inability to consider the possibly higher hurdles keeping other Newarkers down.

Indeed, Lou Levov is described as a typical first-generation product of the Jewish ghetto, "a father for whom everything is an unshakable duty, for whom there is a right way and a wrong way and nothing in between . . . men quick to be friendly and quick to be fed up." In this characterization of the virtues of moral absolutes, Roth reveals his Newarkers will be unlikely to consider whether Weequahic, or Howard Street, the old ghetto that Jewish Newarkers had by and large by Roth's teenage years abandoned to African-Americans, was possibly to other Newarkers never such a paradise, even in the 1940s. It is always possible that someone else's Utopia can be another race's hell, but not for characters who speak in absolutes of right and wrong like Lou Levov.[19]

Swede (the nickname to which fair-haired, athletic Seymour answers among old Newark friends) follows his father as president of the glove factory, sticks with the city of Newark through good times and bad, and is destroyed when the encroaching tides of racial change and pie-eyed liberalism swamp his world. Yet, even in the novel's first pages, selective memory is at work that glosses quickly over some of white ethnic Newarkers', such as the Levovs', complicity in the decline of their city and the invisible racism that allows some Newarkers to rise and others to cluster in the slum. Zuckerman/Roth recalls Keer Avenue, where the Levovs and other "rich Jews lived—or rich they seemed to most of the families who rented apartments in the two-, three- and four-family buildings." Unlike the immigrant generation, "which had recreated around Prince Street in the impoverished Third Ward" a Yiddish-speaking slum, the narrator recalls that their more affluent progeny were on the fast track to full-bore Americanism. "The Keer Avenue Jews, with their finished basements, their screened-in porches, their flagstone front steps, seemed to be at the forefront, laying claim like audacious pioneers to the normalizing American amenities."[20]

But those "normalizing amenities" were off-limits to blacks, who were barred from the federal benefits that largely began immigrants' slow climb up into the middle class—Social Security benefits, for example, were not extended to agricultural workers and domestic servants, the two largest categories of black employees. And the Federal Housing Administration began its infamous redlining policy of denying federally insured mortgages to residents of "Negro-majority" and "Negro-threatened" areas. Middle-class black attempts to move out of the ghetto were stymied. In Newark, the black residents of the Central (old Third) Ward in 1950 complained that banks refused to make loans available to prospective home buyers in what was now the majority-black slum of their city. Those screened-in porches, purchased in many cases with Uncle Sam's assistance, were unavailable to blacks in Newark and other American cities.[21]

Moreover, the move to quasi-suburban Weequahic that Roth celebrates played a large role in turning the area around Prince and Howard Streets into a ghetto. The already decaying apartment buildings of this slum—which produced the notorious gangsters Abner "Longy" Zwillman, Joseph "Doc" Stacher, and others—were, beginning in the 1920s, abandoned by those second-generation Jewish success stories Roth celebrates, so that as early as 1940 the city's Jewish Welfare Board noted that only twenty-three hundred Jewish residents remained in the old Third Ward. Already by 1948, the Board noted that suburbanization was beginning among Newark's Jewish community.[22]

Taking their place in the Central Ward were the black migrants to the city, who moved into the slums where housing stock was now in most cases fifty or more years old. Many buildings had no indoor plumbing, toilets were still outhouses, and central heating and even running water were often missing. A federal report in 1944 acknowledged that Newark's Central Ward rental housing was some of the worst in the country, and one-third of the units were regarded as substandard by any criteria. Slumlords "gouged these tenants mercilessly," the report asserted, with five thousand houses "unfit to live in," a finding borne out later as the black population swelled to seventy-five thousand in 1950 but still was relegated chiefly to the Central Ward, which was the densest, most noxious part of a city that overall had the third-highest population density in the nation. The 1944 report noted that ghetto landlords still blithely rented out more than five thousand buildings unfit to live in by any object criteria, a situation by and large uncorrected in 1966, when urban planner George Sternlieb again condemned "the tenement landlord" of Newark as chiefly responsible for the deplorable conditions of the slum. And when federal public housing was first created in Newark, it didn't alleviate the situation for the black ghetto dwellers. Baxter Terrace House was opened with the whites-only color bar firmly in place, a situation that fit in neatly with the city's hypersegregated theaters, Salvation Army, municipal pools and bath houses, and other facilities.[23]

While in *The Human Stain* Roth's retired black teacher, Ernestine Silk, does get around to deploring segregated schools in south Jersey, the Jim Crow Light situation in the Newark of the author's youth goes unmentioned. The texture of the indignities blacks suffered in Newark's slum, instead, can be found in the oral histories of African-American Newarkers collected in *When I Was Comin' Up*, but since Weequahic quite accurately was separated from the Central Ward by only a few miles but nevertheless a chasm of de facto segregation in the 1940s, very few such voices make it into *American Pastoral*. Such uncomfortable memories are banished from the Eden of 1940s Newark.[24]

Other hints are given in the novel, however, that the city's industrial magnates were already withdrawing from their golden city years, if not decades, before the scapegoated 1967 riots. After cataloging Lou Levov's success at establishing Newark Maid Gloves as a fixture at the city's downtown L. Bamberger's, Zuckerman notes that,

Little more than a decade later, with the opening of a factory in Puerto Rico in 1958, the Swede would himself become the young president of the company, commuting every morning down to Central Avenue from his home some thirty-odd miles west of Newark, out past the suburbs—a short-range pioneer living on a hundred-acre farm on a back road in the sparsely habitated hills beyond Morristown, in wealthy, rural Old Rimrock, New Jersey, a long way from the tannery floor where Grandfather Levov had begun.[25]

The American Dream has been attained for this individual, surely, but the way in which he enjoys his private success has serious public ramifications for Newark. Like many companies, the Levovs' fictitious Newark Maid was already fleeing the city years before the supposedly singular cataclysm of the riots drove a stake into the city's heart.

Journalist William Adler documents a similar process in the nearby real-time city of Paterson, New Jersey, in which the industries and residents that had supported a thriving downtown circa 1940 were fleeing in the postwar years. Manufacturer Archie Sergey at first was committed to Paterson, but then opened a fluorescent lighting factory in low-wage, nonunionized Mississippi to forestall the high wages and other demands made by his Paterson workforce's union. This move was completed by a later owner, who closed the Paterson factory altogether and opened a maquiladora factory in Mexico. For taking dozens of jobs out of a U.S. city, he was generously compensated with federal tax breaks, as presumably Swede Levov is, too, when he starts his retreat from Newark.

In the 1950s, as Adler's *Mollie's Job* documents, Paterson businessman Archie Sergey himself bought a suburban ranch house in Fair Lawn, at about the time *American Pastoral* has Swede, in 1952, make the move to a far-distant ex-urban address, and this move, too, mirrored the situation in the real Newark. As Joseph Conforti notes, the city's industrial decline had already been evident in the 1940s, for although the wartime escalation of needed industries staved off decline, the city's industrial base had already shrunk by the 1950 census. Moreover, for every white ethnic family such as the Levovs that moved to the suburbs, more tax dollars and consumer spending went with them. Until 1976, New Jersey did not have a state income tax, and cities relied exclusively on property taxes to fund city services (funding inequities remain today, but they were greater prior to the introduction of the income tax). And families in the suburbs increasingly avoided older urban downtowns in favor of suburban shopping malls such as Paramus's Garden State Plaza and Bergen Mall, which opened in 1957.[26]

These residential and business moves were in full swing fifteen or so years before the riots that were later blamed for Newark's cataclysmic fall from grace, and were the result, as George Lipsitz, Kenneth Jackson, and other historians document, of federal subsidies and the generous long-term mortgage policies of lending institutions, rather than of supposed black rioting. The result of such practices was to leave Newark and other older cities increasingly as the preserve of poorer residents, bereft of the municipal services that city halls bled of tax revenue could not afford, and cut off from well-paying jobs, which were heading to suburban, if not already overseas, locations.[27]

Thousands of families did as Swede does in Roth's novel. The present author's Newark-born Italian-American mother and his father, from the woolen mill city of Garfield, New Jersey, accepted Uncle Sam's largesse and bought a house in a virtually all-white suburb soon after their 1960 marriage. The result of these wise personal decisions was less tax revenue and shopping activity in older downtowns such as Newark's once-fabled Four Corners. By the 1950s, the city's mayor and council nervously worried that stores were leaving the city in favor of outlying mall locations, and those stores and theaters that did remain in the downtown closed after dark, since customers deserted the city after five in favor of their suburban domiciles. Moreover, the Short Hills Mall in suburban Millburn, New Jersey, for example, financed by Newark's Prudential Insurance Co., offered elite Fifth Avenue stores in an enclosed, suburban enclave that became the shopping destination for ex-urbanites.[28]

The Levovs, then, are part of larger trends that already were draining the life out of Newark; the glove factory and others like it, we are later told, are outsourced by 1958, and residents have already made moves to the suburbs. Not because Negroes threatened: Rather, Uncle Sam beckoned, an FHA mortgage in one hand and the Interstate Highway Act of 1956 in the other. Zuckerman comments that, after Swede moves into his colonial manse, he is "a long way from Newark," which is true, but the point remains the white flight was already occurring by the early 1950s. When confronted with these facts, facts Roth chooses to ignore, it is easy to see why scholar Clark Taylor referred to Short Hills and the other places urban whites fled to as Newark's "Parasitic Suburbs."[29]

The Newark Maid factory's outsourcing to Puerto Rico, too, it is later mentioned, is to avoid greedy unions, an irony considering it was the unionized paychecks of white ethnic Newarkers, a strong union town, that buttressed the city's downtown until white ethnics took those paychecks and put down payments on those suburban houses. By July 1967 Roth's family, Zuckerman's family, Swede Levov's family, and the present author's Italian-American mother had all already vacated Newark, and the exodus had nothing to do with blacks' destroying an Eden. Rather, the FHA subsidies, mortgages, and higher-education federal largesse for white Americans made it logical for individuals to vacate Newark or Detroit and a thousand other old cities. Decisions that made sense individually, however, in the aggregate played a far larger role in eviscerating the health of older American cities than any perceived African-American lack of family values.

And yet Swede will have none of it. Like his retired father, he blames the city's decline on "taxes, corruption and race." But especially race. "It's the worst city in the world, Skip," he tells Zuckerman.

Used to be the city where they manufactured everything. Now it's the car-theft capital of the world. Did you know that? . . . The thieves live mostly in our old neighborhood. Black kids, forty cars stolen in Newark every twenty-four hours. That's the statistic. . . . And they're murder weapons—once they're stolen, they're flying missiles. The target is anybody in the street—old people, toddlers, doesn't matter. Out in front of our factory was the Indianapolis Speedway to them. That's another reason we left.

After a litany of all the vanished businesses in the city, Swede recounts his experience with carjackers who pointed a gun at his head in front of the sweetshop where he had his first date. The sense of rage and loss, white victimization, could not be more palpable.[30]

And yet a page later, we again hear how the family's glove factory fled to Puerto Rico, at least in part a decade before this scene of urban mayhem, and that other factories similarly fled to the Philippines, Korea, Taiwan, and China. Even the quintessential glove city, Gloversville, New York, beginning in 1952, relocated its production plants to the Philippines. We do not hear who white ex-Gloversvilleans blame for their city's decline, but one can hazard an educated guess. Whether massive offshoring and outsourcing played some role in Newark's decline, though, Swede doesn't say, and no one in the novel thinks to ask him.[31]

Indeed, for all the verbal pyrotechnics and *kibbitzing* of Roth's many characters— and he powerfully evokes a sense of a lost place and time in his many characters' totemic recitations of shuttered theaters, sweet shops, and businesses in the lost city of Newark—the many voices merge into one, for a univocal, communal consensus seems to be created on what killed Newark, and it certainly was not (Zuckerman and Swede and Lou Levov agree) white flight. Indeed, Zuckerman is intent on summoning the heady days of 1945–1950 Newark, too, and in recalling the post-war city, he urges, "Let's remember the energy." He breathlessly summons "the GI Bill inciting them to break out in ways they could not have imagined possible before the war," and recalls the spate of wildcat militancy of workers who "demanded more and went on strike for it," before concluding, "The lid was off. Americans were to start over again, en masse, everyone in it together."[32] Yet black novelist Curstis Lucas in 1946 wrote of a *Third Ward Newark* in which black Newarkers are preyed upon by slumlords, pimps, and murderous saloonkeepers, a city in which a VE celebration plausibly ends in a race riot. Not everyone was in it together, for the GI Bill and other engines of economic mobility by and large barred to Newark's blacks, who judging by Lucas may not have shared Swede's euphoria for the good old days.[33]

Roth seems willfully blind to the degree to which race inflects his notion of Newark and to how certain populations were granted greater access to federal programs, suburban addresses, and other engines of socioeconomic mobility. The wildcat strikes are breathlessly cheered by Zuckerman as part of a time when "everyone was in it together," yet he says not a word of the hate strikes during World War II by white workers who refused to sit in solidarity with African-Americans. And we are later told that it is "the unions" that "had made it more and more difficult for a manufacturer to make any money, you could hardly find people to do that kind of piecework anymore," and so the factories of the city just had to move offshore. After the riots, we are told several times, it proved impossible to get quality glove workers. Aside from the complete amnesia on the role unions played in making Newark a livable, middle-class place for Italians and Jews, this time- and race-sensitive "damn unions" rhetoric questions what sort of pan-Newark loyalty Zuckerman and Levov have when it comes to nonwhite residents.[34]

It is white ethnic grievances that Roth magnifies to the exclusion of any consideration of antiblack racism. In *The Plot against America*, Roth's reimagining of a World War II era in which President Charles Lindbergh takes the country down a fascist road, much is made of the anti-Semitism of real fascist sympathizers like Fritz Kuhn's German-American Bund. Newark's crime boss Longy Zwillman organizes his *shtarkers* into a self-defense force that guards Weequahic against roving anti-Semites, as he did in real life (although as even the narrator of *The Plot*, young Phil Roth, admits, Longy just as often preyed upon Jewish businessmen such as his Uncle Monty by offering them "protection" and hauling "services" they didn't need but couldn't refuse).[35]

But Roth supplants real antiblack rioting with an imagined 1942 wave of pogroms, including a horrific night of smashed synagogue windows, looted Jewish businesses, and assaults on Jews in Detroit. Astonishingly, not one word intrudes into this vision of the real riots—white-on-black assaults on Great Migration workers in the real Detroit of 1943. Beginning with an assault on blacks who had dared venture into Belle Island Park, the city's Central Park, one week of attacks, in which blacks were pulled from streetcars and beaten, convulsed the Motor City. World War II also saw assaults on blacks in Harlem, Philadelphia, and Los Angeles, as well as hate strikes by white workers who refused to allow blacks to join them as trolley car motormen in Philadelphia, for example, and the anti-Mexican zoot suit riots in 1943 Los Angeles.[36]

And a key scene in *The Plot* centers on an ex-Newark Jewish neighbor who is hunted and killed on a road in rural Kentucky. In the rural South, from the 1890s through 1955, nearly six thousand black Americans were lynched in what Grace Elizabeth Hale aptly termed a ritual reassertion of white solidarity. To be sure, some southern and eastern European immigrants were lynched, most infamously Sicilians blamed for the unsolved murder of the New Orleans police chief in 1890, and factory manager Leo Frank in 1915 Georgia. But even in the imagined fascist America of a President Lindbergh one would imagine that the real-time American pariahs—blacks and Hispanics—would be the victims of racist riots, and Roth's imagination again fails him in this regard.[37]

So, too, Jeffrey Eugenides's *Middlesex*, an urban memoir novel of immigrant Detroit, offers great detail on the indignities Greek immigrants faced in a nativist country. The narrator's grandfather is deloused onboard the ship carrying him to America, and when he works at Henry Ford's auto plant, Americanization inspectors visit his home to make sure he is living like a regular American ("Employees should use plenty of soap and water in the home" is the first English-language lesson he learns on the job). And company detectives break up any attempt to resist the speedup ("In 1922 it was still a new thing to be turned into a machine") or to unionize. Yet, when the Depression hits, the narrator's grandmother, Desdemona, recalls, she is appalled by the largest humiliation America hurls at her: " 'And *then*'—hand to heart—'then they make me go to work for those *mavros*. Black people! Oh my God!'" When Desdemona travels by streetcar to her new job in "Black Bottom," she reacts with all the horror of an immigration restrictionist on safari to a Greek or other immigrant neighborhood, yet the fear is now a white-on-black loathing:

Now in the alleys she saw men washing themselves at open faucets. Half-dressed women jutted out hips on second-story porches. Desdemona looked in awe and terror at all the faces filling the windows, all the bodies filling the streets, nearly a half million people squeezed into twenty-five square blocks. . . . Still, more and more were coming every year, every month, seeking jobs in the North. They slept on every couch in every house. They built shacks in the yards. . . . (Over the years, Black Bottom, for all the whites' attempts to contain it . . . would slowly spread, street by street, neighborhood by neighborhood, until the so-called ghetto would become the entire city itself, and by the 1970s, in the no-tax base, white-flight, murder-capital Detroit of the Coleman Young administration, black people could finally live wherever they wanted to. . . .

Desdemona also reacts with horror to black men lounging in front of a barber-shop (this is 1932, the Depression, after all). When they wolf-whistle and call to her libidinously, the stereotype is complete.[38]

Greek immigrants remember every slight—rightfully so—and suggestion by bigoted nativists that southern and eastern Europeans don't know the virtue of soap and water, but no character—not even the otherwise omniscient narrator—sees fit to comment on the irony and sad racialized privilege even Greek-Americans have in this regard. By 1932, a mere ten years after her arrival in Detroit, Desdemona can recite by heart the slights at blacks as lazy, dirty, sexually promiscuous, and incapable of self-help.

And yet when blacks are assaulted by whites or otherwise victimized, Desde-mona and *Middlesex*'s other all-seeing characters suddenly are nearsighted. Eugenides passes over the World War II years with only the briefest mention of the vicious attacks on blacks that rocked the city for a week. In a single paragraph Lefty, Cal's grandfather, is incorrectly told the riot started when a black raped a white, and there is no correction to this canard. To be sure, Lefty refuses to serve some of the white rioters in his diner, but the focus shifts to the slights to him, as a rejected customer shouts, "Why don't you go back to your own country?" We see black poverty, but none of the causes for it, nor any details of the white assaults on blacks that preceded by twenty-four years the July 1967 rebellion. And no character reflects that the hypersegregation that forces "a half million black bodies into twenty-five square blocks" has contributed to the anger, poverty, and resentment at city authorities that Fine, Hahn and Feagin, and others suggest was the unproximate cause of the 1967 rebellion. Such omissions might be one of the indignities that in 1968 Danny, black protagonist of *When the Fire Reaches Us*, swears black Detroi-ters "ain't forgot—not that nor any of the injustices which has been perpetrated on us." The pity is that Eugenides's Greek characters, like real-life white Detroiters, did forget. When the July 1967 riots erupt, characters in *Middlesex*, as in *American Pastoral*, and in the real white enclaves of Newark and Detroit, regard the riots as inexplicable cataclysms that came out of nowhere; as they have forgotten 1943 and all the years in between, it cannot be otherwise.[39]

Other novels have treated this World War II atrocity more sympathetically. Marge Piercy's *Gone to Soldiers* centers on a Jewish family in Detroit. During the 1943 attacks a Jewish storekeeper rescues a black man she knows from the neighborhood from an attack by a white gang, but not before they beat him into unconsciousness. Other characters recall seeing blacks pulled from streetcars and beaten by white hoodlums, as actually occurred in Detroit. A shaken character leaves the bakery:

Alvin was waiting for her in the next doorway. . . . "Everybody's crazy! Wow! We better not tell anybody we helped a *schvartzer*, even Mr. Bates."
   "I don't care. He's a nice man and he works hard."
   "Have you ever seen anything like that? Them, just beating on him?"
   "Yes," Naomi walked more slowly. "But it wasn't colored people they were beating."

In this terrific epiphany, Nazis and racists in America have more in common than other novelists, and many white readers, care to acknowledge.

Other Jewish characters worry about the homegrown fascists Roth elevates to the White House, but fearfully listen to "Father Coughlin on the radio, linking up rationing, always unpopular, and shortages to Jews and colored, stirring up the resentment that seemed endemic to the streets."[40] Anti-Semitism and antiblack animus coexisted in the real city of the 1940s, and *Gone to Soldiers* is more politically and historically savvy than Roth in linking the two.

Characters also note that "there had been hate strikes in several of the plants, when Negroes were hired or when they were let into any positions but the lowest. Just recently a few colored women had been hired at Briggs and some of the white women wanted to walk off in protest. They said all colored women had syphilis." The daughters of the novel's main family can link up anti-Semitism to the even more virulent racism swirling all around them in 1943 Detroit. It is these linkages that are regrettably missing in Eugenides's Detroit or Roth's 1940s Newark.[41]

Here, too, characters note that, compared to some of the white migrants, Detroit's blacks actually have better houses and cleanliness standards. "They talk down the colored all the time, but the colored by me, they keep up their houses fine," one factory workingwoman tells her mates. "They aren't like the colored down in Paradise Valley. They own their houses and they keep their yards nice. They were all born up here and they belong. But those hillbillies, they never saw an inside toilet before. They throw their slops out in the yard to stink."[42] In its complexities and contradictions, *Gone to Soldiers* is a much more sympathetic white-ethnic account of the plight of blacks than is presented in Eugenides or Roth.

Proletarian novelists writing in the World War II era recognized some of white ethnics' situation in America, at once pariahs and despised industrial mules and Hunkies, and yet carrying with them the fortunate passport to privileged Americanism that came with a white skin. Thomas Bell's masterful novel of three generations of Slovak steelworkers, *Out of This Furnace*, has the old immigrant grandfather and his oldest friend travel down memory lane to the Old First Ward of Braddock, Pennsylvania. "You should've seen it twenty years ago when it was full of stores," the grandpa tells his grandson. ". . . There was more friendliness. It was good then."

Then the old-timers sigh and set about blaming the usual suspects. "So it goes," Dorta says. "It's too bad the niggers had to come. They never bother me, but some of my neighbors have moved, especially the ones with daughters. The men are always getting drunk, and fighting, and you hear women screaming during the night. They all live together like so many animals. And so dirty!" "They're poor," the grandson says. "How much does soap and water cost?" "I know. But I was just thinking that once it was the Irish looking down on the Hunkies and now it's the Hunkies looking down on the niggers. The very things the Irish used to say about the Hunkies the Hunkies now say about the niggers. And for no better reason." Dorta shrugged but didn't say anything.[43]

Like Desdemona, the characters bemoan the perceived filth of the new "niggers" living down in the old First Ward, previously a Slavic enclave. But unlike in Eugenides, or in Roth, at least some Slovaks are aware of the sad ironies present in nostalgic and insidious comparisons between immigrant then and black now.

To return to Roth's angry Swede: *American Pastoral* is a novel predicated on nostalgia, and the selective amnesia that comes with it. A key scene in which Zuckerman learns of the tragedies that have befallen Swede is set at that most myopic and self-fabricated of American ceremonies—the high school reunion. Who wouldn't remember an idyllic Newark at such a moment,—whether it actually ever existed, and whether what went wrong for one's family—or the once-somewhat (partially) grand city of Newark—was the fault of a subsequent black rebellion. But it is only personal "mythologizing" that the narrator, Zuckerman, cares to examine.

The reunion is held in suburban Livingston, "far from the futility prevailing in the streets of our crime-ridden, drug-infested childhood home," a move that makes it easier for white ex-urbanites who never visit their old stomping grounds to know for a certainty that everything is chaotic there with "them" now, and perfect back with "us" in "our" Newark. (When Zuckerman does visit Swede's old house after the reunion, he's certain that even stepping out of his car would be sure suicide.[44] When the present author has visited his grandparents' old South Eighteenth Street, Newark, neighborhood, by now African-American, he has emerged without a scratch.) Still, as everything has moved to suburban bastions like Livingston and nearby Short Hills, it might be plausible to have at least one character ponder whether a reinvestment of some kind in the here-and-now Newark might be possible or laudable.

But the only musing on fabricated histories of better then and miserable now occurs around individual stories. A classmate confides to Zuckerman that his father had an enormous influence on the troubled teen, but Zuckerman can't place this classmate. "As much as I was remembering that day of all that had once happened, far more was so beyond recall that it might never have happened," Zuckerman muses. He also allows that "we don't just forget things because they don't matter but also forget things because they matter too much," and admits that one person's recollections might seem to another person "willful excursions into mythomania."[45] And yet none of these same hesitations or doubts arise on whether Swede or Lou

Levov or Zuckerman are correctly remembering the communal narrative of a functioning 1945 Newark and a senseless riot in 1967. On these matters there rests a consensus from white ex-Newarkers. Zuckerman's musing on the selectivity of memory, the convenience of forgetting the unpleasant, only focuses on personal issues, such as who was happy in high school.

Sociologist Sherry Ortner, herself a product of a slightly later Weequahic High School class, offers a different impression of her Newark childhood. Attending her own high school reunion, she allows that although many of her classmates had successful careers, variables of race and class shaped, if not automatically determined, the circumstances for her African-American classmates. Their families were cut off from some of the most lucrative aspects of New Deal social programs from their very creation, and since socioeconomic mobility, in any case, is generational, Newark blacks were cut out of riding the engine of economic growth during its most dynamic years of 1945–1973. By the time some redress was made and Newark's African-Americans elected the city's first black mayor, Kenneth Gibson, in 1970, the city's deindustrialization was just about complete. Happy memories of homeroom coincide, in Ortner's recounting of her high school reunion, with these uncomfortable facts.[46]

Moreover, even for Ortner's white classmates, good old Newark was not necessarily a sunny city. The idyllic bygone Newark saga was given the lie by classmates' recollections of broken homes, business failures, fathers who abandoned mothers and children, suicide, and even, in one instance, a father murdered by underworld associates. As we'll see in the next chapter, organized crime ran roughshod over Newark, with Italian and Jewish gangs run by Ritchie "The Boot" Boiardo and Abner "Longy" Zwillman given easy access to city hall and carte blanche in controlling numbers, drugs, extortion, and protection rackets well into the 1950s. These grimmer notes in the Newark saga present a fuller portrait of the stresses and dysfunctionalities that existed in Essex County well before July 1967.[47]

Still, it is the loss of a bygone city, robbed by black violence, the permissive society, and overall lack of standards that Roth presents. In *American Pastoral*, Swede's father-in-law, an Irish-American plumber from nearby Elizabeth, New Jersey, religiously recites the vanished businesses (Singer Sewing Machine, Burry Biscuits), theaters, ballparks, and ethnic parishes of his youth, just as Lou Levov angrily recounts the decline of his Newark. At a dinner party at Swede's country retreat, Lou angrily cuts off any suggestion that "the trash" (read, the 1960s writ large) that has inundated him is inevitable. " 'It leaks in, Mr. Levov,' Bill Orcutt said to him pleasantly, 'whether we like it or not. . . . It's not the same out there anymore, in case you haven't heard.' "

But Lou is having none if it. "Oh, I heard sir. I come from the late city of Newark. . . . Look, the Irish ran the city, the Italians ran the city, now let the coloreds run the city. That's not my point. I got nothing against that. It's the colored people's turn to reach into the till? I wasn't born yesterday. In Newark corruption is the name of the game." Seemingly, Lou is a realist on these matters, and since it was

Italian-American Mayor Hugh Addonizio and Jewish and Italian councilmen who in real-time 1969 had been indicted and convicted for complicity with Italian organized crime in the city, Lou would have had to have been blind not to know what was what in Newark.[48]

Yet, almost immediately, Lou's jeremiad denounces the new "corruption" and "high taxes" that are killing Newark, not granting for a moment that the thirty years of white ethnic political corruption prior to 1967 may have bled the city dry, not Gibson's ascension as the city's first African-American mayor. Indeed, even earlier, Lou, for all his protestations that a "colored" mayor is OK with him, rants that "a whole business is going down the drain because of that son of a bitch LeRoi Jones, that Peek-A-Boo-Boopy-Do, whatever the hell he calls himself in that goddamn hat. I built this with my hands! With my blood! . . . But they took that city and now they are going to take that business and everything that I built up a day at a time." The distinction between "builders "and "takers" is driven home by this white ethnic rant, although for the record, Amiri Baraka (LeRoi Jones) "took" the city by helping organize a black and Puerto Rican coalition that in 1970 placed Ken Gibson in the mayoralty. This form of taking is called an election.[49]

Lou goes on to denounce those burning down their own homes, never considering that slumlords' tenements were not considered "their" homes by many ghetto dwellers, nor allowing that much of the destruction in Newark occurred as a result of state police, city police, and white vigilante retaliation at blacks after the looting had subsided. Indeed, when Swede's black forelady places a "blacks work here" sign in his factory window, the building is promptly shot up by white vigilantes who, Swede suspects, are off-duty cops. As Ron Porambo's exposé of the suppression of the riots, *No Cause for Indictment*, suggests, this is a plausible scenario. Not all the destruction of "the late city of Newark" was at the hands of black looters.[50]

Moreover, at the 1972 dinner, Lou's continued rant belies some of the causes of the city's decline: the suburbanization and outsourcing of businesses and residences by white middle-class entrepreneurs such as his own family. "General Electric already moved out in 1953. GE, Westinghouse, Breyer's, down on Raymond Boulevard, Celluloid, all left the city. Every one of them big employers, and before the riots, before the racial hatred, they got out. Race is just the icing on the cake." And Lou continues with the signs of decline: poor schooling, no city services, dropouts, "and the projects, don't get me started on the projects."[51]

One has to wonder whether capital flight subsidized by state and federal government, and residents' exodus in the early 1950s played a significant role in the city's inability to clean the streets or educate the children to Lou's satisfaction. Indeed, Swede, at an earlier point, notes that in 1952, the year he moved out to the country, "Everybody else who was picking up and leaving Newark was headed for one of the cozy suburban streets in Maplewood or South Orange." Questions of where the decline started and who out in Old Rimrock might be implicated in that decline never get addressed.[52]

To be sure, Swede's angry musing on his entitlement to live out in the WASP horse country resonates with that of many white ethnics of the second or third generation who began to move into suburban New Jersey communities. "Why shouldn't I be where I want to be? Why shouldn't I be with who I want to be? Isn't that what this country's all about? . . . That's what being an American is—isn't it?" Yet, in 1952, blacks, as we've seen, were violently resisted when they endeavored to "be where they wanted to be," as other Americans (surely not Swede) thought part of being an American was having the right to exclude whom they wanted.[53]

Yet, implausibly, no one at a table of self-proclaimed McGovern liberals contradicts Lou, or even suggests some of this complex intertwining of personal choice and communal decline. When the riots come up at the Levov table, someone might have mentioned that the proximate cause was the police's breaking of black cabdriver John Smith's ribs for the high crime of having an expired driver's license and that the National Commission on Civil Disorders and the New Jersey governor's investigation suggested as contributing factors blacks' resentment of urban renewal, political corruption in the Addonizio administration (which had appointed a white city council crony superintendent of schools, passing over a qualified black applicant in a school district already 75 percent black), and a long history of police brutality toward blacks. None of these objections are raised in 1972 by the "liberals" in attendance.[54]

One significant shortcoming in the Newark of *American Pastoral*—and as I'll argue below, even in Roth's later *The Human Stain*—is that no credible black voice is permitted to disrupt the communal consensus. It might strain credulity to have a black guest who's coming to dinner in Old Rimrock, but even elsewhere in urban memoirs black voices are rarely permitted a genuine speaking role Yet, when they are, surprising epiphanies arise. In *Canarsie*, Jonathan Rieder's study of Jewish and Italian Brooklynites bemoaning the decline of their beloved East New York and Brownsville neighborhoods, a similar wail about vanished ethnic businesses on Pitkin Avenue and the ravages of crime, drugs, and other signifiers of urban malaise rises from old-timers. With barely a half sentence devoted to "Of course, there was Murder Inc.," the omnipresent organized crime syndicate that ran Brownsville, a much-maligned slice of the city in the 1930s and 1940s, the rest of the narrative as agreed upon by the white informants paints a similar story of a stolen Eden.

Finally, a black resident of Canarsie (a quasi-suburbanized part of Brooklyn whose white residents feel very much under siege by the mid-1970s) gets his turn at bat. "The people of Canarsie are right to be nostalgic. The neighborhoods *were* terrific. They were fabulous neighborhoods. . . . Now it's not the same as they knew it in the '50s, so they mourn it. It's a shame. But there's only one problem with that. I mean, the Canarsie people forget one thing: *I* didn't destroy *their* Brownsville." Indeed, in Rieder's work we learn that most white ethnics fled Brownsville and East New York in the early 1950s, when home ownership became available elsewhere, and thus played a contributing role in the ghettoization of the old neighborhoods. It would perhaps cause ex-Brownsville residents more psychic trauma than they could handle, as it would be a burden for ex-Newarkers, to acknowledge that they voluntarily left their Eden, in many cases as soon as they were able to after World War II. The lone black voice from Canarsie reminds us of this missing piece in urban memoirs of old neighborhood decline. Similar intrusions of counternarratives, however, are missing in *American Pastoral*.[55]

At the dinner party, as throughout the novel, all voices seem in consensus that what has occurred is "a total vandalization of our world." Although what spurs this comment from Swede is his father's news that "developers from the suburbs" are stealing copper pipes, ornate cornices, stained glass, and even cobblestone streets from the carcass of Newark, in order to build suburban dream castles for fleeing white yuppies much like his son. More evidence that, as Clark Taylor suggested, in 1972, the year of Swede's ill-fated dinner party, "parasitic suburbs" had contributed more than their share to the city's decline. When Lou Levov and Mr. Dwyer sit down and reminisce and complain about "those people" "vandalizing" their cities, we are told, "Two great memories meet, and it is futile to try to contain them."[56] No character in the novel makes much of an effort, and while their recollections of old Newark are richly textured, accurate re-creations of white ethnic parts of "the late city of Newark," the angry diatribes that univocally explain the supposed reasons for the city's decline are imperfect at best.

There are no black voices in Roth or in Eugenides's *Middlesex* that aren't ventriloquized; that is, they serve to essentially agree with the novels' white protagonists' point of view. In *American Pastoral*, Vicky, a loyal black forelady, sticks by Swede during the riots, telling Swede, "This is mine too. You just own it." During the riots Vicky acts "in order to appease any rioters who might be heading from South Orange Avenue with their torches." She places signs alerting rioters to the fact that "most of this factory's employees are NEGROES," but this only provokes white backlash, as vigilantes or "Newark cops in an unmarked car" shoot up Swede's factory. Amazingly, Swede's rage and anger are still directed against those black "takers," and even after Vicky imperils her own life by standing up to National Guardsmen firing indiscriminately into the windows of the black ghetto, Swede still is certain that the National Guardsmen's tanks, not courageous blacks, are what saved his factory and city. What Vicky thinks of this race-inflected myopia, we don't hear.[57]

Instead, we again hear from white Newarkers. Swede characterizes the black looters as "looting crowds crazed in the streets . . . Newark's burning Mardi Gras streets, a force is released that feels redemptive, something purifying is happening, something spiritual and revolutionary perceptible to all." This quickly gives way to the police overkill of blowing away innocent passersby: "A police car opens fire into the bar across the street, out his window he sees a woman go down, buckle and go down, shot dead right on the street, a woman killed right in front of his eyes." And white vigilantes again are described blowing out his factory windows because of Vicky's "Negroes here" sign, and yet Swede does not redirect his rage at the police overkill that resulted in twenty-six deaths, most of them after the black looting had been contained.[58]

In *The Human Stain* the ventriloquism is raised to a whole different level. Ernestine Silk, the retired schoolteacher sister of Coleman Silk, who has passed for white his whole professional life, comes to give Nathan Zuckerman her analysis of why urban America has declined, and it sounds a whole lot like Zuckerman talking to himself in blackface. She blames, in rapid succession, Black History Month, lack of standards in the schools, the end of the classics, the permissive society, and urban renewal. Her list of culprits sounds very unlikely coming from a self-described proud race woman:

But everything there now is black this and black that. . . . Years ago, East Orange High was excellent. Kids coming out of East Orange High, especially out of the honors program, would have their choice of colleges. Oh, don't get me started on this subject. . . . Today the student asserts his incapacity as a privilege. . . . There are no more criteria, Mr. Zuckerman, only opinions. I often wrestle with this question of what everything used to be. What education used to be. What East Orange High used to be. What East Orange used to be. Urban renewal destroyed East Orange, there's no doubt in my mind. . . . Then 280 and the parkway cut our little town in quarters. The parkway eliminated Jones Street—the center of our colored community the parkway eliminated altogether . . . nice houses along Oraton Parkway, Elmwood Avenue, Maple Avenue . . . Central Avenue . . . the Fifth Avenue of the Oranges.

In cataloging the great shopping district that used to exist in East Orange, Ernestine sighs, "All of life was there in East Orange."[59]

One has to wonder again if the disappearance of B. Altman and Saks from downtown East Orange (a city bordering Newark) is the fault of the permissive, liberal society, or of suburbanization and the construction of megamalls in Short Hills, Wayne, and the like, which further immiserated increasingly minority Newark and East Orange already in the late 1950s. Clark Taylor notes that when the Short Hills Mall opened, many stores fled Newark to open branches in the suburbs, but when minority children from Newark arrived in search of the traditional gifts from Santa, mall security guards barred the black urchins from entering. Such scenarios make one wonder just who had "vandalized" the city of its downtown shopping core.[60]

So, too, when Ernestine decries Black History Month for killing East Orange's fabulous school system, where students don't even read *Moby-Dick* anymore, alarm bells should ring. Throughout the 1970s, 1980s, and beyond black and white educators alike lobbied for, advocated, and sued for redressing the property-tax base for education funding, which has created a chasm between such affluent suburban districts as Cherry Hill and Short Hills and cities such as Camden and Newark. In New Jersey such efforts were taken to the state supreme court, where the inequitable funding mechanisms were declared unconstitutional. Nevertheless, as Jonathan Kozol has demonstrated in *Savage Inequalities*, in New Jersey and elsewhere, cities have continued to receive the short end of the educational stick. Kozol notes, for example, that schools in affluent suburbs such as Cherry Hill, only miles from Camden, have indoor swimming pools, new tracks, and computer labs, while in Camden utility closets often double as classrooms. A race woman such as Ernestine would likely recognize that school districts strapped for funds and facing crumbling buildings, some more than eighty years old in districts such as Newark, likely didn't make a free decision to scrap *Moby-Dick*.[61]

But Zuckerman clearly agrees with Ernestine that giving in to black anger killed East Orange and Newark: "All of life was there in East Orange. And when? Before. Before urban renewal. Before the classics were abandoned. Before they stopped giving out the Constitution to high school graduates. Before there were remedial classes in the colleges teaching kids what they should have learned in ninth grade. Before Black History Month. . . . That's when it was all different—before. And, she lamented, it will never be the same again, not in East Orange or anywhere else in America."[62]

Ernestine is the reassuring, sensible older black woman who comforts Zuckerman, and the white ethnic reader, that he is not racist for casting his rage at the decline of Newark where he does. Ernestine, like her brother, who passes as white, and chooses a striving Jewish academic persona with which to do so, ventriloquizes a sense of different-sameness, the older black woman who can proudly stand up to discrimination that "we" all agree was wrong (she offers a litany of segregation's injustices that she and her siblings overcame); nevertheless, "we" recognize permissiveness and lack of standards for the self-destructive foolishness she and Zuckerman are certain they are.

In this regard, her further laments are instructive.

In my childhood, as in yours, it was recommended that each student who graduated from high school in New Jersey get at graduation two things: a diploma and a copy of the Constitution. Do you recall that? You had to take a year of American history and a semester of economics—as, of course, you have to no longer: "have to" is just gone out of the curriculum. . . . Here in America, as far as I can see, it's just getting more foolish by the hour.[63]

"In my childhood, as in yours" gives the game away. Like *American Pastoral*'s unanswered diatribe against black looters' destroying Newark, the sensible-civil-rights-but-no-further-than-1965 vision of Roth's black character is predicated on an essentialism, a normative sameness. We "good" blacks were really not different from you Jews and other white ethnics. We, too, prized learning and standards and respectability. We, too, condemn the permissive society and "these" blacks who demand too much. A comfortable, armchair consensus on how far "these"/"we" people can go in demanding change, and consensus, too, on what tore down a supposedly wonderful city is achieved. This is the essence of the nostalgic urban novel.

But would a black woman who had come through a segregated society really call educators worried about institutional racism "reactionary"? Are these

Zuckerman/Roth's white Newark's words in a black mouth? If Ernestine has been observant in the real 1990s New Jersey, she would have noticed and remarked on those school-funding battles that pitted the Newark–East Orange–Camden part of the state against the affluent, virtually all-white suburbs. She might have noticed that the takeover of Newark's woefully underfunded school district occurred not when it was controlled by Italian and Irish political hacks, such as former City Councilman James Callaghan (who in 1969 would be indicted and eventually jailed for his role in the bribery/corruption scandal of the Addonizio administration), but when it was controlled by African-Americans.[64]

The African-American memories of real-life Newarkers contained in *When I Was Comin' Up* indicate that for real-life blacks, Black History Month and not reading *Moby-Dick* were not the true injustices in Essex County. But if she had suggested such matters, Ernestine might reveal that her agenda, or vision of the past, is not the same as Zuckerman/Roth/White Newark's.[65]

But then, it seems that the real role Roth assigns to Ernestine in *The Human Stain* is to reassure white ex-urbanites that even many older black Newark and East Orange residents don't hold them culpable, and agree with them that the good old days were idyllic and that they are blameless in any of the urban mess we see today. If only more aspired to standards and emulated Weequahic—Coleman Silk, again, chooses for his white role model/masquerade a Jewish Newark (or near-Newark) persona—then couldn't "our" Newark, as it was "in my childhood, as in yours," be great again?

Certainly authors invariably engage in ventriloquism—all the characters' words are, after all, the creation of the author. Nevertheless, there are questions of plausibility, and when an author establishes straw men in abundance to stand in for his ideological and racial adversaries in tearing down pristine, safe old Newark, one has to wonder if we are still reading a novel or an artful screed.

Mikhail Bakhtin has celebrated the novel's heteroglossia, the ability to present a multivocal, carnivalesque depiction of life in which all voices and characters have their say. It seems that the multivocal Bakhtinian novel breaks down under circumstances of conservative politics.[66] For the liberating, chaotic (educational?) possibility of dialogue—multilogue—is precluded when no blacks are invited to the Levov dinner table, and when those characters meant to stand in for racial difference turn out to be thinly veiled masquerades for the master's voice. The novel's possibilities sputter to a halt when dialogue ends, when The Answer as provided by one character (the author, Lou Levov, the angry white Newarker) is regarded as impossible to debate. Newark once contained 420,000 people, more than 75,000 of them by 1950 black, and this substratum of the city in which *American Pastoral* pines for a functioning past is lamentably absent.

The same image emerges in *Middlesex*, which recounts the story of a transgendered Greek-American from Detroit. Here I shall leave aside an exploration of the gender politics of the issues discussed in this book about Cal's discovery that she is a he, and instead discuss Cal's recollections of Detroit before, during, and after the 1967 riots. As in *American Pastoral*, so, too, here the riots are seen as an inexplicable act of vengeance by angry blacks who destroy something rather than make anything of worth. The context for the building frustration in Detroit, ironically considered a "model city" for its attempts to deal with race relations, is missing from Eugenides's urban memoir novel. As noted above, a brief, inaccurate account of the 1943 white assaults on blacks is given, and Black Bottom residents are characterized as dysfunctional, contemptible creatures.

When the riots break out, the Stephanides family, including Cal's restaurant-owning father, Milt, are caught completely by surprise. Cal recalls that her father "kept up a brave front. He hosed down the sidewalk outside the diner and kept the windows spotless. . . . But the Zebra Room's swing music and old-time baseball players couldn't stop time. It was no longer 1940 but 1967. Specifically, the night of July 23, 1967."[67]

When "the all-white Detroit police force" raids "after-hour bars" in an attempt to forestall in Detroit the long, hot summer that had already consumed Newark, something goes wrong, and the riots break out. Milton, who only awhile before was remarking "that it was always something that amazed him about black people," "the contradiction between the perfection of their automobiles and the disrepair of their houses," makes a further comparison, between the functioning, hardworking immigrant neighborhood he knew as a youth, and the chaos he sees now. "On the corner of Sterling and Commonwealth was the old Masonic Temple, where one Saturday afternoon thirty-five years before, Milton had been runner-up in a spelling bee. A spelling bee! . . . That's what used to happen in this neighborhood. Spelling bees! Now ten-year-olds were running in the streets, carrying bricks."[68]

The contrast between the respectable older immigrant cities and the strange scene he sees in the present is the sum total of Milton's, or any other character's, commentary on why Black Bottom has erupted after forty years of racism. Sidney Fine, Thomas Sugrue, and other historians have patiently explained the conglomeration of factors that led to this urban crisis, yet novelists have continued to make insidious comparisons.[69]

Indeed, Cal's family sees the riots as a "block party" more than a riot, suggesting that blacks are up to their old minstrel show irresponsibility. Even attempts to assert that they had regarded their black fellow Detroiters as "just like them" smack of condescension and the sad degree to which Greek newcomers, like other immigrants, have internalized the American white-black binary of normal us and dysfunctional them:

Up until that night, our neighborhood's basic feeling about our fellow Negro citizens could be summed up in something Tessie said after watching Sidney Poitier's performance in *To Sir with Love*, which opened a month before the riots. She said, "You see, they can speak perfectly normal if they want to." That was how we felt. (Even me back then, I won't deny it, because we're all the children of our parents). We were ready to accept the Negroes. We weren't prejudiced against them. We wanted to include them in our society *if they would only act normal!*[70]

As Thomas Sugrue has amply documented, the white ethnic feeling toward "Negro fellow citizens" had more uniformly been one of assault when blacks attempted to move anywhere within an ethnic white neighborhood. Firebombs, cross burnings, and "white citizens' councils" greeted any attempt by blacks to exercise anything like equal citizenship rights throughout the 1940s, 1950s, and early 1960s, and white citizens' councils were a key constituency in the victories of Detroit Mayor Albert Cobo in the 1950s. Blacks acting "normal" in the Detroit of Cal were greeted by firebombs and scorn. Rioting blacks, alas, were now regarded as, prima facie, not like "us," yet again.[71]

Milton, as well as his son/daughter Cal, draws the "correct," or at least predictable, conclusion. When a black resident responds to Milton's befuddlement, "The matter with us is you," Milton sees this statement as an emblem of the entire degenerate 1960s tearing down his beloved Detroit: "'The matter with us is you.' . . . Delivered by Milton in his so-called black accent, delivered whenever any liberal pundit talked about the 'culturally deprived' or the 'underclass' or 'empowerment zones,' spoken out of the belief that this one statement, having been delivered to him while the blacks themselves burned down a significant portion of our beloved city, proved its own absurdity." And yet, only two pages later, the black resident who delivered this condemnation of white-on-black racism endemic in the Motor City (which even Cal admits has an "all white police force," at a time when blacks are half the city's population) is gunned down by police snipers.[72]

Yet Cal asserts, with little evidence, that the police acted with restraint and argues this was a planned black revolution, something disputed by both the 1968 National Advisory Commission on Civil Disorders and the subsequent scholarship of Fine. Still, the novel's omniscient narrator asserts, "Believe what you want. I was seven years old and followed a tank into battle and saw what I saw." The mantra of white ethnic backlash is in full flower in this statement, which rejects any evidence of what it doesn't want to see, and posits the city as functioning before rebellious blacks ruined it for the rest of us.[73]

The riots were the fault of black urbanites themselves, not the lamentable but predictable outcome of decades of racism and inattention to the abuse these residents suffered by city administrations and institutions. What Eugenides misses, too, is the biracial nature of looters in Detroit. This fact, noted by Fine and already memorialized in Tinker's *When the Fire Reaches Us*, is completely unremembered by Eugenides, just as most ex-urbanite commentators on the riots that supposedly drove them from Detroit miss this key component. This is seen as a black imposition, assault, on innocent (yes, Edenic) whites.[74]

It is perhaps not surprising that in a post-civil-rights, social-spending-retrenchment era like the 1990s and the early twenty-first century, both Roth and Eugenides were awarded the Pulitzer Prize for their respective urban-nostalgic memoirs. Much of white America, at least judging by and reflected in the political program of administrations, both Democratic and Republican, preferred to pretend that all questions of racial inequity in America had been solved in or about August 1965, and once voting-rights and civil rights measures had been enacted, any enduring socioeconomic differences between white and black Americans surely could be attributed to supposed black failings. By the time of Eugenides's and Roth's novels, this backlash historiography and homegrown amnesia was in full swing. They captured perfectly a post-civil-rights era that suggested that a supposed lack of family values and other structural problems within black families, not the injustices that were visited upon them, was responsible for the detritus of the ghetto.

Ironically, in *Middlesex* the very next scene following the riots shows the Greek-American family humiliated by a realtor who doubts their fitness (whiteness) as prospective residents in affluent Grosse Pointe. That it was African-Americans, not "Mediterraneans," who experienced the indignities of racial steering, redlining, and worse when they attempted in vain to escape to the suburbs, well into the 1970s, need hardly be remarked at this point. In positing blacks as the eternal destroyers and white ethnics as yet again the oppressed innocents, all within a few pages, Eugenides captures perfectly the dominant narrative of urban decline in the early-twenty-first-century American Zeitgeist. For whatever gender he may be or adapt, the protagonist Cal remains white.[75]

What is absent, too, is any consideration of how thoroughly dysfunctional Jewish and Greek slum dwellers seemed to nativist contemporaries circa 1920. As we've seen, magazine writers, novelists, and then gangster-movie producers offered a disreputable portrait of cities, and in both Roth's and Eugenides's work there are glimpses of an underworld that casts disgrace on immigrant culture, too. Still, when compared to larger transgressions by post-1967, black urbanites, such criminality is excused.

In *Middlesex*, Cal's grandfather and his brother-in-law are bootleggers and gamblers in Prohibition era Detroit, and while they are cast in a nostalgic glow in the novel's overall declension narrative, "respectable" Detroiters certainly were appalled by immigrant bootleggers such as the real-life Bernstein brothers. Likewise, Newark's gangsters under the control of Longy Zwillman and Ritchie "The Boot" Boiardo appear in *The Plot against America*, but since they are defending Weequahic from the Bund and Lindbergh's fictive storm troopers, much is excused. Even this significant element of white Newark's history is predicated on significant erasures of the dystopic aspects of immigrant culture, for Zwillman also introduced heroin, extortion, and other illegal activities, not just defense forces, to Essex County. And while *The Plot*'s narrator notes that Italian hoods extorted money from blacks in Newark's ghetto, no linkage is made here or in other Roth novels to possible black grievances in the good old city.[76]

Indeed, even some of the later ethnic entrepreneurial activity so often celebrated in such memoirs and personal narratives was rooted in criminal activity. The celebrated Kinney Parking Systems business, Gerard Jones asserts, was founded with Zwillman gang money, and comic book publishers also were funded with illicit gang money. And in *The Plot against America*, Phil Roth's brother marries the daughter of Philadelphia restaurant owner William F. Schapp II: "Though Mr. Schapp had himself started out in the twenties as Pinball Billy Schapiro, a two-bit hustler associated with the worst hoods from the most rundown row houses on the most violent streets of the South Philly badlands, . . . by 1942 the return on the pinballs and the slots amounted to upward of fifteen thousand unreported dollars each week and Pinball Billy had been regenerated as William F. Schapp II, highly esteemed member of the Green Valley Country Club, of the Jewish fraternal organization Brith Achim."

Here is an acknowledgment, at long last, that yes, there was a Jewish mob—but almost immediately a big so-what is offered compared to Roth's earlier screed on what blacks have made of the city. Could it be possible to excuse Jewish criminality, and then make the leap to similarly excusing (or at least understanding) where some black and Hispanic illegal activity in the 1990s city came from—in a city with fewer legitimate resources at its disposal?[77]

Indeed, behind many "legitimate" success stories of Jewish and other white-ethnic entrepreneurial activity in Philadelphia, northern New Jersey, Cleveland, and elsewhere sits the seed capital of drugs, gambling, prostitution, bootlegging, and protection rackets. Every time a nostalgic, wistful evocation of a bygone landmark such as Philadelphia's "Original Schapp's" restaurant occurs, perhaps the evoker would do well to reflect that its origins were not so very different, perhaps, from the origins of the hated and demonized Crips and Bloods. One of Weequahic's favorite restaurants, The Tavern, was apparently a Zwillman-controlled front. And on a grander scale, in Philadelphia, too, newspaper publisher Moe Annenberg got his start in the protection rackets.[78]

The rapidity with which the Jewish mob is glossed over, valorized by money and social respectability, with no screed or denunciation by Roth, is remarkable. Country club membership evidently excuses all, and here, *The Plot against America* sees the bigger threats in America's homegrown anti-Semites and fascists. In *American Pastoral* and *The Human Stain* the bigger threats are blacks and loss of "standards." White ethnics are privileged and valorized, and if beginnings in crime are acknowledged, the glint of pride in "making it" into respectable and comfortable affluent whiteness glosses over them.

White violence is cast here as "sensible"—determination to escape the ghetto by strivers such as Schapp/Schapiro, or determination to resist bigots, as when Uncle Morty and the narrator's father are recalled as defenders against Irish thugs running into the Third Ward with lead pipes circa 1917, and Zwillman's "Jewish Police" are recalled as watching out for Fritz Kuhn, and beating up the Bund. Black violence, however, in *American Pastoral* remains inexplicable and destroys lovely old Newark.[79]

In general, white ethnic criminality in the nostalgic urban memoir is excused, and as we'll see next chapter, often in nostalgic recollections, it remains a source of white ethnic pride. It is only in earlier works, such as the 1930 proletarian novel *Jews without Money* by Mike Gold, that Jewish gangsters are the slum-created hoodlums, the gangstas of their day, without the sepia-toned glow. Gold's acknowledgment of the slums, sins, and inequities of New York's Lower East Side is an unflinching look at the hellish nature of the immigrant city, not because of immigrants' lack of "values," but because of the predatory practices of industrialists, landlords, and the like. Such awareness is completely missing from Roth's Newark and Eugenides's Detroit, which must shine if they are to stand in contrast to the black metropolis that follows.[80]

In the urban memoir, the problem, as Tinker's Danny Sands laments in *When the Fire Reaches Us*, is that we are still talking past each other. "Wall-eyed looks" of mutual recrimination persist from urbanites of various backgrounds. And in contemporary HBO series, such as *The Wire* and the recently concluded *The Sopranos,* the nostalgic longing for a bygone city continues to resonate in ways that would exasperate Danny.

In the crime drama *The Wire*, these mutually passing stories are presented sensitively, but still, in the show's Baltimore, white and black characters facing desperate circumstances in a postindustrial city are walled apart from each other. They never quite meet and speak to one another or articulate a way to construct paths out of their various dead ends. Particularly in Season 2, *The Wire* focuses on two mutually distressed urban groups, underemployed, primarily white ethnic port workers, and the African-American drug dealers of stereotypically bleak projects. But it is only the white ethnics' plight that is articulated in a political framework of deindustrialization, disinvestment, and other of scholar Jerry Herron's "humiliations" against the city.[81]

In the opening episode of Season 2, the maverick cop McNulty glumly looks out across the deindustrialized, rotting factories and vacant piers of the ungentrified part of Baltimore Harbor. "My father used to work there," McNulty's new partner tells him. "In the shipyards, in the steel, yeah. Had an uncle who was a supervisor there. Got laid off in '78, though." "'73 for my Dad," McNulty replies. Within minutes, we are introduced to the bleak opportunity structure that exists in present-day Baltimore, in which everyone—black, white, and Wigger—is hustling and using whatever marginal, dwindling (or is that swindling?) resources they can to keep destitution at someone else's door.[82]

The degree to which characters articulate this awareness, though, is largely predicated on race, as when the stevedores' union official Frank Sobotka rails at "Ronny the-Union-buster Reagan and half a dozen other sons a bitches," as well as containerization and the city's move to turn the harbor into a gentrified tourist attraction, rather than a working waterfront generating livelihoods for his men. Throughout *The Wire*, white ethnic characters acknowledge that for all its dysfunctions, Baltimore was a better place when the ports were humming with activity. While a few black characters, such as D'Angelo, the introspective nephew of crime chief Avon Barksdale, ruefully observe the futility of drug gangs cutting each other down and hope for a better life, or at least cooperation, between the rival drug gangs, no black characters give voice to the larger socioeconomic factors that have bled their inner cities, too, of economic resources and left them with few other options than hustling drugs. The violence of drive-by drug wars and an innocent child hit by a stray bullet appears, accurate testimony to the brutal conditions in many cities, but a fuller explanation of how the projects got this way is omitted. To be sure, Omar, a robber testifying against drug dealers, tells a sleazy lawyer that they are similar predators—one preying on the system with a gun, the other with a briefcase—but nothing like Sobotka's denunciation of the history that traps him is heard from the projects.[83]

The hypermilitarized, brutal conditions in which even law-abiding public-housing residents live are apparent when police officers Herc, Carver, and Prez decide to pay a 2 a.m. visit to the projects to show them who "owns" them, and Prez pistol-whips a teen for lounging on his car. At that point the projects fight back, hurling bottles, televisions, and garbage out the high-rise windows at the oc-cupying cops. As in real-life 1967 Newark, police brutality triggers an aggrieved response, and the project people fight back. So, too, art imitates life when the squad's black commanding lieutenant, Daniels, coaches Prez on the story of "fear-ing for his safety" that he'll take before the investigations board to justify his un-provoked attack.[84]

Moreover, the largest of the few crumbs left in Baltimore invariably go to white ethnics first. The cynical Polish-American police major, Valchek, explains how his incompetent, trigger-happy son-in-law Prez will rise through the ranks no matter what, courtesy of family and connections. Meanwhile, on the docks it is apparent that most of the heavy work is still being performed by the few black dockworkers, and the no-show and union official positions go to the Polish- and Italian-American old-timers. Sobotka's son, Zig, messes up and loses a container (and at other times conspires with his father and other white stevedores to bring drugs, prostitutes, and other contraband through the port), but Frank looks the other way and saves Zig's job. A black dockworker teases Sobotka and his buddies: "Y'all need to crawl back down in them holes. Remind yourself of who you is and where you come from." Although it's said in a joshing manner, later an African-American stevedore, Nat, angrily confronts Sobotka and asks how come it isn't time, as he'd been promised, for a black man to run for president of the local.[85]

Race still matters, and it simmers just below the surface, as at a mixed-race meeting of dockworkers, where Nat, an older black man, says, "That Polack mother f****r" might grab the grainery for condos, not industrial use." The black workers nod in agreement, but Horse, Sobotka, and the other white men mutter, "Whoa whoa whoa," and a fast "Hey, no offense," by Nat defuses the situation. But when Nat is angry that a black man has again been passed over for nomination for the union presidency, Sobotka says, "Black, white, what's the difference, Nat? Until we get that f*****g canal dredged, we're all niggers. Pardon my French." To which Nat snaps, "Or Polacks. Pardon mine." Race continues to shape life chances for the characters, and raw wounds are still just below the surface. As Eric Arnesen has demonstrated, on the docks of New Orleans and other southern cities such as Baltimore, whites and blacks cooperated tenuously to protect their jobs, but with racialized privilege lurking just beneath the surface. In moments of crisis, such as the one Sobotka tries to manage as best he can, the scabs often were ripped bloody.[86]

Throughout the series it is the white ethnic connections forged in Locust Point that enable certain characters to get by in the city, as when Sobotka donates a

stained-glass window to a parish and asks for some "face time" with the senator
from the Polish priest. When a young stevedore laments he only worked "five
days last month, that's all," and is "parking that piece of shit Buick two blocks
from the house, hoping for a lazy repo man," Sobotka tells him to go have a shot
and a beer, on him, and arranges for a stack of cash, "his change," to be waiting
for him at the bar. One hand still washes the other in the old neighborhood, even
if Sobotka's attempts to save his port will ultimately end in disaster. The show's
African-American characters, by and large without these connections downtown,
must fend for themselves, in the illegal drug trade of the projects.[87]

More jovially, when the stevedores gather for a shot and a beer at Dolores's tiny
row-house bar, a consensus develops around the good old days, and one stevedore
sighs, "It ain't never gonna be what it was." The younger workers, Nick and Ziggy,
tease the older ones about this epic nostalgia, but the characters do miss their
sense of purpose and rootedness in a functioning working-class community. The
frustration, though, among younger folks in Locust Point is apparent, as the good
times seem to have dried up with the portside jobs. Zig tells his father, "I remember everything. . . . All sitting around the kitchen table and talking shit about this
gang and that gang. Who's better with the break bulk, who could turn around
faster, and who was lazy. . . . I remember when youse all went down to picket
them scabs down in Covington Piers. . . . Everything. Everything." The nostalgia
here is no less embittered than in *American Pastoral*, but it's those outsourcing
factory owners such as the Swede, not black scapegoats, who are more likely to be
blamed for the decline of "the late great city of Baltimore."[88]

Sobotka expresses this rage, too, when a lobbyist explains to him the harbor
improvements are still not a sure thing, even after the boxes full of money he's
taken from the union to grease politicians. When the lobbyist objects to Sobotka's
implications that he's a sellout, saying his great-grandfather was a knife sharpener
on Preston Street, Sobotka asks,

You're talking history, right? I'm talking now. Because down here, it's still, "Who's your
old man?" Until you got kids, and then it's, "Who's your son?" But after the horror movie
I seen today—Robots! Piers full of robots! My kid will be lucky if he's even punching
numbers five years from now. And while it don't mean shit to me that I can't take my steak
knives to DeBiago and Sons, it breaks my f*****g heart that there's no future for the
Sobotkas on the waterfront![89]

Mercifully, in *The Wire*, for the most part at least, the white ethnic characters, who
do face disaster, do not blame the blacks for robbing them of their livelihood, but
correctly target the forces of deindustrialization—"piers full of robots," corrupt
politicians in bed with developers, and drug dealers alike—as well as the new forces
of gentrification. The old rhetoric of "we never locked our doors," the tropes used to
stigmatize minority urbanites, seems less than irrelevant in such circumstances.

The squeeze characters feel is from above and below. When Nick and his
girlfriend look at a row house they're thinking of buying, it turns out it was Nick's

aunt's old place, when the area was Locust Point. Now that it's an "up-and-coming" area, though, the realtor is offering it at a six-figure price to BMW-driving yuppies. More outside forces are pressing the Locust Point residents' backs to the wall. And by Season 3, the city has recovered sufficiently for city hall to be recaptured by an earnest Italian-American mayor. Control of the chocolate cities of George Clinton are reverting to white ethnics' control, with the complicity of conniving black pols such as the show's Senator Clay Davis; the neighborhoods, black and white, are still the losers.[90]

The Wire sensitively portrays the plight of these white ethnics, many of whom are complicit in drug dealing and smuggling as much as the African-Americans of the projects, but again, their grievances are more fully expressed than those of the minorities from the other side of the tracks. Sadly, Nick is determined, even as he's dealing drugs, not to seem "like some project nigger," and we do get some hints of the racial animosity that infuses the show's Baltimore. When black drug dealers beat up and rob Ziggy over an unpaid debt, and then torch his beloved Camarro, Zig enlists his black dockworker friend to help get him out of trouble but nonetheless hurls racial epithets when telling his cousin of his plight. Race is an agonizing dilemma in the show's Baltimore, but the larger economic pain both communities face is nevertheless at the forefront. *The Wire* is deft in its depiction of a city in which the characters, white or black, are left with few other options now that living-wage jobs have indeed long-fled Locust Point and West Baltimore alike, and for all concerned, "It ain't never gonna be what it was." When Sobotka wants out of the smuggling arrangement he has with the Greeks, Nino calmly looks across the harbor at the moribund factories. "They used to make steel there, no?" he asks, and the message is clear. As in Bruce Springsteen's "My Home Town," the jobs are going, boys, and they won't be back; Sobotka, Nick, and, across the city, D'Angelo and Barksdale, too, can deal drugs and hustle swag in the shadows of the rusting dinosaurs, or starve.[91]

For all that the show's police concentrate on Barksdale and the other black drug dealers in the projects, ironically it turns out the drug action in West Baltimore is ultimately controlled by a mysterious "Greek," who also runs the portside smuggling operation. As in nineteenth-century city mysteries, and many gangster movies of the 1930s, it's higher-ups who control the public face of crime, but such characters can hide in luxury penthouses and, in the case of the Greek, slip out of the country and regroup when Daniels's task force is ready to sweep in. Drug dealers, and the poor deindustrialized dockworkers, are caught in the police net, but the real masterminds walk free. Moreover, in Season 1's concluding episodes, when Lieutenant Daniels closes in on the drug dealers, he is called off by his higher-ups and a corrupt black politician who is implicated in the trade. Senator Davis, though, has his counterparts in the show's second season; the viewer also sees the cynical, corrupt world of department and machine politics in the white wards of portside Locust Point. The two hungry communities, black and white, are linked, without their even knowing it, although it is only younger whites such as Nick, the conniving stevedore nephew of Sobotka, who provides some of the context for turning to illegal activity in such a desperate city. "You try living on five or six days a month and see how fast it puts you on your ass," he says. "I am on my ass, Uncle Frank." The whole city, black and white, shares his plight, but it is only from Locust Point that such explanations are heard.[92]

That the even more desperate African-American characters turn to drugs—as police officer Herc says, "In this f*****g town, what other crime is there?"—is perhaps understandable, but the context of the city's hypersegregation—black exclusion from the skilled trades that flourished when the Greek's henchman says, "They used to make steel there, no?"—and other factors largely go unremarked by black characters. But *The Wire* does a masterful job of situating early-twenty-first-century urbanites in a city with fewer and fewer options for working-class residents, white or black. In this, its nostalgic look back at a city of "makers" versus "takers" is more nuanced than that contained in the nostalgic urban novels.

The Sopranos, too, employs the mean streets of rusting cityscape in and around Newark to comment on memory, nostalgia, and the ways things used to be back in the white ethnic 'hood. However, since the characters who pine for functioning Newark are loan sharks (and worse), not novelists or glove manufacturers from Weequahic, the memories of the good old days are tinged with sardonic commentary on the futility of comparing a functioning then to a sadder, grimmer urban present.

Throughout the series the old neighborhood, with its sense of rootedness, everyone knowing who they are and where they fit, is clearly preferable to Tony to the McMansions of the affluent suburb where he lives. While hanging out in front of Satriale's or Artie's restaurant back in the old neighborhood, Tony is at home far more than in a deracinated subdivision of "Wonder Bread wops" that can't compare to Newark for warmth or evocative memories.

But the series slyly comments on the falsity that sits behind warm, safe old neighborhoods. Obviously, we know what mayhem goes on in Satriale's back room, so even if the pork sandwiches are good enough to keep FBI Agent Harris coming back until the final episode, the urban village of "safe" streets is only safe if one turns a blind eye to Tony's enterprises.

Even the evocations of the past set up the slipperiness of remembering a better, safer city. Tony is always pining for a Newark that never was. When Tony steps inside a church in Season 1, he is filled with awe for the workmanship he sees around him. "Your great-grandfather and his brother Frank built this," Tony tells his daughter, reverently eying the marble altar his family had a hand in building. "Yeah, right, two guys," Meadow scoffs. "No, they were part of a crew, they didn't design it, but they knew how to build it. You go out today and find me two guys who can put grout in your bathtub." But we know that it was loan sharking, not stone masonry, that lifted the Soprano family out of the ghetto.[93]

Later, Tony again makes a reverent pilgrimage to the old Italian First Ward and shows his son the church his family built, but A.J. is similarly unimpressed. "We're talking history here, A.J." Tony says, in almost the same words that Sobotka uses to cut down the yuppie lobbyist. But here it's clear Tony misses his old ethnic neighborhood back in the city. "Your family's history, Newark's history." "Yeah, well who gives a shit about Newark?" his son asks.

Tony stresses the Italian pride that used to keep the neighborhood beautiful and safe, but ironically, viewers have already by this point seen flashbacks to Italian Newark, when Tony's father and Uncle Junior were not above beating deadbeats in a brutal way. In this flashback to "Down Neck" (a working-class area of the city east of the railroad tracks), we see girls skipping rope in front of their brick row houses, far from the riots on Springfield Avenue that Tony's mother watches on television. Livia may regard the rioters as the real lawless element (and as she irons, a television set shows the scenes of mayhem, an announcer saying that "the toll now stands at 11 dead and 600 wounded, as well as hundreds of businesses set ablaze"). And yet, in functioning, safe white Newark, for all the evocative fin-tailed Cadillacs, Junior and Johnny Boy put a deadbeat in traction. Later, too, as they are arrested for fencing fur coats at an amusement park, a gangster sullenly asks the police, "La fongool! Why don't you go lock up the moolinans! They're the ones that are burning down Newark!" Again, the kinds of white crime that the real Boiardo mob and the fictional Sopranos commit is given a pass when compared to ostensibly more dangerous threats. But clearly Tony's old Down Neck neighborhood is no poster child for civic virtue.[94]

References are made to 1967 in another scene, when Tony and his corrupt assemblyman pal connive with a black businessman, Maurice, to run a slum housing scam with government money. Any role that housing scams or the crime syndicate that Tony's father earlier ran might have played in bleeding Newark dry go unremarked in this episode.

In recalling his Newark youth, Assemblyman Zellman says, "Then came 1967," again summoning the annus horribilis for all white Newark. "What a f*****g summer that was!" Tony's mob henchman recalls. "Hey, were you around for Tony Imperiale? The White Knight?" Tony asks Maurice, his new black partner. Maurice replies, "Around, who do you think he was organizing against?" Tony adds, "Italian pride. Keep Newark white." Maurice answers, "Inspired Klansmen, some of those boys." Like Roth's Swede, Tony wants to have it both ways. He wants to be ethnic— Italian pride, and invested in the great specialness of his hardworking old, immigrant parish—and just "normal," that is, white. Either way, his recollections of Newark as a grand old place are predicated on forgetting its dysfunctions (to which his family significantly contributed, in 1967, as well as in the twenty-first century via HUD scams). And his teasing equation of Tony Imperiale with a defender ethos is one that African-Americans such as Maurice clearly don't share. Tony is elated to discover that he and his black business partner grew up near each other—"We were practically neighbors!" Tony gushes; "Yeah," a mob henchman smirks, "that's why you moved"—and the sense of a harmonious past has been disrupted.[95]

In another episode the present-day Newark is visited by a befuddled, senile Uncle Junior, who searches for his lost city. He wanders far into the by-now desolate slum in his bathrobe. As he stares up at the shuttered Pabst Blue Ribbon

Brewery, with its iconic three-story-high "beer bottle," an ancient black prostitute, who may or may not know Junior from the old days, comes along and asks for a ride. Junior asks if he knew her from the Jupiter Club, which she replies burned down years ago. The vacated past leers far above Junior, in the form of that desolate brewery, but down on the ground, aging blacks carry on in his old neighborhood.

Still, the aged gangster is certain someone has stolen his city from him, although here, unlike in *American Pastoral*, this white ex-Newarker's search is pathetically the result of his onrushing senility, and African-Americans aren't blamed for the brewery's closing.

When Junior further wanders into a storefront church, he demands to see "Johnny Soprano, goddammit, I'm his brother!" The black Newarkers have no idea who or what this ghost from the city's crime-ridden past is talking about, and a black minister coaching his young parishioners in a scam wants to get rid of Junior. Another older black man, though, eventually recalls, "Back in the day, when this was an Italian neighborhood, some fellas kept their jukeboxes here." Uncle Junior searching for his deceased brother is the counterpart of Zuckerman, only here we recognize, if Junior can't, the impossibility of returning home; if one could, one might discover that white ethnics ran many scams that impoverished places such as Newark.[96]

The sense of aggrievedness at a city stolen from its rightful white owners comes back again when Silvio organizes a counterprotest against "Chief Del Red Clay" and other Native American activists who are demonstrating in front of Newark's Columbus Park. When Silvio, Artie Bucco, and other angry Italian-Americans show up and find an effigy hanging, Sil hollers, "That better not be Columbus up there!" to which a protester hollers, "He's gonna burn, just like our ancestors did!" and the boys prepare to clash with the protesters. "They've got a permit, Sil," a white Newark cop tells him, to which the gangster replies, "I'm gonna remember this, Joey." The old rules of white hegemony no longer apply in twenty-first-century Newark.

Tony at least has the presence of mind to cut Silvio off when he plays the angry-oppressed-white-man card. To be sure, Tony has throughout the series lashed out at blacks he is sure are "Affirmative Action c**ks*****s" and his daughter's Jewish-black boyfriend, the "Hasidic homeboy," but here he stops Silvio's white ethnic screed. "Did you get what you got because you're Italian? No, you got it because you're you, because you're smart, because you're talented, whatever." Such epiphanies are rare, but they at least give *The Sopranos* a sophisticated sense of the complicated factors sitting behind urban America's changing face, a factor mostly lacking in urban nostalgic novels.[97]

Tony, though, knows he has come in at the tail end of something, and it is not just the mob but the old ethnic city that is altering beyond recognition. As Newark passes from its Italian-Americans' control, we also see the evisceration of the few traditions that preserve a memory of the older city. At Paulie Walnuts's old parish, the feast and saint's procession must continue without the revered "golden hat of

Saint Alzere," when the parish's new, non-Italian priest won't play by the old rules and wants to be cut in for a bigger piece of the proceeds. When Paulie refuses to comply, the procession continues without the "holy raiment." "They forgot his hat!" one old-timer cries, but in a few years it's uncertain whether anyone will remember.[98]

Gentrification is already lapping at Tony's North Newark doors, and an upscale juice franchise displaces the Italian live poultry store. When the franchise manager won't pay protection to gangster Patsy Parisi, he mutters, "What's happening to this f*****g neighborhood?" The realtor with whom Tony does business tells him, too, that she's moved into a luxury condo in "the old glove factory"; perhaps Swede Levov has cashed in yet again. In any event, yuppies supplant the old neighborhood every bit as perniciously as minorities, evidently, although in the next-to-last episode of all time it's clear that Little Italys in the city are also making way for ethnic newcomers. As some of New York boss Phil Leotardo's thugs walk through New York's Little Italy, a tour bus informs the paying customers that although Little Italy once covered forty square blocks, it is now only two streets long. Indeed, when a gangster doesn't pay attention as he's talking on his cell phone, he wanders into an Asian immigrant neighborhood, a look of hopeless confusion on his face. In the modern city he is clearly out of his element.[99]

In *The Sopranos*, the recollections of a happier Newark coexist with ironic evidence that all was not well back in the day. For all the lovely Jefferson Airplane melodies that play under Tony's recollections of Uncle Junior's nifty 1967 Cadillac, corruption was a constant in the old city. Moreover, unlike in the urban nostalgic novels of Roth, there are telling suggestions that nonwhite Newarkers such as Maurice might not have regarded the city as all that accommodating in the Edenic past. And if the city is disappearing from older white ethnics' grasp, suburbanization and urban yuppie pioneers may be just as much to blame as minority scapegoats. In any event, a seat at the tables in front of Satriale's remains an appealing perch from which to swap fables about an imagined city, a slice of heaven in Italian North Newark.

For many transplanted, aging urbanites, the appeal of such imaginative cityscapes of ethnic rootedness as those that rush by in the opening *Sopranos* montage is palpable. Pizza Land. Satriale's. Pulaski Savings & Loan—who wouldn't live in such a world of inviting icons of the bygone urban village? Fortunately, one needn't take a blood oath to Tony's crew to indulge in a nostalgic re-creation of the past. We are all popular cultural producers at the dawn of the twenty-first century, and the Internet has allowed many ex-urbanites to create the kind of cities they've always imagined. Our final chapter, then, is a tour through the warm and sunny precincts of Virtual Newark.

—6—

"We Never Locked Our Doors at Night": Newark on the Net, minus the Mob

In an episode of the acclaimed HBO series *The Sopranos,* the New Jersey mob boss decides to show his teenage son, A.J., his family's old neighborhood in Newark's First Ward. "We're talking about history here, A.J. Your family's history. Newark's history." His son, though, remains unimpressed. "Well who gives a shit about Newark?" "I'm making a point," Tony counters. "This neighborhood used to be beautiful. A hundred percent Italian." He then laments the state of disrepair, commenting on the filthiness and crime he sees all around him: "I mean, look at, look at all of these buildings around here. Most of them are falling down to the ground." He then points to his family's old parish church, St. Lucy's, a symbol for him of the vanished Little Italy that has been replaced by boarded-up crack dens. "But that church is still standing. You know why?" "The bricks?" A.J. guesses. "Because our people give a shit, that's why. Every Sunday, Italians from the old neighborhood, they drive miles to come here to pray. To keep this place alive." And A.J. counters, "Yeah, so how come we never do?"[1]

The irony of Tony Soprano, violent mob boss, lamenting the intrusion of crime and danger into his formerly safe old neighborhood, which was "a hundred percent Italian," need hardly be remarked. Periodically throughout the series, flashbacks show us that in the 1950s, when the streets were clean and safe, Tony's father and Uncle Junior were not above using baseball bats and meat cleavers to convince business associates of the errors of their ways. And some of what was built by the Italians (and, as we'll see, Jews) in working-class Newark was not exactly sanctioned by the chamber of commerce. Clearly Tony is building for himself a selective and usable past out of the memories that, like the bricks, lie all around him on Garside Street.

Yet there is another irony to Tony's trek to his imagined Newark. "Why don't we come here?" A.J. wonders, and it's evident that for all of Tony's loving evocations of the "old neighborhood," where his people built something, for all his "talking history here," Garside Street and the poverty of life in its cold-water flats are things Tony and his people did everything they could to flee as soon as they could. Yet even if, like Tony, most white ex-Newarkers for the most part avoid the city in favor of the leafy green suburbs of McMansions to which many of them have escaped, thousands of former city residents do return to the city of their youth—virtually.

New technologies, particularly the Internet, have enabled exiles from urban America to creatively "keep this place alive" from the comfort of their cul de sacs, without having to traverse city streetscapes they imagine as demonstrably more dangerous and lethal than they were in their youth. One such imaginative re-creation is www.virtualnewarknj.com, a cornucopia of oral histories, photos, and historical vignettes of Newark's theaters, ethnic shops and neighborhoods, fire companies, restaurants, parks, and much else that gave texture to New Jersey's largest city in the era from roughly 1910 to 1967. Newark is not alone here, as the phenomenon of the virtual city has become a common one. As Alessandro Aurigi and Stephen Graham have documented, in Europe especially, virtual cities have arisen as the new combination virtual city hall and chamber of commerce, where one can "access" an array of shopping, entertainment, city services, information, and options, all without ever having to step over a homeless person or negotiate along gridlocked streets. The point of such virtual cities, they argue, is to present urbanism's thrills and cultural amenities without the poverty and contestation that may disconcert or threaten upscale computer users in "real time." (Of course, Aurigi and Graham note that the problems of poverty and unequal access to resources or political influence persist "off-screen.")[2]

In the United States, other cities' Web sites offer a mix of historical vignettes and information on current amenities in the "real" cities they virtually replicate. Thus, in the virtual analogue of Jersey City, information on the current offerings at Liberty State Park coexists with Frank "I Am the Law" Hague, who has not held sway at city hall since 1947. A somewhat more sanitized, and celebratory, past is presented at a site dedicated to the 125th anniversary of Passaic, New Jersey. While the site offers a virtual tour of historic Passaic, as well as links to the Passaic High School reunion site, with a virtual jukebox of 1950s doo-wop songs, it seems there is nothing whatsoever at this site related to the city's epic year-long textile strike of 1926–1927, or earlier labor strife, a bloody story of confrontation that scholars such as Paul Murphy and David J. Goldberg have so amply documented.[3]

It is in this selective vein that www.virtualnewarknj.com (recently redubbed www.oldnewark.com) purports to present its version of the past. The site endeavors to offer the "visitor" a reconnect to a vanished time and place—historical memories, pictures, and information on New Jersey's largest city as it purportedly existed in the past—without making reference to the city as it currently exists, at least explicitly. This is a Newark for those who no longer live or work in the city.

One has to admire this labor of love, which has re-created a multilayered streetscape in a telling example of Dolores Hayden's "Power of Place," and still feel that something has been edited out, in order to serve an insidious political purpose in the here and now.[4] The blood on Newark's bygone pavements has been whitewashed by the categories the site's managers deem relevant to re-creating a seemingly conflict-free city. What's lurking in the shadows of Virtual Newark's alleys, though, are the real (as opposed to virtual) models for Tony Soprano, the mobsters who controlled, well, virtually everything in the city during the 1920s–1950s. The site is for the most part silent on Ruggiero "Ritchie the Boot" Boiardo, head of Newark's Mafia, but the Jewish mob has recently been added to the site. As Virtual Newark is a work in progress, at least some mention of organized crime has been added in the person of Abner "Longy" Zwillman, head of the New Jersey branch of Murder Inc.[5] These tales and reminiscences of certain mobsters have been added to Virtual Newark since I began visiting its "streets."

Still, the stories of Zwillman that make it into Virtual Newark do so in ways that turn him and his pals in Murder Inc. into veritable folk heroes, in ways that contrast his brand of lawbreaking with a more ominous brand of "urban pathology" (at least to the posters) that emerged in post-1967 Newark (and the July 1967 rebellion by African-Americans remains for the most part a nonissue, effaced by the code of omerta from Virtual Newark). Even the mob is selectively recalled in ways that serve insidious political purposes for white ethnic ex-urbanites looking to contrast their city with the twenty-first-century Newark.

Indeed, the Newark of the Internet stands in as a kind of "Lost Atlantis" of harmony, an exemplar set apart from the supposed dystopias of a violent place out of which white ethnics regretfully escaped in the wake of the July 1967 riots. Supposed black and Hispanic criminality is tacitly contrasted with a harmonious city of the past in which "we never locked our doors," for although some less pleasant features of earlier Newark intrude, the dominant leitmotif seems to be a re-creation of a city of hardworking white ethnics on their way to socioeconomic mobility.

This chapter, then, will examine some of the sociopolitical implications of these broader questions of who gets constituted as "belonging" to the faux communities that certain former Newarkers are creating for themselves via technology. A selective airbrushing of problematic or conflict-laden violent pasts has occurred to fabricate the cities that white ethnics would prefer they had come from. Indeed, the flocking to cyberculture is seen by Alison Adam and Eileen Green as an "escape from a world gone wrong."[6] In this respect what is Virtual Newark but an upgrade of the tried-and-true method of "white flight," which, courtesy of the GI Bill, the FHA, and redlining, had already by the 1940s drained Newark of much of its middle class and property tax base, as Kenneth Jackson documents in *Crabgrass Frontier*.[7] Jerry Gafio Watts notes, as well, that the white flight that began as early as the 1940s hastened businesses' escape from the city, too, as employers followed their workforce and benefited from tax breaks in the new suburbs. This process starved the city for ratables, so that by the 1960s, Newark was one of the nation's poorest cities, but paradoxically had one of the highest property-tax rates.[8] After this white flight, former Newarkers have been left, decades later, to make sense of their former city via a cybernarrative that privileges stories of white ethnics' self-sacrifice and law-abiding nature. Indeed, as Peter Way has remarked in a different context, "Ethnic culture made sense of the material here and now by applying the traditional then."[9]

This certainly seems to be the case in this virtual city. The site is divided into various features, including a chat room, a discussion group, images of Newark (with city businesses, churches, restaurants, parks, public buildings, and images of people), information on the city's cemeteries, a feature on "your ancestor's neighborhood" that allows for a street-by-street visit to the city's old wards, and information on the history of Newark's ethnic communities. Only four options are listed for ethnic communities, however—German, Italian, Jewish, and Irish— suggesting already that Virtual Newark is a selective glimpse at the real city, which is now roughly 70 percent African-American and Hispanic. But as a map of the city's "nationalities" commissioned in 1911 by Presbyterian church leaders, re- produced on the site, makes clear, already by that early date the city was home to significant numbers of African-Americans, living adjacent to the predominantly Jewish Third Ward neighborhoods and Weequahic. As Watts notes, while blacks only reached majority status in Newark circa 1966, they were an early and sig- nificant (albeit politically and economically powerless) percentage of the city's population quite early. While only 2.7 percent of the city's 347,469 residents in 1910, by 1920 Newark African-Americans numbered 16,977. By 1940 they were 11 percent of the city's population, and by 1950 (the heyday of nostalgic Virtual Newark), they accounted for 17 percent of the city's population.[10] These commu- nities of color, though, are almost wholly absent from the precincts of Virtual Newark. The Newark that is represented here is more emblematically represented by a 1964 photo submitted of the all-white champion bowling team from Golda's Bar, or the similarly monochromatic 1940s Lions' Club from the city's Roseville section.[11]

It is while searching through another of Virtual Newark's features that this African-American absence, as well as the selective reshaping of Italian and Jewish Newark, becomes most apparent. Visitors are invited to post "Your Newark Memories," and dozens of recollections are grouped by Newark neighborhoods. But it's a fair question just whose Newark is being remembered, and how a communal consensus has sent even 1940 Newark's seamy side to the trash bin. A typical posting is one by Angela DeGennaro Lucas, who refers to the city's predominantly Italian old First Ward centered on Eighth Avenue: "I grew up in the First Ward. Everyone knew everybody else. They all looked after anyone's kids. There were no doors locked. We slept on the fire escapes in the summer while watching people below." In a second posting, she repeats, "Together, we were all one big family" on Garside Street "until urban renewal took away our house," going on to laud the ethnic businesses such as Megaro Funeral Home, Andy Monda's Grocery, Gerardo the fruit seller, Mattia's Chicken Market, "Gennarino's, where we bought a five-cent coke in a bottle," and her own grandparents' tavern, "the Trecolle Club (meaning three peaks)."

This evocation of ethnic businesses is almost totemic, a religious invocation of the reality of the neighborhood's former "vibrancy" and warmth that is repeated by other posters referring to Prince Street, the city's main Jewish shopping thoroughfare (accompanying the recollections of the street's bakeries and clothing stores is a photo of the pushcart-lined street from circa 1910, evocative of New York's more famous Hester Street). DeGennaro Lucas sums up the communal consensus, that this litany of stores is likely to convey for other posters and readers: "The street was mostly Italians from the same province, Avellino. Everyone knew one another and watched out for each other." Leonard Fabiano recalls the First Ward of his youth in much the same way, adding his homage to the ethnic businessmen of Eighth Avenue: "They worked incredibly hard and built up their lives for their family and to serve the neighborhood." And Ronald Mangine, referring to Garside Street, remembers "Watching the old-timers play boccie or modra with their fingers for wine, it was called boss and underboss, oh, the arguments from those games."[12]

All of these recollections of life on Garside are no doubt accurate, so far as they go. And in this respect, at least, a recollected Newark has some glimmer of connection to its historical past, unlike such postmodern faux-ethnic tourist venues as Detroit's deracinated Greektown, so scathingly deconstructed by Jerry Herron as not too Greek, and never much of a town. "Although most people choose to live elsewhere," Herron notes, "they haven't been able to abandon the city imaginatively, whether out of nostalgia or guilt or a combination of the two." Yet when "old things—warehouses, machine shops, lofts, cheap hotels—are made to look new again," they become upscale bars and restaurants, not sites of contestation such as they often were in industrial Detroit or Newark. This is what is lacking from both re-created urban playlands such as Greektown and virtual cities such as cyber Newark.[13]

There is nothing in Virtual Newark that questions the context in which many of these warm memories took place. While "boss and underboss" are recalled, there is nothing in Virtual Newark on the real boss of the First Ward, mobster Ruggiero "Ritchie the Boot" Boiardo. His name appears only in a passing reference in a story told about the head of the city's Jewish crime syndicate, Abner "Longy" Zwillman, but none of the posters discuss in any detail the bloody career of Boiardo, even when referring, as Mangine does, to the First Ward restaurants "The Victoria Castle and later the Sorrento," both Boiardo hangouts, as Michael Immerso's book, *Newark's Little Italy*, demonstrates. Immerso notes that Boiardo still controlled much of northern New Jersey's organized crime in the 1950s, and that his rule was far from gentle.[14] Omitted are the violent end that awaited certain North Jersey mobsters caught on the wrong side of turf wars, such as Willie Moretti, murdered in a Cliffside Park restaurant in 1951, or a description of the brutal methods by which Boiardo maintained control of the First Ward crime syndicate in the 1930s, 1940s, and 1950s.[15]

Indeed, there is no detailed description of Italian organized crime in Virtual Newark, and only a brief intrusion into Leonard Fabiano's sepia-toned recollections of the First Ward's best restaurant, "the Victoria Castle, where my oldest sister had her wedding reception. Very regal at the time. Joe DiMaggio, Frank Sinatra and many Mafiosi dined there."[16] Even if amnesia suddenly arises, and no names can be summoned to add to the luminaries "DiMaggio, Sinatra, and . . . many Mafiosi," this is more than other informants care to recall, nor does the fact appear that a 1965 Essex County grand jury "issued a presentment indicating a lack of law enforcement in the area of organized crime. It was discovered that there was actual overlapping in the payrolls of the Newark Police Department and an underworld related enterprise."[17]

Nor do the kickbacks Boiardo provided to Congressman and later Newark Mayor Hugh Addonizio quite make it into the collective consciousness of the site's cybercitizens. As John T. Cunningham notes in his book, *Newark*, Addonizio, the "law and order" mayor who invited the National Guard in to restore "order" during the July 1967 "riots," would later do time in the federal pen for accepting bribes and kickbacks in a scheme worked out with Anthony "Tony Boy" Boiardo of the mob.[18] The overlap between the mob and city hall was rumored to have been a long-standing one, as Jerry Gafio Watts notes in his cultural biography of Amiri Baraka. Black politicians such as Councilman Irvine Turner allied themselves with the Third Ward Political Club of both Murder Inc.'s "Longy" Zwillman and former Mayor Meyer Ellenstein, and in return illegal activity such as numbers running went unmolested in black areas of the city. However, when Zwillman was briefly imprisoned in the early 1950s, the Italian branch of organized crime represented by Ritchie "The Boot" Boiardo stepped into the numbers racket of the black precincts of the Central (formerly Third) Ward. This takeover was facilitated, Watts argues, because Boiardo was close to the new mayor, Ralph Villani.[19] Instead of such seamier memories of Newark, nights sleeping on fire escapes and unlocked doors—not protection rackets and contract hits—give texture to the virtual tour of the First Ward.

And if we must have criminality, it takes the guise of a tip-off to an annoying intrusion into the "victimless" scheme of "playing the numbers." Bob Certo recalls his grandparents' running a numbers game out of a candy store. They never were caught, however, because his grandmother's sister was married to a Newark cop who inevitably let them know of upcoming raids. What we get, then, in Virtual Newark is the creation of a communal narrative built on a consensus that hardworking, honest white ethnics kept the neighborhood safe. South Sixteenth Street is re-created by Rose LaBruno as "a street of lovely two- and three-family homes where people of all nationalities got along beautifully," while Sharon of Vailsburg insists, "We very rarely locked our doors and we played out in the streets. . . . We would walk down the Avenue late at night and never worried about our safety." Any discussion of criminality in Italian Newark is rendered as playful recollections of warm and fuzzy criminality, and it's by no means certain that running a numbers racket is even regarded as all that immoral.[20]

While the streets may have been safe, many informants in other venues own up to an economic perilousness in 1950s Newark that they might not at first confess. Anthropologist Sherry B. Ortner, herself a 1958 graduate of Newark's predominantly Jewish Weequahic High School, interviewed her former classmates for her study, *New Jersey Dreaming*. She notes of Weequahic, the neighborhood where middle-class strivers moved, that "the Weequahic neighborhood in the fifties was the proverbially quiet and peaceful place, with clean, tree-lined, and above all, safe streets." Yet she notes that "many people remember loving the neighborhood, . . . but social distinctions lurking in these kinds of streets became increasingly salient to the class of '58 as they grew up."

Judging from the recollections Ortner gleaned in her interviews, it seems dysfunctions were always there, causing much private pain behind closed doors. One informant notes, "My family consisted of my mother, my sister, and I; my father kind of abandoned us when I was six years old, so I really grew up without a father in a sense." Two other members of Weequahic High's class tell similar tales of parental abandonment, while another relates that his father was "totally absent as a father, except to be destructive and negative." Another man recalls that his father was a compulsive gambler who lost everything, and went bankrupt in the late 1940s. Another graduate relates the story of a seemingly successful legitimate businessman who was rumored to have been murdered by the mob. Other tales of family dissolution and poverty, which was more prevalent than even Ortner herself imagined, are recalled as having been kept behind closed doors, and such memories even today are burdened with a great deal of shame. While they may have eventually been shared in person with an anthropologist whom one had known in high school, these tales of personal trauma have not made it onto the streets of Virtual Newark. Even in cyberspace these matters are too shameful to be paraded in broad daylight; thus the virtual city, which for many older Newarkers is the only city that matters anymore, is a selective reconstruction that privileges the safe streets, not the stresses of life, in even one of 1950s Newark's more desirable neighborhoods. It may be that the venues in which certain forms of oral history are practiced today, as on the Web, are predisposed only to capture a triumphalist narrative.[21]

Virtual Newark has recently proven a little more forthcoming in owning up to the city's Jewish organized-crime figures, but in ways that only serve in the end to buttress the construction of a narrative of hardworking, ambitious white ethnics striving to improve their communities. A frequent poster to Virtual Newark, Nat Bodian, has recently added an account of "Longy Zwillman, the notorious gangster from Newark's Third Ward." Bodian notes that "Abner 'Longy' Zwillman [was] one of the organizers and a founding member of the nationwide crime syndicate known as Murder, Inc. . . . He was forced to quit school to help support his mother and six brothers and sisters after his father died suddenly." Taking up a produce wagon, Zwillman "soon saw there was more money to be made selling lottery numbers than in selling produce. So he started his own numbers bank. . . . Eventually, with the aid of hirelings and musclemen, he controlled the numbers business in most of Newark."[22]

Even this brief synopsis of "the notorious gangster" is an odd mixture of admission of illegal methods—"hirelings and musclemen"—with a barely concealed admiration for entrepreneurship and seizing the main chance: —"one of the organizers and founding members" (of Murder Inc., but let's pass over that), who "soon saw" where the money was to be made. Then, too, there's the revealing detail that it was only the death of Longy's father that "forced" him to quit school, thus preventing perhaps a more praiseworthy use of his "organizational" genius.

Bodian goes on to acknowledge that Zwillman branched out into bootlegging during Prohibition "with the aid of Third Ward hirelings," and that his "criminal enterprises were vastly expanded, ultimately, to include all types of crime, including gambling, prostitution and control of some labor unions." The flavor of this recollection of the Third Ward gangster, though, quickly moves in another direction. In describing Zwillman's February 1959 funeral (Longy either hung himself or was rubbed out by associates who sought to make his death appear a suicide, as the FBI was closing in), Bodian writes, "Although Zwillman had ranked as one of the nation's top crime bosses, and one of the six bosses of Murder Inc., he had maintained his lifelong roots in Newark's old Third Ward and his connections with Newark." Bodian states that "Zwillman and his gang had protected Jewish merchants from marauding attacks by anti-Semites," a novel spin on the gangster, indeed, one that is followed up elsewhere on the site by assertions that Zwillman's Third Ward gang provided vigilantes for assaults on rallies by the German-American Bund in nearby Irvington. In this scenario, we are quickly moving away from Zwillman's houses of prostitution and labor racketeering, and he becomes almost a neighborhood hero protecting his people from those even bigger hoodlums, Fritz Kuhn and Adolf Hitler. Bodian continues in this vein, asserting that "his generosity to fellow Newarkers was legendary. He funded the Mount Carmel Guild downtown soup kitchen through seven depression years. He provided needy Newark Jews with food baskets during Jewish holidays." However Longy came by his money, his charitable activities are quickly the focus of this recollection, and he becomes something of a Robin Hood for the Third Ward. Indeed, the site reproduces a program book from a 1928 banquet at the Third Ward Political Club (dominated already by Zwillman), which lauds him as the ward's benefactor.[23]

Yet what passed for politics in Newark was often little distinguishable from organized crime. It has already been noted that Mayor Addonizio was eventually imprisoned for his connection to the Boiardo mob. In 1954, the FBI likewise documented Zwillman's long-standing, mutually remunerative relationship with the Essex County (Newark) Democratic Party. A letter to J. Edgar Hoover, dated January 28, 1954, alleged that Longy had close ties to two former Newark mayors, Meyer Ellenstein and Ralph Villani, as well as the Essex County Democratic Party chairman. It was reported that in 1940 Ellenstein, Jersey City Mayor Frank Hague, and Zwillman divvied up jobs at the Brewster Aircraft Company, which held a sweetheart lease at the Newark Airport. The report cited "a confidential informant, of known reliability," saying that

Zwillman had acquired a substantial block of stock in the Brewster Aircraft Corporation in late 1939 or early 1940, and at this time Zwillman was allegedly operating a racket with one Frank Corbally, then the local WPA Administrator who was supplying WPA labor to Brewster. It was also stated that as of April 17, 1940, no lease had been negotiated by Brewster Corporation for the use of the Newark Airport; as a result, the corporation was having free use of the property.

Also in 1940, after Ellenstein was acquitted of alleged misconduct in office, Zwillman threw him a grand party, and the subsequent reorganization of the Newark Police Department "was re-organization by Zwillman." A second informant alleged that Zwillman was allowed to operate his rackets unimpeded because he served as the money man for the Essex County Democratic Party chairman every November.

Zwillman's reach extended beyond his home turf, for he was also alleged to have aided Jersey City's Mayor John V. Kenny. Kenny, though, denied that Zwillman had contributed fifty thousand dollars to his mayoral campaign in 1949, blaming his rival, former Mayor Frank Hague, for spreading the rumor. If so, this may have been sour grapes on Hague's part, for during the latter part of his thirty-year run as mayor of Jersey City, an agent noted in a 1954 "memorandum, general investigative intelligence file," that "it was reported that former Mayor Frank Hague of Jersey City also obtained a sizeable cut of each weekly take" on gambling operations in Bayonne. The agent noted that it was reported in 1945 that Zwillman apparently obtained a thousand dollars weekly, which was divided "among the powers in Hudson County." The familiarity that New Jersey politicians had with Third Ward citizens such as Longy is relatively unexamined in Virtual Newark.[24]

Recently, though, a more unsavory Jewish mob figure has been added to the virtual city. The exploits of Max "Puddy" Hinkes, Longy's numbers enforcer for the city, provides a less sanitized glimpse at the underworld. Yet, even here, Bodian gives prominent play to Hinkes's time with the "Minute Men," the group of vigilantes led by "a former prize fighter, Nat Arno" that violently confronted the German-American Bund during the 1930s. "Max took pleasure in cracking heads," the poster notes, and he and the Minute Men were "remarkably effective in making the Jewish neighborhoods safe from Nazi harassment." Still, Hinkes's earlier career, the poster admits, was "dedicated to hijacking, burglary, breaking and entry, stickups, extortion, shake downs, and working both sides of labor disputes as an enforcer. . . . Max was loyal only to money." It is at this point that one must ask why Virtual Newarkers were so foolish as never to lock their doors with a character like Puddy prowling the streets. And yet Puddy's exploits do not interfere with this and other posters' insistence that the streets of pre-1967 Newark were absolutely safe. The "usable" past of a safe and functioning white-ethnic city distorts and omits the "unusable" past.

This "unusable" past, too, may very well have contributed to the city's decay. "During the time that . . . Zwillman controlled the rackets, Puddy was the guy who collected from the numbers to deliver the bag to City Hall to keep the mayor and his cronies happy." Later the poster notes that Puddy "was the disciple of David 'Quincy' Lieberman, . . . a local power broker whose connections extended from gangsters to the cops on the beat, to the local ladies of the night, right up to the office of the Mayor." It is noteworthy that, in another posting, Bodian lauds 1930s Newark mayor, Meyer Ellenstein, as "the champion of the city," designating him "certainly the most colorful, charming, and talented city leader in Newark's history through the World War II era." Ellenstein continued to serve as the city commissioner responsible for the Department of Revenue and Finance until 1954, the heyday of the era when Longy's bagman was splitting the take with the "cronies" at city hall. Any reflection on the symbiosis between the rackets and city hall, both run out of the Third Ward Political Club of which Zwillman was president, and the role such closeness may have played in the city's precipitous decline, is absent. The selective remembrances are still being created, seventy years later.[25]

Elsewhere posters lovingly recall city businesses such as the Riviera Hotel and the famed Tavern Restaurant, only parenthetically remarking that both were part-owned by "silent partner" Longy Zwillman. In an homage to the Tavern, it is only in a footnote that readers learn that "at the end of Prohibition, Zwillman invested in a number of reputable, established business enterprises. The Tavern was among his investments." Like much else about Zwillman on this site, this makes him sound like just a shrewd and ambitious Third Ward "investor," which, in a sense, he was.[26]

Elsewhere the language practically *kvells*. From a "modest numbers operation," Zwillman and Joseph "Doc" Stacher become "big names in organized crime."[27] As Rachel Rubin and Rich Cohen have argued in their work, it seems that Jewish gangsters are translated in the communal narrative into admirable businessmen— granted, on the wrong side of the law, but as Cohen's title has it, "Tough Jews" who are admired in the neighborhood for not being pushed around or accepting their humble place in the ghetto.[28] As in Jonathan Rieder's account of Canarsie, Brooklyn's white-flight refuge for those fleeing Brownsville and East New York, mention of Murder Inc. is embedded in an evocation of the safe and functional neighborhood and eventual upward mobility along Pitkin Avenue. As a Canarsie informant tells Rieder of 1930s Brownsville, "I remember a vital, active community of small shopkeepers and garment workers. Of course, there was Murder Inc., but they stayed in their own poolroom, and we weren't too aware of them." Of course, Murder Inc.'s infiltration of the garment industry was the stuff of tabloid headlines in the 1920s, 1930s, and 1940s, as well as much despair on the part of union officials such as Sidney Hillman. Surely garment workers along Pitkin Avenue knew as much. This amnesia on the part of Rieder's informant is telling, yet vital if former Canarsieans, like fleeing Newarkers, are to have their safe, clean, painless past. Another Canarsie informant adds, "We lived in a ghetto, maybe, but it wasn't such a slum!" The comparison to what current African-American residents of Brownsville have made "such a slum," is apparent. So, too, the word on the street in Virtual Newark is similarly ambivalent about their branch of Murder Inc. Most kids from Jewish Newark became doctors and lawyers and accountants, and hey, some were mighty smart gangsters, too.[29]

However, even a cursory glance at some of the 747 pages in Zwillman's FBI file indicates that there was a less charitable, chamber of commerce side to him.

A June 7, 1950, letter to J. Edgar Hoover documenting Zwillman's "criminal activities" notes that "Zwillman first became a feared man when in 1923 he shot Leo Kapus in the leg. Kapus was at that time in the bootlegging business . . . and controlled what was commonly referred to as 'Bootlegger's Row' in Newark." Arrests in Newark in 1927 and 1928 on charges of "atrocious assault and battery with intent to kill" are noted in Zwillman's file. The letter also cryptically notes the violence between the Boiardo and Zwillman mobs during the 1930s, omitting the fact that Boiardo was shot, likely on Longy's orders, simply noting that "Al Capone reportedly came to Newark to straighten out the difference between Boiardo and Zwillman." Other feuds are more graphically detailed. The FBI letter notes that rival bootleggers Max Hassel and Max Greenberg "were planning to eliminate Zwillman from the picture, but that Zwillman had learned of the plan. On April 12, 1933, both Hassel and Greenberg were murdered in the Elizabeth Carteret Hotel in Elizabeth, N.J. The two murders are unsolved." Maybe somebody should have urged Hassel and Greenberg to lock their doors.

The letter also notes the most sensational Newark mob hit, that on Arthur Flegenheimer, aka "Dutch Schultz," a celebrated piece of gang lore from 1935 that, so far as Virtual Newark's residents are concerned, never happened. The FBI, however, notes that the morning after the hit in a Newark tavern, the Palace Chophouse, Longy "had in his possession photostats of all papers found on Schultz's body," and that Longy was questioned by the Newark police in regard to the Schultz murder, as well as in regard to other missing persons or "fugitives." Perhaps because Longy had Philip Kull, a former Newark police officer, on his Third Ward gang payroll, no charges ever came from this investigation.

The 1950 letter also notes that a rival "liquor traffic along the Jersey Shore" resulted in the murder of Al Lillian and that when his brother, William, sought to switch to servicing restaurants with cigarette-vending machines, he ran afoul of another Zwillman enterprise, the Public Service Tobacco Co. William was convinced to sell out to Longy after a "severe beating." Longy bought William Lillian out, "although it was rumored that Zwillman threatened to kill Lillian if he didn't give up the business. Unfavorable publicity resulted from the purchase of this business as to the methods used by Zwillman to gain control of the enterprise." The letter also notes Zwillman's association with Jacob "Gurrah" Shapiro, Meyer Lansky, Louis "Lepke" Buchalter, Benjamin Siegel, Moe Wolensky, and Moe Dalitz. A subsequent addition to Longy's file notes, "The theory has been advanced that the top mobsters in the country, including Luciano, Costello, Buchalter, Shapiro, Zwillman, and Siegel, were apprehensive about the return of Dutch Schultz to the New York area, inasmuch as they had assumed management of Schultz's gang. It has been suggested that several of the above mobsters did a favor for certain Kansas City mobsters and had Michael James Lacapra killed, and that gunmen were furnished by Kansas City to dispose of Dutch Schultz."[30]

The FBI also noted that heroin was being dealt out of the Riviera Hotel, one of those "legitimate" enterprises remembered so fondly by posters to Virtual Newark.[31] As with much of the grittier, unpleasant aspects of Newark, the violent methods by which Zwillman controlled his empire, as well as its specific shady enterprises, are omitted from Virtual Newark.

We needn't even go to the top of the organized-crime hierarchy to find evidence of criminality or dysfunctional behavior in earlier, predominantly white times and areas of Newark. The 1958 classmates whom Sherry Ortner interviewed recalled several Jewish kids from 1950s Weequahic who did jail time for dealing drugs, and who later hung out in rough gangs. Those Jewish working-class boys who hung out at a neighborhood hot dog stand called Syd's were recollected as using drugs and likely dealing them, too. These are not the kinds of neighborhood memories likely to make it into Virtual Newark, either.[32]

Rather, Syd's hot dogs is remembered in Virtual Newark in a quite different way. The denizens of Syd's from the early 1950s who the poster chooses to recall are slightly more praiseworthy:

During the Bratter era of Syd's ownership, in the early 1950s, . . . you were likely to find Philip, Jack, or Bernie at Syd's. It was their favorite neighborhood hang-out. 'Philip' was Philip Roth, who would later become a famous novelist. . . . 'Jack' was Jack Kirsten, who would later become a notable and widely and highly-regarded Essex County Superior Court judge. 'Bernie' was Bernie Marcus, who would later found the 2,000+ store chain, "Home Depot" with more than 50 billion dollars in annual sales.

Whoever was meeting in the alley out back, the site cares not to say.[33]

If the blood on the Third Ward's streets has been whitewashed, Virtual Newark is equally vague as to precisely when the golden age was supposed to have existed. Exact recollections of years and dates are often omitted, in a way that creates a consensus on the mythic stability of "the old days." Like many others, Ron Mangine's recollections exist apart from a specific fixed year or date. They are the magical no-time/all-time of the old neighborhood before it went bad. He concludes his story of the First Ward, "What a magical time and place lost forever except in my heart and mind"—without ever indicating what year precisely that "magical time" was.[34]

Years are often omitted, even if an internal clue (year graduated from high school, for example) can sometimes fix a posting as referring to a specific date. For the most part, though, postings refer to a nebulous era somewhere between Pearl Harbor and July 1967, the end time so far as white ethnic Newark is concerned, that is, "the riots." All recollections of a neighborhood in which "we never locked our doors," then, exist in a mythic no-time/all-time, "the good old days." Specificities such as a particular year or an analysis of actual crime figures from 1950 are unnecessary. All the confirmation required is in other posters' reiterations that "we all felt safe no matter what time we came home."[35]

The "all," though, are virtually all-white, and no consideration of the poverty of the city's black community is given. While mention of the city's slums is omitted on the site, such black poverty was already amply documented by 1939 Farm Security Administration and 1944 Newark Housing Authority housing-survey photographs of the crumbling wood-frame shacks of the black sections of the old Third (Central) Ward, as well as the homeless colonies that persisted on the city's periphery.[36] As Nathan Wright noted in his 1968 study, *Ready to Riot*, "Typical of conditions faced by black arrivals was housing blight, with Newark's decaying slums among the worst in the nation. Nearly one-third of all the dwelling units in Newark in 1944 were reported to be below minimum standards of health and decency."[37] When members of Students for a Democratic Society, including Tom Hayden, established an antipoverty program (the Newark Community Union Project) in the city, they documented their efforts in a 1966 film, *Troublemakers*. The grainy black-and-white film convincingly portrays the hurdles they faced, in terms of both the enormity of the poverty in the city's black slums and the unresponsiveness of the corrupt administration of Mayor Hugh Addonizio, who makes a brief appearance in the film.[38]

On Virtual Newark, no link is made between such poverty and the exclusion of blacks from any meaningful political role in the city as late as the 1960s, or the brutality of a virtually all-white police force toward city minorities, and the conflagration that erupted in July 1967. Indeed, as far as I can tell, there has been only one posting by an African-American, son of a jazz drummer who grew up in the 1960s and 1970s in the projects along formerly Jewish Prince Street. Fortunately, his recollections confirm of his old neighborhood that, "until the ravages of 'white flight,' political corruption and crime converged it was a positive experience."[39]

In other contexts, however, white ex-Newarkers can allow that the wonderful neighborhood where everyone got along with everyone else was predicated on a distinction between white Newarkers and African-Americans. Several of Sherry Ortner's former classmates from 1950s Weequahic High recall differential treatment meted out to the city's blacks. One former classmate is described as "growing up in an open house. The door was always open, kids could come over, play basketball in the driveway. . . . The only time anything happened was when [the informant] brought two Black kids home to play basketball and his father told him never to invite them again—'after all, your mother and sister are here.'" Other Jewish parents made sure black maids used separate glasses and plates, although two other informants recall having more advanced views on race. One wrote a letter to the *Newark News* about the Emmett Till lynching, "and my part of it was, if this is America, count me out, or something." A second woman says her mother refused to treat black maids as lesser-than. "And nobody had to drink from a jelly glass."[40] A different view of Newark's race relations in the 1950s is presented, too, in the recollections of Amiri Baraka, who recalls "mini race riots" after nearly every school day as he tried to make it home without a beating from white schoolmates, and learning to curse in Italian as a counter to the racial epithets his white classmates at McKinley School and Barringer High hurled at him.[41] The point is not that some Newarkers were racist and others not, but merely that the real brick-and-concrete city of circa 1955 was a site of contestation and varying degrees of harmony, which is not the way the seamless story of safe streets presents it on Virtual Newark.

Indeed, the city's present perilous state is used as a point of contrast with the supposedly conflict-free past. A few posters contrast their recollected version of Newark with recent visits to their old neighborhoods, "now like a war zone," without questioning how the city got that way. Nat Bodian, a frequent poster to Virtual Newark on all aspects of the city's Jewish community, and responsible for the entries on Zwillman, is the one poster who has elected to directly address July 1967, recently adding "A Recollection of Newark of 1939 and . . . AFTER THE RIOTS": "I hold vivid recollections of the riots, which I believe was a major turning point in Newark's 20th-century history." Yet there is no discussion of the circumstances surrounding the beating of cabdriver John Smith by Newark policemen, or the battles over "slum clearance" plans surrounding the proposed expansion of a medical school, major catalysts for the riot/rebellion (along with poverty, generalized police brutality, Mayor Addonizio's unwillingness to appoint a black as secretary to the city's school board, and housing inadequacies in the Central Ward).[42] Instead, the "riot" is presented as an inexplicable natural disaster to which a white Newarker could only react with horror. "During the riots, I had sat on the front porch of my Hillside home, just 800 feet from the Newark line, listening to the gunfire . . . and being turned back at the Newark-Hillside line by rifle-toting National Guardsmen." Later, "I listened to stories of victimized . . . Newark merchants, how businesses had been stripped bare, buildings set afire . . . even one account of a Newark butcher who had locked himself in his ice box for protection. He had vowed to me that he would never go back to his former business site."[43] Omitted from this account is the fact that twenty-five of the twenty-six fatalities in the July 1967 disturbances were blacks who were shot by city police or New Jersey National Guardsmen. Yet it is (white) Newark merchants who are portrayed as "victimized."

The mood of the nervous adjacent white communities might be summed up by Elizabeth Mayor Thomas Dunn's infamous order that police were to "shoot to kill" potential looters—an order that Ron Porambo forcefully argues was executed in Newark, too.[44]

Virtual Newark's account goes on to assert that "up until that summer in 1967, I continued to regard Newark as a great city," before inevitably returning to the "golden time," at least this time fixed by a set year, "back in 1939, when I could walk up to my Third Ward home on Montgomery Street from downtown Newark in the late-night hours without looking over my shoulder. Newark's streets, as I recall them pre–World War II, were relatively safe to one and all." That the same cybercitizen of Virtual Newark can gloss over Zwillman's colorful career, with no mention of the murders of Moretti, Flegenheimer, Hassel, and Greenberg, or Puddy Hinkes's various assaults, break-ins, and stickups, and condemn the lawlessness of blacks in July 1967 as a tragedy is, to say the least, remarkable. Nor do we get a comparative reflection on the percentage of the 1939 loan-sharking operations concentrated in Newark. Instead, the poster suggests that the riots were the moment when crime was first intruded into Newark: "From published statistics I learned that in 2001, for example, Newark crime . . . was 34% higher than the national average. Car theft was 3.57 times the national average." Bodian adds, "I have no idea what the 1939 statistics were, but I lived with the *feeling* that Newark at that time offered a safe, secure environment in which to live and work."[45]

Similar contrasts are set up by former white residents of Brooklyn's "changed" neighborhoods. Jonathan Rieder details the litanies of disenchanted "pilgrims" to the old neighborhood: "I couldn't believe it. The houses were all marked up, the streets were filthy, and there was garbage and graffiti everywhere. There was no respect for property. It was very sad, and I started to cry." Another informant cried out, "I used to walk Flatbush Avenue when I was dating my wife. It was all white then. . . . It was all one big happy Flatbush family. But now? Ninety-five percent of them have been mugged and moved away. Is it my fault?"[46] It is this contrast between the feeling of safeness in old Newark (old Brooklyn, "old neighborhoods" everywhere)—a repeated, consensual feeling, given the concreteness of Tony Soprano's "bricks" when repeated by some ex-Newarkers—that is set up in contrast to the certainty that black Newark today is more violent and dangerous than anything they were a part of. This dichotomy between safe then and hideous now, I would argue, is Virtual Newark's hidden reason for being.

The riots of 1967 and their aftermath seem to be the one chapter of the city's history that no one can address honestly. Again, in turning to Newark's fictionalized favorite son, Tony Soprano, when the topic turns to "the Newark riots," or any other topic even tangentially related to race, black and white former residents alike can only speak in elliptical code words. As noted, Tony's bought-and-paid-for politician brings up "the summer of '67," and Tony asks a black minister, "Maurice, were you around for Anthony Imperiale? The White Knight?" "Around?" he replies, "Who do you think he was fighting against?" "Italian pride! Keep Newark white!" The minister can only mutter, "Inspired Klansmen, some of those boys."[47] It is perhaps not surprising that in Virtual Newark there is no in-depth discussion of the factors leading up to July 1967, nor of the role that Imperiale—who rode white backlash into the Newark City Council and then the New Jersey Senate—played in fanning the flames in that long, hot summer and after.[48]

A different reading of the riots, though, was current, at least among some white Newarkers, shortly after 1967. Journalist Ron Porambo offers a different perspective on who the real victims were in the Newark riot. He provides, in a 1971 account, sobering details of looters and even African-American bystanders shot in the back by law-enforcement authorities, and even National Guardsmen shooting up black-owned stores in retaliation for the supposed riot, days after the initial neighborhood anger over the police beating of black cabdriver John Smith had died down. Indeed, Porambo paints a scathing and convincing portrayal of official retaliation and violence directed at the blacks of the city's Central Ward, presenting evidence that most reports of sniping and arson could be laid at the doorstep of trigger-happy and panicky city policemen and New Jersey National Guardsmen.[49]

John Cunningham, too, notes that even then-Police Director Dominick Spina commented, "I think a lot of the report of snipers was due to the, I hate to use the word, trigger-happy guardsmen, who were firing at noises, and firing indiscriminately at times, it appeared to me, and I was out in the field at all times." The enormity of this "indiscriminate" fire cannot be overstated. Cunningham notes that "State Police and National Guard gunfire . . . expended nearly 15,000 rounds of ammunition between them in less than three days of occupation."[50]

Porambo's book *No Cause for Indictment* is an exposé of official neglect of the Central Ward, violent suppression of the initial looting after Smith's beating, and subsequent failure to address the convincing charges of police brutality. As even the official report to Governor Richard Hughes remarked, "The damage caused within a few hours early Sunday morning, July 16, to a large number of stores marked with 'Soul' signs to depict non-white ownership and located in a limited area reflects a pattern of police action for which there is no possible justification. . . . It embittered the Negro community as a whole at a time when the disorders had begun to ebb."[51]

As Porambo reported, he was told by Eric Mann, a teacher and organizer with the Newark Community Union Project,

Essentially there were two riots in Newark. One was started by black people and one by the State Police. The first riot was over in two days. It took very few lives but a hell of a lot of property. The second riot was pure retribution on the part of the National Guard and the State Police. For instance, the first three days not a black store was touched. It can be documented that systematically, starting on Friday night and primarily on Saturday and Sunday nights, the State Police went to each black store and smashed its windows.

It was thirty-one hours after the looting that the first fatality occurred.[52]

None of this sort of recollection of Newark or of a contested meaning to the riot/rebellion has made it into the precincts of Virtual Newark. It might be asking a lot of a Web site operated by devoted amateur historians (I use the words advisedly) to capture all aspects of the city's past. And in many other respects the site has done an admirable job of capturing the texture and specificity of an exciting and vibrant immigrant city. But the amnesias and omissions that form the consensus narrative of the riot's tragic and appalling nature for white Newark are too striking to be a mere accident. If more voices from black and Hispanic Newarkers, those who saw the events along Springfield Avenue from a different perspective, had been added to the site, a more contentious Newark would have been captured. As Beth Kolko argues, it is not just economic issues of access to the Web and computer ownership and literacy that have created a cyberdivide to mirror the many other American divides along race lines. Rather, she argues that in cyberspace the default race remains set at white, mirroring the supposed normative concerns of America as a whole while continuing to treat minorities' voices in a cursory fashion.[53] Again, I am not seeking to castigate unduly the posters to Virtual Newark, a site that holds much to thrill someone like me, who fondly recalls keeping score for boccie games in Vailsburg Park. Rather, I am merely suggesting that this virtual slice of nostalgia is selective and has pushed non-European-descent Newarkers to the margins, as they perhaps felt in 1967 Vailsburg.

To open history up to interpretation would be to reintroduce contestation into the city. But perhaps this is the very thing—conflict—that such Web sites seek to avoid. The contestation over resources between racial and ethnic groups (most starkly illustrated by the real battles of July 1967) has indeed been removed from the streets of Virtual Newark. As Aurigi and Graham argue, such virtual cities have the danger of becoming "pseudo communities," "traditional communities transformed into safe, unthreatening, impersonal associations." They argue that "virtual cities need to recognize and encourage the clash of viewpoints and discourses that are an essential element of urban life." This clash, a recognition that there was trouble in paradise, seems the very recognition from which citizens of Virtual Newark are fleeing. Replacing a real city with a virtual, selective, nostalgified one only exacerbates this problem. As Aurigi and Graham note, some cyberspace optimists see the Internet as the new public space, and the physical decay of the built environment need not concern us so long as we have these "electronic analogies for the real, material urban areas that host them."[54]

Nor can specific details on the root causes of the changes that Newark has undergone "concern" the posters to Virtual Newark. No discussion appears of the post–World War II federally subsidized white flight to the suburbs, courtesy of the FHA, or the deindustrialization of the country's thousands of Newarks that may perhaps go a long way toward explaining the decline of the city. Nowhere on Virtual Newark is it remarked that, as Nathan Wright noted in his 1968 study, *Ready to Riot,* even "between 1938 and 1944 industries left [Newark] at such a pace as to represent a loss to the City of Newark of $300,000,000 in assessed valuation," a process that only accelerated after the war.[55]

Porambo notes that by the time of the riot/rebellion, what remained in the business district were a few office towers filled with service industries, notably insurance. At the same time, forty thousand units of substandard housing existed in the city; yet Newark pinned its hopes for revitalization on twenty new office buildings in the downtown. This faith-based investment in the business core's renewal occurred at a time when "the poor of black Newark live[d] with the highest proportion rates of infant and maternal mortality, venereal disease and tuberculosis in the nation." Of the two faces of Newark, the still-healthy nine-to-five downtown and the hollowed-out neighborhoods, Porambo concluded, "This dichotomy had failed to attract the attention of the mass media prior to the 1967 explosion, but, after it was too late, its coverage was plentiful." Forty years later the dichotomy seems to be growing again, between Newark as some imagine it to have been and what remains at the tail end of a long process of white flight and deindustrialization.[56]

The real streets of Newark, then, can be safely ignored so long as they can be made to fit into a communally sanctioned narrative, and even Italian and Jewish criminality of an earlier era can be glossed as ambitious ethnic outward-boundism, even if of a slightly shady sort. Having one's city at a safe distance by clicking on a mouse seems to be the trend; a virtual city removes the mess of current urban "pathologies." Yet those included in this community are a relatively small stratum of elite, technologically savvy computer owners (disproportionately male, disproportionately white). Beyond that, the kinds of narratives privileged on such sites

are tales of past harmony, safe streets, and hard work, where everyone knew everyone else and looked out for each other: the virtual cybernetic urban villagers.

What are the sociopolitical implications of maintaining a Virtual Newark, when
the real Newark, and its three hundred thousand now largely African-American
and Hispanic residents and their pressing political and economic needs, lies only
a few miles from some of those logging on to lament the "vanished city" they are
busy creating? Who gets counted as a cybercitizen, then, within the precincts of
Virtual Newark? Sherry Ortner has argued that one way that ethnic and racial
groups that have been left behind in places such as Newark may function for those
"making it" is as a projection of their not-so-recent pasts, and a reminder of just
how tenuous their entry into the middle class may be:

From the point of view of a group that has advanced itself in class terms, or is seeking to
do so, lower-status groups may represent their own past, only recently and tenuously shed.
This often means that boundaries must be drawn, literally and figuratively. Rising up is not
only a matter of gaining positive goods . . . but also drawing negative lines between one's
own group and those below it. Such drawing of lines is quite irrational, invested with fears
of social pollution and danger.[57]

Moreover, it is even the tenuous nature of this rise into the middle class, and
one's ambivalence as to whether the game was worth the candle, that may cause
psychic overload for the aging strivers who abandoned Newark. Safe streets and
good schools in the suburbs may not sufficiently compensate for the vanished
sense of belonging among one's own class and ethnic kind back in the familiar
streets of Weequahic. Anxiety may perhaps have to find an outlet, so those who
took advantage of FHA-backed mortgages in the suburbs now refashion the narrative to say they "had to" leave Newark when it "turned bad." A similar tale is
told by the Jews and Italians of Canarsie, who recall Brownsville—a seedy slum
community even in the 1920s, when it fostered Bugsy Siegel and other denizens
of the underworld—as a wonderful place out of which they were unwillingly
driven by blacks.[58] Wendell Pritchett observes that rather than the haven they recall, Brownsville had quite unsettling connotations for "respectable" New Yorkers
in the 1920s–1940s. Brownsville's juvenile delinquency rate in 1939 was 25
percent higher than New York City's norm, and had the highest rates of assault,
robberies, and total crime in Brooklyn. Its most famous native son was Murder
Inc.'s Abe "Kid Twist" Reles. To be sure, the area was also home to hardworking,
honest garment workers and unionists, civic-improvement activists, and others. This
is merely to suggest that, as in Virtual Newark, loving evocations of Brownsville
before it "went bad" are only partially accurate at best.[59]

Yet a reliance on a virtual past, a partial past, can shield the reminiscers from
unsettling political implications, an awareness that perhaps Newark in 2007 is just
as multivocal as the Newark or Brownsville of 1940. A virtual past operates as
a screen filtering, as well, any unpleasant confrontations with the Newark of
Zwillman, Boiardo, and Addonizio. As Sherry Turkel argues, "Computer screens

are the new locations for our fantasies, both erotic and intellectual." And to that list of fantasies, I would add "historical." Increasingly, the screen is the site, Turkel argues, onto which simulacra are projected, "worlds without origins" or "copies that no longer have originals." She further suggests that it is the very anomie of suburbanized, shopping-mall society, with its lack of a sense of history or community center, that has caused such longing for virtual communities,[60] a phenomenon that Jerry Herron has documented in the case of suburban thrill seekers returning (tentatively) to a historically "humiliated" Detroit.[61]

The refuge they seek is in an imagined old neighborhood, though, in a past where they still have a future. For too closely examining some of the urban pathologies (1950 vintage) would suggest that the city's later decline already had some of its seedbeds in the Weequahics and Vailsburgs they wish to remember as idyllic. Thus gangsters for the most part disappear from this streetscape, and if they must darken the doorsteps of the Riviera Hotel or the Tavern Restaurant, they are quietly acknowledged as "bootleggers," with most of their more violent activities swept up in a hurried whisper of "Murder Inc."

After this unpleasantness is out of the way, one can then discuss Longy Zwillman's beneficence to neighborhood youth, and his charitable activities on behalf of the Mount Carmel soup kitchen. Yet the Newark of the 1940s and 1950s that they have reconstructed has no place for African-Americans, either, and is one in which "the riots of 1967" just tragically happened, wiping out the timeless harmony of their recollections. As Turkel says when referring to life in on-screen virtual communities, "We reconstruct our identities on the other side of the looking glass."[62] And perhaps this imaginative, for the most part violence-free, re-creation of bygone Newark as a warm and fuzzy city free of pathological mayhem and racial and ethnic strife is simply another case of those who control the modem controlling the past. But whether Virtual Newarkers really believe the communal self they are creating—that they literally never locked their doors and the streets were safe until 1967 just sort of happened—the poses they assume have deeper cultural salience in setting the framework for discussions of resource allocation and diminishing commitment to urban America on the "real" side of the computer screen. This realm includes a Newark that, minor league baseball stadium and performing-arts center notwithstanding, could perhaps use the moxie of a Longy Zwillman in standing up for its interests.

Conclusion

The United States has always had an ambivalent attitude toward cities, seeing them as symbols of progress and entertainment, but also vice and "foreignness." The thrills the city had to offer in the nineteenth century were often presented as illicit, and voyeuristic magazine and novel treatments of the foreigner in the midst of a big-city slum were often designed to titillate middle-class readers as much as they might instruct.

Later, at the dawn of the talkies, one of the most popular genres was the gangster film, through which the city was often portrayed as a powerful force that sent poor souls to their doom. In other cases, the gangster's very foreignness was a marker for the depths into which Depression era Manhattan or Chicago had plunged. With the urban disturbances of the 1960s, popular culture took another look at the city and decided that, from Detroit to Watts to Harlem, the problem had a different face. Blaxploitation classics, such as *Shaft,* and television crime dramas offered a visual exclamation point to the famous New York *Daily News* headline "Ford to New York: Drop Dead!"

In our own day this problem of rendering the city and its residents "exotic" has only been exacerbated in a political climate of dwindling resources and commitment to helping those not in the six-figure income bracket. Authors of films, novels, and TV shows and now Web site posts continue to give fictional voice to a city of demons and delights, and such depictions go a long way in shaping the political climate in which city residents, from 9-11 New Yorkers to Katrina's New Orleanians, battle for aid and comfort.

Yet ironically, from around 1990, the urban past has often been depicted in nostalgic vignettes as functioning urban villages, where hardworking immigrants helped each other, the streets were safe, and people never locked their doors. Novels that have drawn identity and inspiration from their fictional and historical homes, such as Eugenides's *Middlesex* and Roth's Newark novels, as well as shows such as *The Sopranos*, give a partial view of the city that reinforces racial redlining, cognitively and substantively. Nostalgically functioning fictive cities of the past may have made it easier for cultural consumers (in other regards, voting citizens) to write off present-day cities, whose residents are perceived in these works as somehow less thrifty, hardworking, and deserving of full citizenship as former white ethnic urbanites.

This trend has recently been taken a step further: Yesterday's foreign threat to the body politic is today's jaded suburbanite, and in recent "cybercities" urban exiles use their computers to reimagine through the haze of nostalgia the cities of their youth as safe warm and fuzzy places. The city continues to thrill and repulse, and even the Internet once again reduces the "mean streets" to a titillating story arc, and the bygone city is now often the vanished Eden with which present-day cities are negatively contrasted. Progressive Era reformers and journalists, who often reacted with horror to the Italian, Jewish, and Slavic immigrant quarters of New York, Chicago, Detroit, and Newark, might be amused to discover that the streetscapes they viewed as a problem are now believed to have been the seat of family values.

For all the insidious comparing in these works, though, they offer loving re-creations of bygone places that continue to entice cultural consumers. Indeed, it is time to confess that even urban memoir novels such as Roth's *American Pastoral* and *The Plot against America* delight me with their evocations of vanished ethnic businesses, recreation sites, and institutions. While reading such novels, a reader such as myself with Newark ties might imagine her or his own Italian-American grandparents patronizing some of the businesses or theaters named in the book, and yes, a warm and fuzzy recollection of keeping score for hotly contested boccie games in Vailsburg Park usually follows as soon as I enter the precincts of Virtual Newark.

It is the implications, though, that this city was somehow stolen from white ethnic urbanites, and that nothing unseemly ever occurred in these bygone cities, with which I take issue. As the insidious comparisons of functioning Greektown, Detroit, or Jewish Weequahic and Little Italy, Newark, and "pathological" present-day cities build, the unsettling, unanswered question that resonate with me is whether nostalgia can ever be progressive. Can a remembered vanished city summon among its current and former residents the will to commit politically and personally to rebuilding those cities? George Sánchez has noted that for a time in the 1950s the Jewish residents of Boyle Heights, a Los Angeles neighborhood changing to a black and Hispanic enclave, opened their ethnic institutions to residents of all races and backgrounds, in an attempt to foster mutual understanding. Likewise in Los Angeles, Dolores Hayden notes that a multiethnic memory project led to a museum display of the multimemories of L.A. from varying ethnic and racial groups. Such projects may lead to the excavation of more accurate, and sympathetic, cityscapes, fostering intergroup commitment to the city's present, not just its memory.[1]

Perhaps such imaginative, empathetic readings of the popular-culture city have occurred among many readers, too, but judging by the disinvestment in and neglect of many older American cities ongoing in the early twenty-first century, the cognitive leap between a nostalgia of loss and one of progressive empathy and commitment to the present-day city, whatever its demographics, has not yet occurred.

The first step in such a project might be to remember the American city in its long, ambivalent image, rejecting binaries of working then and dysfunctional now. Can we remember the former immigrant and second-generation white ethnic enclaves in cities in all their complexities, the poverty and the hard work, the tight-knittedness that at its worst bred an insularity exploding into antiblack rioting in places such as 1943 Detroit and 1954 Deering Park, Chicago? Can we recall, too, that such cities were often unpleasant places for excluded African-Americans, who have now inherited cities bled of state and federal resources, from which many businesses and stable middle-class residences and institutions have long fled? And if homages to Newark and Detroit as they once were can evoke a commitment to the city as it accurately was, good and bad, and an honest evaluation of its present state of abandonment, maybe ex-urbanites can redirect their anger at the degeneration that has occurred in their cities to a commitment to rebuilding them for their current occupants. If nostalgia ever can become such a progressive force, then perhaps at long last Newark's Nathan Zuckerman, and his real-life counterparts, can hold their next reunion in the real Newark, and not turn away from the city with loathing.

It is time at last.

Notes

CHAPTER 1: INTRODUCTION

1. Samuel Johnson in James Boswell, *Life of Johnson*, Vol. 6, Chap. 9, 1777; *Taxi Driver* (1976, directed by Martin Scorsese).

2. "The Sidewalks of New York," words and music by Charles B. Lawlor and James W. Blake, 1894; "Rosie O'Grady," words and music by Maude Nugent, 1896; "Manhattan," words by Lorenz Hart, music by Richard Rodgers, 1925.

3. George Lippard, *Quaker City, or The Monks of Monk Hall*, New York: Odyssey Press, 1970 (originally published 1844), 373, 375, 379.

4. Paul J. Erickson, *Welcome to Sodom: The Cultural Work of City-Mystery Fictions in Antebellum America*, Austin: University of Texas dissertation, 2006; Albert Johannsen, *The House of Beadle and Adams and Its Dime and Nickel Novels: The Story of a Vanished Literature*, Norman: University of Oklahoma Press, 1950–1962.

5. Glenn Altschuler, *Rude Republic: Americans and Their Politics in the 19th Century*, Princeton, N.J.: Princeton University Press, 2000. For workers' belief in American egalitarianism, see, too, Sean Wilentz, *Chants Democratic: New York City and the Rise of the American Working Class, 1788–1850*, New York: Oxford University Press, 1986.

6. Morton G. White, *The Intellectual versus the City: From Thomas Jefferson to Frank Lloyd Wright*, New York: Oxford University Press, 1977.

7. Frederick Jackson Turner, *The Frontier in American History*, New York: Henry Holt, 1947 (originally published 1893).

8. Jack Beatty, *The Rascal King: The Life and Times of James Michael Curley, 1874–1958*, Reading, Mass.: Addison-Wesley, 1992; Robert Wiebe, *The Search for Order, 1877–1920*, New York: Hill & Wang, 1967; Lincoln Steffens, *The Shame of the Cities*, New York: Sagamore Press, 1957 (originally published 1904); David Hammack, *Power and Society: Greater New York at the Turn of the Century*, New York: Columbia University Press, 1987; George Templeton Strong, *Diary*, New York: Octagon Books, 1974 (originally published 1875); Edward K. Spann, *The New Metropolis: New York City, 1840–1857*, New York: Columbia University Press, 1981; S. J. Kleinberg, *The Shadow of the Mills: Working-Class Families in Pittsburgh, 1870–1907*, Pittsburgh: University of Pittsburgh Press, 1989, especially 268–302.

9. David R. Roediger, *Working toward Whiteness: How America's Immigrants Became White*, New York: Basic Books, 2005; Matthew Frye Jacobson, *Whiteness of a Different Color: European Immigrants and the Alchemy of Race*, Cambridge, Mass.: Harvard University Press, 1996; Noel Ignatiev, *How the Irish Became White*, New York: Routledge, 1995; Robert M. Zecker, " 'Negrov Lynčovanie' and the Unbearable Whiteness of Slovaks: The Immigrant Press Covers Race," *American Studies* 43 (2): 43–72 (Summer 2002); Karen Brodkin, *How Jews Became White Folks and What That Says about Race in America*, New Brunswick, N.J.: Rutgers University Press, 1998.

10. Burton J. Hendrick, "The Great Jewish Invasion," *McClure's Magazine* 28: 307–321 (January 1907), warned that New York was fated in a few years to become not just overwhelmingly Jewish but therefore "Asiatic." For visual representations of German anarchist tendencies, see cartoons in *Puck*, such as February 18, 1885, 400, "Gotham's Gospel Needs." For violent Irish, see *Puck*, January 21, 1885, 336, "O'Donovan Rossa's Shooting-Gallery for Irish Dynamiters," and on Italian vagrants and annoying peddlers, see *Puck*, December 3, 1884, 224, "The Decline of Italian Opera in New York—Will It Have to Go A-Begging?"

11. Helen Campbell, *Darkness and Daylight: Lights and Shadows of New York Life*, Detroit: Singing Tree Press, 1969 (originally published 1895).

12. Finley Peter Dunne, *Mister Dooley on Ivrything and Ivrybody*, New York: Dover, 1963. For the character of Bridgeport, see William Tuttle, *Race Riot: Chicago in the Red Summer of 1919*, New York: Atheneum, 1970, and James T. Farrell, *Studs Lonigan, a Trilogy*, Urbana: University of Illinois Press, 1993 (originally published 1935).

13. J. A. Mitchell, *The Last American, a Fragment from the Journal of Khan-li, Prince of Dimph-yoo-chur and Admiral in the Persian Navy*, New York: F. A. Stokes, 1889.

14. Theodore Dreiser, *Sister Carrie*, New York: Penguin Books, 1987 (originally published 1900); Frank Norris, *McTeague: A Story of San Francisco*, Greenwich, Conn: Fawcett Publications, 1966 (originally published in 1899); Upton Sinclair, *The Jungle*, New York: Doubleday and Co., 1906.

15. Olivier Zunz, *The Changing Face of Inequality: Urbanization, Industrial Development and Immigrants in Detroit, 1880–1920*; Beatty, *The Rascal King*.

16. Neal Gabler, *Winchell: Gossip, Power and the Culture of Celebrity,* New York: Knopf, 1994; Burton B. Turkus and Sid Feder, *Murder Inc.: The Story of the Syndicate*, Cambridge, Mass.: DaCapo Press, 2003 (originally published 1951); Thomas Reppetto, *American Mafia: A History of Its Rise to Power*, New York: Henry Holt, 2004; Rich Cohen, *Tough Jews*, New York: Simon & Schuster, 1998; Jonathan Rieder, *Canarsie: The Jews and Italians of Brooklyn against Liberalism*, Cambridge, Mass.: Harvard University Press, 1985, 21, 25.

17. Thomas Sugrue, *The Origins of the Urban Crisis: Race and Inequality in Postwar Detroit*, Princeton, N.J.: Princeton University Press, 1996; Dan Georgakas, *Detroit: I Do Mind Dying: A Study in Urban Revolution*, New York: St. Martin's Press, 1975; Jerry Herron, *AfterCulture: Detroit and the Humiliation of History*, Detroit: Wayne State University Press, 1993; Arnold Hirsch, *Making the Second Ghetto: Race and Housing in Chicago, 1940–1960*, Chicago: University of Chicago Press, 1998 (originally published 1983); Thomas Philpott, *The Slum and the Ghetto: Neighborhood Deterioration and Middle-Class Reform, 1880–1930*, New York: Oxford University Press, 1978; Michael Harrington, *The Other America: Poverty in the United States*, Baltimore: Penguin Books, 1969 (originally published 1962).

18. On antiblack riots in the 1940s and 1950s Detroit and Chicago, see Sugrue, *The Origins of the Urban Crisis*, and Hirsch, *The Making of the Second Ghetto*. On the 1967 Newark riot, see Ronald Porambo, *No Cause for Indictment: An Autopsy for Newark*, New York: Holt, Rinehart & Winston, 1971. For the perceived decline of 1960s–1970s New York, see Vincent J. Cannato, *The Ungovernable City: John Lindsay and His Struggle to Save New York*, New York: Basic Books, 2001, and Jim Sleeper, *The Closest of Strangers: Liberalism and the Politics of Race in New York*, New York: Norton, 1989.

19. www.heidelberg.org; www.thed.us/heidelberg.html; www.agilitynut.com/h/heidelberg.html; Wendy S. Walters, "Turning the Neighborhood Inside Out: Imagining a New Detroit in Tyree Guyton's Heidelberg Project," *TDR: The Drama Review* 45 (4): 64–93 (Winter 2001); Tyree Guyton, Rebecca Margolis, and Jerry W. Ward, Jr., "Triangulation," *Literature and Medicine* 15 (1): 74–87 (Spring 1996); Herron, *AfterCulture*, 198–201.

20. On the creation of Soho, New York, as an artists' colony, and the subsequent gentrification of this once-dowdy factory area, see Sharon Zukin, *Loft Living: Culture and Capital in Urban Change*, Baltimore: Johns Hopkins University Press, 1982. For Detroit's faux ethnic tourist area, Greektown, see Jerry Herron, *AfterCulture*.

21. *A Bronx Tale*, 1993, directed by Robert De Niro. For white ethnics' perceptions of the 1960s as a time of decline, see Rieder, *Canarsie*; Sleeper, *The Closest of Strangers*; Allen Matusow, *The Unraveling of America: A History of Liberalism in the 1960s*, New York: Harper & Row, 1986; Michael Novak, *The Rise of the Unmeltable Ethnics: Politics and Culture in the Seventies*, New York: Macmillan, 1972; Cannato, *The Ungovernable City*; Matthew Frye Jacobson, *Roots Too: White Ethnic Revival in Post-Civil Rights America*, Cambridge, Mass.: Harvard University Press, 2006.

22. Philip Roth, *The Plot against America*, Boston: Houghton Mifflin, 2004; Roth, *The Human Stain*, Boston: Houghton Mifflin, 2000; Roth, *The Facts: A Novelist's Autobiography*, New York: Farrar, Straus & Giroux, 1988; Roth, *American Pastoral*, New York: Vintage Books, 1998.

23. Jeffrey Eugenides, *Middlesex*, Toronto: Vintage Canada, 2003.

24. *The Sopranos*, Season 4, Episode 7.

25. *The Wire*, Season 4.

26. *The Sopranos*, Season 6, Episode 8. When the upscale juice store manager spurns his demand for protection money, Patsy also sadly concludes, "It's over for the little guy!"

27. See www.virtualnewarknj.com, as well as www.cityofjerseycity.org, www.geocities.com/senafp/Passaic125thCelebration.html. See, too, Alessandro Aurigi and Stephen Graham, "The 'Crisis' in the Urban Public Realm," in Brian D. Loader, ed., *Cyberspace Divide: Equality, Agency and Policy in the Information Society*, New York: Routledge, 1998; Stephen Graham and Simon Marvin, *Splintering Urbanism: Networked Infrastructures, Technological Mobility and the Urban Condition*, New York: Routledge, 2001. The quotation is from Alison Adam and Eileen Green, "Gender, Agency, Location and the New Information Society," in Loader, *Cyberspace Divide*.

28. *On the Town*, 1949, directed by Stanley Donen and Gene Kelly; *Meet Me in Saint Louis*, 1944, directed by Vincente Minnelli.

29. *Annie Hall*, 1977, directed by Woody Allen.

30. Edward Alsworth Ross, *The Old World in the New*, New York: Century, 1914, 291.

31. *The Public Enemy*, 1931, directed by William A. Wellman.

32. On anticomics crusaders, see Gerard Jones, *Men of Tomorrow: Geeks, Gangsters and the Birth of the Comic Book*, New York: Basic Books, 238–242, 261–266, 270–280.

On the Hays Code in Hollywood, see Leonard J. Leff and Jerold L. Simmons, *The Dame in the Kimono: Hollywood, Censorship and the Production Code,* Lexington: University of Kentucky Press, 2001.

CHAPTER 2: NEXT STOP, THE GHETTO: TOURS OF ETHNIC EXOTICA IN THE POPULAR PRESS

1. George Lippard, *Quaker City, or The Monks of Monk Hall*, New York: Odyssey Press, 1970 (originally published 1844), 45.

2. Lippard, 61.

3. Lippard, 80.

4. "Philadelphia City Prostitutes' Register," 1863, Philadelphia City and County Archives.

5. Jacob A. Riis, *How the Other Half Lives*, New York: Scribner's, 1890.

6. Lippard.

7. Lippard, 477–478; *Puck*, February 18, 1885, 400.

8. Lippard, 479.

9. Noel Ignatiev, *How the Irish Became White*, New York: Routledge, 1995; Eric Lott, *Love and Theft: Blackface Minstrelsy and the American Working Class*, New York: Oxford University Press, 1995; Michael Rogin, *Blackface, White Noise*, Berkeley: University of California Press, 1996; Robert M. Zecker, "'Negrov Lynčovanie' and the Incredible Whiteness of Slovaks: The Immigrant Press Covers Race," *American Studies*, 43 (2):43–72 (Summer 2002).

10. Lippard, 482.

11. Ignatiev, *How the Irish Became White*, 125–139, 148–158.

12. Philip Hone, *The Diary of Philip Hone, 1828–1851*, New York: Dodd, Mead, 1889; George Templeton Strong, *The Diary of George Templeton Strong*, New York: Octagon Books, 1974 (originally published 1835–1875).

13. Herman Melville, *The Confidence-Man, His Masquerade*, Evanston, Ill.: Northwestern University Press, 1984 (originally published 1857).

14. Glenn Altschuler, *Rude Republic: Americans and Their Politics in the Nineteenth Century*, Princeton, N.J.: Princeton University Press, 2000.

15. Sam Alewitz, *Filthy-Dirty: A Social History of Unsanitary Philadelphia in the Late Nineteenth Century*, New York: Garland, 1989.

16. Carroll D. Wright, *The Slums of Baltimore, Chicago, New York and Philadelphia*, Washington, D.C.: Government Printing Office, 1894; Emily Dinwiddie, *Report on the Housing Conditions in Philadelphia* (1904), Octavia Hill Association, Philadelphia. A series of case studies of people in Northern Liberties conducted in October 1946 by the Friends' Neighborhood Guild of Fourth and Green indicates that in the 800s of North Orkney and 900s of North Hancock, most homes still had outdoor toilets. Friends' Neighborhood Guild Settlement House papers, Swarthmore College. See, too, John F. Sutherland, "Housing the Poor in the City of Homes: Philadelphia at the Turn of the Century," in Allen F. Davis and Mark H. Haller, eds., *The Peoples of Philadelphia*, Philadelphia: Temple University Press, 1973.

17. "WPA Ethnic Group Survey, the Poles in Philadelphia" (1939), microfilm at the Pennsylvania Historical and Museum Commission, Harrisburg.

18. "A Ramble in Old Philadelphia," *The Century* 23 (5): 655–667 (March 1882).

19. Fredric M. Miller, Morris J. Vogel, and Allen F. Davis, *Philadelphia Stories: A Photographic History, 1920–1960,* Philadelphia: Temple University Press, 1988, 5–6, 26;

Alewitz, *Filthy-Dirty*, 14–15, 40, 60–63, 71–73, 85, 99–103, 127; Sam Bass Warner, *The Private City: Philadelphia in Three Periods of Its Growth*, Philadelphia: University of Pennsylvania Press, 1968, 183–185; W.E.B. DuBois, *The Philadelphia Negro: A Social Study*, Philadelphia: University of Pennsylvania Press, 1996 (originally published 1899). See, too, Howard Gillette, "The Emergence of the Modern Metropolis," in William W. Cutler III and Howard Gillette, eds., *The Divided Metropolis: Social and Spatial Dimensions of Philadelphia, 1800–1975*, Westport, Conn.,: Greenwood Press, 1980, 7–8; John F. Sutherland, "Housing the Poor in the City of Homes: Philadelphia at the Turn of the Century," in Allen Davis and Mark Haller, eds., *The Peoples of Philadelphia,* Philadelphia: Temple University Press, 1973; Carroll D. Wright, *The Slums of Baltimore, Chicago, New York and Philadelphia*, Washington, D.C.: Government Printing Office, 1894; Friends Neighborhood Guild, Reports and Case Studies, 1946, 1947, housed in Swarthmore College Archives. See also Emily Dinwiddie, *Housing Conditions in Philadelphia: An Investigation*, Philadelphia: Octavia Hill Association, 1904; The Northern Soup Society, papers, 1903–1906, and the Public Baths Association of Philadelphia papers, 1895–1927, both housed in the Historical Society of Pennsylvania, Philadelphia. For middle-class, native-born Philadelphians' efforts to distance themselves spatially and psychically from poor, foreign-born sections of the city, see John Henry Hepp IV, *The Middle-Class City: Transforming Space and Time in Philadelphia, 1876–1926*, Philadelphia: University of Pennsylvania Press, 2003. For immigrant Detroit's similarly unsanitary condition, see Olivier Zunz, *The Changing Face of Inequality*, Chicago: University of Chicago Press, 1982; for Pittsburgh, see S. J. Kleinberg, *In the Shadow of the Mills*: *Working-Class Families in Pittsburgh, 1870–1907*, Pittsburgh: University of Pittsburgh Press, 1989.

20. Warner, *The Private City*; DuBois, *The Philadelphia Negro*.

21. "Philadelphia City Prostitutes' Register." For New York, see Timothy Gilfoyle, *City of Eros: New York City, Prostitution and the Commercialization of Sex, 1790–1920*, New York: W. W. Norton, 1992.

22. Lippard, *Quaker City*.

23. Eli K. Price, *History of the Consolidation of the City of Philadelphia*, Philadelphia: J. B. Lippincott, 1873, 55, 113; Daniel H. Mahony, *Historical Sketches of the Catholic Churches and Institutions of Philadelphia*, Philadelphia, 1895, 48, 57; Noel Ignatiev, *How the Irish Became White*, New York: Routledge, 1995, 125–139, 148–158; Howard Gillette, Jr., "The Emergence of the Modern Metropolis: Philadelphia in the Age of Its Consolidation," in William W. Cutler III and Howard W. Gillette, Jr., eds., *The Divided Metropolis: Social and Spatial Dimensions of Philadelphia, 1800–1975*, Westport, Connecticut: Greenwood Press, 1980, 7–8.

24. Lippard, 424.

25. Lippard, 262.

26. Lippard, 266–267. Ignatiev, *How the Irish Became White*, and Daniel H. Mahony, *Historical Sketches of the Catholic Churches and Institutions of Philadelphia*, Philadelphia, 1895, detail the anti-Catholic violence for which Philadelphia became famous. Mahony gives a vivid depiction of the riot and the burning of St. Augustine's and St. Michael's in 1844, pp. 48, 57.

27. George G. Foster, *Celio, or New York above Ground and under Ground*, New York: Dewitt & Davenport, 1850; Stuart M. Blumin, *The Emergence of the Middle Class: Social Experience in the American City, 1760–1900* , New York: Cambridge University Press, 1989, 15–16; George G. Foster, *New York by Gas-Light: With Here and There a Streak of Sunshine,* New York: M.J. Ivers, 1850, 5, as cited in Blumin.

28. Paul J. Erickson, *Welcome to Sodom: The Cultural Work of City-Mysteries Fiction in Antebellum America*, Austin: University of Texas dissertation, 2005, 30; Ned Buntline, *The Mysteries and Miseries of New York: A Story of Real Life*, New York: Berford, 1848; George Lippard, *The Empire City, or New York by Night and Day: Its Aristocracy and Dollars*, Philadelphia: T. B. Peterson, 1864; Lippard, *New York: Its Upper Ten and Lower Million*, Cincinnati: H. M. Rulison, 1854.

29. Erickson, 34.

30. Erickson, 27–35, 42–44, Blumin, 15. See, for example, John Chumasero, *Life in Rochester, or Sketches from Life: Being Scenes of Misery, Vice, Shame and Oppression, in the City of the Genesee, by a Resident Citizen*, Rochester, N.Y.: D. M. Dewey, 1848; Eugene Sue, Jr., *The Mysteries of Charleston*, Charleston, S.C.: Typographical Depository, 1846; "Argus," *Norton, or The Lights and Shades of a Factory Village*, Lowell, Mass.: Vox Populi Office, 1849; Philip Penchant, *The Mysteries of Fitchburg*, Fitchburg, Mass.: Charles Shepley, 1844; Frank Hazelton, *The Mysteries of Troy*, Troy, N.Y.: Troy Publishing Company, 1847; Osgood Bradbury, *Mysteries of Lowell*, Boston: E. P. Williams, 1844.

31. James Fenimore Cooper, *The Deerslayer*, New York: Washington Square Press, 1961 (originally published 1841); Cooper, *The Pioneers*, New York: New American Library, 1980 (originally published 1823).

32. Edmund Morgan, *American Slavery, American Freedom: The Ordeal of Colonial Virginia*, New York: Norton, 1975; Daniel J. Boorstin, *The Americans: The Colonial Experience*, New York: Vintage, 1964; Boorstin, *The Americans: The Democratic Experience*, New York: Vintage, 1974; Sean Wilentz, *Chants Democratic: New York City and the Rise of the American Working Class*, New York: Oxford University Press, 1984; Bruce Laurie, *Working People of Philadelphia, 1800–1850*, Philadelphia: Temple University Press, 1980; Laurie, *Artisans into Workers: Labor in Nineteenth-Century America*, New York: Hill & Wang, 1989; Eric Arnesen, Julie Greene, and Bruce Laurie, eds., *Labor Histories: Class, Politics and the Working Class Experience*, Urbana: University of Illinois Press, 1998. On class differences in Cooper's hometown, see Alan Taylor, *William Cooper's Town: Power and Persuasion on the Frontier of the Early American Republic*, New York: Vintage Books, 1996.

33. On the artisan theory of independent self-sufficiency and its collision with industrial America's "wage slavery," see Wilentz, *Chants Democratic*, Laurie, *Artisans into Workers*; Altschuler, *Rude Republic*. On the demonization of the poor in nineteenth-century America, see Michael B. Katz, *In the Shadow of the Poorhouse: A Social History of Welfare in America*, New York: Basic Books, 1986.

34. Wilentz, *Chants Democratic*; Laurie, *Artisans into Workers*; Laurie, *Working People of Philadelphia*.

35. Eric Foner, *Free Soil, Free Labor, Free Men: The Ideology of the Republican Party before the Civil War*, New York: Oxford University Press, 1995; Eric Foner, *A Short History of Reconstruction*, New York: Harper & Row, 1990; James McPherson, *Battle Cry of Freedom*, Princeton, N.J.: Princeton University Press, 1988.

36. Blumin, *The Emergence of the Middle Class*, 107, 11–122; Foster, *New York by Gas-Light*, as cited in Blumin, 107.

37. Blumin, 143–144.

38. Herbert Asbury, *The Gangs of New York: An Informal History of the Underworld*, New York: Paragon House, 1990 (originally published 1928); *Gangs of New York*, 2002, directed by Martin Scorsese. See, too, Tyler Anbinder, *Five Points: The 19th-Century New York City Neighborhood That Invented Tap Dance, Stole Elections and Became the World's Most Notorious Slum*, New York: Free Press, 2001.

39. Wilentz, *Chants Democratic*; Blumin, *The Emergence of the Middle Class*. See, too, Tyler Anbinder, *Five Points*.

40. Lawrence Levine, *Highbrow, Lowbrow: The Emergence of Cultural Hierarchy in America*, Cambridge, Mass.: Harvard University Press, 1988; Edward K. Spann, *The New Metropolis: New York City, 1840–1857*, New York: Columbia University Press, 1981; Blumin, *The Emergence of the Middle Class*, 145; Wilentz, *Chants Democratic*.

41. Wilentz, *Chants Democratic*, 300–301; Foster, *New York in Slices*, New York: William H. Graham, 1849, 43–47, cited in Wilentz; John W. Ripley, "Account of Astor Place Riot of 1849" (1897), cited in Wilentz. Foner, *A Short History of Reconstruction*, 14–15.

42. Blumin, *The Emergence of the Middle Class*; Joe R. Feagin and Harlan Hahn, *Ghetto Revolts: The Politics of Violence in American Cities*, New York: Macmillan, 1973, 72–74; McPherson, *Battle Cry of Freedom*, 609–611.

43. *New York Times*, July 13–17, 1863; McPherson, *Battle Cry of Freedom*, 609–611; Frank Towers, "Job Busting at Baltimore Shipyards: Racial Violence in the Civil War-Era South," *Journal of Southern History* 66 (2): 221–256 (May 2000); Feagin and Hahn, *Ghetto Revolts*, 72–74.

44. Feagin and Hahn, *Ghetto Revolts*, 72–74; McPherson, *Battle Cry of Freedom*, 609–611; *New York Times*, July 13–17, 1863.

45. Wilentz, *Chants Democratic*.

46. John Higham, *Strangers in the Land: Patterns of American Nativism, 1860–1925*, Westport, Conn.: Greenwood Press, 1981; William Preston, *Aliens and Dissenters: Federal Suppression of Radicals, 1903–1933*, Urbana: University of Illinois Press, 1994; Matthew Frye Jacobson, *Barbarian Virtues: The United States Encounters Foreign Peoples at Home and Abroad, 1876–1917*, New York: Hill & Wang, 2000.

47. Stephen Crane, *Stories and Tales*, New York: Vintage Books, 1955. *Maggie: A Girl of the Streets* and "The Men in the Storm" were originally published in 1893; "George's Mother" in 1896.

48. Crane, "The Men in the Storm," 21.

49. Crane, "An Experiment in Misery."

50. Jacob Riis, *How the Other Half Lives*, New York: Scribner's, 1890; Helen Campbell, *Darkness and Daylight in New York, or Lights and Shadows of New York Life*, New York: A. D. Worthington, 1892, 39–40. See, too, Helen Campbell, *Prisoners of Poverty: Women Wage-Workers, Their Trades and Their Lives*, Westport, Conn.: Greenwood Press, 1970 (originally published 1887).

51. Mick Moloney, "McNally's Row of Flats: Irish American Songs of Old New York." The song was composed in 1874.

52. Campbell, *Darkness and Daylight in New York*. For social Darwinist thinking regarding the poor, see Michael B. Katz, *In the Shadow of the Poorhouse*; David Ward, *Poverty, Ethnicity and the American City, 1840–1925: Changing Conceptions of the Slum and the Ghetto*, New York; Cambridge University Press, 1989.

53. Campbell, *Darkness and Daylight in New York*. Progressive reformer's attitude toward immigrant cleanliness might be summed up by sociologist Edward Alsworth Ross's assertion that "a Slav can live in dirt that would kill a white man." Ross, *The Old World in the New*, New York: Century, 1914. See, too, Jacobson, *Barbarian Virtues*. On post–World War II white ethnics' similar slurs toward African-Americans living in public housing, see Thomas Sugrue, *The Origins of the Urban Crisis: Race and Inequality in Postwar Detroit*, Princeton, N.J.: Princeton University Press, 1996; Rhonda Y. Williams, *The Politics of Public Housing: Black Women's Struggles against Urban Inequality*, New York: Oxford University Press, 2004.

54. Crane, "An Experiment in Misery," 38.

55. Crane, *Maggie: A Girl of the Streets*; Katz, *In the Shadow of the Poorhouse*; Ward, *Poverty, Ethnicity and the American City*.

56. Theodore Dreiser, *Sister Carrie*, New York: Doubleday, Page, 1900.

57. Frank Norris, *McTeague: A Story of San Francisco*, Greenwich, Conn.: Fawcett, 1966 (originally published 1899).

58. Campbell, *Darkness and Daylight in New York*, 224, 358–359.

59. Campbell, *Darkness and Daylight in New York*, 112, 153.

60. Campbell, *Darkness and Daylight in New York*.

61. Hutchins Hapgood, *The Spirit of the Ghetto: Studies of the Jewish Quarter of New York*, New York: Funk & Wagnalls, 1902.

62. Stanley Nadel, *Little Germany: Ethnicity, Religion and Class in New York City, 1845–1880*, Urbana: University of Illinois Press, 1990; James Green, *Death in the Haymarket: A Story of Chicago, the First Labor Movement and the Bombing that Divided Gilded Age America*; New York: Pantheon Books, 2004; Paul Avrich, *The Haymarket Tragedy*, Princeton, N.J.: Princeton University Press, 1984; Philip Foner, ed., *The Autobiographies of the Haymarket Martyrs*, New York: Humanities Press, 1969; *Puck*, December 3, 1884, 214, "A Lost Opportunity"; December 12, 1888, 272, "The Proper School for 'Anarchists'": November 30, 1887, 232, "The Countryman and the Snake": April 24, 1889, 136, "After One Hundred Years": October 12, 1887, 116, " 'Free' America," which shows German anarchists easily entering America, while skilled mechanics are turned away; and December 21, 1887, 268, "Ten Little Anarchists," which includes the lines "Nine little anarchists, boiling over with hate, One tried to make a bomb, and then there were eight," and, "Six little anarchists, meeting in a dive, One talked himself to death, and then there were five."

For the threat Irish dynamiters supposedly posed, see *Puck*, July 3, 1889, 306, "A Fourth of July Firecracker," in which Uncle Sam explodes a fire cracker, "Public Indignation": "That would send the Clan na Gael Irishmen back where they came from . . ." Also, *Puck*, June 26, 1889, 304, "The Mortar of Assimilation," shows Lady Liberty mixing immigrants in a pot, "Citizenship," into which one rebellious Irishman won't mix.

63. *Puck*, "O'Donovan Rossa's Shooting-Gallery for Irish Dynamiters," January 21, 1885, 336; also see *Puck*, "The Irrepressible Conflict," October 23, 1895, 145, in which an Irishman armed with a saber, "Clan na Gael," threatens Britain from the safety of the United States. Also, *Puck*, "Saint Patrick's Day in the Evening," March 16, 1892, 55; February 1885, 354, "The Coming Industry for Shantytown," in which an Irishman discovers "Anybody can make dynamite. All that is needed is lard and nitric acid"; on Irish shanty squalor in uptown Manhattan, see May 20, 1885, 187, "A Gala Occasion"; September 2, 1885, 3, "The New Law vs. the Poor" (An' is it puttin' thim wires unthergrounds they're after doin'?" an Irish washerwoman hanging her laundry on the telephone pole outside her shanty demands. "Faith if Oi hang me claus up undtherground the divvil'll be after 'em"); and September 26, 1888, 69, "A Lament from Harlem," in which Grogan and Mrs. Cassidy deplore the new apartments bringing "rich parvaynoos crowding out th' ould families uptown here!" in their squalid Harlem shanty village.

64. "Italian Life in New York," *Harper's New Monthly Magazine* 62 (371): 676–684 (April 1881).

65. "Italian Life in New York," *Harper's New Monthly Magazine*, 62 (371): 676–684 (April 1881). For anti-Italian sentiment in America circa 1900, see, too, Preston, *Aliens and Dissenters*; Ross, *The Old World in the New*; Madison Grant, *The Passing of the Great Race, or, The Racial Basis of European History*, New York: C. Scribner's Sons, 1921;

Lothrop Stoddard, *The Revolt against Civilization: The Menace of the Under Man*, New York: C. Scribner's Sons, 1922. On the Dillingham Commission, see Robert F. Zeidel, *Immigrants, Progressives and Exclusion Politics: The Dillingham Commission, 1900–1927*, DeKalb: Northern Illinois University Press, 2004.

66. "Italian Life in New York," *Harper's New Monthly Magazine* 62 (371): 676–684 (April 1881). On Lewis Hine, see Mary Panzer, *Lewis Hine*, New York: Phaidon, 2002. The remark on Italians' "backless skulls" is from Ross, *The Old World in the New*.

67. "Italian Life in New York," *Harper's New Monthly Magazine* 62 (371): 676–684 (April 1881).

68. Riis, *How the Other Half Lives*, 26–27.

69. Riis, *How the Other Half Lives*.

70. Bruno Lasker, "Fagots and Furnaces," *Survey* 40: 368 (1917); Ruth S. True, "Boyhood and Lawlessness," *West Side Studies* 1: 15–16 (1914); Sophonisba Breckinridge, *New Homes for Old*, New York: Harper & Brothers, 1921, 18; Katharine Anthony, "Mothers Who Must Earn," *West Side Studies* 1: 10 (1914); *New York Times*, December 20, 1907, 16; "The Rent Strike Grows," *The Charities and the Commons* 19: 1379 (1907); Phil Davis, "The Kosher Meat Strike," *Survey* 37: 638 (1917); Esther Packard, "My Money Won't Reach," *Survey* 39: 122 (1918); "Americanization by Starvation," *Survey* 44: 284 (1920); *The Philadelphia Inquirer*, February 22, 1917; February 23, 1917; February 25, 1917; March 2, 1917; March 7, 1917, for kosher foods riots in South Philadelphia and Northern Liberties, two immigrant neighborhoods. For Slovak children's pilferage to aid the family economy before and during the Depression in Philadelphia, see Robert M. Zecker, " 'Not Communists Exactly, but Sort of like Non-Believers': The Hidden Radical Transcript of Slovak Philadelphia, 1890–1954," *The Oral History Review* 29(1): 1–37 (Winter/Spring 2002).

71. Riis *How the Other Half Lives;* Edward Said, *Orientalism*, New York: Vintage Books, 1994.

72. H. C. Brunner, "Jersey and Mulberry," *Scribner's Magazine* 13 (5): 641–649 (May 1893).

73. *Puck,* February 11, 1885, 378, "Easily Satisfied," shows an Irish nationalist next to a map of both the Western and Eastern Hemispheres labeled Ireland: "Begorra thin, that's all we want!"

On Italian and German urban nuisances, see *Puck*, July 24, 1889, 365, "His Lullaby"; November 13, 1889, 179, "A Mean Case of Peanut Politics"; February 22, 1888, 414, "The Downfall of Italian Music"; December 3, 1884, 224, "The Decline of Italian Opera in New York—Will It Have to Go A-Begging?"; August 10, 1892, 395, "The Rise of Pietro and Jacopo"; November 16, 1887, 183, "A Grinding Italian Monopoly."

74. Robert Orsi, *The Madonna of 115th Street: Faith and Community in Italian Harlem, 1880–1950*, New Haven, Conn.: Yale University Press, 2002; Robert Orsi, "The Religious Boundaries of an Inbetween People: Street *Feste* and the Problem of the Other in Italian Harlem, 1920–1990," *American Quarterly* 44 (3): 313–347 (September 1992).

75. Orsi, *The Madonna of 115th Street*; Orsi, "The Religious Boundaries of an Inbetween People"; Michael Immerso, *Newark's Little Italy: The Vanished First Ward*, New Brunswick, N.J.: Rutgers University Press, 1997. For attitudes toward Slavic immigrants by native-born Americans, as well as the primarily Irish Roman Catholic hierarchy, see M. Mark Stolarik, *Immigration and Urbanization: The Slovak Experience, 1870–1918*, New York: AMS Press, 1989; Victor Greene, *For God and Country: The Rise of Polish and Lithuanian Ethnic Consciousness in America, 1860–1910*, Madison: State Historical Society of

Wisconsin, 1975; Victor Greene, *The Slavic Community on Strike: Immigrant Labor in Pennsylvania Anthracite*, Notre Dame, Ind.: University of Notre Dame Press, 1968.

76. H. C. Brunner, "Jersey and Mulberry," *Scribner's Magazine* 13 (5): 641–649 (May 1893).

77. Robert F. Foerster, *The Italian Emigration of Our Times*, New York: Arno Press, 1969 (originally published 1924); Humbert Nelli, *Italians in Chicago, 1880–1930*, New York: Oxford University Press, 1970; Lydio F. Tomasi, ed., *The Italian in America: The Progressive View, 1891–1914*, New York: Center for Migration Studies, 1972.

78. Brunner, "Jersey and Mulberry." For the wary proximity of Italian and Slovak and other Slavic immigrants in Nicetown, a steel-mill neighborhood of North Philadelphia, see Robert M. Zecker, " 'Where Everyone Goes to Meet Everyone Else': The Translocal Creation of a Slovak Immigrant Community," *Journal of Social History* 38 (2): 423–453 (Winter 2004).

79. Riis, *How the Other Half Lives*; Hutchins Hapgood, *The Spirit of the Ghetto: Studies of the Jewish Quarter of New York*, with commentary by Harry Golden, New York: Schocken, 1966 (originally Funk & Wagnalls, 1902). For Riis's photography, see Maren Stenge, "Jacob Riis and Urban Visual Culture: The Lantern Slide Exhibition as Entertainment and Ideology," *Journal of Urban History* 15 (3): 274 (May 1989); Gregory S. Jackson, "Cultivating Spiritual Sight: Jacob Riis' Virtual-Tour Narrative and the Visual Modernization of Protestant Homiletics," *Representations* 83: 126–166 (Summer 2003); Bill Hug, "Walking the Ethnic Tightwire: Ethnicity and Dialectic in Jacob Riis' *How the Other Half Lives*," *Journal of American Culture* 20 (4):41–53 (Winter 1997); Susan D. Moeller, "The Cultural Construction of Urban Poverty: Images of Poverty in New York City, 1890–1917," *Journal of American Culture* 18 (4): 1–17 (Winter 1995). For similarly selective images in photographic essays of East London poverty, see Gillian Rose, "Engendering the Slum: Photography in East London in the 1930s," *Gender, Place and Culture* 4 (3): 277–300 (November 1997). For similar selectivity among Depression era photographers documenting rural poverty in America, see William Stott, *Documentary Expression and Thirties America*, Chicago: University of Chicago Press, 1986. The 1888 quotations from Riis are from "Flashes from the Slums, Pictures Taken in Dark Places by the Lightning Process," *New York Sun*, February 10, 1888, 10, and *New York Morning Journal*, December 12, 1888, both cited in Stenge, "Jacob Riis and Urban Visual Culture." "The New York Dives" illustration from *National Police Gazette*, December 12, 1846, is also cited in Stenge.

80. Hutchins Hapgood, *The Spirit of the Ghetto: Studies of the Jewish Quarter of New York*, New York: Funk & Wagnalls, 1902.

81. Jacob Riis, "How the Other Half Lives: Studies Among the Tenements," *Scribner's Magazine* 6 (6): 643–663 (December 1889); Riis, "Light in Dark Places: A Study of the Better New York," *The Century* 53 (2): 246–253 (December 1896).

82. Riis, "How the Other Half Lives."

83. "Uncle Sam's Lodging House," cartoon, *Puck*, June 7, 1882.

84. Lincoln Steffens, *The Shame of the Cities*, New York: Sagamore Press, 1957 (originally published 1904); "A Ramble in Old Philadelphia," *The Century* 23 (5): 655–665 (March 1882).

85. Riis, "How the Other Half Lives"; David Hammack, *Power and Society: Greater New York at the Turn of the Century*, New York: Columbia University Press, 1987.

86. Hammack, *Power and Society*; Sam Bass Warner, *The Private City*; Warner, *Streetcar Suburbs: The Process of Growth in Boston*, Cambridge, Mass.: Harvard University Press, 1962; Becky Nicolaides, *My Blue Heaven: Life and Politics in the Working-Class*

Suburbs of Los Angeles, 1920–1965, Chicago: University of Chicago Press, 2002; Kenneth Jackson, *Crabgrass Frontier: The Suburbanization of the United States*, New York: Oxford University Press, 1985. For the degree to which even in the 1870s native-born middle-class Protestant residents had fled increasingly "foreign," Irish and German sections of Manhattan, see Kenneth Scherzer, *The Unbounded Community*, Durham, N.C.: Duke University Press, 1992.

87. Orsi, "The Religious Boundaries of an Inbetween People"; Foerster, *The Italian Emigration of Our Times*; Jacobson, *Barbarian Virtues*. See, too, "Italian Life in New York," *Harper's Magazine* 62 (371): 676–684 (April 1881).

88. On a nineteenth-century view of America's Chinese communities, see *Puck*, "Imitation Is the Sincerest Form of Flattery," October 14, 1885, 102; "Joy in Mott Street," April 22, 1885, 118; "An Ordinary Transaction," October 30, 1889, 148; and "True, If Rather Tardy," December 12, 1888, 258, in which two Chinese men discuss the recent presidential election: "Who in Soupee Now?" a gloating fan of "Hallison" asks. His friends replies, "Lats!" (Rats).

89. Gilfoyle, *City of Eros*; "Prostitutes' Register of the City of Philadelphia"; on Jewish criminality in turn-of-the-century New York, see Irving Howe, *World of Our Fathers: The Journey of the East European Jews to America and the Life They Found and Made*, New York: Simon & Schuster, 1976, 133–134; Jenna Weissman Joselit, *Our Gang: Jewish Crime and the Jewish Community, 1900–1940*, Bloomington: Indiana University Press, 1983; Albert Fried, *The Rise and Fall of the Jewish Gangster in America*, New York: Holt, Rinehart & Winston, 1980.

90. Riis, "How the Other Half Lives;" Said, *Orientalism*; *Puck*, February 8, 1893, 396, "One of the Family"; November 23, 1887, 211, "Striking an Average"; May 9, 1889, 177, "A Subterfuge"; May 6, 1891, 167, "Pleasant Recollections"; November 28, 1894, 234, "Happy Dreams"; March 17, 1897, "The Hit of the Night"; March 3, 1897, "Disgraced"; November 7, 1894, 180, "Making Use of Nature"; June 2, 1897, "The Story of a Toy." For the patriotic impersonator of a regular Yankee descendant of Lafayette, see *Puck*, April 24, 1889, 134, "Harvest Time." On foreign neighborhoods, see *Puck*, July 3, 1889, 308, "No Wonder" ("Misfortune, sir; I put all my money into a store on Avenue A, and I couldn't speak German!"); *Puck*, August 22, 1906, 3, "Broadway on a Jewish Holiday" (in which a deserted street is guarded by one lone policeman in front of stores marked "Schwindlheim and Stecklemeyer, Silk and Satin Goods and Rubber Boots" among others).

91. Riis, "How the Other Half Lives"; Ross, *The Old World in the New*.

92. Riis, "How the Other Half Lives"; Abraham Cahan, *Yekl and the Imported Bridegroom and Other Stories*, New York: Dover Publications, 1970 (originally published 1896); *Hester Street* 1975, directed by Joan Micklin Silver). On Progressives' attempts to reform the "foreign" cities circa 1880–1920, see Robert Wiebe, *The Search for Order, 1877–1920*, New York: Hill & Wang, 1967; Hammack, *Power and Society*.

93. Riis, "How the Other Half Lives"; Henry Adams, *The Education of Henry Adams*, Boston: Houghton Mifflin, 1974 (originally published 1918), 238, 457; Henry James, *The American Scene,* London: Chapman & Hall, 1907, 71, 131, 265–266.

94. Udetta D. Brown, "A Survey of Housing Conditions in Passaic, N.J.—Prepared for the Housing Committee of Passaic Board of Trade," March–May 1915; "WPA Ethnic Group Survey, the Poles in Philadelphia" (1939). Becky M. Nicolaides, *My Blue Heaven*, 33–34, for keeping of livestock by native-born blue-collar residents of a Los Angeles suburb in the 1920s. Jim Barrett, *Work and Community in the Jungle: Chicago's Packinghouse Workers, 1894–1922*, Urbana: University of Illinois Press, 1987; Robert Slayton, *Back of the Yards: The Making of a Local Democracy*, Chicago: University of

Chicago Press, 1986; Ewa Morawska, *For Bread with Butter*, New York: Cambridge University Press, 1985, 133–135, for Slavic immigrants keeping animals in Johnstown, Pa. WPA Ethnic Group Survey, "Tin-Town, New Castle, Pa., Slovaks," microfilm at the Pennsylvania Historical and Museum Commission, Harrisburg. Mildred Allen Beik, *The Miners of Windber*, University Park: Pennsylvania State University Press, 1996, 99–100, notes the same phenomenon in coal-mining communities in central Pennsylvania. Oral histories note the growing of crops on vacant industrial land, as occurred in Philadelphia and steel cities such as Homestead, Pa. "Another thing, when he would go huckstering, he would be gone sometimes for a couple of days. It was one less mouth to feed . . . ," Anne Yurcon interview, Homestead Oral History Project, University of Pittsburgh, Archives of Industrial Society, AIS/OH 76:25. Gary R. Mormino and George E. Pozzetta, *The Immigrant World of Ybor City: Italians and Their Latin Neighbors in Tampa, 1885–1985,* Urbana: University of Illinois Press, 1987, 273–280. *The Sopranos*, Season 6, Episode 8. The quotation on "bad investments" refers to Slovak immigrants, who Henry Cabot Lodge argued had "too much in common with the Chinese" to contribute anything to the United States," Henry Cabot Lodge, "The Restriction of Immigration," *North American Review* 152 (1891). On immigrants' food ways and how they were disparaged by native-born Americans, see Hasia R. Diner, *Hungering for America: Italian, Irish and Jewish Foodways in the Age of Migration*, Cambridge, Mass.: Harvard University Press, 2001.

95. Israel Zangwill, *The Melting Pot,* New York: Arno Press, 1975 (originally performed 1908); Irving Howe, *World of Our Fathers*, 133–134.

96. Stephen Jay Gould, *The Mismeasure of Man*, New York: W. W. Norton, 1996; Jacobson, *Barbarian Virtues*; Matthew Frye Jacobson, *Whiteness of a Different Color*, Cambridge, Mass.: Harvard University Press, 1996; Frank Norris, *McTeague*. An impressive collection of the skulls of different European "races" is on display at the Mutter Museum of Medical Science, Philadelphia.

97. Riis, "How the Other Half Lives."

98. Michael Miller Topp, *Those without a Country: The Political Culture of Italian American Syndicalists*, Minneapolis: University of Minnesota Press, 2001; for Slovaks, see Robert M. Zecker " 'Not Communists Exactly, but Sort of Like Non-Believers': The Hidden Radical Transcript of Slovak Philadelphia, 1890–1954," *Oral History Review* 29 (1): 1–37 (Winter/Spring 2002). The reference to the workers' mandolin band is in *Rovnost L'udu* (*Equality for the People*), November 18, 1924, 1. On various immigrant groups' radicalism, see Paul Buhle and Dan Georgakas, eds., *The Immigrant Left in the United States*, Albany: State University of New York Press, 1996.

99. Riis, "How the Other Half Lives."

100. Nathan Glazer and Daniel P. Moynihan, *Beyond the Melting Pot: The Negroes, Puerto Ricans, Jews, Italians and Irish of New York City*, Cambridge, Mass.: M.I.T. Press, 1970.

101. Pietro Di Donato, *Christ in Concrete*, New York: Bobbs-Merrill, 1939; Henry Roth, *Call It Sleep*, New York: Avon, 1964 (originally published 1934); Mike Gold, *Jews without Money*, New York: Avon, 1965 (originally published 1930).

102. On Fasanella, see the catalog of a powerful retrospective of Fasanella's work offered in both New York and Cooperstown, N.Y., Paul S. D'Ambrosio, *Ralph Fasanella's America*, Cooperstown, N.Y.: Fenimore Art Museum, 2001, and Patrick Watson, *Fasanella's City: The Painting of Ralph Fasanella with the Story of His Life and Art*, New York: Knopf, 1973. Riis, "How the Other Half Lives"; Foerster, *The Italian Emigration of Our Times*.

103. James T. Farrell, *Studs Lonigan, A Trilogy*, New York: Modern Library, 1932. On the 1918–1919 race riots in Chicago and elsewhere, see William Tuttle, *Race Riot: Chicago in the Red Summer of 1919*, Urbana: University of Illinois Press, 1996; James Barrett and David Roediger, "Whiteness and the Inbetween Peoples of Europe," *Journal of American History* 16 (3): 3–45 (Summer 1997); Robert M. Zecker, " 'Negrov Lynčovanie' and the Unbearable Whiteness of Slovaks: The Immigrant Press Covers Race," *American Studies* 43 (2): 43–72 (Spring 2002).

104. Farrell, *Studs Lonigan*, 306.

105. Riis, "How the Other Half Lives"; Farrell, *Studs Lonigan*; *Puck*, February 4, 1885, 360–361; *Puck*, "A Hint to Irish Modesty," May 9, 1888, 175; also March 14, 1888, 42, "Incidents of the 17th," and March 16, 1892, 64, "McGrath's First St. Patrick's Day in America," showing a top-hatted Irish marching society with banners, "Fourth Ward Descendants of Kings" and "Society of Sons of the Sod." See, too, *Puck*, May 27, 1896, in which a feisty Irishman answers the question, "What is liberty?" "It's th' roight to make somebody ilse vote wid de gang, begorra!"

106. Many magazine writers of the turn of the century depicted geographically constricted immigrant communities in various American cities. Among them are Ivan Ardan, "The Ruthenians in America," *Charities and the Commons* 13: 246–252 (December 4, 1904); John R. Commons, "Slavs in the Bituminous Mines of Illinois," *Charities and the Commons* 13: 227–229 (December 4, 1904); John Daniels, "Americanizing Eighty Thousand Poles," *Survey* 14: 373–385 (June 4, 1910); William E. Davenport, "The Italian Immigrant in America," *Outlook* 73: 29–37 (January 3, 1903); Phillip Davis, "Making Americans of Russian Jews," *Outlook* 80: 631–637 (July 8, 1905); Laura B. Garrett, "Notes on the Poles in Baltimore," *Charities and the Commons* 13: 235–239 (December 4, 1904); Burton J. Hendrick, "The Great Jewish Invasion," *McClure's Magazine* 28: 307–321 (January 1907); Owen R. Lovejoy, "The Slav Child: A National Asset or a Liability," *Charities and the Commons* 14: 882–884 (July 1, 1905); Peter Roberts, "The Sclavs in Anthracite Coal Communities," *Charities and the Commons* 13: 215–222 (December 4, 1904); P. V. Rovnianek, "The Slovaks in America," *Charities and the Commons* 13: 239–245 (December 4, 1904); Mary Buell Sayles, "Housing and Social Conditions in a Slavic Neighborhood," *Charities and the Commons* 13: 257–261 (December 4, 1904); Edward A. Steiner, "The Russian and the Polish Jew in New York," *Outlook* 72: 528–539 (November 1, 1902); Steiner, "The Slovak and the Pole in America," *Outlook* 73: 555–564 (1903).

107. Peter Roberts, "The Sclavs in Anthracite Coal Communities," 215.

108. Frank Julian Warne, *The Slav Invasion and the Mine Workers*, Philadelphia: J. B. Lippincott, 1904, 113.

109. Victor Greene, *The Slavic Community on Strike*; Katherine Mayo, *Justice to All: The Story of the Pennsylvania State Police*, New York: Putnam's, 1917; P. V. Rovnianek, "The Slovaks in America," 244. For coverage of the strike-breaking actions by "Cossack" state police, see Mildred Allen Beik, *The Miners of Windber*, 219; Robert M. Zecker, " 'Not Communists Exactly, but Sort of Like Non-Believers.' " See also *Jednota*, November 5, 1919, 5; *Národné Noviny*, September 5, 1912, "Ta svoboda americka" ("That American Freedom"), November 20, 1913; *Amerikansky Russky Viestnik*, October 17, 1912.

110. Warne, *The Slav Invasion and the Mine Workers*, 112.

111. Edward Steiner, "From Ephrata to Whisky Hill," *Outlook* 88: 778–784 (April 4, 1908), 780. See, too, Henry Edward Rood, "A Pennsylvania Colliery Village: A Polyglot Community," *The Century* 55 (6): 809–829 (April 1898).

112. Ross, *The Old World in the New*, 126.

113. Ross, *The Old World in the New*, 138; Thomas Bell, *Out of This Furnace*, Pittsburgh: University of Pittsburgh Press, 1976 (originally published 1941); Ewa Morawska, *For Bread with Butter*.

114. Ross, *The Old World in the New*, 139.

115. Lothrop Stoddard, *The Revolt against Civilization*. See, too, Alfred P. Schultz, *Race or Mongrel: A Brief History of the Rise and Fall of the Ancient Races of Earth; A Theory That the Fall of Nations Is Due to Intermarriage with Alien Stocks; A Demonstration That a Nation's Strength Is Due to Racial Purity; A Prophecy That America Will Sink to Early Decay Unless Immigration Is Rigorously Restricted*, Boston: L. C. Page, 1908.

116. Katherine Hoffman, "In the New York Ghetto," *Munsey's Magazine* 23: 608–619 (August 1900), 608.

117. Hoffman, "In the New York Ghetto," 615.

118. Robert Haven Schauffler, "The Island of Desire," *Outlook* 100: 666–673 (March 23, 1912), 673.

119. E. S. Martin, "East Side Considerations," *Harper's Magazine* 96: 853–863 (1898), 855; Hutchins Hapgood, *The Spirit of the Ghetto*, with commentary by Harry Golden.

120. Stephen Greenblatt, "Resonance and Wonder," in Ivan Karp and Steven D. Lavine, eds., *Exhibiting Cultures*, Washington, D.C.: Smithsonian Institution Press, 1991. See, too, Marianna Torgovnick, *Gone Primitive: Savage Intellects, Modern Lives*, Chicago: University of Chicago Press, 1990; Raymond Corbey, "Ethnographic Showcases 1870–1930," *Cultural Anthropology* 8 (3): 338–369 (August 1993); Meg Armstrong, "A Jumble of Foreignness: The Sublime Musayums of Nineteenth-Century Fairs and Expositions," *Cultural Critique* 23: 199–250 (Winter 1992); Rosemarie Bank, "Representing History: Performing the Columbian Exposition," *Theatre Journal*, 54 (4): 589–606 (December 2002); Roslyn Poignant, *Professional Savages: Captive Lives and Western Spectacle*, New Haven, Conn.: Yale University Press, 2004.

121. Zecker, " 'Negrov Lynčovanie' and the Unbearable Whiteness of Slovaks." See, too, Jacobson, *Whiteness of a Different Color;* Finley Peter Dunne, *Mr. Dooley on Ivrything and Ivrybody*, New York: Dover Publications, 1963, 8–9.

122. *Puck*, December 19, 1888, 278, "A Night of Disaster"; October 2, 1889, 88, "Almost Flustered"; February 24, 1892, 7, "Soulful Longings." See, too, *Puck*, August 21, 1889, 431, "A Defender of Civilization," in which O'Reagan tells his friend, "Oi wish, Teddy, that instead av sittin' here in this Park we was only on wan av thim Sout' Sea Oislands where there's nothin' to do bat slape and ate fruit!" To which his friend, Casey, replies, "Bedad, Oi'm ashamed to hear a civilized man talk loike dat! Phwere could yez get any thing to drink, ye haythen!"

123. E. S. Martin, "East Side Considerations," 854–855; *Jednota*, February 17, 1904, 4; Burton J. Hendrick, "The Great Jewish Invasion," *McClure's Magazine* 28: 307–321 (January 1907).

124. *Národný Kalendár,* 1907, 93, 109; *NK,* 1916, 38, 43, 57–61; *NK,* 1918, 57; *Národné Noviny*, February 10, 1910; March 10, 1910. See, too, June Granatir Alexander, *Ethnic Pride, American Patriotism: Slovaks and Other New Immigrants in the Interwar Era*, Philadelphia: Temple University Press, 2004.

125. Upton Sinclair, *The Jungle*, New York: Doubleday, 1906; Lincoln Steffens, *The Shame of the Cities*; for conditions in Chicago's Back of the Yards, Barrett, *Work and Community in the Jungle: Chicago's Packinghouse Workers, 1894–1922*; Slayton, *Back of the Yards*; Lizabeth Cohen, *Making a New Deal: Industrial Workers in Chicago, 1919–1939*, New York: Cambridge University Press, 1990.

126. Abraham Cahan, *The Rise of David Levinsky*, New York: Harper, 1917.

127. Abraham Cahan, *Yekl and the Imported Bridegroom*. On urban entertainment circa 1900, see Kathy Peiss, *Cheap Amusements: Working Women and Leisure in Turn-of-the-Century New York*, Philadelphia: Temple University Press, 1986; David Nasaw, *Going Out: The Rise and Fall of Public Amusements,* Cambridge, Mass.: Harvard University Press, 1999.

128. Elizabeth Ewen, *Immigrant Women in the Land of Dollars: Life and Culture on the Lower East Side, 1890–1925*, New York: Monthly Review Press, 1985, 53–55, 119–121.

129. Anzia Yezierska, *Hungry Hearts*, New York: Grosset, 1920, 264, 263.

130. *Slovak v Amerike*, August 25, 1908, 3.

131. Anzia Yezierska, *Bread Givers*, New York: Persea Books, 1970 (originally published 1925), 30–31.

132. Yezierska, *Bread Givers*, 26, 27.

133. Yezierska, *Hungry Hearts*, 67, 68, 73, 82, 83; Mike Gold, *Jews without Money*.

134. Katherine Stubbs, introduction to Anzia Yezierska, *Arrogant Beggar*, Durham, N.C.: Duke University Press, 1996 (originally published 1927), xiv, xx.

135. Hapgood, *The Spirit of the Ghetto*; Henry Roth, *Call It Sleep*.

136. J. A. Mitchell, *The Last American*, New York: F. A. Stokes, 1889; Edward Bellamy, *Looking Backward*, New York: Houghton, Mifflin, 1887.

137. Mitchell, *The Last American*. For the views on the "mongrelization" that mass immigration was supposedly bringing to America, see Schultz, *Race or Mongrel*.

138. Mitchell, *The Last American;* Hendrick, "The Great Jewish Invasion"; Ross, *The Old World in the New*; Warne, *The Slav Invasion and the Mine Worker*; Cabot Lodge, "The Restriction of Immigration." *Puck*, March 13, 1913, cover, "As to Japanese Exclusion. Perhaps If They Came in Kimonos, the Real Undesirables Might Be Kept Out." Earlier, in its 1893 answer to "The Immigration Question," *Puck* suggested that a fictitious crooked ward boss, "Michael Doolan," would answer, "Kape thim all out except the Oirish—Home Rule must not be interfered wid." *Puck,* February 15, 1893, 422.

139. *Puck*, January 11, 1893, 331; *Puck*, "A Hint to the Hebrews," May 11, 1881, 178; *Puck*, "O'Donovan Rossa's Shooting–Gallery for Irish Dynamiters," January 21, 1885, 336; also see *Puck*, "The Irrepressible Conflict," October 23, 1895, 145, in which an Irishman armed with a saber, "Clan na Gael," threatens Britain from the safety of the United States. Also, *Puck*, "Saint Patrick's Day in the Evening," March 16, 1892, 55.

140. Finley Peter Dunne, *Mr. Dooley on Ivrything and Ivrybody*, 1.

141. Dunne, *Mr. Dooley*, 29. For the view that the Irish now controlled the streets, and it was the Italians who dug them up, see *Puck*, January 4, 1893, 312, "A Progressive Race."

142. Dunne, *Mr. Dooley*, 32–34.

143. Dunne, *Mr. Dooley*, 29–30, 33, 34, 59–61, 66, 73, 78, 79. On Chicago gangs, see William Tuttle, *Race Riot*; James Barrett and David Roediger, "Whiteness and the Inbetween Peoples of Europe,"

CHAPTER 3: "A PROBLEM THAT WE, THE PUBLIC, MUST SOLVE": THE GANGSTER FILM

1. Kathy Peiss, *Cheap Amusements: Working Women and Leisure in Turn-of-the-Century New York*, Philadelphia: Temple University Press, 1986; David Nasaw, *Going Out: The Rise and Fall of Public Amusements,* Cambridge, Mass.: Harvard University Press, 1999.

2. *The Public Enemy* (1931, directed by William A. Wellman); *Little Caesar* (1931, directed by Mervyn LeRoy); *Scarface, The Shame of a Nation* (1932, directed by Howard Hawks).

3. John Springhall, "Censoring Hollywood: Youth, Moral Panic and Crime/Gangster Movies of the 1930s," *Journal of Popular Culture* 32 (3): 135–154 (Winter 1998).

4. Paul J. Erickson, *Welcome to Sodom: The Cultural Work of City-Mysteries Fiction in Antebellum America*, Austin: University of Texas dissertation, 2005.

5. See, for example, the aristocratic cabal ruling 1844 Philadelphia in George Lippard, *Quaker City, or The Monks of Monk Hall*, New York: Odyssey Press, 1970 (originally published 1844). For later wealthy "big bosses" controlling the rackets, see *Bullets or Ballots* (1936, directed by William Keighley).

6. On the newfound political strength of southern and eastern European Americans in the 1930s, see Lizabeth Cohen, *Making a New Deal: Industrial Workers in Chicago, 1919–1939*, New York: Cambridge University Press, 1990. Useful, too, in this regard is Thomas Bell's novel of Slovak steelworkers, who by the 1930s no longer accepted being referred to by foremen as "Hunkies" and started organizing through the Congress of Industrial Organizations and President Roosevelt's Democratic Party: Bell, *Out of This Furnace*, Pittsburgh: University of Pittsburgh Press, 1976 (originally published 1941). Gangster films with somewhat admirable ethnic characters in subplots are *Little Caesar*; *The Last Gangster* (1937, directed by Edward Ludwig), and *City for Conquest* (1940, directed by Anatole Litvak).

7. On post–World War II efforts to contain the city and promote suburbanization via redlining, highway construction, and other federal programs, see Thomas Sugrue, *The Origins of the Urban Crisis: Race and Inequality in Postwar Detroit*, Princeton, N.J.: Princeton University Press, 1996; Kenneth Jackson, *Crabgrass Frontier: The Suburbanization of the United States*, New York: Oxford University Press, 1985; Arnold Hirsch, *Making the Second Ghetto: Race and Housing in Chicago, 1940–1960*, Chicago: University of Chicago Press, 1998; George Lipsitz, *The Possessive Investment in Whiteness: How White People Profit from Identity Politics*, Philadelphia: Temple University Press, 2006. On the depiction of the communist menace in popular culture, see Ellen Schrecker, *Many Are the Crimes: McCarthyism in America*, Boston: Little, Brown, 1998, especially Chap. 4, "They Are Everywhere," 119–153; Margot Henriksen, *Doctor Strangelove's America: Society and Culture in the Atomic Age*, Berkeley: University of California Press, 1997; Cyndy Hendershot, *Anti-Communism and Popular Culture in Mid-Century America*, Jefferson, N.C.: McFarland, 2003. *Kiss of Death* (1947, directed by Henry Hathaway); *Panic in the Streets* (1950, directed by Elia Kazan); *Pickup on South Street* (1953, directed by Samuel Fuller). For city criminals menacing the suburbs, see *The Desperate Hours* (1955, directed by William Wyler).

8. Giorgio Bertellini, "Black Hands and White Hearts: Italian Immigrants as 'Urban Racial Types' in Early American Film Culture," *Urban History* 31 (3): 375–399 (2004). Maxine Schwartz Seller, ed., *Ethnic Theatre in the United States*, Westport, Conn.: Greenwood Press, 1983.

9. Giorgio Bertellini, "Black Hands and White Hearts," *Urban History* 31 (3): 375–399 (2004). The quotation is on 388.

10. Reviews in *Moving Picture World*, January 30, 1909, 125, and November 16, 1912, 668, as cited in Bertellini, "Black Hands and White Hearts," 390.

11. *Training Day* (2001, directed by Antoine Fuqua); *Inside Man* (2006, directed by Spike Lee); *The Siege* (1998, directed by Edward Zwick).

12. Bertellini, "Black Hands and White Hearts." Madison Grant, *The Passing of the Great Race; or, The Racial Basis of European History*, New York: Scribner's, 1921; Madison Grant and Charles Stewart Davison, *The Alien in Our Midst: or, 'Selling Our Birthright for*

a Mess of Pottage,' New York: Galton, 1930; Lothrop Stoddard, *The Revolt against Civilization: The Menace of the Under Man*, New York: Scribner's, 1922; Stoddard, *The Rising Tide of Color against White World Supremacy*, New York: Scribner's, 1920; Robert F. Foerster, *The Italian Emigration of Our Time,* Cambridge, Mass.: Harvard University Press, 1924; Robert F. Zeidel, *Immigrants, Progressives and Exclusion Politics: The Dillingham Commission, 1900–1927*, DeKalb: Northern Illinois University Press, 2004. For the view of southern Italians' and Sicilians' innate criminality, even from an elite Italian criminologist's perspective, see Cesare Lombroso, *Crime, Its Causes and Remedies*, Boston: Little, Brown, 1911; Lombroso, *The Criminal Anthropological Writings of Cesare Lombroso*, Lewiston, N.Y.: Edwin Mellen Press, 2004.

13. Cited in Matthew Frye Jacobson, *Whiteness of a Different Color: European Immigrants and the Alchemy of Race*, Cambridge, Mass.: Harvard University Press, 1996, 184.

14. *Kiss of Death* (1947, directed by Henry Hathaway).

15. *Regeneration* (1915, directed by Raoul Walsh).

16. On the settlement houses, see Jane Addams, *Twenty Years at Hull House*, Boston: Bedford/St. Martin's, 1999 (originally published 1915); Lillian Wald, *The House on Henry Street*, New York: Holt, 1915; Allen Davis, *Spearheads for Reform: The Social Settlements and the Progressive Movement, 1890–1914*, New Brunswick, N.J.: Rutgers University Press, 1984; *Regeneration* (1915, directed by Raoul Walsh); *The Public Enemy* (1931, directed by William A. Wellman); *The Roaring Twenties* (1939, directed by Raoul Walsh).

17. *Regeneration* (1915, directed by Raoul Walsh). For Riis's photography, see Maren Stenge, "Jacob Riis and Urban Visual Culture: The Lantern Slide Exhibition as Entertainment and Ideology," *Journal of Urban History* 15 (3): 274 (May 1989).

18. Stephen Crane, *Stories and Tales*, New York: Vintage Books, 1955, includes *Maggie: A Girl of the Streets,* and his other Bowery Tales. Jacob Riis, "The Passing of Cat Alley," *The Century* 57 (2): 166–176 (December 1898); *The Musketeers of Pig Alley* (1912, directed by D. W. Griffith).

19. Christopher Shannon, "Public Enemies, Local Heroes: The Irish-American Gangster Film in Classic Hollywood Cinema," *New Hibernia Review* 9 (4): 48–64 (Winter 2005). *The Public Enemy*; *The Roaring Twenties* (1939, directed by Raoul Walsh); *Angels with Dirty Faces* (1938, directed by Michael Curtiz).

20. Lippard, *The Quaker City*.

21. George Kibbe Turner, "Tammany's Control of New York by Professional Criminals," *McClure's Magazine* 33 (2): 117–134 (June 1909), as cited in Albert Fried, *The Rise and Fall of the Jewish Gangster in America*, New York: Columbia University Press, 1993, 61–71; Herbert Asbury, *The Gangs of New York: An Informal History of the Underworld*, New York: Knopf, 1928. For similar tight working relationships between politicians and crime gangs in nineteenth–century Philadelphia, see Noel Ignatiev, *How the Irish Became White*, New York: Routledge, 1995, 148–176.

22. James T. Farrell, *Studs Lonigan, A Trilogy*, New York: Modern Library, 1932; Finley Peter Dunne, *Mr. Dooley on Ivrything and Ivrybody*, New York: Dover, 1963.

23. *Chicago Tribune*, November 12, 1924, 8, as cited in Daniel McDonough, "Chicago Press Treatment of the Gangster, 1924–1931," *Illinois Historical Journal* 82: 17–32 (Spring 1989). Even earlier, though, the Chicago press had portrayed the heavily Jewish West Side area around "Bloody Maxwell Street" as a den of vice, violence and urban pathology. Fried, *The Rise and Fall of the Jewish Gangster in America*, 90. For a further condemnation of corrupt Chicago, see W. T. Stedman, *If Christ Came to Chicago! A Plea for the Union of All Who Love in the Service of All Who Suffer*, Chicago: Laird & Lee, 1894.

24. *Chicago Tribune,* June 1, 1925, 8; September 10, 1928, 12; September 13, 1928, 12, all cited in McDonough, "Chicago Press Treatment of the Gangster." See Lothrop Stoddard, *The Revolt against Civilization*; Robert Foerster, *The Italian Emigration of Our Time*; *Little Caesar* (1931, directed by Mervyn LeRoy). For the complex phenomenon of social banditry, in which some predators on the wealthy are indeed regarded as folk heroes, in Sicily and elsewhere, see Eric J. Hobsbawm, *Primitive Rebels: Studies in Archaic Forms of Social Movement in the 19th and 20th Centuries,* New York: Praeger, 1963.

25. Paul Kavieff, *The Purple Gang: Organized Crime in Detroit, 1910–1945,* Fort Lee, N.J.: Barricade Books, 2005; Fried, *The Rise and Fall of the Jewish Gangster in America,* 103–108. Bertolt Brecht and Kurt Weill, *Aufstieg und Fall der Stadt Mahagonny: Oper in drei Akten,* Vienna: Universal Edition, 1969 (originally performed 1930).

26. *Metropolis* (1927, directed by Fritz Lang); *Doctor Mabuse* (1922, directed by Fritz Lang); *M* (1931, directed by Fritz Lang).

27. Siegfried Kracauer, *From Caligari to Hitler: A Psychological History of the German Film,* Princeton, N.J.: Princeton University Press, 2004 (originally published 1947); Kracauer, *The Mass Ornament: Weimar Essays,* Cambridge, Mass.: Harvard University Press, 1995.

28. *Metropolis* (1927, directed by Fritz Lang); *Modern Times* (1936, directed by Charley Chaplin). For "Taylorism" and its discontents, see Frederick Winslow Taylor, *The Principles of Scientific Management,* New York: Harper, 1911; Robert Kanigel, *The One Best Way: Frederick Winslow Taylor and the Enigma of Efficiency,* Cambridge, Mass.: M.I.T. Press, 2005; Bernard Doray, translated by David Macey, *From Taylorism to Fordism: A Rational Madness,* London: Free Association, 1988. For resistance to Taylorism in the Passaic textile mills, see the 1926–1927 issues of the *Passaic Textile Strike Bulletin,* New York Public Library; Passaic Textile Strike Committee, *Hell in New Jersey,* Passaic, NJ: General Relief Committee Textile Strikers, 1926, and the strike committee's 1926 film, *The Passaic Textile Strike.*

29. *Modern Times* (1936, directed by Charley Chaplin); Karel Čapek, translated by Paul Selver, *R.U.R. (Rossum's Universal Robots),* Garden City, N.Y.: Doubleday, 1923; *Bladerunner* (1982, directed by Ridley Scott).

30. *The Front Page* (1931, directed by Lewis Milestone); *Scarface* (1932, directed by Howard Hawks); *The Beast of the City* (1932, directed by Charles Brabin); *Crime without Passion* (1934, directed by Ben Hecht and Charles McArthur); *Angels with Dirty Faces* (1938, directed by Michael Curtiz); *Kiss of Death* (1947, directed by Henry Hathaway).

31. *Underworld* (1927, directed by Joseph Von Sternberg); *Angels with Dirty Faces*; *The Roaring Twenties*. *Kiss of Death* (1947, directed by Henry Hathaway), also features a mob lawyer, Howser, described by the assistant DA as "another intimate shyster with connections . . ."

32. *Silk Stocking Sal* (1924, directed by Tod Browning); *Three Wise Crooks* (1925, directed by F. Harmon Weight). On the Bowery B'hoy Mose and Lize characters, see Stuart M. Blumin, *The Emergence of the Middle Class: Social Experience in the American City, 1760–1900,* New York: Cambridge University Press, 1989, 107, 111–122.

33. *Underworld* (1927, directed by Joseph Von Sternberg).

34. *The Dragnet* (1928, directed by Joseph Von Sternberg); see, too, *Thunderbolt* (1929, directed by Joseph Von Sternberg). Damon Runyon, *More Guys and Dolls: Thirty-Four of the Best Short Stories,* Garden City, N.Y.: Garden City Books, 1951. The Broadway play *Guys and Dolls* was produced in 1950, with the film version following in 1955, directed by Joseph L. Mankiewicz.

35. Albert Fried, *The Rise and Fall of the Jewish Gangster in America*; Rich Cohen, *Tough Jews*, New York: Simon & Schuster, 1998; Jenna Weissman Joselit, *Our Gang: Jewish Crime and the New York Jewish Community, 1900–1940*, Bloomington: University of Indiana Press, 1983.

36. Timothy J. Gilfoyle, *City of Eros: New York City, Prostitution and the Commercialization of Sex, 1790–1920*, New York: W. W. Norton, 1992; David J. Pivar, *Purity and Hygiene: Women, Prostitution and the 'American Plan,' 1900–1930*, Westport, Conn.: Greenwood Press, 2002; Margit Stange, *Personal Property: Wives, White Slaves and the Market in Women*, Baltimore, Md.: Johns Hopkins University Press, 1998; Barbara Meil Hobson, *Uneasy Virtue: The Politics of Prostitution and the American Reform Tradition*, New York: Basic Books, 1987. For a 19th-early 20th-century memoir by a prostitute, see Josie Washburn, *The Underworld Sewer: A Prostitute Reflects on Life in the Trade*, Lincoln: University of Nebraska Press, 1997 (originally published 1909).

37. *The Docks of New York* (1927, directed by Joseph Von Sternberg). For the rough life of dockworkers in New York, see Howard Kimeldorf, *Reds or Rackets? The Making of Radical and Conservative Unions on the Waterfront*, Berkeley: University of California Press, 1988, and Calvin Winslow, ed., *Waterfront Workers: New Perspectives on Race and Class*, Urbana: University of Illinois Press, 1998. For "black and tans," see Jacob Riis, *How the Other Half Lives*, New York: Scribner's, 1890. Ironically, a 1927 exposé of the evils of prostitution, *Is Your Daughter Safe?* features a cameo by Big Bill Thompson, mayor of Chicago, a city with a reputation as black as New York's. *Is Your Daughter Safe?* (1927, directed by Louis King and Leon Lee).

38. *Me, Gangster* (1928, directed by Raoul Walsh).

39. *Me, Gangster; White Heat* (1949, directed by Raoul Walsh); *The Public Enemy; Angels with Dirty Faces*.

40. *The Racket* (1928, directed by Lewis Milestone). On Chicago corruption, see Daniel McDonough, "Chicago Press Treatment of the Gangster, 1924–1931"; James L. Merriner, *Grafters and Goo Goos: Corruption and Reform in Chicago, 1833–2003*, Carbondale: Southern Illinois University Press, 2004; Dick W. Simpson, *Rogues, Rebels and Rubber Stamps: The Politics of the Chicago City Council, from 1863 to the Present*, Boulder, Colo.: Westview Press, 2001; Richard Lindberg, *To Serve and Collect: Chicago Politics and Police Corruption from the Lager Beer Riots to the Summerdale Scandal*, New York: Praeger, 1991. For a contemporary view of Big Bill Thompson, see John Bright, *Hizzoner Big Bill Thompson, An Idyll of Chicago*, New York: J. Cape & H. Smith, 1930.

41. *The Racket; Little Caesar* (1931, directed by Mervyn LeRoy); *Bullets or Ballots* (1936, directed by William Keighley).

42. F. Scott Fitzgerald, *The Great Gatsby*, New York: Scribner's, 1925; *Little Caesar*. On Rothstein, see Nick Tosches, *King of the Jews*, New York: Ecco Press, 2005; Donald Henderson Clarke, *In the Reign of Rothstein*, New York: Vanguard Press, 1929.

43. Turkus and Feder, *Murder, Inc.*; "Reminiscences of William O'Dwyer, Oral History 1962," Columbia University Oral History Project, Butler Library, Columbia University; George Walsh, *Public Enemies: The Mayor, the Mob and the Crime That Was*, New York: W. W. Norton, 1980.

44. Herbert Mitgang, *Once upon a Time in New York: Jimmy Walker, Franklin Roosevelt and the Last Great Battle of the Jazz Age*, New York: Free Press, 2000; Gene Fowler, *Beau James: The Life and Times of Jimmy Walker*, New York: Viking Press, 1949; Gerald Leinwand, *Mackerels in the Moonlight: Four Corrupt American Mayors*, Jefferson, N.C.: McFarland, 2004 (the four are Chicago's Thompson, New York's Walker, Boston's

James M. Curley and Jersey City's Frank "I Am the Law" Hague). On Newark and political corruption, see Ron Porambo, *No Cause for Indictment: An Autopsy of Newark,* New York: Holt, Rinehart & Winston, 1971, 60–63, 69–72, 258–266; Jerry Gafio Watts, *Amiri Baraka: The Politics and Art of a Black Intellectual,* New York: New York University Press, 2001, 350–351, and FBI documents pertaining to ties between New Jersey gang bosses Abner "Longy" Zwillman, Ruggerio "Ritchie the Boot" Boiardo, and Willie Moretti and Newark mayors Meyer Ellenstein, Ralph Villani, and Hugh Addonizio, as well as Jersey City mayors Frank Hague and John Kenny, at www.foia.fbi.gov/zwillman.htm. On Moretti's career and demise, see Thomas Reppetto, *American Mafia: A History of Its Rise to Power,* New York: Henry Holt, 2004, 141–145, 151, 161, 216–218, 233, 248, 265–267. For a more positive assessment of Newark mayors Ellenstein and Villani, see Harold Kaplan, *Urban Renewal Politics: Slum Clearance in Newark*, New York: Columbia University Press, 1963.

45. *The Racket*; Mario Puzo, *The Godfather*, New York: Putnam, 1969. On the theory that Cermak was assassinated on the orders of the Capone gang, see Reppetto, *American Mafia*, 128–129. For a more laudatory assessment of Cermak by his fellow Czech Chicagoans, see Gustav Drnec, *Náš Čermak: úžasná životní a mučednická smrt českoamerického přistěhovalce, starosty města Chicaga ("Our Cermak: The Amazing Life and Sad Death of a Czech-American Immigrant, the Mayor of the City of Chicago),* Chicago: Spravedlnosti, 1933. Bronx gangster "Dutch Schultz" in 1935, too, did plot to assassinate Special Prosecutor Thomas Dewey, but his colleagues in Murder Inc. feared such a murder would bring too much heat on them, and instead arranged for Schultz's murder at Newark's Palace Chop House. Burton B. Turkus and Sid Feder, *Murder, Inc.: The Story of the Syndicate*, Cambridge, Mass.: DaCapo Press, 1979 (originally published 1951), 128–151. See, too, Albert Fried, *The Rise and Fall of the Jewish Gangster in America*, 188–189, 196.

46. *The Wire*, Season 1, Episode 12.

47. *The Racket* (1928, directed by Lewis Milestone).

48. *The Public Enemy*. Views of corrupt and immoral Chicago from the turn of the century include W. T. Stedman, *If Christ Came to Chicago!* George Kibbe Turner, "The City of Chicago, A Study of the Great Immoralities," *McClure's Magazine* 28 (1): 576–579 (April 1907).

49. *The Public Enemy*.

50. John Springhall, "Censoring Hollywood: Youth, Moral Panic and Crime/Gangster Movies of the 1930s," *Journal of Popular Culture* 32 (3): 135–154 (Winter 1998).

51. This and other newspaper editorials on gangster movies are cited in Springhall, "Censoring Hollywood." On the *Newark Star-Ledger*, see Carol Felsenthal, *Citizen Newhouse: Portrait of a Media Merchant*, New York: Seven Stories Press, 1998.

52. Henry James Forman, *Our Movie Made Children*, New York: Macmillan, 1933.

53. Springhall, "Censoring Hollywood."

54. *The Public Enemy*; *Angels with Dirty Faces*.

55. *The Public Enemy*.

56. George Kibbe Turner, "The Daughters of the Poor," *McClure's Magazine* 33 (4): 45–61 (November 1909), as cited in Fried, *The Rise and Fall of the Jewish Gangster in America*, 66–67. See, too, Peiss, *Cheap Amusements*, and Nasaw, *Going Out*. Abraham Cahan, *Yekl and the Imported Bridegroom and Other Stories*, New York: Dover, 1970 (originally published 1896); *Hester Street* (1975, directed by Joan Micklin Silver).

57. *The Public Enemy*. On settlement houses, see Addams, *Twenty Years at Hull House*, and Davis, *Spearheads for Reform*.

58. *The Roaring Twenties* (1939, directed by Raoul Walsh); Neal Gabler, *Walter Winchell: Gossip, Power and the Culture of Celebrity*, New York: Alfred Knopf, 1994, 188–189; Fried, *The Rise and Fall of the Jewish Gangster in America*, 109–110; Turkus and Feder, *Murder, Inc.*, 264–294.

59. Joe Krause, "The Jewish Gangster: A Conversation Across Generations," *American Scholar* 64 (1): 53–65 (Winter 1995); Rachel Rubin, "Gangster Generation: Crime, Jews and the Problem of Assimilation," *Shofar: An Interdisciplinary Journal of Jewish Studies* 20 (4): 1–17 (2002).

60. *The Public Enemy*; *The Roaring Twenties*.

61. Mark Stuart, *Gangster Number Two: Longy Zwillman, the Man Who Invented Organized Crime*, Secaucus, N.J.: Lyle Stuart, 1985, documents the opposite career trajectories of Zwillman and Sir Joseph Reinman.

62. *The Public Enemy*.

63. *Little Caesar* (1931, directed by Mervyn LeRoy); *The Cocoanuts* (1929, directed by Robert Florey); *Animal Crackers* (1930, directed by Victor Heerman). For the Marx Brothers' playful subversion of ethnic stereotypes, see Daniel Lieberfeld and Judith Sanders, "Here under False Pretenses: The Marx Brothers Crash the Gates," *American Scholar* 64 (1): 103–108 (Winter 1995).

64. Mitgang, *Once upon a Time in New York*; Fowler, *Beau James*; Leinwand, *Mackerels in the Moonlight*.

65. *Little Caesar*; *The Wire*, Season 2.

66. *Little Caesar*; *Bullets or Ballots* ; *The Last Gangster*.

67. *Little Caesar*; *Bullets or Ballots*; *Racket Busters* (1938, directed by Lloyd Bacon).

68. *The Little Giant* (1933, directed by Roy Del Ruth); *A Slight Case of Murder* (1938, directed by Lloyd Bacon).

69. *The Doorway to Hell* (1930, directed by Archie Mayo); *The Public Enemy*.

70. *Little Caesar*; on *festa*, see Robert Orsi, *The Madonna of 115th Street: Faith and Community in Italian Harlem, 1880–1950*, New Haven, Conn.: Yale University Press, 2002; Robert Orsi, "The Religious Boundaries of an Inbetween People: Street *Feste* and the Problem of the Other in Italian Harlem, 1920–1990," *American Quarterly* 44 (3): 313–347 (September 1992); Michael Immerso, *Newark's Little Italy: The Vanished First Ward*, New Brunswick, N.J.: Rutgers University Press, 1997.

71. *Little Caesar*; Daniel McDonough, "Chicago Press Treatment of the Gangster."

72. *Angels with Dirty Faces;* on crime in 1920s–1940s Brooklyn, see Jonathan Rieder, *Canarsie: The Jews and Italians of Brooklyn against Liberalism*, Cambridge, Mass.: Harvard University Press, 1985, 20–26, 90–94; on Murder Inc.'s infiltration of the New York garment industry, as well as the Amalgamated Clothing Workers of America, see Turkus and Feder, *Murder Inc.*, 331–362, and Steven Fraser, *Labor Will Rule: Sidney Hillman and the Rise of American Labor*, Ithaca, N.Y.: Cornell University Press, 1991, 242–258. Wendell Pritchett observes that, rather than the haven some former residents recall, Brownsville had quite unsettling connotations for "respectable" New Yorkers in the 1920s–1940s. Brownsville's juvenile delinquency rate in 1939 was 25 percent higher than the New York City's norm, and Brownsville had the highest rates of assault, robberies, and total crime in Brooklyn. Its most famous native son was Murder Inc.'s Abe "Kid Twist" Reles. Wendell Pritchett, *Brownsville, Brooklyn: Blacks, Jews, and the Changing Face of the Ghetto*, Chicago: University of Chicago Press, 2002, 42–49. Richard Gambino, *Blood of My Blood: The Dilemma of the Italian-Americans*, New York: Guernica, 1996, especially 274–312; Reppetto, *American Mafia*, 33, 37–38, 49; *Goodfellas* (1990, directed by Martin Scorsese); Daniel

McDonough, "Chicago Press Treatment of the Gangster"; Rich Cohen, *Tough Jews*; Joe Krause, "The Jewish Gangster"; Rachel Rubin, "Gangster Generation."

73. *Little Caesar.*

74. *The Public Enemy*; *Little Caesar*; *The Roaring Twenties*. *Some Like It Hot* (1959, directed by Billy Wilder) features George Raft as gangster "Spats" Colombo, but in a broad-brushed caricature of the kinds of roles he seriously played in the 1930s and 1940s. Jeffrey Eugenides, *Middlesex*, New York: Farrar, Straus & Giroux, 2002. On Detroit's Purple Gang, see Kavieff, *The Purple Gang.*

75. Both quotations cited in Jonathan J. Cavallero, "Gangsters, Fessos, Tricksters and Sopranos: The Historical Roots of Italian American Stereotype Anxiety," *Journal of Popular Film and Television* 32 (2): 50–63 (Summer 2004). See Matthew Frye Jacobson, *Whiteness of a Different Color*; Jennifer Guglielmo and Salvatore Salerno, eds., *Are Italians White? How Race Is Made in America*, New York: Routledge, 2003; Thomas A. Guglielmo, *White on Arrival: Italians, Race, Color and Power in Chicago, 1890–1945*, New York: Oxford University Press, 2004; Madison Grant, *The Passing of the Great Race*; Lothrop Stoddard, *The Revolt against Civilization.*

76. Hasia R. Diner, *Hungering for America: Italian, Irish and Jewish Foodways in the Age of Migration*, Cambridge, Mass.: Harvard University Press, 2001, 77–83.

77. *Scarface, The Shame of the Nation*; *The Last Gangster* (1937, directed by Edward Ludwig).

78. *The Last Gangster*; *The Desperate Hours* (1955, directed by William Wyler).

79. *Scarface*; *Little Caesar.*

80. Cavallero, "Gangsters, Fessos, Tricksters and Sopranos"; John Springhall, "Censoring Hollywood"; *Scarface.*

81. *The Last Gangster.* Although Krozac's nationality isn't stated, the surname suggests a Yugoslavian background. If this is the case, an intriguing parallel may be made to the career of Louis Adamic, who published the story of his return to his Slovenian home village as a distinguished writer in his 1934 memoir, *The Native's Return: An American Immigrant Visits Yugoslavia and Discovers His Old Country*, New York: Harper, 1934. On Lewis Hine, see Mary Panzer, *Lewis Hine*, New York: Phaidon, 2002.

82. *The Last Gangster.*

83. *Národné Noviny* article, "Rezolúcianaochranu prist'ahovalkcov" ("Resolution in Defense of Foreigners"), *Národné Noviny*, 1937 (no further date), in National Slovak Society papers, Box 168, Immigration History Research Center, University of Minnesota; "A Protest: To the Senators and Representatives of the Commonwealth of Pennsylvania, March 11, 1935," by the National Slovak Society (NSS) similarly denounced a proposal by Pennsylvania State Senator William Rodgers to "deny the right for [workmen's] compensation to non-resident aliens—[as] un-American," NSS papers, Box 168, IHRC. Such vociferous protests by the NSS may explain why this national fraternal society was being investigated as early as 1938 for suspected communist infiltration. Letter, from Representative Harold Velde, Chairman, House Un-American Activities Committee, to Senator Edward Martin, July 2, 1954, in NSS papers, Box 169, file, "Communism," IHRC. Dies's suggestion is cited in Cavellero, "Gangsters, Fessos, Tricksters and Sopranos," 55.

84. *Bullets or Ballots*; Cavallero, "Gangsters, Fessos, Tricksters and Sopranos"; *Marked Woman* (1937, directed by Lloyd Bacon) featured Italian actor Eduardo Ciannelli in the role of Vanning.

85. *Bullets or Ballots.*

86. In *Racket Busters* (1938, directed by Lloyd Bacon), the crusading special prosecutor tells his staff that he is dissatisfied with their work so far, because he's not interested in "small fry." Still, he notes that they have managed to imprison "Lucky Lugano."

87. Burton B. Turkus and Sid Feder, *Murder, Inc.: The Story of the Syndicate*, Cambridge, Mass.: DaCapo Press, 1979 (originally published 1951), 331–362; Neal Gabler, *Walter Winchell: Gossip, Power and the Culture of Celebrity*, New York: Knopf, 1994, 274–280.

88. *Racket Busters.*

89. *Racket Busters; Bullets or Ballots; The Roaring Twenties;* Stephen Curry, "Dewey Defeats the Dutchman," *American History* 37 (5): 38–46 (December 2002). Turkus and Feder, *Murder, Inc.;* Fried, *The Rise and Fall of the Jewish Gangster in America.*

90. *Bullets or Ballots*; *The Wire*, Season 2, Episode 12. On Roosevelt's stigmatization of "economic royalists" during the Second New Deal, see Lizabeth Cohen, *Making a New Deal*; Steve Fraser and Gary Gerstle, eds., *The Rise and Fall of the New Deal Order, 1930–1980*, Princeton, N.J.: Princeton University Press, 1989.

91. *Bullets or Ballots*; *The Last Gangster*; *The Roaring Twenties*. For municipal corruption in New York, see Turkus and Feder, *Murder, Inc.*; "Reminiscences of William O'Dwyer, Oral History 1962," Columbia University Oral History Project, Butler Library, Columbia University; Walsh, *Public Enemies*; Mitgang, *Once upon a Time in New York*; Fowler, *Beau James.* On Newark and political corruption, see Porambo, *No Cause for Indictment.*

92. *Kiss of Death* (1947, directed by Henry Hathaway); *The Maltese Falcon* (1941, directed by John Huston); *On the Waterfront* (1954, directed by Elia Kazan). *On the Waterfront* followed close on the heels of the well–publicized New York State crime commission hearings on corrupt waterfront unions, and also coincided with the McClellan and Kefauver hearings on mobster influence in unions. See Lee Bernstein, *The Greatest Menace: Organized Crime in Cold War America*, Amherst: University of Massachusetts Press, 2002; Kimeldorf, *Reds or Rackets?*

93. *Dead End* (1937, directed by William Wyler).

94. *Angels with Dirty Faces*. For the acceptance of pilferage in immigrant working–class culture, see Bruno Lasker, "Fagots and Furnaces," *Survey* 40: 368 (1917); Ruth S. True, "Boyhood and Lawlessness," *West Side Studies* 1: 15–16 (1914); Sophonisba Breckinridge, *New Homes for Old*, 18; Katharine Anthony, "Mothers Who Must Earn," *West Side Studies* 1: 10 (1914); "The Rent Strike Grows," *Charities and the Commons* 19: 1379 (1907); Phil Davis, "The Kosher Meat Strike," *Survey* 37: 638 (1917); Esther Packard, "My Money Won't Reach," *Survey* 39: 122 (1918); "Americanization by Starvation," *Survey* 44: 284 (1920). For kosher food riots in South Philadelphia and Northern Liberties, two immigrant neighborhoods, see the *Philadelphia Inquirer*, February 22, 1917; February 23, 1917; February 25, 1917; March 2, 1917; March 7, 1917. For Slovak children's pilferage to aid the family economy before and during the Depression in Philadelphia, see Robert M. Zecker, " 'Not Communists Exactly, but Sort of Like Non-Believers': The Hidden Radical Transcript of Slovak Philadelphia, 1890–1954," *The Oral History Review* 29 (1): 1–37 (Winter/Spring 2002).

95. *Angels with Dirty Faces*; Hobsbawm, *Primitive Rebels.*

96. *Angels with Dirty Faces*. Another cinematic fighting priest is Father Barry in *On the Waterfront,* and both mirror real–life workers' priests such as Pittsburgh's Father Charles Rice and New York's "waterfront priest," Father John Corridan. See Colin Davis, " 'All I Got's a Hook': New York Longshoremen and the 1948 Dock Strike," in Calvin Winslow, ed., *Waterfront Workers.*

97. *Angels with Dirty Faces*; *Dead End*; *The Roaring Twenties*; *A Bronx Tale* (1993, directed by Robert De Niro).

98. *City for Conquest* (1940, directed by Anatole Litvak).

99. *The Last Gangster*. This view of the press is at odds with the crusading crime-fighting reporter, best captured in Humphrey Bogart's quip as Ed Hutcheson in *Deadline U.S.A.* (1952, directed by Richard Brooks): "That's the press, baby, and there's nothing you can do about it!"

100. Karen Brodkin, *How Jews Became White Folks and What That Says about Race in America*, New Brunswick, N.J.: Rutgers University Press, 1998; Lipsitz, *The Possessive Investment in Whiteness*; Kenneth Jackson, *Crabgrass Frontier: The Suburbanization of the United States*, New York: Oxford University Press, 1985; Douglas S. Massey and Nancy A. Denton, *American Apartheid: Segregation and the Making of the Underclass*, Cambridge, Mass.: Harvard University Press, 1993; David Roediger, *Working toward Whiteness: How America's Immigrants Became White: The Strange Journey from Ellis Island to the Suburbs*, New York: Basic Books, 2005.

101. David Roediger, *The Wages of Whiteness: Race and the Making of the American Working Class*, New York: Verso, 1999; Roediger, *Working toward Whiteness*; James Barrett and David Roediger, "Whiteness and the Inbetween Peoples of Europe," *Journal of American History* 16 (3): 3–45 (Summer 1997); Robert M. Zecker, " 'Negrov Lynčovanie' and the Unbearable Whiteness of Slovaks: The Immigrant Press Covers Race," *American Studies* 43 (2): 43–72 (Spring 2002); Matthew Frye Jacobson, *Roots Too: White Ethnic Revival in Post-Civil Rights America*, Cambridge, Mass.: Harvard University Press, 2006; Jacobson, *Whiteness of a Different Color*; Lipsitz, *The Possessive Investment in Whiteness*.

102. *The Last Gangster*.

103. *Kiss of Death*. A title card at the film's beginning declares, "Filmed on location in New York on the actual locale associated with the story."

104. K. A. Cuordleone, " 'Politics in an Age of Anxiety': Cold War Political Culture and the Crisis in American Masculinity," *The Journal of American History* 87 (2): 515–545 (September 2000).

105. *Kiss of Death*; *White Heat*. See, too, eerie evocations of an emasculated upper class as posing a communist takeover threat in *The Manchurian Candidate* (1962, directed by John Frankenheimer).

106. *Kiss of Death*; *On the Waterfront*. Lee Bernstein, *The Greatest Menace*. See, too, Lee Mortimer and Jack Lait, *Washington Confidential*, New York: Crown, 1951, for a contemporary conflation of these two "menaces."

107. *Panic in the Streets* (1950, directed by Elia Kazan).

108. *Pickup on South Street* (1953, directed by Samuel Fuller).

109. *Pickup on South Street*.

110. *Naked City*; *Cops*. On suburbanization see Jackson, *Crabgrass Frontier*.

111. On the attitude of white ethnic Catholics in the urban Northeast and Midwest toward African–Americans, see John McGreevy, *Parish Boundaries*, Chicago: University of Chicago Press, 1996, 89–101, and Eileen McMahon, *What Parish Are You From?* Lexington: University Press of Kentucky, 1995, 118–125. On anti-public-housing animus among white ethnics, see Thomas Sugrue, *The Origins of the Urban Crisis*, Princeton, N.J.: Princeton University Press, 1996, 61–75; Arnold Hirsch, *Making the Second Ghetto*, New York: Cambridge University Press, 1983, 70–72, 80–84, 89, 97–99; Thomas Philpott, *The Slum and the Ghetto*, Belmont, Calif.: Wadsworth, 1991, 160–161, 166–169, 196–197; Jacobson, *Roots Too*; Zecker, " 'Negrov Lynčovanie' and the Unbearable Whiteness of

Slovaks." A particularly amnesiac discussion of "race relations" in the context of resurgent white ethnic pride is Michael Novak, *The Rise of the Unmeltable Ethnics,* New York: Macmillan, 1972.

112. *The Desperate Hours*; *The Last Gangster.*

113. W.E.B. Du Bois, *The Souls of Black Folk*, New York: Vintage Books, 1990 (originally published 1903).

114. Will Herberg, *Protestant, Catholic, Jew: An Essay in American Religious Sociology*, Garden City, N.Y.: Doubleday, 1955. For suburban blending of eastern and southern European ethnics into a generic "white" group, see, for example, Roediger, *Working toward Whiteness.*

115. *A Raisin in the Sun* (1961, directed by Daniel Petrie). "Chicago Fiddles While Trumbull Park Burns," *The Nation*, May 22, 1954. For Slavic Philadelphians' resistance to blacks' moving into the Point Breeze section, see the *Philadelphia Inquirer*, July 8, 1951; Zecker, " 'Negrov Lynčovanie' and the Unbearable Whiteness of Slovaks." Slovak former and current residents of Point Breeze reached a surprising degree of unanimity in saying that it wasn't the Point Breeze and Tasker Homes housing projects per se that "ruined" their old neighborhood, but the uncleanliness of the African–American residents. For resistance by white ethnics in Chicago and Detroit to blacks' moving near them, see Sugrue, *The Origins of the Urban Crisis*; Hirsch, *Making the Second Ghetto*; Jacobson, *Roots Too.*

CHAPTER 4: "CERTAIN SOCIOLOGICAL REALITIES THERE": A CITY FOR THE 1960s AND BEYOND

1. Richard Wright, *Native Son*, New York: Harper & Row, 1940; *East Side/West Side* (1963–1964).

2. *East Side/West Side* (1963–1964); *The Cosby Show* (1984–1992); *All in the Family* (1971–1979). On "relevant" television programs dealing with race in the 1970s, see Kirsten Marthe Lentz, "Quality Versus Relevance: Feminism, Race, and the Politics of the Sign in 1970s Television," *Camera Obscura* 15 (1): 45–93 (2000). On blockbusting and racial steering, see Thomas Sugrue, *The Origins of the Urban Crisis: Race and Inequality in Postwar Detroit*, Princeton, N.J.: Princeton University Press, 1996; Kenneth Jackson, *Crabgrass Frontier: The Suburbanization of the United States*, New York: Oxford University Press, 1985; Arnold Hirsch, *Making the Second Ghetto: Race and Housing in Chicago, 1940–1960*, Chicago: University of Chicago Press, 1998; George Lipsitz, *The Possessive Investment in Whiteness: How White People Profit from Identity Politics*, Philadelphia: Temple University Press, 2006.

3. Donald Bogle, *Primetime Blues: African Americans on Network Television*, New York: Farrar, Straus & Giroux, 2001, 107–113; Jannette Dates and William Barlow, eds., *Split Image: African Americans in the Mass Media*, Washington, D.C.: Howard University Press, 1993, 269, 297.

4. Bogle, *Primetime Blues*, 107–113; *East Side/West Side* (1963–1964).

5. *East Side/West Side*; *Cops* (1989–present).

6. Thomas Philpott, *The Slum and the Ghetto: Immigrants, Blacks and Reformers in Chicago, 1880–1930*, Belmont, Calif.: Wadsworth, 1991; David Chalmers, *And the Crooked Places Made Straight: The Struggle for Social Change in the 1960s*, Baltimore: Johns Hopkins University Press, 1996; Nicholas Lehman, *The Promised Land: The Great Black Migration and How It Changed America*, New York: Vintage Books, 1992; Ronald Formisano, *Boston against Busing: Race, Class and Ethnicity in the 1960s and 1970s*, Chapel Hill: University of North Carolina Press, 2004; J. Anthony Lukas, *Common Ground: A Turbulent Decade in the Lives of Three American Families*, New York: Vintage Books, 1986.

7. Theodore Hershberg, ed., *Philadelphia: Work, Space, Family, and Group Experience in the 19th-Century*, New York: Oxford University Press, 1981; Olivier Zunz, *The Changing Face of Inequality: Urbanization, Industrial Development and Immigrants in Detroit*, Chicago: University of Chicago Press, 1982. A similar pattern held for seemingly mono-working-class neighborhoods in Pittsburgh circa 1900. S. J. Kleinberg, *The Shadow of the Mills: Working-Class Families in Pittsburgh, 1870–1907*, Pittsburgh: University of Pittsburgh Press, 1989.

8. Michael Harrington, *The Other America: Poverty in the United States*, New York: Macmillan, 1962.

9. Arnold Hirsch, *Making the Second Ghetto*; Thomas Philpott, *The Slum and the Ghetto*; "Chicago Fiddles While Trumbull Park Burns," *The Nation*, May 22, 1954.

10. Newton Minow, *Equal Time: The Private Broadcaster and the Public Interest*, New York: Atheneum, 1964; Minow, *How Vast the Wasteland Now?* New York: Gannett Foundation Media Center at Columbia University, 1991.

11. George Lipsitz, *Time Passages: Collective Memory and American Popular Culture*, Minneapolis: University of Minnesota Press, 1990; Lipsitz, *Rainbow at Midnight: Labor and Culture in the 1940s*, Urbana: University of Illinois Press, 1994.

12. Marshall McLuhan, *The Medium Is the Massage*, New York: Random House, 1967; McLuhan, *Understanding Media: The Extensions of Man*, New York: McGraw–Hill, 1964; *Cops* (1989–present); *CSI* (2000–present); *Homicide: Life on the Streets* (1993–1999).

13. *Naked City* (1958–1963); Bogle, *Primetime Blues*, 83, 106, 109.

14. *Naked City*; *The Musketeers of Pig Alley* (1912, directed by D. W. Griffith).

15. *Dragnet* (1951–1959); for the zoot suit riots, see Eduardo Obregon Pagan, *Murder at the Sleepy Lagoon: Zoot Suit Riots, Race, and Riot in Wartime L.A.*, Chapel Hill: University of North Carolina Press, 2003; Mauricio Mazan, *The Zoot-Suit Riots: The Psychology of Symbolic Annihilation*, Austin: University of Texas Press, 1984. For the 1965 rebellion in Watts, see Gerald Horne, *Fire This Time: The Watts Uprising and the 1960s*, New York: DaCapo Press, 1997; Paul Bullock, ed., *Watts, the Aftermath: An Insider's View of the Ghetto, by the People of Watts*, New York: Grove Press, 1969; Eric Priestley, *Flame and Smoke*, Staten Island, N.Y.: Turnaround Printers, 1974; Walter J. Raine, *The Perception of Police Brutality in South Central Los Angeles*, Los Angeles: Institute of Public Affairs, UCLA, 1967; Spencer Crump, *Black Riot in Los Angeles: The Story of the Watts Tragedy*, Los Angeles: Trans-Anglo Books, 1966; Jerry Cohen and William S. Murphy, *Burn, Baby, Burn! The Los Angeles Race Riot, August, 1965*, New York: Dutton, 1966; Frederic C. Coonradt, *The Negro News Media and the Los Angeles Riots*, Los Angeles: School of Journalism, University of Southern California, 1965.

16. *Dragnet* (1951–1959); *Dragnet* (1967–1970).

17. Henry Taylor and Carol Dozier, "Television Violence, African-Americans and Social Control, 1950–1976," *Journal of Black Studies* 14 (2): 107–136 (December 1983); *The Streets of San Francisco* (1972–1977); *The Maltese Falcon* (1941, directed by John Huston).

18. Sidney Fine, *Violence in the Model City: The Cavanagh Administration, Race Relations and the Detroit Riot of 1967*, Ann Arbor: University of Michigan Press, 1989; Joe R. Feagin and Harlan Hahn, *Ghetto Revolts: The Politics of Violence in American Cities*, New York: Macmillan, 1973; Ron Porambo, *No Cause for Indictment: An Autopsy of Newark*, New York: Holt, Rinehart & Winston, 1971; Tom Hayden, *Rebellion in Newark: Official Violence and Ghetto Response*, New York: Vintage Books, 1967; Mike Davis, *City of Quartz: Excavating the Future in Los Angeles*, New York: Vintage Books, 1992, 67–70; *Report*

of the National Advisory Commission on Civil Disorders (the Kerner Commission), Washington, D.C.: U.S. Government Printing Office, 1968.

19. Dragnet (1967–1970); Mike Davis, *City of Quartz*; Lou Cannon, *Official Negligence: How Rodney King and the Riots Changed Los Angeles and the LAPD*, New York: New Times Books, 1997; Tom Owens, *Lying Eyes: The Truth behind the Corruption and Brutality of the LAPD and the Beating of Rodney King*, New York: Thunder's Mouth Press, 1994; Staff of *The Los Angeles Times, Understanding the Riots: Los Angeles before and after the Rodney King Case*, Los Angeles, The Commission, 1992; *Report of the Independent Commission on the Los Angeles Police Department*, Los Angeles, The Commission, 1991.

20. *Car 54, Where Are You?* (1961–1963).

21. *Barney Miller* (1975–1982); Jim Sleeper, *The Closest of Strangers: Liberalism and the Politics of Race in New York*, New York: W. W. Norton, 1990; Vincent J. Cannato, *The Ungovernable City: John Lindsay and the Struggle to Save New York*, New York: Basic Books, 2001.

22. *The French Connection* (1971, directed by William Friedkin); *The Taking of Pelham One Two Three* (1974, directed by Joseph Sargent); *Taxi Driver* (1976, directed by Martin Scorsese); *Barney Miller* (1975–1982); *Welcome Back, Kotter* (1975–1979).

23. *The Untouchables* (1959–1963); Hirsch, *Making the Second Ghetto*; "Chicago Fiddles While Trumbull Park Burns."

24. *The Godfather* (1972, directed by Francis Ford Coppola); *The Godfather: Part II* (1974, directed by Francis Ford Coppola); on perceptions of New York in the 1970s, see Cannato, *The Ungovernable City.*

25. McLuhan, *Understanding Media*; *Naked City*; *East Side/West Side*.

26. Eric Lott, *Love and Theft: Blackface Minstrelsy and the American Working Class*, New York: Oxford University Press, 1993; Michael Rogin, *Blackface, White Noise: Jewish Immigrants in the Hollywood Melting Pot*, Berkeley: University of California Press, 1996; George Lipsitz, "The Meaning of Memory: Family, Class, and Ethnicity in Early Network Television Programs," *Cultural Anthropology* 1 (4): 355–387 (November 1986); Robert M. Zecker, " 'Negrov Lynčovanie' and the Unbearable Whiteness of Slovaks: The Immigrant Press Covers Race," *American Studies* 43 (2): 43–72 (Summer 2002). For Slovak, Ruthenian, Jewish, and German immigrants' minstrel shows, see *Jednota,* October 2, 1918, 6; *Národné Noviny,* April 4, 1912; portraits of minstrel shows performed at St. Michael's Greek (Byzantine) Catholic and St. John's Lutheran churches, Passaic, New Jersey, circa 1919, in author's possession. St. Mary of the Assumption Byzantine Catholic Church, Wilkes–Barre, Pa., "Hundredth Anniversary Souvenir Journal, 1888–1988," includes "Photograph—Parish Plays, Minstrel Shows, 1949." Housed at the Balch Institute for Ethnic Studies. *Slovensky Hlasnik,* November 13, 1947, 1, reports on a minstrel show performed in New Kensington, Pa. *New Yorksky Dennik,* November 22, 1913, 2, reports an enterprising Slovak selling minstrel songs in New York and Brooklyn. Berndt Ostendorf, " 'The Diluted Second Generation': German-Americans in Music, 1870–1920," in Hartmut Keil, ed., *German Workers' Culture in the United States, 1850 to 1920*, Washington, D.C.: Smithsonian Institution Press, 1988, 280–281. On denial of equal relief payments to blacks, see Rhonda Y. Williams, *The Politics of Public Housing: Black Women's Struggles against Urban Inequality*, New York: Oxford University Press, 2004, 27.

27. See cartoons in *Puck,* for example, "Not Explicit," December 4, 1895, 275; "Presence of Mind," March 16, 1892, 58; "Such Is Fame," May 20, 1896, n.p.; "Claim Disallowed," February 9, 1898, n.p.; "The Tableaux at Coon Corners," December 8, 1897, n.p.; "Au Courant," January 1, 1896, 339; "Ceremony," June 17, 1891, 262.

28. Bogle, *Primetime Blues*, 21–41; Lipsitz, "The Meaning of Memory"; *Amos 'n Andy* (1951–1953); on the Talented Tenth, see W.E.B. DuBois, *The Souls of Black Folk*, New York: Vintage Books, 1990 (originally published 1903).

29. *Amos 'n Andy* (1951–1953); *The Birth of a Nation* (1915, directed by D. W. Griffith); *Boyz 'n the Hood* (1991, directed by John Singleton). On *The Birth of a Nation*, see Michael Rogin, "Their Sword Became a Flashing Vision," in Michael Rogin, *Ronald Reagan the Movie and Other Episodes in Political Demonology*, Berkeley: University of California Press, 1987. On hip-hop, see Jeff Chang, *Can't Stop, Won't Stop: A History of the Hip-Hop Generation*, New York: St. Martin's Press, 2005; Jason Tanz, *Other People's Property: A Shadow History of Hip-Hop in White America*, New York: Bloomsbury, 2007.

30. On TV news and dramas of the ghetto, and the Moynihan report, as viewed by a Harlem teenager, see Robin D.G. Kelley, *Yo Mama's Disfunktional! Fighting the Culture Wars in Urban America*, Boston: Beacon Press, 1997.

31. *Amos 'n Andy*; Bogle, *Primetime Blues*, 21–41; Albert Johnson, "Beige, Brown or Black," *Film Quarterly* 13 (1): 38–43 (Autumn 1959); Albert Johnson, "The Negro in American Films: Some Recent Works," *Film Quarterly* 18 (4): 14–30 (Summer 1965). On suburbanization, see Jackson, *Crabgrass Frontier*; Robert Fishman, *Bourgeois Utopias: The Rise and Fall of Suburbia*, New York: Basic Books, 1987, 175–179, 193–194.

32. *I Remember Mama* (1949–1957); *Life with Luigi* (1952–1953); *The Goldbergs* (1949–1956); *The Honeymooners* (1955–1956); Lipsitz, "The Meaning of Memory."

33. Karen Brodkin, *How Jews Became White Folks and What That Says about Race in America*, New Brunswick, N.J.: Rutgers University Press, 1998.

34. For consumerism's equation with Americanism during the 1950s, see Lizabeth Cohen, *A Consumer's Republic: The Politics of Mass Consumption in Postwar America*, New York: Vintage Books, 2004; for white flight and slum creation in Brooklyn, see Walter Thabit, *How East New York Became a Ghetto*, New York: New York University Press, 2003; for the same process in the Bronx, see Jill Jonnes, *South Bronx Rising: The Rise, Fall and Resurrection of an American City*, New York: Fordham University Press, 2002; Lipsitz, "The Meaning of Memory"; Lipsitz, *The Possessive Investment in Whiteness*.

35. Lipsitz, "The Meaning of Memory"; Paul C. Mishler, *Raising Reds: The Young Pioneers, Radical Summer Camps and Communist Political Culture in the United States*, New York: Columbia University Press, 1999; Judy Kaplan and Linn Shapiro, *Red Diapers: Growing Up in the Communist Left*, Urbana: University of Illinois Press, 1998.

36. Lipsitz, "The Meaning of Memory"; *The Goldbergs*; *The Honeymooners*; Paul Buhle and Dan Georgakas, eds., *The Immigrant Left in the United States*, Albany: State University of New York Press, 1996; Kaplan and Shapiro, *Red Diapers*; Mishler, *Raising Reds*.

37. Lipsitz, "The Meaning of Memory"; *East Side/West Side*; *Amos 'n Andy*; *The Life of Riley* (1953–1958); *The Honeymooners*; *The Goldbergs*; Michael Katz, *In the Shadow of the Poorhouse: A Social History of Welfare in America*, New York: Basic Books, 1986; Kaplan and Shapiro, *Red Diapers*; Ellen Schrecker, *Many Are the Crimes: McCarthyism in America*, Boston: Little, Brown, 1998.

38. *The Honeymooners*; Lipsitz, "The Meaning of Memory."

39. David Riesman, *The Lonely Crowd: A Study of the Changing American Character*, New Haven, Conn.: Yale University Press, 1950; William H. Whyte, *The Organization Man*, Garden City, N.Y.: Doubleday, 1957; Jackson, *Crabgrass Frontier*. For the persistence of working-class culture in supposedly uniformly middle-class Eisenhower America, see

Jack Metzgar, *Striking Steel: Solidarity Remembered*, Philadelphia: Temple University Press, 2000.

40. On rent strikes and antieviction campaigns during the 1930s, see Lizabeth Cohen, *Making a New Deal: Industrial Workers in Chicago, 1919–1939*, New York: Cambridge University Press, 1990; Irving Bernstein, *Turbulent Years: A History of the American Worker, 1933–1941*, Boston: Houghton Mifflin, 1969.

41. *The Honeymooners* (1955–1956).

42. Bogle, *Primetime Blues,* 139–140; Johnson, "Black, Brown or Beige"; Johnson, "The Negro in American Films"; National Advisory Commission on Civil Disturbances (Kerner Commission).

43. For the view of late 1960s urban America as out of control, see Alan Matusow, *The Unraveling of America: A History of Liberalism in the 1960s*, New York: Harper & Row, 1984.

44. *N.Y.P.D.* (1967–1969); on Lindsay, see Cannato, *The Ungovernable City*.

45. *N.Y.P.D.*; *East Side/West Side*; *The Mod Squad* (1968–1973); *Hill Street Blues* (1981–1987); *Miami Vice* (1984–1989); *Starsky and Hutch* (1975–1979); Taylor and Dozier, "Television Violence, African-Americans and Social Control 1950–1976"; Giorgio Bertellini, "Black Hands and White Hearts: Italian Immigrants as 'Urban Racial Types' in Early American Film Culture," *Urban History* 31 (3): 375–399 (2004).

46. *Mannix* (1967–1975).

47. *White Heat* (1949, directed by Raoul Walsh); *CSI* (1989–present); *Adam-12* (1968–1975).

48. Hahn and Feagin, *Ghetto Revolts*; Porambo, *No Cause for Indictment*; Sidney Fine, *Violence in the Model City*; National Advisory Commission on Civil Disturbances.

49. *Adam-12*.

50. *The Mod Squad* (1968–1973).

51. Bogle, *Primetime Blues*, 156–159.

52. *Room 222* (1969–1974); *The Blackboard Jungle* (1955, directed by Richard Brooks); for the Killens quotation, see Bogle, *Primetime Blues*, 163.

53. *Room 222*; Jacob Riis, *How the Other Half Lives*, New York: Scribner's, 1890.

54. *Adam-12*; *Baretta* (1975–1978;) *Starsky and Hutch*; Roland Barthes, *Mythologies*, New York: Hill & Wang, 1994 (originally published 1957); for the conflation of TV crime dramas with "reality" in the minds of white teachers in Harlem, see Kelley, *Yo Mama's Disfunktional!*

55. *Mannix*; *Starsky and Hutch*; *The Streets of San Francisco*.

56. *Adam-12*; Taylor and Dozier, "Television Violence, African-Americans and Social Control 1950–1976"; *Dirty Harry* (1971, directed by Don Siegel). On the Rodney King affair, see Lou Cannon, *Official Negligence*; Tom Owens, *Lying Eyes*: Staff of the *Los Angeles Times, Understanding the Riots: Los Angeles before and after the Rodney King Case*, 1992; *Report of the Independent Commission on the Los Angeles Police Department*, 1991.

57. National Advisory Commission on Civil Disturbances; *The Road to Anarchy: Findings of the Riot Study Commission of the New Jersey State Patrolmen's Benevolent Association Inc.*, Trenton, N.J.: 1968. Taylor and Dozier, "Television Violence, African–Americans and Social Control 1950–1976"; *Kojack* (1973–1978); *Baretta*; *Starsky and Hutch*; *Miami Vice*.

58. *Dirty Harry* (1971, directed by Don Siegel); *The Road to Anarchy*.

59. *Dirty Harry*.

60. *Death Wish* (1974, directed by Michael Winner).

61. Jim Sleeper, *The Closest of Strangers*, 253–254, 259; Haynes Johnson, *Sleepwalking through History: America in the Reagan Years*, New York: Doubleday, 1991.

62. Carlo Rotella, *Good with Their Hands: Boxers, Bluesmen and Other Characters from the Rust Belt*, Berkeley: University of California Press, 2002, 105–166; *The French Connection* (1971, directed by William Friedkin).

63. *Watermelon Man* (1970, directed by Mario Van Peebles). On Moreland's career, see Daniel J. Leab, *From Sambo to Superspade: The Black Experience in Motion Pictures*, Boston: Houghton Mifflin, 1975, 121, 132, 186–187, 246; Donald Bogle, *Toms, Coons, Mulattoes, Mammies and Bucks: An Interpretive History of Blacks in American Films*, New York: Continuum, 1994, 71–75, 101–102, 108–109, 129; Thomas Cripps, *Making Movies Black: The Hollywood Message Movie from World War II to the Civil Rights Era*, New York: Oxford University Press, 1993, 43, 48, 129, 133, 143, 145, 180, 184.

64. *A Raisin in the Sun* (1961, directed by Daniel Petrie); *Watermelon Man*.

65. *Sweet Sweetback's Baadasssss Song* (1971, directed by Mario Van Peebles). Bogle, *Toms, Coons, Mulattoes, Mammies and Bucks*, 234–238; Daniel J. Leab, *From Sambo to Superspade*, 242–249; Ed Guerrero, *Framing Blackness: The African-American Image in Film*, Philadelphia: Temple University Press, 1993, 86–91. The quotation is from Guerrero, 86.

66. Guerrero, *Framing Blackness*, 86–91; quotation in Leab, *From Sambo to Superspade*, 248–249.

67. *Shaft* (1971, directed by Gordon Parks, Jr.); *Shaft's Big Score* (1972, directed by Gordon Parks, Jr.); see, too, Leab, *From Sambo to Superspade*, 259; Guerrero, *Framing Blackness*, 91–94, 97; Bogle, *Toms, Coons*, 238–241.

68. *Superfly* (1972, directed by Gordon Parks, Jr.).

69. *Coffy* (1973, directed by Jack Hill); *Foxy Brown* (1974, directed by Jack Hill).

70. Robin D.G. Kelley, *Yo Mama's Disfunktional!*

71. William Julius Wilson, *The Truly Disadvantaged: The Inner City, the Underclass and Public Policy*, Chicago: University of Chicago Press, 1987; *Shaft*; *Dirty Harry*; *Superfly*; *Fort Apache, the Bronx* (1981, directed by Daniel Petrie).

72. Jerry Herron, *AfterCulture: Detroit and the Humiliation of History*, Detroit: Wayne State University Press, 1993; Sidney Fine, *Violence in the Model City*; Thomas Sugrue, *The Origins of the Urban Crisis*; William Adler, *Mollie's Job: A Story of Life and Work on the Global Assembly Line*, New York: Touchstone, 2001, 23–52; Lizabeth Cohen, *A Consumer's Republic;* Jackson, *Crabgrass Frontier*.

73. Bruce Kuklick, *To Every Thing a Season: Shibe Park and Urban Philadelphia, 1909–1976*, Princeton, N.J.: Princeton University Press, 1991.

74. Richard Gambino, *Blood of My Blood: The Dilemma of the Italian-Americans*, New York: Guernica, 1973, 325. Thomas Sugrue, *The Origins of the Urban Crisis*; *Death Wish*; *Superfly*; *Shaft*.

75. *Planet of the Apes* (1968, directed by Franklin J. Schaffner); *Beneath the Planet of the Apes* (1970, directed by Ted Post); John Godey, *The Taking of Pelham One Two Three*, New York: Putnam, 1973; *The Taking of Pelham One Two Three* (1974, directed by Joseph Sargent). See, too, David L. Pike, "Urban Nightmares and Future Visions: Life beneath New York," *Wide Angle* 20 (4): 8–50 (October 1998).

76. *Taxi Driver* (1976, directed by Martin Scorsese); *Midnight Cowboy* (1969, directed by John Schlesinger). On New York's mid-1970s fiscal crisis, see Cannato, *The Ungovernable City*.

77. On Wallace, see Dan T. Carter, *The Politics of Rage: George Wallace, the Origins of the New Conservatism and the Transformation of American Politics*, Baton Rouge: Louisiana State University Press, 2000; Marshall Frady, *Wallace*, New York: Random House, 1996. On Tony Imperiale, see Porambo, *No Cause for Indictment*, 174–189, 267–268, 272–276, 331–339; Edward H. Ransford, "Blue Collar Anger: Reactions to Student and Black Protest," *American Sociological Review* 37 (3): 333–346 (June 1972); Paul Goldberger, "Tony Imperiale Stands Vigilant for Law and Order," *New York Times Magazine,* September 29, 1969; David K. Shipler, "The White Niggers of Newark, *Harper's Magazine* 245: 77–83 (August 1972); Arthur M. Louis, "The Worst American City: A Scientific Study to Confirm or Deny Your Prejudices," *Harper's Magazine* 250: 67–71 (January 1975); John Gizzi, "Anthony Imperiale, R.I.P." *Human Events* 56 (2): 20 (January 21, 2000); "Anthony Imperiale, 68, Dies; Polarizing Force in Newark," *New York Times*, December 28, 1999, B9. On Boston's busing crisis, see Formisano, *Boston against Busing*, and Lukas, *Common Ground.*

78. *Taxi Driver* (1976, directed by Martin Scorsese); *Network* (1976, directed by Sidney Lumet); *Dirty Harry* (1971, directed by Don Siegel).

79. *Escape from New York* (1981, directed by John Carpenter).

80. Mike Davis, *Ecology of Fear: Los Angeles and the Imagination of Disaster*, New York: Metropolitan Books, 1998; Mike Davis, *Beyond Bladerunner: Urban Control, the Ecology of Fear*, Westfield, N.J.: Open Media, 1992; on Giuliani, see Jack Newfield, *The Full Rudy: The Man, the Myth, the Mania*, New York: Thunder's Mouth Press, 2002; Robert Polner, ed., *America's Mayor: The Hidden History of Rudy Giuliani's New York*, Brooklyn: Soft Skull Press, 2005; on private prisons, see Dennis J. Palumbo, "Privatization and Corrections Policy," *Policy Studies Review* 5 (3) (1986): 598–605; Michael Hallett, "Commerce With Criminals: The New Colonialism in Criminal Justice," Review of Policy Research 21 (1) (2004): 49–62.

81. *Escape from New York*; *Beneath the Planet of the Apes*; also, see Pike, "Urban Nightmares and Future Visions."

82. *Escape from New York*. On the disbuilding of urban neighborhoods in the Bronx, Newark, Detroit, and elsewhere, see Camilo Vergara, *The New American Ghetto,* New Brunswick, N.J.: Rutgers University Press, 1995; Camilo Vergara, *American Ruins*, New York: Monacelli Press, 1999.

83. *The Warriors* (1979, directed by Walter Hill); *RoboCop* (1987, directed by Paul Verhoeven); *Johnny Mnemonic* (1995, directed by Robert Longo).

84. *Escape From New York; Shaft; Superfly;* on Reagan era attitudes and policies toward cities, see Haynes Johnson, *Sleepwalking through History*, 116–124, 179–187.

85. *Escape from New York.* On enduring residential segregation by race, see Douglas S. Massey and Nancy A. Denton, *American Apartheid: Segregation and the Making of the Underclass*, Cambridge, Mass.: Harvard University Press, 1993. On gated communities and gentrification, see Mike Davis, *City of Quartz*; Mike Davis, *Ecology of Fear.*

86. *Annie Hall* (1977, directed by Woody Allen); *Manhattan* (1979, directed by Woody Allen); *Hannah and Her Sisters* (1986, directed by Woody Allen).

87. *Smoke* (1995, directed by Wayne Wang); Paul Auster, *The New York Trilogy*, New York: Penguin Books, 1990. On the gentrification of formerly bohemian and downscale spaces in Manhattan, such as the Lower East Side, see Janet L. Abu-Lughod, *From Urban Village to East Village: The Battle for New York's Lower East Side*, Cambridge, Mass.: Blackwell, 1994; Christopher Mele, *Selling the Lower East Side: Culture, Real Estate and Resistance in New York City*, Minneapolis: University of Minnesota Press, 2000; Clayton

Patterson, ed., *Resistance: A Radical Political and Social History of the Lower East Side*, New York: Seven Stories Press, 2007.

88. *Clockers* (1995, directed by Spike Lee); *Four Brothers* (2005, directed by John Singleton); *Boyz 'n the Hood* (1991, directed by John Singleton). Massey and Denton, *American Apartheid*.

89. Donald Bogle, *Primetime Blues: African Americans on Network Television*, New York: Farrar, Straus & Giroux, 2001, 252. *Hill Street Blues* (1981–1987). On urban policies during the 1980s, see Haynes Johnson, *Sleepwalking through History*, 116–124, 179–187.

90. *Hill Street Blues*; *Fort Apache, the Bronx*.

91. On the MOVE disaster, Buzz Bissinger, *A Prayer for the City*, New York: Random House, 1997, 23; John Anderson and Hilary Hevenor, *Burning Down the House: MOVE and the Tragedy of Philadelphia*, New York: W. W. Norton, 1987; Robin Erica Wagner-Pacifici, *Discourse and Destruction: The City of Philadelphia versus MOVE*, Chicago: University of Chicago Press, 1994; Michael Boyette, *"Let It Burn!": The Philadelphia Tragedy*, Chicago: Contemporary Books, 1989. See, too, the John Edgar Wideman novel *Philadelphia Fire*, New York: Holt, 1990. On Diallo, see Kadiatou Diallo, *My Heart Will Cross This Ocean: My Story, My Son*, New York: One World, 2003.

92. Bogle, *Primetime Blues*, 273–274.

93. On King, see Lou Cannon, *Official Negligence*; Tom Owens, *Lying Eyes*; Staff of the *Los Angeles Times, Understanding the Riots; Report of the Independent Commission on the Los Angeles Police Department*.

94. *Jungle Fever* (1991, directed by Spike Lee). On Dinkins and the Giuliani campaign, see Wilbur C. Rich, *David Dinkins and New York City Politics: Race, Images and the Media*, Albany: State University of New York Press, 2007; J. Phillip Thompson, *Double Trouble: Black Mayors, Black Communities, and the Call for a Deep Democracy*, New York: Oxford University Press, 2005.

95. "Jesse Helms Blocks the Racial Integration of the Fourth Circuit Court of Appeals," *Journal of Blacks in Higher Education* 29: 48–49 (Autumn 2000); "North Carolina as the Next Target for the Affirmative Action Abolitionists," *Journal of Blacks in Higher Education* 19: 74–75 (Spring 1998); "Strike Three for a Senior Antiblack Member of the U.S. Senate," *Journal of Blacks in Higher Education* 34: 32 (Winter 2001–2002); Xinshu Zhao and Steven H. Chaffee, "Campaign Advertisements versus Television News as Sources of Political Issue Information," *Public Opinion Quarterly* 59 (1): 41–65 (Spring 1995).

96. On Cabrini Green, see Mischa Gaus, "The Olympic Hustle," *In These Times*, July 2007, 20–23; on Mayor Byrne and her successor, see Paul Kleppner, *Chicago Divided: The Making of a Black Mayor*, DeKalb: Northern Illinois University Press, 1985, 50, 139, 142–143, 154; on SDS volunteers confronting suburban slumlords in Newark, see *Troublemakers* (1966, produced by Newsreel Films); on Koch and homelessness, see Haynes Johnson, *Sleepwalking through History*, 243, 250.

97. *NYPD Blue* (1993–2005); *Homicide: Life on the Street* (1993–1999); *Hill Street Blues*; *The Wire* (2002–present).

98. Rhonda Y. Williams, *The Politics of Public Housing: Black Women's Struggles against Urban Inequality*, New York: Oxford University Press, 2004, 37–47, 58–63, 113–123, 124–154.

99. *NYPD Blue*.

100. *Homicide: Life on the Street*. See, too, Thomas A. Mascaro, "Shades of Black on Homicide: Life on the Street: Progress in Portrayals of African American Men," *Journal*

of Popular Film and Television 32 (1): 56–57 (Spring 2004). On Baltimore's racist history of urban renewal, black displacement, and hyper-segregation of public housing, see Rhonda Y. Williams, *The Politics of Public Housing*; see, too, Sugrue, *The Origins of the Urban Crisis*, for white resistance to black homeowners from the 1940s to the 1960s. Similar resistance occurred in Slavic sections of Philadelphia; see Robert M. Zecker, " '*Negrov Lynčovanie* and the Unbearable Whiteness of Slovaks': The Immigrant Press Covers Race," *American Studies* 43 (2): 43–72 (Spring 2002). For the history of federally subsidized white flight, the best work remains Kenneth Jackson, *Crabgrass Frontier*.

101. Haynes Johnson, *Sleepwalking through History*.

102. Daniel P. Moynihan, *The Negro Family: The Case for National Action*, Washington, D.C.: Office of Policy Planning and Research, U.S. Department of Labor, 1965.

103. Nathan Heard, *Howard Street*, Edinburgh, Scotland: Payback Press, 1998 (originally published 1968); *Boyz 'n the Hood* (1991, directed by John Singleton). On 1980s and 1990s black cinema, see Manthia Diawara, "Noir by Noirs: Towards a New Realism in Black Cinema," *African American Review* 27 (4): 525–537 (Winter 1993).

104. *Boyz 'n the Hood*; *Four Brothers* (2005, directed by John Singleton). See, too, Jerry Herron, *AfterCulture: Detroit and the Humiliation of History*; Dan Georgakas and Marvin Surkin, *Detroit, I Do Mind Dying: A Study in Urban Revolution*, New York: St. Martin's Press, 1975.

105. *Clockers*; Richard Price, *Clockers*, Boston: Houghton Mifflin, 1992. Price sets his novel in a fictionalized Jersey City. On the deliberate ghettoization of high–rise public-housing projects, see Hirsch, *Making the Second Ghetto*; Sugrue, *The Origins of the Urban Crisis*; Williams, *The Politics of Public Housing*.

106. *Clockers;* Richard Price, *Clockers*. See, too, Paula J. Massood, "Which Way to the Promised Land? Spike Lee's *Clockers* and the Legacy of the African American City," *African American Review* 35 (2): 263–279 (Summer 2001). Lee's film *He Got Game* (1998) demonstrates that prison is the only other avenue out of the Coney Island, Brooklyn, projects for those not blessed with Jesus Shuttlesworth's basketball talents.

107. *Jungle Fever.*

108. *Freedomland* (2006, directed by Joe Roth); Richard Price, *Freedomland*, New York: Broadway Books, 1998.

109. On the Kensington neighborhood in Philadelphia, see Bissinger, *A Prayer for the City*, 66–75.

110. *Cops* (1989–present); *Mutual of Omaha's Wild Kingdom* (1963–1988).

111. *The Godfather* (1972, directed by Francis Ford Coppola).

112. Michael Novak, *The Rise of the Unmeltable Ethnics: Politics and Culture in the Seventies*, New York: Macmillan, 1971. See, too, Richard Gambino, *Blood of My Blood: The Dilemma of the Italian-Americans*, New York: Guernica, 1973, for a mid-1970s defense of the moral primacy of the Italian family although Gambino angrily denies the validity to images of Italian criminality in film and elsewhere.

113. *Mean Streets* (1973, directed by Martin Scorsese).

114. *Mean Streets*; *Goodfellas* (1990, directed by Martin Scorsese); *A Bronx Tale* (1993, directed by Robert De Niro).

115. *Goodfellas*. In *A Bronx Tale*, too, characters have colorful nicknames such as JoJo the Whale, Jimmy Whispers, Eddie Mush, and Frankie Coffeecake.

116. *Goodfellas*.

117. *A Bronx Tale*; *Fort Apache, the Bronx*.

118. George Clinton, "Chocolate City"; Lehman, *The Promised Land*.

CHAPTER 5: "ALL OF LIFE WAS THERE BEFORE": THE URBAN NOSTALGIC MEMOIR

1. Barbara Wilson Tinker, *When the Fire Reaches Us*, New York: Modern Literary Editions, 1970, 8.

2. Tinker, *When the Fire Reaches Us*, 23, 33, 41–43, 45–50. On labor-market discrimination in Detroit, see Thomas N. Maloney and Warren C. Whatley, "Making the Effort: The Contours of Racial Discrimination in Detroit's Labor Markets, 1920–1940," *Journal of Economic History* 55 (3): 465–493 (September 1995).

3. Paul Kavieff, *The Purple Gang: Organized Crime in Detroit, 1910–1945*, Fort Lee, N.J.: Barricade Books, 2005; Albert Fried, *The Rise and Fall of the Jewish Gangster in America*, New York: Columbia University Press, 1993, 103–108.

4. Tinker, *When the Fire Reaches Us*, 69, 86.

5. Sidney Fine, *Violence in the Model City: The Cavanagh Administration, Race Relations and the Detroit Riot of 1967*, Ann Arbor: University of Michigan Press, 1989, 56–60, 63, 101, 104–111, 116–117, 120–125, 148–154. See, too, Albert Bergesen, "Race Riots of 1967: An Analysis of Police Violence in Detroit and Newark," *Journal of Black Studies* 12 (3): 261–274 (March 1982); Kenneth O'Reilly, "The FBI and the Politics of the Riots, 1964–1968," *Journal of American History* 75 (1): 91–114 (June 1988); Max Arthur Herman, *Fighting in the Streets: Ethnic Succession and Urban Unrest in Twentieth-Century America*, New York: Peter Lang, 2005, 75–89; Benjamin D. Singer, Richard W. Osborn, and James A. Geschwender, *Black Rioters*, New York: Heath Lexington, 1970; Joe R. Feagin and Harlan Hahn, *Ghetto Revolts: The Politics of Violence in American Cities*, New York: Macmillan, 1973, 152, 153, 161–165, 173, 176–177, 189, 195, 264–265; Tinker, *When the Fire Reaches Us*, 143, 148–149, 171–173.

6. Fine, *Violence in the Model City*, 167, 188, 195, 199–203, 225–232.

7. Tinker, *When the Fire Reaches Us*, 148–149.

8. Tinker, *When the Fire Reaches Us*, 69.

9. Tinker, *When the Fire Reaches Us*, 254.

10. Nathan Heard, *Howard Street*, Edinburgh, Scotland: Payback Press, 1998 (originally published 1968). See, too, Ron Porambo, *No Cause for Indictment: An Autopsy of Newark*, New York: Holt, Rinehart & Winston, 1971; Nathan Wright, *Ready to Riot*, New York: Holt, Rinehart & Winston, 1968; Joseph M. Conforti, "Ghetto or City?" *Society* 9 (10), "Special Issue: The Nation of Newark," 20–34 (September/October 1972); Tom Hayden, *Rebellion in Newark: Official Violence and Ghetto Response*, New York: Vintage Books, 1967.

11. Nathan Heard, *Howard Street*, 18, 41, 64, 93, 114, 137, 170. See, too, Conforti, "Ghetto or City?" 26, 29; Porambo, *No Cause for Indictment*, 60–63, 69–72, 258–266; John T. Cunningham, *Newark*, Newark: New Jersey Historical Society, 1988, 326, 334–335; Wright, *Ready to Riot*.

12. Jerry Herron, *AfterCulture: Detroit and the Humiliation of History*, Detroit: Wayne State University Press, 1993. For Detroiters' resistance to deindustrialization, see, too, Dan Georgakas and Marvin Surkin, *Detroit, I Do Mind Dying: A Study in Urban Revolution*, New York: St. Martin's Press, 1975.

13. Juke Boy Bonner, "Goin' Back to the Country"; John Lee Hooker, "Motor City's Burning."

14. Herron, *AfterCulture*, 198–201; Tyree Guyton, Rebecca Margolis, and Jerry W. Ward, Jr., "Triangulation," *Literature and Medicine* 15 (1): 74–87 (1996); Wendy S. Walters, "Turning the Neighborhood Inside Out: Imagining a New Detroit in Tyree Guyton's Heidelberg Project," *Drama Review* 43 (4): 64–93 (Winter 2001).

15. See Harry Golden on tour buses to the exotic Jewish Lower East Side circa 1910, in Hutchins Hapgood, *The Spirit of the Ghetto: Studies of the Jewish Quarter of New York*, with commentary by Harry Golden, New York: Schocken, 1966 (originally Funk & Wagnalls, 1902).

16. Linda Hamalian, "Kea Tawana: Or Who Would Build a Better Ark Than Noah?" *Black-American Literature Forum* 21 (1–2): 97–112 (Spring/Summer 1987); Holly Metz, "Where Am I Going: Kea's Ark, Newark, New Jersey," *Southern Quarterly* 39 (1–2): 197–216 (2001).

17. Kenneth Jackson, *Crabgrass Frontier: The Suburbanization of the United States*, New York: Oxford University Press, 1985, 274–276.

18. Philip Roth, *American Pastoral*, New York: Vintage Books, 1997, 197; Larry Schwartz, "Roth, Race and Newark," www.eserver.org/clogic/2005/schwartz.html.

19. Roth, *American Pastoral*, 11.

20. Roth, *American Pastoral*, 10.

21. Conforti, "Ghetto or City?" 25; Clement A. Price, "The Struggle to Desegregate Newark: Black Middle Class Militancy in New Jersey, 1932–1947," *New Jersey History* 99 (3–4): 215–228 (1981).

22. Jewish Welfare Board, "Survey of Newark," July 1940, cited in Schwartz, "Roth, Race and Newark."

23. Schwartz, "Roth, Race and Newark." See, too, for poverty in 1940s–1950s Newark, Nathan Wright, *Ready to Riot*; George Sternlieb, *The Tenement Landlord*, New Brunswick, N.J.: Rutgers University Press, 1996; Harold Kaplan, *Urban Renewal Politics: Slum Clearance in Newark*, New York: Columbia University Press, 1963; Conforti, "Ghetto or City?"; Cunningham, *Newark*. See *Troublemakers* (1966, Newsreel Films) for a confrontation with a suburban slumlord by organizers for the Newark Community Union Project (NCUP). See, too, the photographs of Samuel Gottscho and William Schleisner taken for the Newark Housing Authority in 1944, and the Farm Security Administration photos of Newark's 1939 homeless colony, American Memory collection of the Library of Congress, Prints and Photographs Division, photo digital IDs gsc 5a11133, gsc 5a11135, gsa 5a11136, fsa 8b17616, fsa 8b16717, fsa 8b17621.

24. Audrey Olsen Faulkner, ed., *When I Was Comin' Up: An Oral History of Aged Blacks*, Hamden, Conn.: Archon Books, 1982; Philip Roth, *The Human Stain*, New York: Vintage Books, 2000, 322; Roth, *American Pastoral*.

25. Roth, *American Pastoral*, 13–14.

26. William Adler, *Mollie's Job: A Story of Life and Work on the Global Assembly Line*, New York: Touchstone, 2001; Conforti, "Ghetto or City?" Clark Taylor, "Parasitic Suburbs," *Society* 9 (10), "Special Issue: The Nation of Newark": 35–41 (September/October 1972); Cunningham, *Newark*, 299–300. On suburban shopping malls, see Lizabeth Cohen, *A Consumer's Republic: The Politics of Mass Consumption in Postwar America*, New York: Vintage Books, 2004. The Garden State Plaza was developed for the R. H. Macy Co., indicating that some large downtown department stores were already directing their retail space away from places such as Paterson and Newark.

27. Jackson, *Crabgrass Frontier*; George Lipsitz, *The Possessive Investment in Whiteness: How White People Profit from Identity Politics*, Philadelphia: Temple University Press, 2006; Conforti, "Ghetto or City?"

28. Clark Taylor, "Parasitic Suburbs," *Society* 9 (10), "Special Issue: The Nation of Newark": 35–41 (September/October 1972).

29. Taylor, "Parasitic Suburbs."

30. Roth, *American Pastoral*, 24–25.

31. Roth, *American Pastoral*, 27.

32. Roth, *American Pastoral*, 40.

33. Curtis Lucas, *Third Ward Newark*, New York: Ziff-Davis Publishing Co., 1946. See, too, Lipsitz, *The Possessive Investment in Whiteness*. In Newark, middle-class blacks who attempted to move into white areas evidently were fiercely resisted. See Clement Price, "The Struggle to Desegregate Newark."

34. Roth, *American Pastoral*, 40. On 1946's wildcat strike wave, see George Lipsitz, *Rainbow at Midnight: Labor and Culture in the 1940s,* Urbana: University of Illinois Press, 1994, 136–154. On fiction regarding antiblack hate strikes, see Marge Piercy, *Gone to Soldiers*, New York: Summit Books, 1987, 295–296; see, too, Lipsitz, *Rainbow at Midnight*, 69–92.

35. Philip Roth, *The Plot against America*, Boston: Houghton Mifflin, 2004, 250–251. For Zwillman, see Mark Stuart, *Gangster Number Two: Longy Zwillman, the Man Who Invented Organized Crime*, Secaucus, N.J.: Lyle Stuart, 1985.

36. Roth, *The Plot against America*, 237–286. On Detroit's 1943 riots, see Janet L. Langlois, "The Belle Isle Bridge Incident: Legend Dialectic and Semiotic System in the 1943 Detroit Race Riots," *Journal of American Folklore* 96 (380): 183–199 (April/June 1983); Marilyn Johnson, "Gender, Race and Rumor: Re-Examining the 1943 Race Riots," *Gender and History* 10 (2): 252–277 (1998); Domenic Capeci and Martha Wilkerson, "The Detroit Rioters of 1943," *Michigan Historical Review* 16 (1): 49–72 (1990); Sharon McHaney, "Detroit's 1943 Riot," *Michigan History* 77 (3): 34–39 (1993); Karen Huck, "The Arsenal on Fire: The Reader in the Riot, 1943," *Critical Studies in Mass Communications* 10 (1): 23–48 (1993). On the zoot suit riots, see Eduardo Obregon Pagan, *Murder at the Sleepy Lagoon: Zoot Suit Riots, Race, and Riot in Wartime L.A.*, Chapel Hill: University of North Carolina Press, 2003; Mauricio Mazan, *The Zoot-Suit Riots: The Psychology of Symbolic Annihilation*, Austin: University of Texas Press, 1984.

37. Roth, *The Plot against America*, 331; Grace Elizabeth Hale, *Making Whiteness: The Culture of Segregation in the South, 1890–1940*, New York: Vintage Books, 1999.

38. Jeffrey Eugenides, *Middlesex,* New York: Vintage Books, 2002, 92–102, 135–143.

39. Eugenides, *Middlesex*, 169; Tinker, *When the Fire Reaches Us;* Sidney Fine, *Violence in the Model City*; Hahn and Feagin, *Ghetto Revolts*.

40. Marge Piecy, *Gone to Soldiers*, New York: Summit Books, 1987, 330–334. See, too, Domenic Capeci, "Black-Jewish Relations in Wartime Detroit," *Jewish Social Studies* 47 (3–4): 221–242 (1985).

41. Piercy, *Gone to Soldiers*, 295.

42. Piercy, *Gone to Soldiers*, 296.

43. Thomas Bell, *Out of This Furnace*, Pittsburgh: University of Pittsburgh Press, 1976 (originally published 1941), 327–330; see, too, Robert M. Zecker, "'Negrov Lynčovanie' and the Unbearable Whiteness of Slovaks: The Immigrant Press Covers Race," *American Studies* 43 (2): 43–72 (Summer 2002).

44. Roth, *American Pastoral*, 45, 75.

45. Roth, *American Pastoral*, 54–55.

46. Sherry Ortner, *New Jersey Dreaming: Capital, Culture and the Class of '58*, Durham, N.C.: Duke University Press, 2003, 69–71, 86–87, 218–220.

47. Ortner, *New Jersey Dreaming*, 31–37. On Newark organized crime, see Conforti, "Ghetto or City?" 26, 29; Stuart, *Gangster Number Two*; see, too, the 747-page FBI file on Abner "Longy" Zwillman, available at www.foia.fbi.gov/zwillman.htm.

48. Conforti, "Ghetto or City?" 26, 29; John T. Cunningham, *Newark*, 334–336; Porambo, *No Cause for Indictment*; Jerry Gaffio Watts, *Amiri Baraka: The Politics and*

Art of a Black Intellectual, New York: New York University Press, 2001, 350–351; Roth, *American Pastoral*, 345–347.

49. Roth, *American Pastoral*, 163–164. Jerry Gaffio Watts, *Amiri Baraka*, 348–367; John T. Cunningham, *Newark*, 337–338; Fred Barbaro, "Political Brokers," *Society* 9 (10), "Special Issue: The Nation of Newark": 42–54 (September/October 1972); Robert Curvin, "Black Power in City Hall," *Society* 9 (10), "Special Issue: The Nation of Newark": 55–58 (September/October 1972); Mfanya D. Tryman, "Black Mayoralty Campaigns: Running the 'Race,'" *Phylon* 35 (4): 346–358 (1974); Richard Krickus, "Organizing Neighborhoods: Gary and Newark," *Dissent* 19 (1): 107–117 (1972); Robert Curvin, *The Persistent Minority: The Black Political Experience in Newark*, Princeton, N.J.: Princeton University Press, 1975. See, too, the oral histories with Mayor Kenneth Gibson at the New York Public Library, Schomburg Center Oral History Tape Collection, Sc-Audio C-122.

50. Ron Porambo, *No Cause for Indictment*; George Sternlieb, *The Tenement Landlord*, New Brunswick, N.J.: Rutgers University Press, 1966.

51. Roth, *American Pastoral*, 345.

52. Roth, *American Pastoral*, 307.

53. Thomas Sugrue, *The Origins of the Urban Crisis: Race and Inequality in Postwar Detroit*, Princeton, N.J.: Princeton University Press, 1996; Arnold Hirsch, *Making the Second Ghetto: Race and Housing in Chicago, 1940–1960*, Chicago: University of Chicago Press, 1998; George Lipsitz, *The Possessive Investment in Whiteness: How White People Profit from Identity Politics*, Philadelphia: Temple University Press, 2006.

54. Conforti, "Ghetto or City?" 25–26, 28–29; Cunningham, *Newark*, 314–342; Porambo, *No Cause for Indictment*; Hayden, *Rebellion in Newark*.

55. Jonathan Rieder, *Canarsie: The Jews and Italians of Brooklyn against Liberalism*, Cambridge, Mass.: Harvard University Press, 1985, 20–26; 94. See, too, Walter Thabit, *How East New York Became a Ghetto*, New York: New York University Press, 2003.

56. Roth, *American Pastoral*, 235–237, 400; Clark Taylor, "Parasitic Suburbs."

57. Roth, *American Pastoral*, 161–165.

58. Roth, *American Pastoral*, 268–269; Porambo, *No Cause for Indictment*; Tom Hayden, *Rebellion in Newark: Official Violence and Ghetto Response*, New York: Vintage Books, 1967.

59. Philip Roth, *The Human Stain*, New York: Vintage Books, 2000, 330–331.

60. Clark Taylor, "Parasitic Suburbs," *Society* 9 (10), "Special Issue: The Nation of Newark": 35 (September/October 1972).

61. Jonathan Kozol, *Savage Inequalities: Children in America's Schools*, New York: Crown, 1991.

62. Roth, *The Human Stain*, 332. Ironically, it was opposition to urban renewal that in part triggered the 1967 Newark urban disturbances. A plan to bulldoze a large part of the Central Ward to accommodate a university and medical center expansion was bitterly resisted. Joseph M. Conforti, "Ghetto or City?" *Society* 9 (10), "Special Issue: The Nation of Newark": 25–26, 28 (September/October 1972); Cunningham, *Newark*, 315–316.

63. Roth, *The Human Stain*, 328–329.

64. Conforti, "Ghetto or City?" 25–31.

65. Audrey Olsen Faulkner, ed., *When I Was Comin' Up: An Oral History of Aged Blacks*, Hamden, Conn.: Archon Books, 1982.

66. Mikhail Bakhtin, *The Dialogic Imagination: Four Essays*, Austin: University of Texas Press, 1981.

67. Jeffrey Eugenides, *Middlesex*, New York: Vintage Books, 2002, 235.

68. Eugenides, *Middlesex*, 239.

69. Sugrue, *The Origins of the Urban Crisis*; Fine, *Violence in the Model City*; Albert Bergesen, "Race Riots of 1967: An Analysis of Police Violence in Detroit and Newark," *Journal of Black Studies* 12 (3): 261–274 (March 1982); Kenneth O'Reilly, "The FBI and the Politics of the Riots, 1964–1968," *Journal of American History* 75 (1): 91–114 (June 1988); Max Arthur Herman, *Fighting in the Streets: Ethnic Succession and Urban Unrest in Twentieth-Century America*, New York: Peter Lang, 2005, 75–89; Benjamin D. Singer, Richard W. Osborn, and James A. Geschwender, *Black Rioters*, New York: Heath Lexington, 1970; Joe R. Feagin and Harlan Hahn, *Ghetto Revolts: The Politics of Violence in American Cities*, New York: Macmillan, 1973, 152, 153, 161–165, 173, 176–177, 189, 195, 264–265.

70. Eugenides, *Middlesex*, 240.

71. Sugrue, *The Origins of the Urban Crisis,* 209–229, 233–241; Thomas Sugrue, "Crabgrass–Roots Politics: Race, Rights, and the Reaction against Liberalism in the Urban North, 1940–1964," *Journal of American History* 82 (2): 551–578 (September 1995).

72. Eugenides, *Middlesex*, 246, 248.

73. Eugenides, *Middlesex,* 250. National Advisory Commission on Civil Disorders (the Kerner Commission), Washington, D.C.: U.S. Government Printing Office, 1968; Fine, *Violence in the Model City.*

74. Barbara Wilson Tinker, *When the Fire Reaches Us*, New York: Modern Literary Editions, 1970, 192; Fine, *Violence in the Model City.*

75. Eugenides, *Middlesex*, 252–256.

76. Eugenides, *Middlesex*, 110–125; Roth, *The Plot against America*, 174, 250, 270, 281–282, 287–288, 298–300. See, for real–life Detroit gangsters, Paul Kavieff, *The Purple Gang: Organized Crime in Detroit, 1910–1945*, Fort Lee, N.J.: Barricade Books, 2005; Albert Fried, *The Rise and Fall of the Jewish Gangster in America*, New York: Columbia University Press, 1993, 103–108. For Newark's Zwillman, see Mark Stuart, *Gangster Number Two* and www.foia.fbi.gov/zwillman.htm.

77. Gerard Jones, *Men of Tomorrow: Geeks, Gangsters and the Birth of the Comic Book*, New York: Basic Books, 2004, 44–45, 105–106, 265, 311; Roth, *The Plot against America*, 287.

78. Jones, *Men of Tomorrow,* 44–45, 105–106, 265, 311; www.foia.fbi.gov/zwillman.htm.

79. Roth, *The Plot against America*, 174, 250–251, 270–271, 281–282, 287–288, 298–300.

80. Mike Gold, *Jews without Money*, New York: Avon Books, 1965 (originally published 1930).

81. Herron, *AfterShock.*

82. *The Wire*, Season 2, Episode 1.

83. *The Wire*, Season 2, Episodes 6 and 9. On the history of public housing in Baltimore, see Rhonda Y. Williams, *The Politics of Public Housing: Black Women's Struggles against Urban Inequality*, New York: Oxford University Press, 2004.

84. *The Wire*, Season 1, Episode 2. For the proximate cause of the 1967 Newark riot, see Hayden, *Rebellion in Newark.*

85. *The Wire*, Season 2, Episodes 1 and 7.

86. *The Wire*, Season 2, Episodes 6 and 7. On intermittent racial strife and cooperation on the docks of Baltimore and other cities, see Frank Towers, "Job Busting at Baltimore Shipyards: Racial Violence in the Civil War-Era South," *Journal of Southern History*

66 (2): 221–256 (May 2000); Eric Arnesen, *Waterfront Workers of New Orleans: Race, Class and Politics, 1863–1923*, Urbana: University of Illinois Press, 1991; Calvin Winslow, ed., *Waterfront Workers: New Perspectives on Race and Class*, Urbana: University of Illinois Press, 1998.

87. *The Wire*, Season 2, Episodes 1 and 3.

88. *The Wire*, Season 2, Episodes 1 and 6.

89. *The Wire*, Season 2, Episode 7.

90. *The Wire*, Season 2, Episode 5; Season 3.

91. *The Wire*, Season 2, Episodes 3 and 5; Bruce Springsteen, "My Home Town."

92. *The Wire*, Season 2, Episode 4.

93. *The Sopranos*, Season 1, Episode 1.

94. *The Sopranos*, Season 4, Episode 7; Season 1, Episode 7.

95. *The Sopranos*, Season 4, Episode 7. See, too, Christopher Kocela, "Unmade Men: *The Sopranos* after Whiteness," *Postmodern Culture* 15 (2): (January 2005).

96. *The Sopranos*, Season 5, Episode 3.

97. *The Sopranos*, Season 4, Episode 3.

98. *The Sopranos*, Season 6, Episode 9.

99. *The Sopranos*, Season 6, Episode 8; Season 7, Episode 8.

CHAPTER 6: "WE NEVER LOCKED OUR DOORS AT NIGHT": NEWARK ON THE NET, MINUS THE MOB

1. *The Sopranos*, Season 4, Episode 7.

2. Alessandro Aurigi and Stephen Graham, "The 'Crisis' in the Urban Public Realm," in Brian D. Loader, ed., *Cyberspace Divide: Equality, Agency and Policy in the Information Society*, New York: Routledge, 1998, 57–80; Stephen Graham and Simon Marvin, *Splintering Urbanism: Networked Infrastructures, Technological Mobility and the Urban Condition*, New York: Routledge, 2001.

3. http://www.cityofjerseycity.org/; http://www.geocities.com/senafp/Passaic125thCelebration.html. For the Passaic Textile strike, see Paul L. Murphy, *The Passaic Textile Strike of 1926*, Belmont, Calif.: Wadsworth, 1974; David J. Goldberg, *A Tale of Three Cities: Labor Organization and Protest in Paterson, Passaic, and Lawrence, 1916–1921*, New Brunswick, N.J.: Rutgers University Press, 1989; Albert Weisbord, *Passaic: The Story of a Struggle against Starvation Wages and for the Right to Organize*, New York: AMS Press, 1976 (originally published 1926).

4. Dolores Hayden, *The Power of Place: Urban Landscapes as Public History*, Cambridge, Mass.: M.I.T. Press, 1995.

5. www.oldnewark.com/memories/thirdward/bodizwill.htm.

6. Alison Adam and Eileen Green, "Gender, Agency, Location, and the New Information Society," in Loader, ed., *Cyberspace Divide*, 95.

7. Kenneth Jackson, *Crabgrass Frontier: The Suburbanization of the United States*, New York: Oxford University Press, 1985, 201–202, 211–212, 225, 274–276; Nathan Wright, Jr., *Ready to Riot*, New York: Holt, Rinehart & Winston, 1968, 49–59, 82–83.

8. Jerry Gafio Watts, *Amiri Baraka: The Politics and Art of a Black Intellectual*, New York: New York University Press, 2001, 348–354.

9. Peter Way, "Evil Humors and Ardent Spirits: The Rough Culture of Canal Construction Laborers," *Journal of American History* (79 (4):1397–1428 (March 1993).

10. Watts, *Amiri Baraka*, 349–350.

11. www.virtualnewarknj.com/associations/info/roselion/1948image.htm; www.virtualnewarknj.com/busind/images/rest/goldas/bowlingteam.jpg.

12. www.oldnewark.com/memories/firstward/lucas01.htm; www.oldnewark.com/memories/firstward/lucas02.htm; www.oldnewark.com/memories/firstward/fabiano.htm; www.oldnewark.com/memories/firstward/manginerem.htm.

13. Jerry Herron, *AfterCulture: Detroit and the Humiliation of History,* Detroit: Wayne State University Press, 1993, 17–24, 64. Quotation is on 24.

14. Michael Immerso, *Newark's Little Italy: The Vanished First Ward,* New Brunswick, N.J.: Rutgers University Press, 1997. On Zwillman, see www.oldnewark.com/memories/thirdward/bodizwill.htm, as well as Thomas Reppetto, *American Mafia: A History of Its Rise to Power,* New York: Henry Holt, 2004, 142, 161, 204–205, 248–250; Burton B. Turkus and Sid Feder, *Murder, Inc.: The Story of the* Syndicate, Cambridge, Mass.: DaCapo Press, 2003 (originally published 1951), 331–362. On the Victoria Castle and the Sorrento, see www.oldnewark.com/memories/firstward/fabiano.htm.

15. On Moretti's career and demise, see Reppetto, *American Mafia,* 141–145, 151, 161, 216–218, 233, 248, 265–267; Turkus and Feder, *Murder, Inc.,* 351–353; www.rotten.com/library/bio/crime/mafia/willie–moretti.

16. www.oldnewark.com/memories/firstward/fabiano.htm.

17. Nathan Wright, Jr., *Ready to Riot,* New York: Holt, Rinehart & Winston, 1968, 5.

18. John T. Cunningham, *Newark,* Newark: The New Jersey Historical Society, 1988, 326, 334–335. See also Wright, *Ready to Riot,* 105; Ron Porambo, *No Cause for Indictment: An Autopsy of Newark,* New York: Holt, Rinehart & Winston, 1971, 60–63, 69–72, 258–266.

19. Watts, *Amiri Baraka,* 350–351.

20. www.oldnewark.com/memories/west/certobook.htm; www.oldnewark.com/memories/west/labruno.htm; www.oldnewark.com/memories/vailsburg/sharon.htm. On Prince Street, see www.oldnewark.com/memories/thirdward/bodprince.htm; www.oldnewark.com/memories/thirdward/mccolganstores.htm.

21. Sherry B. Ortner, *New Jersey Dreaming: Capital, Culture, and the Class of '58,* Durham, N.C.: Duke University Press, 2003, 31–37.

22. www.oldnewark.com/memories/thirdward/bodizwill.htm.

23. www.oldnewark.com/memories/thirdward/bodizwill.htm; http://www.oldnewark.com/memories/newark/bodianprohibition.htm; www.oldnewark.com/memories/newark/bodinazis.com; www.oldnewark.com/memories/thirdward/bodianfuneral.htm.

24. www.foia.fbi.gov/zwillman.htm.

25. www.oldnewark.com/memories/bios/bodanellen.htm. For a more praiseworthy assessment of Ellenstein's and Villani's role in Newark's slum–clearance policies, see Kaplan, *Urban Renewal Politics: Slum Clearance in Newark,* New York: Columbia University Press, 1963.

26. www.oldnewark.com/memories/thirdward/bodianriviera.htm; www.oldnewark.com/memories/weequahic/bodiantavrest.htm.

27. www.oldnewark.com/memories/thirdward/bodizwill.htm.

28. Rachel Rubin, *Jewish Gangsters of Modern Literature,* Urbana: University of Illinois Press, 2000; Rich Cohen, *Tough Jews,* New York: Simon & Schuster, 1998.

29. Jonathan Rieder, *Canarsie: The Jews and Italians of Brooklyn against Liberalism,* Cambridge, Mass.: Harvard University Press, 1985, 21, 25; www.oldnewark.com/memories/thirdward/bodiannames.htm. On Murder Inc.'s infiltration of the New York garment industry, as well as the Amalgamated Clothing Workers of America, see Turkus and Feder, *Murder Inc.,* 331–362, and Steven Fraser, *Labor Will Rule: Sidney Hillman and the Rise of American Labor,* Ithaca, N.Y.: Cornell University Press, 1991, 242–258.

30. FBI file, Abner Zwillman, available at www.foia.fbi.gov/zwillman.htm.

31. www.foia.fbi.gov/zwillman.htm; www.oldnewark.com/memories/thirdward/bodian-riviera.htm.

32. Ortner, *New Jersey Dreaming*, 64–65, 118.

33. www.oldnewark.com/memories/weequahic/bodiansyds.htm.

34. www.oldnewark.com/memories/firstward/manginerem.htm.

35. www.virtualnewarknj.com.

36. See, for example, the photographs of Samuel Gottscho and William Schleisner taken for the Newark Housing Authority in 1944, and the Farm Security Administration photos of Newark's 1939 homeless colony, in the American Memory collection of the Library of Congress, Prints and Photographs Division, photo digital IDs gsc 5a11133, gsc 5a11134, gsc 5a11135, gsa 5a11136, fsa 8b17 616, fsa 8b17617, fsa 8b17621.

37. Wright, *Ready to Riot*, 14. On slum conditions in Newark, see, too, Harold Kaplan, *Urban Renewal Politics: Slum Clearance in Newark,* New York: Columbia University Press, 1963; George Sternlieb and Robert W. Burchell, *Residential Abandonment: The Tenement Landlord Revisited,* New Brunswick, N.J.: Rutgers University Press, 1973.

38. *Troublemakers* (1966, Newsreel Films). On the Newark Community Union Project and the 1967 rebellion, see, too, Tom Hayden, *Rebellion in Newark: Official Violence and Ghetto Response,* New York: Vintage Books, 1967.

39. www.oldnewark.com/memories/thirdward/devosestella.htm.

40. Ortner, *New Jersey Dreaming*, 61–62.

41. Amiri Baraka, *The Autobiography of LeRoi Jones,* Chicago: Lawrence Hill Books, 1997 (originally published 1984), as cited in Ortner, *New Jersey Dreaming*, 72; Watts, *Amiri Baraka*, 21–22.

42. For the catalysts for July 1967's riot/rebellion, see Porambo, *No Cause for Indictment*; Watts, *Amiri Baraka*, 348–356; Wright, *Ready to Riot*.

43. www.oldnewark.com/memories/newark/bodianriots.htm.

44. On Dunn, see Wright, *Ready to Riot*, 137–138. On the police handling of the Newark riot/rebellion, see Porambo, *No Cause for Indictment*, especially 18–31, 113–153; Cunningham, *Newark*, 314–328. On Dunn's acceptance of political contributions from the DeCavalcante crime family, see Porambo, 30.

45. www.oldnewark.com/memories/newark/bodianriots.htm.

46. Rieder, *Canarsie*, 90, 93.

47. *The Sopranos*, Season 4, Episode 7.

48. Porambo, *No Cause for Indictment*, 174–189, 202–203, 272–276.

49. Porambo, *No Cause for Indictment*.

50. Cunningham, *Newark*, 321–322.

51. Porambo, *No Cause for Indictment*; *Report for Action* (Newark: Governor's Select Commission on Civil Disorders, 1968), as cited in Cunningham, *Newark*, 323.

52. Porambo, *No Cause for Indictment*, 118–119; Cunningham, *Newark*, 314–328.

53. Beth Kolko, "Erasing Race: Going White in the (Inter)Face," in Beth Kolko, Lisa Nakamura, and Gilbert B. Rodman, eds., *Race in Cyberspace*, New York: Routledge, 2000, 213–232.

54. Aurigi and Graham, "The 'Crisis' in the Urban Public Realm," 66.

55. Wright, *Ready to Riot*, 14.

56. Porambo, *No Cause for Indictment*, 302–309.

57. Ortner, *New Jersey Dreaming*, 52.

58. Rieder, *Canarsie*, especially 20–26, 90–94.

59. Rieder, *Canarsie*; Wendell Pritchett, *Brownsville, Brooklyn: Blacks, Jews, and the Changing Face of the Ghetto,* Chicago: University of Chicago Press, 2002, 42–49.

60. Sherry Turkel, *Life on the Screen: Identity in the Age of the Internet,* New York: Touchstone, 1995, 26, 47.

61. Herron, *AfterCulture: Detroit and the Humiliation of History*, especially 155–201.

62. Turkel, *Life on the Screen*, 177.

CONCLUSION

1. George Sánchez, " 'What's Good for Boyle Heights Is Good for the Jews': Creating Multiracialism on the Eastside during the 1950s," *American Quarterly* 56 (3): 633–662 (September 2004); Dolores Hayden, *The Power of Place: Urban Landscapes as Public History*, Cambridge, Mass.: M.I.T. Press, 1995. Of interest here, too, are Camilo Vergara's thirty–year photographic projects documenting the alteration occurring in various American cities, such as Detroit, Newark, Camden, and the Bronx. It might be possible to replace the loathing that such denuded cityscapes produce with a commitment to restoring one's former city to past glories. Camilo Vergara, *The New American Ghetto*, New Brunswick, N.J.: Rutgers University Press, 1995; Camilo Vergara, *American Ruins*, New York: Monacelli Press, 1999.

Index

"Abie Kabibl," 92

Adam, Alison, 10, 203

Adam-12, 134–37

Adams, Henry, 49–50

Addams, Jane, 53, 88

Adler, William, 174

Addonizio, Hugh, 169, 182–83, 206, 208, 213–14

The Adventures of Lieutenant Petrosino, 74

African-Americans: absence from television and film, 129; assaults on by whites, 6, 17–20, 22, 27–28, 53–54, 114–19, 121, 126, 138–140, 152, 156, 161–62, 167, 176–79, 182–85, 189, 193, 213, 215–16, 223, 249 n.115, 257 n. 100; in Baltimore, 152, 192–93, 195; and black and tans, 30, 35, 45, 47–48; in blaxploitation films, 139–42, 147, 159; as blues artists, 7, 169; in Chicago, 53–54, 115–17, 223; in Detroit, 165–68, 177–79, 188–89, 223; and Draft Riots, 27–28; and drug gangs, 10, 166, 169, 192, 195; excluded from suburbs, 114–16, 118, 172, 185, 187; fears of fraternization with whites, 16–17, 30, 35, 45, 47–48, 52, 62, 131, 156, 159, 161–63, 178, 213; and the Great Migration, 11, 119, 166; in Los Angeles, 133–35, 140–41, 153–55, 168, 177, 222; as maids in film, 111, 114–15; in New York, 27–28, 45, 47–48, 50, 117–19, 127–29, 131, 133, 138–39, 144, 146–47, 150–51, 153, 155–56, 160–62, 175, 183; in Newark, 165, 167–69, 172–73, 177, 181–85, 197–98, 203–4, 206, 212–16; in Philadelphia, 20, 133, 150; and police brutality, 146, 150, 154, 166–67, 169, 182–85, 189, 193, 206, 214–16; as police in fiction, 74, 84–85, 133–34, 149–52, 154; and prostitution, 20, 166–69; in public housing, 152, 155–56, 173, 192–93, 195, 213; and redlining, 114–16, 118, 130, 172; and riots in 1960s, 133, 137, 165–70, 182, 184, 188–89, 197, 203, 206, 214–16; and slum housing, 117–18, 135, 168, 172–73, 177–80, 182, 210, 212–13, 215; stereotypes of, 127–29, 131, 177–78; as urban underclass, 52, 156–58, 175, 190

Agnew, Spiro, 11, 145

Alaska, 68

Albany, N.Y., 68

Alcatraz, 101, 110

Alewitz, Sam, 19

Allen, Woody, 1, 2, 8, 10, 148–49

B. Altman & Co. Department Store, 185

Altschuler, Glenn, 3, 19

American Mutoscope and Biograph Co. *See* Biograph Co.

American Pastoral, 163, 171–76, 178, 180–88, 191, 194, 198, 222

Amos 'n' Andy, 127–29, 131
Anarchists, 4, 17, 34, 36, 41
Angels with Dirty Faces, 6, 77, 80–82,
    87–88, 96, 106–8
Animal Crackers, 92
Annenberg, Moses, 191
Annie Hall, 10, 148
Anti-Catholicism, 19, 21–22, 26–28,
    40–41, 66–67
Anti-communism, 72, 102, 106, 112–13,
    131, 246 n.83
Anti-Irish riots, 19, 21, 22
Anti–Semitism, 10, 18, 34, 48, 60, 67, 92,
    179
Anti-urbanism, 3, 4, 6, 11–13
The Apollo Theater, 128
Arnesen, Eric, 193
Arno, Nat, 209
Arrogant Beggar, 64
Asbury, Herbert, 26, 52, 77
Asbury Park, N.J., 133
Association for the Improvement of the
    Condition of the Poor, 47
Astor Place Riots, 26–27
Atlanta, 119
Aurigi, Alessandro, 202, 217
Auster, Paul, 148
Avellino, Italy, 205
Ayres, Lew, 94–95

Back of the Yards (Chicago neighbor-
    hood), 61, 85, 87–88
Bacon, Lloyd, 94
Bacon's Rebellion, 23
Baker, Benjamin, 25
Bakhtin, Mikhail, 187
Baltimore, 9, 12, 14, 19, 27, 55, 84–85,
    105, 152–53, 192–95
Baltimore Sun, 152
L. Bambergers & Co. Department Store
    (Newark), 142, 173
Bancroft, George, 80–82
Baraka, Amiri (LeRoi Jones), 182, 206, 213
Baretta, 136–37
Barney Miller, 125, 149
Barthes, Roland, 136
Baxter Terrace House (Newark housing
    project), 173

Bayonne, N.J., 209
Beadle and Co., 2
Beame, Abraham, 136
The Beast of the City, 80
Beban, George, 75
Bell, Thomas, 57, 179
Bellamy, Edward, 66
Belle Island Park (Detroit), 177
Beneath the Planet of the Apes, 143
Bennett, Lerone Jr., 141
Bensonhurst (Brooklyn neighborhood),
    131, 133, 156
The Bergen Mall, 174
Berlin, 79
Berman, Otto "Abbadabba," 81
Bernstein Abe, 79, 98, 166, 190
Bernstein, Lee, 112
Bertellini, Giorgio, 73–75
Bingham, Theodore, 48, 51, 138
Biograph Co., 73
The Birth of a Nation, 76, 128
"Black and tans," 16, 30, 35, 45, 47, 82
Black Bottom (Detroit neighborhood),
    177–78, 188
The Black Hand, 8, 11, 36, 73–74, 78
The Black Hand, 73
The Blackboard Jungle, 6, 135
Bladerunner, 80
Blaxploitation films, 125, 128, 139–42,
    147, 159, 221
"Blind pigs," 20, 23, 62, 77, 167
Blockbusting, 118–19, 140
Blumin, Stuart, 22, 23, 27
Boardinghouses, 32, 51, 57, 62–63
Boas, Franz, 75
Bochco, Steven, 149–50
Bogart, Humphrey, 6, 13, 71, 81–82, 91,
    102, 108, 114
Bogle, Donald, 128–29, 135, 149
Boiardo, Anthony, 206
Boiardo, Ruggiero, 169, 181, 190, 197,
    203, 205–6, 208, 211, 218
Bonner, Juke Boy, 7, 169
Booth, Elmer, 76
Borgnine, Ernest, 146
Borneo, 60
Boston, 4, 6, 19, 28, 46, 52, 66, 109, 119,
    145, 156

"Bowery B'hoys," 25–27, 34, 35, 58, 81
"Bowery Tales," 30–31, 33, 36
Boyle Heights (Los Angeles neighbor-
  hood), 222
Boyz 'n the Hood, 2, 128, 149,
  153–55
Brace, Charles Loring, 4
Braddock, Pa., 57, 179
Bread Givers, 63
Brecht, Bertolt, 79
Bremer, Arthur, 145
Brent, Evelyn, 81
Brewster Aircraft Corp., 208–9
Breyers Ice Cream Co., 182
Bridgeport (Chicago neighborhood), 5, 53,
  68, 85
Brodkin, Karen, 111, 130
Bronson, Charles, 138, 143
The Bronx, 53, 104, 108, 130, 146,
  159–62, 266 n.1
A Bronx Tale, 108, 159–62
Brook, Clive, 81
Brooklyn: in crime dramas, 125, 139, 155;
  fears of racial change in, 183–84, 210,
  215, 218; in gangster films, 2, 96,
  159–60; Italian immigrants in, 2, 41,
  159, 183–84, 218; Jewish immigrants in,
  148, 183–84, 218; and Murder Inc., 96,
  116, 157, 159, 210, 218; nostalgia and,
  218; suburbanization and, 183–84, 210;
  in television sitcoms, 125, 129, 132–33
Brooklyn Bridge, 44, 46, 65
Brown, Udetta, 50
Browning, Tod, 86
Brownsville (Brooklyn neighborhood), 96,
  116, 183–84, 210, 218
Brunner, H.C., 40, 42, 44
Bryan, William Jennings, 3–4
Buchalter, Louis "Lepke," 6, 103, 211
Bullets or Ballots, 72, 83, 93–94,
  102–5
Buntline, Ned, 22, 26, 28, 45
Burry Biscuits Co., 181
Byrne, Jane, 151

CSI, 11, 122, 134
Cabrini Green (Chicago housing
  project), 151

Cagney, James, 6, 13, 71–72, 77, 82,
  86–87, 91, 95, 109, 134
Cahan, Abraham, 49, 62, 88
Call It Sleep, 52, 65
Callaghan, James, 187
Cambridge, Godfrey, 139
Camden, N.J., 185–87, 266 n.1
Campbell, Helen, 30–32, 34, 36, 81
Canada, 91
Canarsie (Brooklyn neighborhood),
  183–84, 210, 218
Canarsie, 183
Čapek, Karel, 80
Capone, Al, 70, 71, 78, 80, 84, 87, 93, 96,
  101, 126, 211
Capra, Frank, 98
Car 54, Where Are You?, 124–25
Carnegie, Andrew, 31
Carpenter, John, 145, 147
Carter, Jimmy, 125, 143
*Celio, or New York Above Ground and
  Under Ground*, 22
Celluloid Manufacturing Co., 182
The Century magazine, 4, 20, 29, 33, 37,
  44, 56, 63, 69, 125
Cermak, Anton, 54, 84, 87, 92
Chaney, Lon, 86
Chaplin, Charlie, 79–80
Charities and the Commons, 56, 63
"Charley Chan," 140
Cherry Hill, N.J., 185–86
Chicago: African-Americans in, 53–54,
  115–17, 119, 223; fears of racial change
  in, 53–54, 60, 115–17, 119, 121, 151,
  223; in gangster films, 6, 80, 87–88, 90,
  92, 94–97, 100, 152; and gangsters, 71,
  78–85, 87, 90, 96, 126; and Gilded Age,
  5, 33, 36, 68–69; and immigration restrictionism, 78; Irish immigrants in, 5,
  53–55, 60, 68–69; Italian immigrants in,
  78, 80, 84, 96, 100; political corruption
  in, 53–55, 79, 82–84, 96; public housing
  in, 151; Slavic immigrants in, 50, 54,
  61, 68; slums in, 85, 87–88, 117, 149;
  and strikes, 36; World's Columbian
  Exposition and, 60
Chicago Herald and Examiner, 71
Chicago Tribune, 78, 83, 96, 97

China, 175

Chinese immigrants, 35, 47–48, 50, 52, 61, 67

"Chocolate City," 7, 162

Christ in Concrete, 52

City for Conquest, 72, 109

"City mysteries," 2, 4, 5, 9, 11, 13, 22–24, 72, 77, 86, 93, 195

City of Eros, 48

Clan na Gael, 41

Cleveland, 58, 79, 89, 146, 156, 191

Cliffside Park, N.J., 205

Clinton, George, 7, 162

Clockers, 149, 155

Cobo, Albert, 189

The Cocoanuts, 92

Coffy, 139, 141

Cohen, Rich, 210

Coll, Vincent "Mad Dog," 89

Columbia Avenue riots (Philadelphia), 133

Columbia University, 148

Columbus, Christopher, 198

Comic books, 13, 190

Comic strips, 4–5, 92

Compson, Betty, 82

Compton, Calif., 155

Comstock, Anthony, 47

Coney Island (Brooklyn neighborhood), 109, 148

Conforti, Joseph, 169, 174

Confidence-Man, 19

Congress of Industrial Organizations, 240 n.6

Conrad, Michael, 149

Converse, Frank, 133

Cook, Tommy, 112

Cooper, James Fenimore, 23

Coppola, Francis Ford, 13

Cops, 7, 11, 52, 114, 119, 122, 157

Corbally, Frank, 208

Correll, Charles, 127

Corridan, Father John, 247 n.96

Cosby, Bill, 118

Costello, Frank, 83, 89, 103

The Cotton Club, 89

Coughlin, Father Charles, 179

Coward, Noel, 1

Coxey, Jacob, 36

Crabrass Frontier, 203

Crane, Stephen, 4, 29–30, 33, 34, 36–37, 44, 45, 76

Crime: African-Americans and, 134–136, 141–42, 144–49, 152–54, 156, 160, 165–68, 175, 178, 180, 183, 192; in Baltimore, 152–53, 192, 195; in Chicago, 69, 84–85, 87, 89–91; in Detroit, 165–68, 178; in gangster films, 71–77, 82, 85–87, 89–91, 102, 107, 160; in German film, 79; in the Gilded Age, 31–32, 34–35, 47, 51–52, 67, 69, 107; and immigration restrictionism, 51, 74, 102; Irish immigrants and, 69, 77; Italian immigrants and, 35, 51, 73–75, 77, 84, 217–18; Jewish immigrants and, 48, 51, 138, 191, 209, 211–12, 217–18; in Los Angeles, 134–136, 153–55, 168; in New York, 31–32, 34–35, 47, 51–52, 75–77, 96, 124–25, 139, 145–49, 155, 160, 183, 191; in Newark, 168, 175, 180, 183, 197–98, 201, 206, 209, 211–15, 217; and nostalgia, 203, 206, 213–15, 218; in Philadelphia, 191; and police brutality, 146, 149–50, 156, 167, 183; and political corruption, 77–78, 82, 84, 209; in postwar film, 137–39, 141–42, 144–49, 153–55; in San Francisco, 34; Slavic immigrants and, 56; in television dramas, 7, 124–26, 134–36, 149–50, 152–53, 157, 192, 195, 197–98, 201

Crime without Passion, 80

"Cross of Gold" speech, 3–4

Cunningham, John T., 206, 215

Curley, James M., 4

The Dago, 75, 78

Daily News (N.Y.), 52, 221

Dalitz, Moe, 89, 211

Dance halls, 62, 76, 82, 86, 88

Darkness and Daylight, 31–32, 34

Davis, Miles, 161

Dead End, 6, 106, 108

The Dead End Kids, 106–7

Death Wish, 125, 138, 141, 143

DeCavalcante crime family, 265 n.44

Dee, Ruby, 118

Deering Park (Chicago neighborhood), 121, 223

Deindustrialization, 116, 123, 141, 162, 223; in Baltimore, 152–53, 192, 194–95; in Detroit, 7–8, 120, 170, 178, 192; in Newark, 173–75, 181–82, 192, 203, 217; in Paterson, N.J., 174; in Reagan administration, 149–50; subsidized by government, 120–21, 153, 174–76, 182; in television dramas, 152–53, 192, 194–95

Del Ruth, Roy, 94

The Dempsey Bill, 102

De Niro, Robert, 158–160

Denton, Nancy, 148

The Desperate Hours, 99, 114–15

The Detectives of the Italian Bureau, 74

Detroit: African-Americans in, 165–68, 177–79, 188–89, 192, 223; and blues artists, 7, 169–70; in crime dramas, 147, 149, 155; deindustrialization in, 266 n.1; fears of racial change in, 115–16, 156, 177–79, 187–90, 223; and gangsters, 79, 98, 116; gentrification in, 205, 219; German immigrants in, 120; Greek immigrants in, 98, 177–78, 187–90, 205; and Heidelberg Project, 7–8, 170; and Hudson's Department Store, 142; Irish immigrants in, 120; Italian immigrants in, 116; Jewish immigrants in, 116, 178–79, 190; and nostalgia, 13, 98, 163, 205; Polish immigrants in, 120; slums in, 165–68, 177–78; suburbanization and, 142, 190; and white flight, 8–9, 13, 142

Detroit Institute of the Arts, 7, 170

Detroit riots (1943), 177–179, 223

Detroit riots (1967), 7, 9, 11, 134, 136, 139, 142, 165, 167–68, 178, 188–89

Dewey, George, 60

Dewey, Thomas, 6, 92, 103–4, 108, 244 n.45

Diallo, Amadou, 146–47, 150

Dies, Martin, 102

Dillingham Immigration Commission, 38

DiMaggio, Joe, 98, 205–6

"Dime novels," 2, 4, 9, 34–35

Dinkins, David, 151

Dirty Harry, 7, 137–38, 141, 145

The Docks of New York, 81–82

Doctor Mabuse, 79

The Doorway to Hell, 94–95

Dorismond, Patrick, 146

Down Neck (Newark neighborhood), 197

Dozier, Carol, 123

Dracula, 86

Draft Riots, 27–28

The Dragnet (film), 81

Dragnet (television show), 122–24, 133

Dreiser, Theodore, 4, 33, 34

Drugs: in Baltimore, 9, 105, 192–96; in blaxploitation films, 141, 158; Chinese immigrants and, 48, 52; in Detroit, 166; in gangster films, 157–58, 160; in the Gilded Age, 47–48, 52; Jewish immigrants and, 212; in Los Angeles, 154–55; in New York, 47–48, 52, 17, 141, 157–58; in Newark, 169, 180–81, 183, 190–91, 211–12; in Philadelphia, 156, 191; in postwar crime films, 137, 141, 154–55; prostitution and, 48; in San Francisco, 137; in television crime dramas, 9, 105, 117, 135, 149, 192–96

Du Bois, W.E.B., 115

Dundee (neighborhood of Passaic, N.J.), 50

Dunn, Thomas, 214, 265 n.44

Dunne, Finley Peter, 60, 68, 78

East Harlem (New York neighborhood), 41

East New York (Brooklyn neighborhood), 159, 183, 210

East Orange, N.J., 185–87

East Saint Louis, Ill., 53

"East Side Considerations," 59

East Side/West Side, 117–19, 122, 124, 126, 133

Eastman, Monk, 77

Eastwood, Clint, 137

Easy Rider, 162

Eisenhower, Dwight, 6, 116, 121, 126, 130, 132

The El Fay Club, 89

Elizabeth, N.J., 181, 211, 214

Elizabeth Carteret Hotel (Elizabeth, N.J.), 211

Ellenstein, Meyer, 79, 84, 207, 208–10

Ellis Island, 101, 163
The Embassy Club, 89
Emmett, Dan, 17
The Empire City, 22
Epstein, Jacob, 43
Erickson, Paul, 23
Escape from New York, 145–48
Essex County, N.J., 181, 187, 190, 206,
    208–9, 212
Ethnic stereotypes: African-American, 10,
    74, 111, 127–29, 139–41, 169, 178, 196,
    213; Chinese, 35, 48; German, 34, 36,
    41; Irish, 4, 10, 28, 33–35, 37, 41, 60,
    62, 67–68; Italian, 8, 10, 35, 37–38, 41,
    62, 67, 73–75, 78, 92–93, 97–99;
    Japanese, 67; Jewish, 10, 18, 34, 48, 60,
    67, 92; Slavic, 41, 57, 67–68, 111
Eugenides, Jeffrey, 8, 13, 98, 163, 165,
    177–80, 184, 187, 190, 192, 221
"An Experiment in Misery," 30–31, 32, 36

Fair Lawn, N.J., 174
Fairbanks, Douglas Jr., 97
Farm Security Administration, 212, 259 n.23
Farrell, James T., 53–55, 78
Fasanella, Ralph, 53
Feagin, Joe, 27, 28, 137, 178
Feature Photoplay Co., 74
Federal Bureau of Investigation, 113, 208,
    210–11
Federal Communications Commission, 121
Federal Housing Administration, 73,
    113–14, 116, 118, 218; in Newark, 130,
    171, 175, 203, 217; in Paterson, N.J., 130
Feldon, Barbara, 118
Fiji, 60
Film noir, 6, 72, 112
Fine, Sidney, 167, 178, 188–89
Fire companies, 19, 25, 26, 38, 167, 202
Fitchburg, Mass., 23
Fitzgerald, F. Scott, 83
Fitzgerald, John, 4
Five Points (New York neighborhood),
    22–23, 26, 27, 30, 34–35, 50, 73, 77
"Flashes from the Slums," 43
Flatbush (Brooklyn neighborhood), 215
Flegenheimer, Arthur. *See also* Schultz,
    "Dutch"

Flophouses, 29–31, 32, 33, 44, 45, 51,
    96, 98
Foerster, Robert, 53, 78
Food ways, immigrant, 50, 58, 99
Ford, Gerald, 144–45, 158, 221
Ford, Henry, 177
Fordham (Bronx neighborhood), 8, 160–61
Forman, Henry James, 86
Forrest, Edwin, 26
Fort Apache, the Bronx, 7, 142, 149, 162
Foster, George, 22–23, 25–26, 28, 44, 45,
    49, 72, 81
Four Brothers, 149, 155
Fox News, 52
Foxy Brown, 141
Frank, Leo, 177
Frankford (Philadelphia neighborhood), 20
Franz, Dennis, 153
Freedomland, 156
The French Connection, 125, 139
The Front Page, 80

The GI Bill, 176, 203
G-Men, 104
Gambino, Richard, 96
Gambling, 8, 20, 31, 79, 83, 103, 160, 169,
    181, 190–91, 206–9
Gangs of New York (film), 26, 28
The Gangs of New York (book), 26, 77
Gangsta rap, 12, 128, 159
Gangsters, 11, 72, 221; African-American,
    141, 147, 150, 153–54; in the Bronx,
    160–63; in Brooklyn, 96, 116, 157, 183,
    210; in Chicago, 13, 53, 70–71, 78–84,
    87, 89–91, 96–97, 125–26; in Cleveland,
    79; in Detroit, 70, 79, 116, 190; as for-
    eign menace, 6, 13, 51, 74, 78, 93, 97,
    99–102; Irish, 53, 70, 77–78, 89; Italian,
    50, 70, 73–75, 77–78, 81, 83, 89, 93–97,
    99–102, 108, 116, 126, 141, 157–58,
    160–63, 169, 181–82, 190, 203, 205–6,
    208, 265 n.44; Jewish, 51, 70, 79, 81,
    83, 91, 93–94, 96, 116, 181, 190–91,
    203, 205–12, 219; and labor racketeer-
    ing, 72, 102–3, 106, 208, 210, 247 n.92;
    in Los Angeles, 153–54; in New York, 6,
    8, 13, 51, 70, 75–77, 83–84, 103, 108–9,
    126, 141, 147–48, 158, 160; in Newark,

8, 50, 79, 84, 91, 94, 104–5, 169, 181–82, 190–91, 197, 203, 205–12, 219; night-clubs, control of, 89, 105; and nostalgia, 125–26, 157–58, 160–63, 199, 206; in Philadelphia, 190–91; and political cor-ruption, 77–79, 82–84, 103–105, 108, 181–82, 191, 206, 208–11, 265 n.44; as role models, 13, 86, 96, 100–102

The Garden State Plaza, 174, 259 n.26

Garfield, N.J., 174

Gates, Darryl, 124

General Electric Co., 182

Genna, Angelo, 78, 80–81, 96

Gentrification, 11, 184; in Baltimore, 192, 194–95; in Chicago, 151; in Detroit, 205; in Los Angeles, 155; in New York, 8, 148–49, 255–56, n.87; in Newark, 9, 198–99

"George's Mother," 29

Georgia, 177

German immigrants, 4, 17, 36, 41, 48, 120, 204

German–American Bund, 176, 190–91, 208–9

Gershwin, George, 72, 89, 109

Gibson, Kenneth, 181–182

The Gilded Age, 33, 35–36, 45, 66

Gilder, Richard Watson, 33

Gilfoyle, Timothy, 48

Gish, Lillian, 76

Giuliani, Rudolph, 146, 150–51

A Glance at New York, 25

Gloversville, N.Y., 176

Goddard, Paulette, 80

Godey, John, 143

The Godfather, 126, 157

Goetz, Bernie, 138–39

"Goin' Back to the Country," 7, 169

Gold, Mike, 53, 64, 191

Goldberg, David, 202

The Goldbergs, 129–31, 133

Golden, Harry, 43, 59

Gone to Soldiers, 178–79

Goodfellas, 2, 96, 159–60

Gordon, C. Henry, 100

Gosden, Freeman, 127

Gossett, Louis Jr., 135

Gould, Jack, 119

Graham, Stephen, 202, 217

Grant, Madison, 54, 75, 98

The Great Depression, 6, 57, 86, 89, 94, 119, 177–78, 208, 221

The Great Gatsby, 83

The Great Migration, 118–119, 166, 177

"The Great Jewish Invasion," 61

The Great Society, 133, 138

Greek immigrants, 98, 177–78, 187–88, 190

Greektown (Detroit neighborhood), 205, 222

Green, Eileen, 10, 203

Green Valley Country Club (Philadelphia), 191

Greenberg, Max, 211, 214

Greenblatt, Stephen, 59

Greene, Victor, 55

Grier, Pam, 139, 141

Griffith, D.W., 74, 76–77, 122, 128

Grosse Pointe, Mich., 7, 166, 190

Grosz, George, 79

Guinan, "Texas," 89

Guys and Dolls, 81

Guyton, Tyree, 170

Guzik, Jacob "Greasy Thumb," 81

Hague, Frank, 202, 208–9

Hahn, Harlan, 27, 28, 137, 178

Hale, Grace Elizabeth, 177

Hammack, David, 46

Hannah and Her Sisters, 148

Hansberry, Lorraine, 115

Hapgood, Hutchins, 35, 43–44, 59, 65

Harlem (New York neighborhood): black riots in, 133; in blaxploitation films, 141–42; gangsters and, 89, 157; gentrifi-cation in, 148; in postwar crime films, 139; slum housing in, 117; in television comedies, 127–29; in television dramas, 117; white assaults on blacks in, 177

Harper, James, 28

Harper's magazine, 29, 37–39, 60, 69, 125

Harrigan, Ned, 31

Harrington, Michael, 6, 121

Hassel, Max, 211, 214

Hate strikes, 176–77, 179

Hawaii, 60
Hawkins, Yusef, 156
Hayden, Dolores, 202, 222
Hayden, Tom, 169, 213
Hayes, Helen, 85
Hayes, Isaac, 147
Haymarket Square Massacre, 36
Hays Production Code, 12, 71–72, 76, 82, 86, 90, 111, 152
Hays, Will, 86, 100
Heard, Nathan, 154, 165, 168–69
Hearst, William Randolph, 67
Hebrew Immigrant Aid Society, 44
Hecht, Ben, 80, 152
Heidelberg Project, 7–8, 170
Hellman, Lillian, 106
Helms, Jesse, 151
Hendrick, Burton J., 61, 67–68
Herberg, Will, 115
Herron, Jerry, 169, 192, 205, 219
Hershberg, Theodore, 119
Hester Street, 49, 88
Hill Street Blues, 134, 149–53
Hill, Walter, 147
Hillman, Sidney, 210
Hillside, N.J., 214
Hine, Lewis, 38, 101
Hinkes, Max "Puddy," 209, 214
Hip-hop, 7, 86, 128, 159
Hirsch, Arnold, 116
Hitler, Adolf, 208
The Hobbes Bill, 102
Hoboken, N.J., 106
Hobsbawm, Eric, 108
Hoffman, Katherine, 58
Hollywood, 67, 72, 77, 85–87, 94, 112, 114, 127
Home Depot, 212
Homelessness, 5, 16–17, 29–30, 32, 33, 34, 36, 45, 52, 64, 213
Homestead, Pa., 36, 57, 61
Homicide, 122, 152–53
Homosexuality, 112
Hone, Philip, 18, 22
The Honeymooners, 129, 131–33
Hooker, John Lee, 7, 169–70
Hooks, Robert, 133
Hoover, J. Edgar, 208, 211

House Un-American Activities Committee, 11, 102, 112
How the Other Half Lives, 39–40, 43–45
Howard Street, 154, 165, 168–69
Hudson County, N.J., 106, 209
Hug, Bill, 43
Hughes, Richard, 216
Hull House, 53, 88
The Human Stain, 14, 173, 183, 185–87, 191
Hungry Hearts, 63–64
Hyman, Earle, 118

I Remember Mama, 129
Immerso, Michael, 205
Immigration Restriction League, 66, 71
Immigration restrictionism, 2–3, 70–71, 83, 101; and Asians, 60–61; and Irish, 4–5, 28, 54–55, 60, 66–67; and Italians, 11, 29, 39, 42, 47, 61, 74–75, 78, 98–100, 102; and Jews, 11, 29, 47, 49, 61; in political cartoons, 5, 49, 60; and Slavs, 54–55, 57–58, 61
Imperiale, Anthony, 27, 145, 197, 215
"In the New York Ghetto," 58
Indianapolis, 114–15
Industrial Revolution, 17
Inside Man, 74
The Internet, 9, 11, 67, 163, 199, 202–3, 217, 222
Interstate Highway Act, 175
Irish immigrants: and anti-black rioting, 27–28, 53–54; in Chicago, 53–54, 60, 68–69; in Detroit, 120; and Draft Riots, 27–28; as dynamiters, 17, 36, 41; and gangsters, 77, 89; and immigration restrictionism, 19, 21–22, 25, 28, 67–68; and minstrelsy, 17; in New York, 25, 27–28, 33–35; in Philadelphia, 19, 21–22; in political cartoons, 5, 17, 36, 41, 45, 54, 60, 68; and political corruption, 4, 10, 53–54, 67–69; and poverty, 35–36; and prostitution, 5; in San Francisco, 33–34; and www. virtualnewarknj.com , 204; whiteness, questioned, 60
Irvington, N.J., 208
"The Island of Desire," 59
The Italian, 75

Italian Blood, 74

Italian immigrants: and anti-black rioting, 156, 161–62, 183, 213, 215; in the Bronx, 53, 160–62; in Brooklyn, 41, 96, 156–57, 183, 218; in Chicago, 50, 78, 85, 93, 97; and crime, 4, 10–11, 36, 73, 97, 100, 157, 163; and food ways, 50; and gangsters, 11, 74–75, 77–78, 85, 89, 92–93, 96–97, 99–102, 157–63, 169, 181, 183, 205–6, 218; Gilded Age magazine depictions, 35–42, 44, 48–50; and immigration restrictionism, 45, 49, 67, 74–75, 78, 97–102; and labor unions, 44, 52–53; in New York, 37–42, 44, 48–50, 52, 73–74, 77, 158, 196–198; in Newark, 9, 50, 169, 181, 196–97, 201, 204–6, 213, 215; and nostalgia, 9, 50, 157–58, 160–162, 183, 196–98, 201, 204–6, 215, 218; in Paterson, N.J., 52; in political cartoons, 41, 45; and political corruption, 181–82, 206; and prostitution, 48, 169; and slum housing, 50; in Tampa, 50; in television comedies, 129; and www.virtualnewarknj.com , 204–6

"Italian Life in New York," 37–39

Jackson, Kenneth, 130, 153, 171, 174, 203

Jacobson, Matthew Frye, 98, 111, 116

James, Henry, 49–50

Japanese immigrants, 60–61, 67

Jefferson, Thomas, 3, 4, 18

Jefferson Airplane, 199

Jeffersonian self-sufficiency, 3, 4, 16, 18–19, 23, 24–25, 28

"Jersey and Mulberry," 40–42

Jersey City, 6, 156–157, 202, 208–9

Jewish immigrants: activism of, 40, 63–65, 130–31; and boardinghouses, 63; in Brooklyn, 183, 210, 218; and crime, 51; and dance halls, 62; in Detroit, 166, 178–79; and gangsters, 77, 83, 93, 157, 163, 166, 172, 177, 181, 190–91, 205–12, 218; Gilded Age magazine depictions, 39–40, 59–61, 67–68, 163; interracial cooperation, 213, 222; and labor unions, 43, 65; in Los Angeles, 222; in New York, 35, 39, 59–65, 67, 77, 129–31,

191; in Newark, 171–72, 177, 181–83, 187, 190–91, 201, 204–14; and nostalgia, 157–58, 171–72, 181–83, 191, 207, 210, 214, 218; in novels, 62–65, 171–72, 177–79, 181–83, 187, 190–91; in Philadelphia, 190–91; in political cartoons, 68; and political corruption, 77, 182, 206, 209–10; poverty of, 39–40, 63–64, 207, 218; and prostitution, 48, 62, 77; suburbanization and, 111, 129–31, 171–72, 182–83; in television comedies, 129–31; and www.virtualnewarknj.com, 204–7, 209–10, 214; whiteness, achieved, 111; whiteness, questioned, 4, 11, 48, 60–61, 67–68, 127

Jews without Money, 53, 64, 191

J.L. Hudson & Co. Department Store (Detroit), 142

Johnny Mnemonic, 147

Johnson, Albert, 129

Johnson, Lyndon Baines, 155

Johnson, Samuel, 1–2

Johnstown, Pa., 50

Jolson, Al, 71

Jones, Gerard, 190

Jones, James Earl, 117

Jones, LeRoi. *See* Baraka, Amiri

The Jungle, 61

Jungle Fever, 151, 155–56

The Kalem Co., 74

Kansas City, 211

Kapus, Leo, 211

Kazan, Elia, 112

Kelley, Robin, 142

Kennedy, Arthur, 72, 109

Kenny, John V., 209

Kensington (Philadelphia neighborhood), 18, 19, 21, 156

Kentucky, 177

Kerner, Otto, 137

The Kerner Commission, 133, 183, 189

Killens, John Oliver, 135

King, Martin Luther Jr., 119

King, Rodney, 124, 137, 150

Kingsley, Sidney, 106

Kinney Parking Systems, 190

Kirsten, Jack, 212

Kiss of Death, 72, 75, 80, 83, 103, 105–6,
   111–13
Koch, Edward, 151
Kojack, 137
Kolko, Beth, 216
Korea, 175
Kosher food riots, 40
Kozol, Jonathan, 185
Krupa, Gene, 143–44, 146
Kuhn, Fritz, 176, 191, 208
Kull, Philip, 211

Labor racketeering, 72, 83, 102–3, 106,
   160, 191, 208–10, 247 n.92
Labor unions: African-Americans excluded, 166, 193; in antebellum America,
   18, 23–25; in Baltimore, 192–94; In the
   Bronx, 53, 130–131; in Brooklyn, 210,
   218; in coal mines, 55–56; In Chicago,
   36; and deindustrialization, 174–76,
   192–94; in Detroit, 166, 177; and
   gangsters, 106, 177, 208, 210; in Gilded
   Age, 36; in Homestead, Pa., 36; in
   Hudson County, N.J., 106; and Italian
   immigrants, 44, 52–53; and Jewish
   immigrants, 43–44; middle class, role in
   building, 57, 106, 120, 175, 240 n.6; in
   New York, 43–44, 106; in Newark,
   175–77; and offshoring, 174–76; in Passaic, N.J., 202; in Paterson, N.J., 174; in
   Philadelphia, 18; and Slavic immigrants,
   55–57, 240 n.6; and speedup, 80; in
   steel mills, 57, 240 n.6; suppressed, 36,
   56, 177, 192, 202; urban decline,
   blamed for, 175; virtual cities, absence
   from, 202
Lacapra, Michael James, 211
Lackawanna, Pa., 56
Landsmanshaften, 43, 191
Lang, Fritz, 79–80
Lansky, Meyer, 6, 70, 83, 105, 211
Las Vegas, 89, 134
The Last American, 5, 65–66
The Last Gangster, 72, 93, 99, 101–2,
   109–11
The Last of the Mafia, 74
Laurie, Bruce, 24
Lawrence, Mass., 18

Lee, Spike, 148–49, 151, 155
LeRoy, Mervyn, 91
Lester, Julius, 128
Levittown, 113–14, 120, 132
Lewis, Daniel Day, 26
Liberty State Park (Jersey City), 202
Lieberman, David "Quincy," 209
Life magazine, 65, 98
Life in Rochester, 23
The Life of Riley, 131
Life with Luigi, 129
"Light in Dark Places," 44
Lillian, Al, 211
Lillian, William, 211
Limbaugh, Rush, 149
Lincoln, Abraham, 25, 111
Lindbergh, Charles, 176–77, 190
Lindbergh, Charles Jr., 110
Lindsay, John V., 133, 137, 143
Lingle, Jake, 84
Lippard, George, 2, 12, 15–19, 21, 22, 24,
   25, 29, 45, 66, 81, 141
Lipsitz, George, 111, 127–28, 131, 174
Lithuanian immigrants, 61
Little Caesar, 6, 71–72, 85–86, 89, 91–99
The Little Giant, 94
Little Italy, 74
Livingston, N.J., 180
Locust Point (Baltimore neighborhood),
   193–96
Loeb, Philip, 131
Lodge, Henry Cabot, 43, 55, 67
Lombroso, Cesare, 51, 75
London, 1
Looking Backward, 66
Lorre, Peter, 79
Los Angeles: assaults on blacks in, 123;
   black political power in, 151; black riots
   in, 133–34, 150, 168; in blaxploitation
   films, 140; interracial cooperation in,
   222; police brutality in, 124, 137, 150,
   154; in postwar crime films, 149,
   153–55; science fiction and, 80; subur-
   banization and, 46; in television crime
   dramas, 122–123, 134–37; and Zoot
   Suit riots, 123, 177
Los Angeles Police Department, 123–24,
   134–37

Lott, Eric, 17, 127
Louima, Abner, 150
Lowell, Mass., 18, 23, 45
Lower East Side (New York neighborhood): activism among Jewish immigrants in, 40, 63–65; boardinghouses, 63; crime, 35, 77, 88; dancing academies in, 62, 88; family abandonment in, 63; and gangsters, 77, 88, 191; in gangster films, 76–77, 106, 109; gentrification, 148; Gilded Age magazine depictions, 7, 43, 47–49, 58–59, 63, 69, 76, 136, 170; in immigrant novels, 53, 62–65; large immigrant families in, 49; and nostalgia, 35, 88; in political cartoons, 49; political corruption, 77, 88; prostitution, 48, 77, 88; slum housing, 47, 49, 53, 63, 106, 191; and tourism, 43, 58–59, 170
Lucas, Curtis, 176
Luciano, Salvatore "Lucky," 83, 96, 102–3, 105, 158, 211
Lynchings, 177
Lynn, Jeffrey, 81

M, 79
MOVE, 150
MTV, 62
Macready, William, 26
Madden, Owney, 70
Madison, James, 3
Mafia, 73–74, 78, 97, 141, 152, 203, 206
Maggie: A Girl of the Streets, 4, 29, 33, 36, 76
Mahanoy City, Pa., 55
Malden, Karl, 123
Manayunk (Philadelphia neighborhood), 18, 20
"Manhattan" (song), 1
Manhattan (film), 148
Mann, Eric, 216
Mannix, 7, 134, 136
Mantle, Mickey, 161
Maplewood, N.J., 171, 182
Marcus, Bernie, 212
Marked Woman, 102
Martin, E.S., 59–61
The Marx Brothers, 92
Mason, Jackie, 151

Massey, Douglas, 148
Mature, Victor, 112
Mayfield, Curtis, 159
Mayfield Road gang, 79
McArthur, Charles, 80
McCarthy, Joseph, 113
McCarthyism, 112–13, 131, 246 n.83
McClure's magazine, 29, 61, 67, 77
McGovern, George, 183
McKinley, William, 60
McLuhan, Marshall, 121, 126
"McNally's Row of Flats," 31
McTeague, 33–34, 51
Mean Streets, 158–59
Meet Me in Saint Louis, 10
"The Melting Pot," 51
Melville, Herman, 19
"The Men in the Storm," 29–30
Metropolis, 79–80
Mexican immigrants, 123, 177
Mexico, 120, 140, 174
Meyer Brothers Department Store (Paterson, N.J.), 142
Miami, 84, 134
Miami Vice, 134
Middlesex, 8, 14, 98, 163, 165, 177–79, 184, 187–90, 221
Midnight Cowboy, 144
Milestone, Lewis, 84
Millburn, N.J., 174
Miller, Glenn, 146
Minneapolis, 41
Minnelli, Vincente, 10
Minow, Newton, 121
Minstrelsy, 17, 97, 127, 139–40, 185, 188, 251 n.26
Mississippi, 174
Mister Dooley, 5, 60, 68–69
Mitchell, J.A., 65–67
Moby–Dick, 185–87
The Mod Squad, 134–36, 153
Modern Times, 80
Mollie's Job, 174
Molly Maguires, 56
The Moran gang, 84
Morawska, Ewa, 57
Moreland, Mantan, 140
Moretti, Willie, 205, 214

Morton, Samuel "Nails," 81, 90
Moses, Robert, 106
Mostel, Zero, 112
Motion Picture Producers and Distributors
    of America, 86
Motion Picture Production Code. *See also*
    Hays Production Code
Motion Picture Research Council, 86
"Motor City's Burning," 7, 169–70
Motown, 159
Moving Picture World, 74
Moynihan, Daniel Patrick, 6, 52, 129, 140,
    154, 168
Muckrackers, 4
Mulberry Bend (New York neighborhood):
    boardinghouses in, 51; Gilded Age mag-
    azine depictions, 5, 8, 40, 42–43, 45, 47,
    50–51; Italian immigrants as "non-
    whites" in, 47, 50–51; Italian immi-
    grants as spectacle in, 40, 42; saloons in,
    45; in silent films, 73; slum housing
    conditions in, 43, 50–51
Muni, Paul, 71, 82, 99–100
Munsey's magazine, 29, 58–60, 69
Murder Inc.: and bootlegging, 91; in
    Brooklyn, 96, 116, 157, 159, 183, 210,
    218; in gangster films, 8, 159; and labor
    racketeering, 210; in Newark, 91, 203,
    206–8, 210; and nostalgia, 183, 210; as
    role models, 96, 218; and "Dutch"
    Schultz's murder, 104; and www.virtual-
    newarknj.com, 207–8, 210, 219
Murphy, Paul, 202
Murphy Brown, 12
The Musketeers of Pig Alley, 76–77, 122
Mutual of Omaha's Wild Kingdom, 157
My Lai massacre, 135
"My Home Town," 195
The Mysteries and Miseries of New York,
    22

N.Y.P.D., 133
NYPD Blue, 152–53
Naked City, 113–14, 122, 126, 133
Národné Noviny, 60–61
Národný Kalendár, 61
Nast, Thomas, 53
The Nation, 116, 118

National Advisory Commission on Civil
    Disorders. *See also* Kerner Commission
National Association for the Advancement
    of Colored People, 127–29
National Police Gazette , 43
National Slovak Society, 56, 102, 246 n.83
Native Son, 117
Nativism, 21–22, 26, 27–28
Ness, Elliot, 126
Network, 145
Neutral Film Co., 74
The New Deal, 47, 61, 106, 163; blacks
    excluded from benefits, 127, 181; and
    "economic royalists," 105; and toler-
    ance, 111; suburbanization and, 120;
    white ethnics and, 72, 120, 129, 240 n.6
New Jersey, 174, 183, 185–87, 191, 203,
    205, 211, 215
New Jersey Dreaming, 207
New Jersey State Patrolmen's Benevolent
    Association, 137–38
New Orleans, 112–13, 177, 193, 221
New York: African-Americans in, 27–28,
    35, 45, 47, 117, 133, 139, 141, 144, 147,
    151, 156; antebellum depictions, 18,
    22–27, 34–35; and Astor Place Riots,
    26–27; in blaxploitation films, 139, 141,
    147; and "Bowery B'hoys" 25–27,
    34–35, 58; Chinese immigrants in, 35,
    47–48, 52; in city mysteries, 22–25, 28,
    49; in comic films, 8, 10, 148; and
    crime, 32, 47–48, 52, 138–39, 144–47;
    and dance halls, 88; deindustrialization;
    in, 141; and Draft Riots, 27–28; and film
    noir, 113; and gangsters, 8, 26, 33,
    73–74, 77, 83, 103–4, 141, 147, 157–58,
    191, 211, 218; and gangster films, 6, 8,
    73–75, 103–4, 106, 126, 157–59; and
    gentrification, 148; German immigrants
    in, 49; Gilded Age depictions, 5, 8,
    29–39, 42–49, 52, 58–59, 61, 63, 68;
    and homelessness, 29–32, 34, 36, 44–45,
    151; immigrant activism in, 53, 63–64;
    in immigrant novels, 52–53, 63–64, 191;
    and immigration restrictionism, 28,
    38–39, 49, 61, 68; Irish immigrants in,
    26–29, 33–35, 37; Italian immigrants in,
    29, 34–35, 37–39, 42, 44–45, 47, 52–53,

73–74, 126, 158; Jewish immigrants in, 35, 39, 43–44, 47–49, 52–53, 58–59, 61, 63, 68, 77, 83, 88, 191; and nostalgia, 8, 35, 49, 88, 126, 143, 146–47, 157–59, 218; police brutality in, 28, 146, 158; political corruption in, 4, 45–46, 53, 77, 82–84; in postwar crime films, 138–39, 141, 143; and Prohibition, 83; and prostitution, 29, 33, 35, 47–48, 52, 77, 81–82, 88; and saloons, 27, 32, 35, 45, 47–48, 53, 82; in science fiction, 143, 145–48; Slavic immigrants in, 59; and slum housing, 31–32, 39, 42–44, 46–47, 49, 52, 106, 117; suburbanization and, 46; in television comedies, 124–25, 132–33; in television crime dramas, 113–14, 117, 122, 126, 133, 152; and tourism, 43, 48, 59

New York: Its Upper Ten and Lower Million, 22

New York by Gas-Light, 22–23

New York Daily Graphic, 52

New York Daily Mirror, 6, 52, 71

New York Police Department, 133, 138

New York Press, 30, 36

New York Public Library, 147

New York Sun, 43

New York Times, 28, 118–19

New York Trilogy, 148

New York Yankees, 161

New Yorker, 98

Newark: African-Americans in, 124, 154, 165, 168–69, 172–73, 176, 181, 184–85, 187, 190, 197–98, 204, 213; and city manager government, 6; crime, 175, 180, 214; deindustrialization in, 173–76, 181–82, 203, 217; and gangsters, 8–9, 50, 79, 91, 104, 169, 172, 176–77, 181–82, 190–91, 196–98, 201, 203, 205–12, 219; and gangster films, 86; and gentrification, 184, 199; and homelessness, 213, 259 n.23; Italian immigrants in, 9, 50, 171, 175, 181, 190, 196–99, 201, 203–6, 211; Jewish immigrants in, 8, 79, 171–72, 176–77, 182, 190–91, 203–11; and nostalgia, 8–9, 13, 50, 163, 165, 171–73, 176, 180–81, 184, 186, 196–99, 201–6, 210, 212–19, 222; in

novels, 8, 13–14, 154, 163, 165, 168–69, 171–76, 179–88, 190; police brutality in, 134, 167, 169, 182–85, 193, 214–16; police–community relations in, 124, 134; political corruption in, 79, 84, 88, 169, 181–83, 206, 208–10, 213; and Prohibition, 91, 210–211; and prostitution, 88, 168, 208; and public housing, 173, 213; science fiction and, 147; segregation in, 173, 176, 183, 185, 213; and slum housing, 9, 169–70, 172–73, 176, 182, 201, 212–14, 259 n.23, 266 n.1; suburbanization and, 130, 142, 171–75, 180, 182–85, 196–97, 202–3, 217, 259 n.26; in television dramas, 9, 12, 50, 163, 196–99, 201, 215; urban renewal and, 183, 214, 261 n.62; and virtual cities, 9–10, 199, 201–2, 204–19, 222; white flight and, 130, 142, 169, 173–75, 185, 202–3, 217; white political conservatism in, 143, 145, 182, 197–98, 215

Newark, 206

Newark Ark, 170

Newark Community Union Project, 213, 216, 259 n.23

Newark Evening News, 213

Newark Housing Authority, 212, 259 n.23

Newark International Airport, 208–9

Newark Ledger, 86

Newark Police Department, 209

Newark Riots, 7, 11: and biracial looting, 167; and nostalgia, 197, 212–15; in novels, 165, 168, 171, 173, 176, 181–85; and police brutality, 167, 182–85, 193, 206, 213, 215–16; and police–community relations, 134, 213; and political corruption, 183; and slum housing, 170, 182, 217; in television dramas, 197, 215; in television news reports, 136, 139; and urban renewal, 183, 217, 261 n.62; and www.virtualnewarknj.com, 203, 212–14, 216, 219

Newark's Little Italy, 205

Nickelodeons, 62, 71, 73, 76, 78, 86

Nightclubs, 89, 92–93, 105

Nitti, Frank, 84

Nixon, Richard, 136, 142

No Cause for Indictment, 182, 216

Norris, Frank, 4, 33–34, 51
Northern Liberties (Philadelphia neighbor-
    hood), 19–20, 21
Norwegian immigrants, 129
Nostalgia, 143, 146–47, 223: and Brook-
    lyn, 218; and crime, 203, 206, 213–15,
    218; and Detroit, 13, 98, 163, 205; and
    gangsters, 125–26, 157–58, 160–63,
    183, 199, 206, 210; and gangster films,
    8, 157–58, 160–62; in Gilded Age, 35;
    and Italian immigrants, 9, 50, 157–58,
    160–62, 183, 196–98, 201, 204–6, 215,
    218; and Jewish immigrants, 157–58,
    171–72, 181–83, 191, 207, 210, 214,
    218; and Lower East Side, 35, 88; and
    Murder Inc., 183, 210; and Newark,
    8–9, 13, 50, 163, 165, 171–73, 176,
    180–81, 184, 186, 196–99, 201–6, 210,
    212–219, 222; in novels, 8, 14, 163,
    165, 170–71, 176, 179–81, 183–84, 186,
    188–89, 191, 221; and Prohibition, 8,
    98, 125, 190, 219; in television dramas,
    9, 14, 125–126, 152, 163, 192, 194,
    196–97, 201–2; in virtual cities, 9, 14,
    163, 202–6, 209–10, 212–219
Novak, Michael, 157–158

O'Bannion, Dion, 78, 80, 89
O'Dwyer, William, 6, 84
Ohio State University, 86
The Old World in the New, 56–57
O'Neal, Frederick, 124
On the Town, 10
On the Waterfront, 106, 112
Once upon a Time in America, 8
Orsi, Robert, 41
Ortner, Sherry, 181, 206–7, 212–13, 218
The Other America, 121
Our Movie Made Children, 86
Out of This Furnace, 57, 179–80

Pabst Brewing Co., 197–98
Palace Chophouse (Newark restaurant),
    104, 211
Palermo, 74
Panic in the Streets, 72, 112–13
Paradise Valley (Detroit neighborhood), 179
Paramus, N.J., 174

Parks, Gordon, 139, 141
Passaic, N.J., 50, 61, 202
Passaic textile general strike, 202
"The Passing of Cat Alley," 76
Paterson, N.J., 52, 130, 142, 174, 259 n.26
Peiss, Kathy,
Pennsylvania Constabulary, 56
Pesci, Joe, 162
Petrosino, Joseph, 74, 100, 134
Philadelphia: African–Americans in, 17,
    53, 116, 119, 150, 156, 177; anti-black
    riots in, 17, 53, 116, 119, 177, 249
    n.115, 257 n.100; black riots in, 6; anti-
    Catholic riots in, 21; in city mysteries, 2,
    15–19, 21–22; and drugs, 156; and
    gangsters, 190–91; Gilded Age magazine
    depictions, 20; and immigrant food
    ways, 50; and Industrial Revolution, 17;
    Irish immigrants in, 21, 68; MOVE con-
    troversy, 150; and police brutality, 150;
    and political corruption, 46, 55, 61, 68;
    and prostitution, 16, 20–21, 48, 88; pub-
    lic housing in, 116, 249 n.115, 257
    n.100; sanitary conditions, 19–20;
    Slavic immigrants in, 116, 249 n.115,
    257 n.100; and suburbanization, 46,
    142; white political conservatism in, 142
The Philippines, 60, 175
Pickup on South Street, 72, 113
Piecework, 38, 176
Piercy, Marge, 178
Pilferage, 40, 87, 106–7, 247 n.94
Pittsburgh, 20, 36, 58
Pittsfield, Mass., 23
The Planet of the Apes, 65, 143, 146
The Plot against America, 8, 14, 176–77,
    190–91, 222
Point Breeze (Philadelphia neighborhood),
    116, 249 n.115
Poitier, Sidney, 188
Police: in antebellum cities, 27; in blax-
    ploitation films, 140; in Chicago, 69, 83,
    96; in Detroit, 167–68, 188–89; in Draft
    Riots, 28; and gangster films, 73, 83–84,
    94, 96, 99, 104, 160–61; in German
    film, 79; in Gilded Age, 69; and Italian
    immigrants, 74; in Los Angeles, 123–24,
    140, 150; and Mafia, 74; in New York,

28, 74, 133, 138–39, 146; in Newark, 169, 182–85, 206, 209, 211, 213–16; in novels, 167–69, 184–85, 188–89; in Philadelphia, 150, 156; and political corruption, 83, 96, 206, 209; in postwar crime films, 137–42, 145, 153–54, 156; in science fiction, 145–47; as strikebreakers, 56; in television comedies, 124–25; in television crime dramas, 122–24, 133–34, 137, 149–53, 157, 192–93, 195–98

Polish immigrants, 41, 54, 55–56, 58, 120, 193–94

Political cartoons, 5, 17, 36, 41, 45, 48–49, 53, 54–55, 60, 67–68, 78, 79, 127

Political corruption: in antebellum cities, 19, 35; in Boston, 4; in Chicago, 53–54, 69, 78–79, 82–84, 90; in gangster films, 77, 82–83, 85, 93–94, 96, 103–6, 108; in Gilded Age magazines, 45–46, 54–55, 69, 77; and Irish immigrants, 38, 53–55, 68–69; and Jewish immigrants, 77; in New York, 4, 35, 45–46, 77, 82–84; in Newark, 79, 84, 86, 169, 181, 183, 187, 206, 208–10, 213; in novels, 53–55, 68–69, 169, 181–83; in Philadelphia, 55, 61; in postwar crime films, 155; and prostitution, 77; in television dramas, 84–85, 194–95, 197

The Polo Grounds, 142

Pool halls, 88, 107

Porambo, Ron, 167, 169, 182, 214–17

Powell, William, 81

Price, Richard, 155

Priestly, Jack, 122

Pritchett, Wendell, 218

Prohibition: in Chicago, 53, 78–79, 81, 83–85, 90, 125; in Cleveland, 79; in Detroit, 79, 98, 190; and the foreign menace, 6, 70, 77; and gangsters, 53, 70–71, 77–79, 83–84, 89–91, 98, 208, 210–11, 219; and gangster films, 6, 71–72, 81, 83–85, 89–91, 94, 104–5; and Greek immigrants, 190; and Irish immigrants, 53, 70, 78, 84, 89; and Italian immigrants, 70, 78, 83–85, 105, 190, 211; and Jewish immigrants, 70, 79, 83, 90–91, 98, 105, 190–91, 208, 210–11; in

New York, 83; in Newark, 79, 91, 105, 190, 208, 210–11, 219; and nightclubs, 89; and nostalgia, 8, 98, 125, 190, 219; in novels, 98, 190; and political corruption, 77–79, 84–85, 105; in television crime dramas, 125; and www.virtual-newarknj.com, 208, 210–11, 219

Prosky, Robert, 149

Prostitution: and African-Americans, 20, 118–19, 140, 165–68; in blaxploitation films, 140, 158; in Chicago, 88; Chinese immigrants and, 48, 52; in city mysteries, 15–16, 24; and dance halls, 88; in Detroit, 165–68; fears of race mixing and, 48, 52; and gangsters, 77, 88, 191, 208–9; in gangster films, 81–82; in Gilded Age, 5, 29, 33, 35–36, 47–48, 52; Irish immigrants and, 29, 33, 36; Italian immigrants and, 35; Jewish immigrants and, 77, 88, 191, 208–9; in Los Angeles, 140; in New York, 29, 33, 35–36, 47–48, 52, 77, 81–82, 88, 118–19; in Newark, 88, 208–9; in novels, 165–68; in Philadelphia, 15–16, 20, 48, 88; and police brutality, 167; and political corruption, 77, 82, 209; in television dramas, 105, 118–19, 193; and www.virtualnewarknj.com, 208–9

Prudential Insurance Co., 175

The Public Enemy, 6, 12, 71, 76–77, 82, 85–91, 95

Public housing: in Baltimore, 152, 192–93; in Brooklyn, 155; in Chicago, 151; in film, 155–56; and gentrification, 151; in Newark, 173, 213; in novels, 156, 182; in Philadelphia, 116, 249 n.115, 257 n.100; and police brutality, 156, 193; segregation in, 152, 173, 192, 257 n.105; in television crime dramas, 150–51, 192–94; and www.virtualnew-arknj.com, 213; whites' opposition to, 116, 152, 156, 249 n.115, 257 n.100

Public Service Tobacco Co., 211

Puck, 5, 17, 36, 41, 45, 48, 54–55, 60, 67–69

Puerto Rico, 173, 175

Pulitzer, Joseph, 67

The Pure Food and Drug Act, 61–62

The Purple Gang, 79, 98, 116, 166

Quaker City, or The Monks of Monk Hall, 2, 15–19, 21–22, 77
Quayle, Dan, 12

R.U.R., 80
Race mixing, fear of: in city mysteries, 16–17; in gangster films, 159, 161–62; in Gilded Age magazines, 35, 45, 47–48; in McCarthy era, 131; in Newark, 213; in novels, 178
The Racket, 82, 84–85
Racket Busters, 83, 94, 103
Raft, George, 13, 92
A Raisin in the Sun, 115, 140
"A Ramble in Old Philadelphia," 20
Randolf, Anders, 82
Ready to Riot, 213, 217
Reagan, Ronald, 136, 147, 149–51, 154, 192
The Red Badge of Courage, 29
Redlining, 6, 73, 113–14, 130, 153, 172, 190, 203, 222
Regeneration, 75–77
Reles, Abe, 218
Rent strikes, 40, 63, 131–32
"Republic of the Bowery," 25
The Revolt against Civilization: The Menace of the Under Man, 58
R.H. Macy Co. Department Store, 259 n.26
Rice, Father Charles, 247 n.96
Rieder, Jonathan, 183, 210, 215
Riis, Jacob, 30–31, 34, 39–40, 43–54, 56, 59, 61–63
Ripley, John W., 26
The Rise and Fall of the City of Mahagonny, 79
The Rise of David Levinsky, 62
The Rise of the Unmeltable Ethnics , 157–58
Riviera Hotel (Newark), 210–11, 219
Rizzo, Frank, 11, 27, 142, 145
The Roaring Twenties, 6, 76–77, 81, 83, 89, 90–91, 98, 103–5, 109
Roberts, Peter, 55
Robinson, Edward G., 13, 71, 82, 91, 93–94, 97, 100–1, 104

RoboCop, 147
Rochester, N.Y., 23
Rockefeller, John D., 31
Roediger, David, 111
The Rookies, 153
Room 222, 135
Roosevelt, Franklin, 84, 105, 247 n.90
Roosevelt, Theodore, 5, 60
Roseville (Newark neighborhood), 204
"Rosie O'Grady," 1
Ross, Edward Alsworth, 11, 39, 49, 56–58, 67
Rotella, Carlo, 139
Roth, Henry, 52, 65
Roth, Joe, 156
Roth, Philip, 13, 165, 189, 192, 212, 221: *American Pastoral*, 163, 171–72, 175–76, 181–84, 186, 191, 222; *The Human Stain*, 173, 183, 185–87, 191; *The Plot against America*, 8, 176–77, 179, 190–91, 222
Rothstein, Arnold, 81, 83, 93
Roundtree, Richard, 139
Rovnianek, Peter V., 56
Rovnost L'udu, 56
Rubin, Rachel, 210
Rugged individualism, 3
Runyon, Damon, 81, 94
Russell, Nipsey, 124

Said, Edward, 40, 48
Saint Louis, 60
Saks Fifth Avenue Department Store, 185
Saloons: in antebellum cities, 16, 20, 23, 25, 27; in Chicago, 53, 60, 68–69; in city mysteries, 16, 23; in Detroit, 166–67; in gangster films, 87, 90, 105, 158–160, 162; in Gilded Age, 45, 51–52, 60, 68–69; and Irish immigrants, 53, 60, 68–69; in New York, 25, 27, 45; in novels, 53, 166–67, 169; in Philadelphia, 20; and political corruption, 53, 105; and prostitution, 82; and race mixing, 16, 45, 52
San Francisco, 33–34, 51, 61, 129, 135, 137, 145
Sánchez, George, 222

Sanitary conditions, 19–20, 50, 177–80, 217
Savage Inequalities, 185
Scarface, 6, 71, 93, 98–100, 102–3
Schauffler, Robert Haven, 59
Schultz, "Dutch," 70, 89, 104, 108, 211, 214
Schwartz, Larry, 171
Scorsese, Martin, 2, 8, 13, 26, 28, 91, 143, 158
Scott, Cynthia, 166–67
Scott, George C., 117, 131
Scribner's magazine, 29, 37, 39, 42, 44
Sergey, Archie, 174
Settlement houses, 4, 19, 40, 49, 53, 64, 76, 88–89
Shaft, 139, 141–43, 147, 221
Shaft's Big Score, 141
The Shame of the Cities, 46
Shannon, Christopher, 77, 89
Shapiro, Jacob "Gurrah," 6, 211
Shays' Rebellion, 23
Shibe Park, 142
The Shirelles, 159
Short, William, 85–86, 100
Short Hills, N.J., 171, 175, 180, 185
The Short Hills Mall, 174–75, 185
Shreveport, La., 119
"The Sidewalks of New York," 1
The Siege, 74
Siegel, Benjamin "Bugsy," 13, 89, 92, 211, 218
Silk Stocking Sal, 81
Simon, David, 152
Sinatra, Frank, 205–6
Sinclair, Upton, 5, 61
Singer Sewing Machine Co., 181
Singleton, John, 149, 153–54
Sister Carrie, 33
The Slav Invasion and the Miner, 55
Slavic immigrants: anti-black attitudes, 60, 116, 179–80; and anti-communism, 113; in Chicago, 54; and film noir, 113; food ways, 50; fraternal societies, 41, 56, 61, 102; in gangster films, 109–11; in Gilded Age magazines, 59; and immigration restrictionism, 11, 49–50, 54–58, 67–68, 102; labor activism, 52, 55–56; in New York, 59; nostalgia and, 179–80;

in novels, 57, 179–80; in Philadelphia, 116, 247 n.94; and pilferage, 247 n.94; and political corruption, 54; slum housing and, 56; suburbanization and, 110–11; whiteness of, 60, 111, 127, 179–80
Sleepy Lagoon murder case, 123
A Slight Case of Murder, 94
Slovak v Amerike, 56, 63
Slum housing conditions: in Brooklyn, 210; in coal–mining communities, 56; in Chicago, 85, 87; in Detroit, 166, 177–79, 188; and gangsters, 210; in gangster films, 85, 87, 106–9, 159; Gilded Age depictions of, 31–32, 34, 36, 38–40, 43–44, 46–47, 49–50, 52; and Italian immigrants, 38–40, 49–50; and Jewish immigrants, 39, 43, 49, 62–63, 191; in Los Angeles, 135; in New York, 31–32, 34, 36, 38–40, 43–44, 46–47, 49–50, 52, 62–63, 109, 118, 159, 191; in Newark, 172–73, 180, 182, 201–2, 212–14, 217, 259 n.23; and nostalgia, 179–80, 210, 214; in novels, 62–63, 166, 177–80, 188, 191; in Philadelphia, 19–20, 191; and Slovak immigrants, 56, 179–80; in television dramas, 118, 122, 135, 151, 201–2; in virtual cities, 214
Smith, John, 183, 214, 216
Smith, "Silver Dollar," 77
Smith, Susan, 156
Smoke, 148
Social bandits, 107–8
Social Darwinism, 31–33, 39, 51, 73, 75, 94, 100
Social Security, 172
Society for the Prevention of Cruelty to Children, 51
Some Like it Hot, 98
The Sopranos, 9, 11, 12, 50, 163, 192, 196–99, 201–3, 215, 222
The Sorrento (Newark restaurant), 205
The South Bronx (Bronx neighborhood), 125
South Orange, N.J., 182
Southwark (Philadelphia neighborhood), 15, 19, 20
Special Agent, 104

Spencer, Herbert, 32
Spina, Dominick, 215
Springhall, John, 86
Springsteen, Bruce, 195
Stacher, Joseph "Doc," 172, 210
Stack, Robert, 126
Staggalee, 141, 147
Stalin, Joseph, 113
Starsky and Hutch, 134, 136–37
Steffens, Lincoln, 46, 55, 61
Steiner, Edward, 56
Stenge, Maren, 43
Sternlieb, George, 173
Stewart, James, 110
Stoddard, Lothrop, 58, 75, 78, 98
The Stork Club, 89
"Street arabs," 5, 34, 76
The Streets of San Francisco, 123–24, 136, 153
Strong, George Templeton, 18, 22, 34
Stuart, Charles, 156
Stubbs, Katherine, 64
Students for a Democratic Society, 213, 259 n.23
Studs Lonigan, 53–55, 68
Sturges, Preston, 147
Suburbanization, 6, 8, 142, 219: and black exclusion, 114, 115, 118, 120, 130, 146, 156, 162, 172, 183, 190; and Brooklyn, 183–84; and Cleveland, 146, 156; and Detroit, 190; and federal subsidies, 113–14, 118, 120, 130, 172, 203, 217–18; in gangster films, 72, 73, 75, 109–12, 114–15; in the Gilded Age, 46, 171; and Newark, 130, 171–75, 180, 182, 184–85, 196, 203, 259 n.26; in novels, 172–73, 175, 180, 182–84, 190; and Paterson, N.J., 130, 174, 259 n.26; and school-funding inequities, 186–87; and Slavic immigrants, 109–11; in television comedies, 129–30, 133; in television dramas, 118, 196; and whiteness, 111, 114–15, 130, 190
Sugrue, Thomas, 116, 153, 188–89
Sumner, William Graham, 32
Superfly, 139, 141–44, 147, 161
Survey, 40
Sweatshops, 5, 43, 62, 88

Sweet Sweetback's Baadasssss Song, 139–41, 161
Syd's Hot Dogs (Newark restaurant), 212

Taiwan, 175
The Taking of Pelham One Two Three, 125, 143, 146
Tammany Hall, 4, 45–46, 53, 77, 83, 105, 108
Tampa, 50
Tarantino, Quentin, 33, 91
The Tavern (Newark restaurant), 191, 210, 219
Tawana, Kea, 170
Taxi Driver, 1, 125, 143–46
Taylor, Clark, 175, 184–85
Taylor, Frederick Winslow, 79
Taylor, Henry, 123
Taylorism, 79–80
Third Ward Democratic Club (Newark), 79, 105, 206, 208, 210
Third Ward Newark, 176
Thompson, William, 79, 82, 84
Three Wise Crooks, 81
Till, Emmett, 213
Tin Pan Alley, 1, 31
Tinker, Barbara Wilson, 165–66, 168–69, 189, 192
To Sir, with Love, 188
Topp, Michael Miller, 52
Training Day, 74
Troublemakers, 213
Trumbull Park (Chicago neighborhood), 116
Turkel, Sherry, 218–19
Turner, Frederick Jackson, 3
Turner, George Kibbe, 77–78, 82, 88
Turner, Irvine, 206
Tweed, William M., 53
24, 137
Twist, Kid, 77
Tyson, Cicely, 117, 131, 133

Underworld , 80–81
The Untouchables, 125
Upper West Side (New York neighborhood), 1, 10
Urban renewal, 166, 183, 185, 214, 217, 257 n.100, 261 n.62

Vailsburg (Newark neighborhood), 206, 216, 219, 222

Vailsburg Park (Newark), 216, 222

Van Peebles, Melvin, 139–41

Vaudeville, 31, 62, 97, 125, 127

Vergara, Camilo, 266 n.1

The Victoria Castle (Newark restaurant), 205

Villani, Ralph, 206, 208

Violence in the Model City, 167

Virtual Cities, 9–10, 14, 163, 199, 202, 217–18, 222

Volstead Act, 77

Von Sternberg, Joseph, 80–81, 86

The Wagner Act, 57, 106

Walker, James J., 82, 84, 92

Wallace, George, 27, 142–43, 145

Walsh, Raoul, 75, 82

Warden, Jack, 133

Warne, Frank Julian, 55–56, 67–68

The Warriors, 147

Washington, Denzel, 74

Washington, George, 21, 26, 46, 67

Washington, D.C., 36, 67

Watermelon Man, 139–40

Watts, Jerry Gafio, 203–4, 206

Watts (Los Angeles neighborhood), 7, 123–24, 133, 135, 139, 168

Watts riot, 123–24, 133, 135, 139, 168

Way, Peter, 203–4

Wayne, N.J., 185

Webb, Jack, 134, 137

Weequahic (Newark neighborhood): and African-Americans, 181, 204, 213; and drugs, 212; and gangsters, 8, 181, 190–91, 207, 212, 219; and nostalgia, 181, 212, 218, 222; in novels, 8, 171–73, 176, 181, 187, 190–91; and Weequahic High School, 181, 206–7, 213

Weill, Kurt, 79

Welcome Back, Kotter, 125

Wellman, William A., 90

West Baltimore (Baltimore neighborhood), 195

West Orange, N.J., 171

Westinghouse Electric Corp., 182

When I Was Comin' Up, 173, 187

When the Fire Reaches Us, 165–68, 178, 189, 192

Whiskey Hill, Pa., 56

Whiskey Rebellion, 23

White flight, 8, 116, 176: and Brooklyn, 183–84, 210; and Detroit, 190; and federal subsidies, 113–14, 130, 203, 217–18; in gangster films, 114; and Newark, 130, 175, 197; in novels, 175, 190; and Paterson, N.J., 130; in television dramas, 197

White Heat, 82, 112, 134

Whiteness: in comic films, 139–40; and criminology, 51, 75; and gangsters, 78; in gangster films, 75, 98, 110–12, 115; and Greek immigrants, 190; and imperialism, 60–61; and Irish immigrants, 4, 17, 54, 60, 67; and Italian immigrants, 4, 11, 47, 75, 78, 98, 111–12, 1197–98, 215; and Jewish immigrants, 4, 11, 47, 49, 60–61, 64, 67–68, 75, 130, 191; and minstrelsy, 17, 127, 139–40; in novels, 190–91; in political cartoons, 17, 60, 68; and prostitution, 48; and Slavic immigrants, 54, 60–61, 67–68, 110–12; and suburbanization, 110–12, 115, 130, 174, 190; in television drama, 197–98, 215

Widmark, Richard, 112–13

Wilentz, Sean, 24

Williams, Clarence III, 135

Williams, Rhonda, 152

Wilson, William Julius, 40

Winchell, Walter, 6, 89, 103, 126

The Wire, 2, 9, 10, 11, 12, 14, 84–85, 93, 105, 152, 163, 192–96

Wolensky, Moe, 211

The Wop, 75

World's Columbian Exposition, 60

World's fairs, 59–60

Works Progress Administration, 19–20, 208

Wright, Bruce, 138

Wright, Carroll, 19

Wright, Nathan, 169, 213, 217

Wright, Richard, 117

www.oldnewark.com. *See also* www .virtualnewarknj.com

www.virtualnewarknj.com, 10, 202, 204–19, 222

Yekl, 49, 62
"Yellow Peril," 60
Yellow press, 67
Yezierska, Anzia, 62–64
Yorkville (New York neighborhood), 59
Young, Coleman, 178

Zangara, Giuseppe, 84
Zangwill, Israel, 51
Zoot Suit riots, 123

Zunz, Olivier, 120
Zwillman, Abner "Longy": and drug dealing, 181; and legitimate businesses, 190–91, 210–12; in novels, 8, 172, 176–77, 190–91; and political corruption, 79, 105, 181, 206, 208–11; and Prohibition, 105, 208–211; and prostitution, 208; and slums, 208; and www.virtualnewarknj.com, 203, 205, 207–10, 214, 218–19

About the Author

ROBERT ZECKER is Professor of History at Saint Francis Xavier University in Nova Scotia. He has taught courses on immigration and ethnicity, race in America, U.S. social movements, class, and urban studies, and has published numerous articles and a book chapter on immigration.